hip: the history

hip:
the history

John Leland

ecco

An Imprint of HarperCollins*Publishers*

HarperCollins books may be purchased for educational, business, or sales promotional use. For information, please write: Special Markets Department, HarperCollins Publishers Inc., 10 East 53rd Street, New York, NY 10022.

FIRST EDITION

Designed by Cassandra J. Pappas

Library of Congress Cataloging-in-Publication Data is available upon request.

ISBN 0-06-052817-6

04 05 06 07 08 BVG / BVG 10 9 8 7 6 5 4 3 2 1

shout outs

For the accomplices who made this book possible, many thanks, condolences and state immunity are in order.

My agent, Paul Bresnick, thought there should be a book on the history of hip. My editor, Dan Halpern, helped craft it, providing sage counsel and a poet's touch. Hip friends John Capouya, Bill Adler, Phil Everson, Greg Milner, Drew Keller (my roughneck peeps upstate) and Trent Gegax generously put their hands on all or parts of the manuscript. They invented the remix. Jordan Leland helpfully reminded me that I was full of shit. Donna Ranieri gathered the photographs; we should all live within their world. My *Times* colleagues, especially Barbara Graustark, kindly overlooked the perpetual bags under my eyes.

Much love and gratitude to Risa and Jordan, who endured neglect from their husband and father while I was busy writing about neglectful husbands and fathers. This book is for them.

contents

hip: the history

preface

getting hip

I know your type.... This is the worst nightmare. I've dreamed of this
on the subway.... If you weren't a journalist you'd never be invited to
anything hip.   —LOU REED

The proper way to read this book, of course, is from the back, checking to
see if your name is in the index. If it is not there (and let's face it, what are
the chances?), my apologies. Somehow your hang time at the Six Gallery
in North Beach or Northsix in Williamsburg, your matted coif or ironic
eyeglasses, your collection of white-label vinyl or Bukowski first editions,
fell through one of the many holes in this book. Perhaps the hip guy you
knew in high school or wished you knew at the needle exchange is not in
here, either. Hip is an elusive thing, and sometimes must be its own reward. Take comfort that you are in good company. If all the hipsters omit-
ted from these pages were gathered together, they could fill the back room
of Max's Kansas City from now until the next Velvet Underground re-
union. With luck, no one would pay his or her tab, and only a sucker
would eat the chickpeas.

   If you *are* in the index, another sort of apology is in order. This is not
a conventional history, faithfully reporting the experiences of the people
who lived it. Instead, it is a history of a public perception, which by its nature is sometimes awry. Its distortions are part of what makes hip. If you

think of Eric Dolphy onstage at the Five Spot, or Rakim writing rhymes in Long Island, you might imagine that they are thinking very hip thoughts, but it is this imagination, and the actions that arise from it, that determine hip's course. Hip is a romantic idea, not a catalog of facts. The accounts of lives and events in this book are intended to capture these myths, noting when necessary how far they stray from the facts. Hip's truths are literary but not always literal.

I've chosen to tell this history through public figures not because they are hipper than other people—no one who has seen Bob Dylan blow "Hava Nagila" on the Lubavitcher Hasidim telethon can believe in the infallibility of celebrities—but because the public perception of their hipness affects so many people at once. The celebrities are just focal points for broader phenomena. *Hip: The History* is about the waves that ripple through the big pond, not the composition of the stone that causes the wave. In truth, many of these celebrated figures led melancholy and isolated lives—hip to think about, but tough for those who lived them. Someday more advanced pharmacology may make hip obsolete. In the meantime, there is perhaps just one way to reconcile Neal Cassady's decision to freeze to death beside a railroad track in Mexico with the actions of those who followed him on the road, drawn by their image of him as a "wild, yea-saying overburst of American joy"—and that is to note that hip's history, and the world we live in, proceeds from that misperception, not from the reality of Mexican cold.

Like other histories, this book indulges in the cheat of hindsight. In judging what is hip and what is not, I've sided with things that shaped or predicted whatever came next. This is admittedly a form of cherry picking: nothing is easier than identifying prescience in the past. Thus, Keith Butler, the Brit folkie who screamed "Judas!" when Dylan played electric at a 1966 concert in Manchester, does not have a place in this book, but Jim Carroll—who can be heard on the Velvet Underground's *Live at Max's Kansas City* asking, "Is that a down? What is it? A Tuinal? Give me it immediately"—will forever belong in hip's lore. History abandoned the acoustic purists, but smiled on urban poets with an appetite for pills. And so, therefore, did hip.

But enough about other people. After seeing that your name is not in the index, how are you supposed to proceed? With a grudge. After all, hip is a competitive sport. The proper reason to read this book is for the satisfaction of knowing that your hipness is hipper than whatever knowledge passeth herein. Surely the book calls for no less. It is in the nature of hip that it is always tearing down shibboleths, including its own, in order to bring more noise. This is why it endures, why it is important. It is always seeking a smarter way. So if you must, raise a glass of Hatorade. I would. But please remember the words of Ice-T, and don't hate the player, hate the game.

As for me, you will not find my name in the index, either. There is something inescapably nerdy about compiling a history of hip. My kind can only console ourselves, like my former colleague singled out in the epigraph above, that we are with Lou Reed in his dreams. As the saying goes, those who can, do. Those who can't . . . well, you know the rest. And if you are riding the subway, pleasant dreams.

introduction

what is hip?
superficial reflections on america

> [T]he Negro looks at the white man and finds it difficult to believe
> that the "grays"—a Negro term for white people—can be so absurdly
> self-deluded over the true interrelatedness of blackness and
> whiteness.   —RALPH ELLISON

The Oakland soul group Tower of Power asked the question in a 1973
song called "What Is Hip?" The band had a reputation as wordsmiths, inventing terms like *honkypox,* for listeners who could not get on the good
foot. But on the Hip Question, they found themselves on slippery terrain,
as poets before them trying to define soul or swing or love. The language
curled back on itself:

> Hipness is—What it is!
> And sometimes hipness is
> What it ain't!

Swaddled in nasty horns and a backbeat, this was a coy put-on, staged for
the benefit of the honkypox. Everybody knows what hip is.

Or at least, everyone can name it when they see it. For something that

Miles Davis

is by definition subjective, hip is astoundingly uniform across the population. It is the beatitude of Thelonious Monk at the piano, or the stoic brutality of Lou Reed and the Velvet Underground, performing songs of drugs and sadomasochism as a projector flashed Andy Warhol's films on their black turtlenecks. It is the flow of Jack Kerouac's "bop prosody" or Lenny Bruce's jazzed-out satire, or the rat-a-tat tattoo of James Ellroy's elevated pulp lit. Walt Whitman was hip; Lord Buckley was hip; Karen O of the Yeah Yeah Yeahs is too hip for her own good. Hip is the way Miles Davis talked, dressed, played or just stood—and the way Bob Dylan, after his own style, followed in kind (though both men strayed into injudicious leather in the 1980s). The streets of Williamsburg in Brooklyn or Silver Lake in Los Angeles comprise a theme park in the key of hip. Its gaze is the knowing, raised eyebrow of Dawn Powell or Kim Gordon, bassist in the downtown band Sonic Youth—skeptical but not unkind.

Clarence Major, in his study *Juba to Jive: A Dictionary of African-American Slang*, traces the origins of hip to the Wolof verb *hepi* ("to see") or *hipi* ("to open one's eyes"), and dates its usage in America to the 1700s. So from the linguistic start, *hip* is a term of *enlightenment*, cultivated by slaves from the West African nations of Senegal and coastal Gambia. The slaves also brought the Wolof *dega* ("to understand"), source of the collo-quial *dig,* and *jev* ("to disparage or talk falsely"), the root of *jive.* Hip be-gins, then, as a subversive intelligence that outsiders developed under the eye of insiders. It was one of the tools Africans developed to negotiate an alien landscape, and one of the legacies they contributed to it. The feed-back loop of white imitation, co-optation and homage began immedi-ately.

From these origins, hip tells a story of black and white America, and the dance of conflict and curiosity that binds it. In a history often defined by racial clash, hip offers an alternative account of centuries of contact and emulation, of back-and-forth. This line of mutual influence, which we seldom talk about, is not a decorative fillip on the national identity but one of the central, life-giving arteries. Though the line often disappears in daily life—through segregation, job discrimination and the racial split in any school cafeteria—it surfaces in popular culture, where Americans col-lect their fantasies of what they might be. The center of American culture runs through Mark Twain and Louis Armstrong, and it is impossible to imagine either's work without both African and European roots. Born in radically different circumstances and separated by history, they have as much in common with each other as with their peers from what either might call the ancestral homeland. Both are classicists and bluesmen, masters of language, breakers of the rules that would hold them apart. What they have in common is hip.

For better and worse, hip represents a dream of America. At its best, it imagines the racial fluidity of pop culture as the real America, the one we are yearning to become. As William Burroughs said, revolution in Amer-ica begins in books and music, then waits for political operatives to "im-plement change after the fact." At its worst, hip glosses over real division and inequity, pretending that the right argot and record collection can outweigh the burden of racial history. White hipsters often use their inter-est in black culture to claim moral high ground, while giving nothing back. When Quentin Tarantino tosses around the word *nigger,* he is claim-ing hipster intimacy while giving callous offense. Really that high ground lies elsewhere. Hip can be a self-serving release from white liberal guilt, of-fering cultural reparations in place of the more substantive kind. This is white supremacy posing as appreciation. Neither of these verdicts on hip is strong enough to cancel the other out. Hip serves both functions: it is an ennobling force that covers for ignominy. Steeped in this paradox, it tells a story of synthesis in the context of separation. Its métier is ambiguity and contradiction. Its bad is often good.

Only a small fraction of the population at any time lives in full commitment to hip; for most of us, work, school, family, rehab or the alarm clock gets in the way. Yet we all participate in its romance. Its Q rating is to die for. Hip permeates mainstream daily life at the level of language, music, literature, sex, fashion, ego and commerce. During the 1992 presidential campaign, Bill Clinton made hip a campaign pitch, working sunglasses and sax on *The Arsenio Hall Show;* for his troubles, both Toni Morrison and Chris Rock anointed him America's first black president. (A decade later Al Sharpton refined this title, quipping, "There is a difference in being off-white and being black.")

If hip is a form of rebellion—or at least a show of rebellion—it should want something. Its desires are America's other appetite, not for wealth but for autonomy. It is a common folk's grab at rich folks' freedom—the purest form of which is freedom from the demands of money. It is an equalizer, available to outsiders as to insiders. Anyone can be hip, even if *every*one can't. In a nation that does not believe in delayed gratification, hip is an instant payoff. You may need years of sacrifice to get to heaven or build a retirement fund, but hip yields its fruit on contact. It is always new but never going anywhere special—a present tense reclaimed from the demands of past and future.

Like other manifestations of the blues, hip keeps its meaning limber. John Lennon, pursuing his domestic bliss in New York City, saw hip as a drag. "Nowadays it's hip not to be married," he said in 1980. "I'm not interested in being hip." For the surreal comic Richard "Lord" Buckley, on the other hand, the word "hip" signified a rain of good fortune. In his rewrite of Mark Antony's funeral oration from *Julius Caesar,* he unlocked Shakespeare's inner hipster, riffing, "Yea, the looty was booty and hipped the treasury well." For Lennon, hip was a prison; for His Lordship, it was whatever was needed, as long as you didn't have to work for it. But even Lennon would have acknowledged that the looty was booty.

The booty, in turn, has bounty. Hip sells cars, soda, snowboards, skateboards, computers, type fonts, booze, drugs, cigarettes, CDs, shoes, shades and home accessories. As Lord Buckley suggested, it serves the treasury well. By bringing constant change and obsolescence, it creates ever-new needs to buy. Though it grabs ideas from the bottom of the economic ladder, hip lives in luxury. Poor societies worry about growing enough corn; rich societies can worry about being corny. Hip shapes how we drive, whom we admire, whose warmth we yearn for in the night. Its scent transforms neighborhoods from forbidding to unaffordable. The fashion designers Imitation of Christ built a thriving label by murmuring a mantra of hip over thrift store clothes, then selling them for hundreds of dollars. Hip brings the intelligence of troublemakers and outsiders into the loop, saving the mainstream from its own limits. What's in Williamsburg today will be in the mall tomorrow; today's *Vice* magazine or *Lucha Libre* Mexican wrestling is tomorrow's *Good Housekeeping* or *SmackDown.* Like the advertising world that grew up alongside it, hip creates value through image and style. In its emphasis on *being watched,* it anticipated the modern mediascape, which values people not for what they produce or possess but for their salience as images. For all its professed disregard for wealth, hip would not have thrived unless it was turning a profit.

Hip is a social relation. You cannot be hip in the way you might be tall, handsome, gawky, nearsighted or Russian. Like camp, its unruly nephew, it requires an audience. Even at its most subterranean, it exists in public view, its parameters defined by the people watching it. You decide what is hip and what is not. Hip requires a transaction, an acknowledgment. If a tree falls in the forest and no one notices its fundamental dopeness, it is not hip.

There is no instruction manual for hipsters, and this book is definitely not one. But there are archetypes of hip. Mark Twain, P. T. Barnum, Miles Davis, Muhammad Ali, Bob Dylan, Richard Pryor, Terry Southern, Richard Hell—these are the tricksters of hip, characters a society invents to undermine its own principles. When Robert Johnson sold his soul to the devil, it was really a trickster who taught him the blues. Gertrude Stein, Andy Warhol and Mickey Ruskin, legendary host of Max's Kansas City, are the facilitators of hip. For them, hip is a team sport. Herman Melville, Charlie Parker, Jack Kerouac and Big Daddy Kane are the fierce soloists, blowing their lives into mad rhythm. Walt Whitman, Raymond Chandler, Dizzy Gillespie, Allen Ginsberg and KRS-One are the theoreticians and explainers, often playing sidekick to their enigmatic brethren. Stephen Foster, Irving Berlin, Al Jolson, Mezz Mezzrow, Carl Van Vechten, Elvis and Eminem are the white boys who stole the blues, or at least that is one way of looking at them. Much of our story revolves around their love and theft.

The word "hip" is commonly used in approval, but this glosses its many limitations. Though it likes a revolutionary pose, hip is ill equipped to organize for a cause. No one will ever reform campaign finance laws under hip's banner, nor save the environment. A hipper foreign policy will not get us out of this fix. Hip steps back. In the fall of 1965, a group called the Vietnam Day Committee asked Ken Kesey to speak at a Berkeley rally against the war, and the results were one small step for hip, one predictable travesty for the movement. As eager souls yearned to be inspired, Kesey abstained: "There's only one thing to do . . . there's only one thing that's gonna do any good at all . . . And that's everybody just look at it, look at the war, and turn your backs and say . . . Fuck it." And he sawed "Home on the Range" on harmonica. Hip had met the enemy, and it was engagement.

Hip is not genius, though it is often mistaken for such by people who ought to know better. As an artistic flame, hip appears to burn hot and short. It glorified the self-destruction of Jackson Pollock, Charlie Parker, Dorothy Parker, Tupac Shakur and Kurt Cobain. Gwendolyn Brooks, in her 1960 poem "We Real Cool," took terminal hipness as a literal state, tweaking the self-destructiveness of the cool pose: "Jazz June. We / Die soon." Hip rationalizes poor life choices; it squanders money, love, talent, lives. This is not a book about devoted fathers, good husbands or community pillars. Hip is a convenient excuse for fuckups. It can also be corrosive and small-minded. In his 1967 short story "You're Too Hip, Baby," Terry Southern skewers an aspiring hipster named Murray. When a black jazzman asks him whether they should listen to Charlie Parker or Béla Bartók, he really is too hip: " 'Bartók, man,' said Murray, and added dreamily, 'where do you go after Bird?' " He reduces genius to sumptuary correctness. This is hipness unto negation, narrowing the universe to an orthodoxy as rigid as the one Murray purports to reject. As a goal in itself, hip is self-defeating or kitsch. The Rat Pack, new and old, are kitsch; the Strokes walk the line. As Leonard Cohen says about poetry, hip is a verdict, not an intention. It becomes its antithesis if made to work too hard.

Through its changes, hip maintains some constants: a dance between black and white; a love of the outsider; a straddle of high and low culture; a grimy sense of nobility; language that means more than it says. People who have never seen a Jim Jarmusch movie or an arty music video can recognize either as an articulation of hip. Specifically, what they recognize is this: the elevation of style and background as narrative and foreground. Hip is the difference between Frank Miller's brooding *Dark Knight* comics and the traditional *Batman* lines; between the X Games and the Olympics; between Allen Iverson and Kobe Bryant; Snoopy and Linus; a Glock and a Colt.

From a proprietary standpoint, hip is a mess. Ralph Ellison, writing about black bohemianism, threw up his hands in dismissal: wasn't bohemianism a white rip-off of black styles? But this is the way hip travels. It is like a game of telephone. African Americans were copied by white Americans, who were copied by French existentialists, who were copied by white intellectuals, who were copied by black hipsters, who were copied by Jewish rappers, who were copied by Brazilian street kids, who were—well, I think you know where this is taking us. It is taking us to the Jungle Club in Tokyo, where Japanese hipsters wear dreadlocks and emulate the funk

Lindyhoppers at Savoy Ballroom, 1941

musician Bootsy Collins. No one along the way can really take full credit for this evolutionary development, and yet here we are—you, me and Bootsy. As Mr. Collins would say, ain't nothing but a party, y'all.

At its most pure, hip is utterly mongrel. Which is to say, purism has no place in hip. Instead, hip comes of the haphazard, American collision of peoples and ideas, thrown together in unplanned social experiment: blacks, whites, immigrants, intellectuals, hoodlums, scoundrels, sexpots and rakes. It feeds off antennae as well as roots. Born in the dance between black and white, hip thrives on juxtaposition and pastiche. It connects the disparate and contradictory. For example, Andy Warhol formally became the patron to the Velvet Underground in the backseat of a limousine on their way up-town to see James Brown at the Apollo Theater in Harlem—three schools of hip joined by one limo ride. Such is the hospitality of hip. It is inclusive, open. When people try to get too pure about it, hip leaves the building.

Hip has a lexicon of surrogates: cool, down, beat, fresh, rad, phat, tight, dope (but under no circumstances, gnarly, bodacious or neat). But really, hip is hip, enduring through all permutations. Anyone who leaves the house with bed head has an idea of where its light shines.

So what is hip?

Perhaps it is best to begin at the beginning. As Amiri Baraka has noted, the Africans who were brought to America encountered a world that was doubly foreign: not just the dislocations of slavery, which had long existed in West Africa, but those presented by America as well. Survival meant using the distance as a source of autonomy and dignity. Hip begins, then, in private language, shaped to the circumstances of the new land.

From colonial times Americans have cobbled a vernacular language that, like the Wolof of the slaves, multiplies the world through a kaleidoscope of meaning. It belongs to the underworld, the streets, the back room, the geeky realms of the digital frontier, where enlightenment requires its own lingo. Walt Whitman celebrated slang as "the lawless germinal element . . . behind all poetry," and sought to celebrate, in contrast to the formal language of England, the "real genius underneath our speech, which is not what the school men suppose, but wild, intractable, suggestive." From his mouth to Flava Flav's ear.

A 1930 lexicon called *American Tramp and Underworld Slang* proposed, somewhat dubiously, that the vernacular use of *hip* came from "having one's hip boots on—i.e., the way in which they protect the wearer from bad weather or dangerous currents is analogous to the way in which awareness or sophistication arms one against social perils." This is a suspect etymology, but a beautiful metaphor for the actions of hip, a stillness amid chaotic motion.

Words, of course, are not frozen in their origins, and hip has had a storied journey through history. It turns with the times. Norman Mailer took on the Hip Question in his famous 1957 essay "The White Negro: Superficial Reflections on the Hipster," a work more widely maligned than read. "Hip," he wrote, "is the sophistication of the wise primitive in a giant jungle," which is a particularly loaded way to think of African Americans but a useful metaphor for hip. He argued that hip emerged after World War II as a quintessentially American response to the orderly atrocities of the Nazi death camps and the nuclear bomb. Faced with such civilized inhumanity, he wrote, the proper reaction was to regress into pathology and homegrown existentialism.

> [I]f the fate of twentieth-century man is to live with death from adolescence to premature senescence, why then the only life-giving answer is to accept the terms of death, to live with death as immediate danger, to divorce oneself from society, to exist without roots, to set out on that uncharted journey into the rebellious imperatives of the self.

By these lines, hip is not so much enlightenment as a response to the looming unknowable. It is a strategy for survival in the face of terror.

It is a long way from *hepi* to Hiroshima, from the shores of Gambia to Mailer's rebellious imperatives of the self. Yet the two definitions suggest a line of thought that parallels the evolving society around it. Hip shaped itself in response to the culture; the culture adapted to the dimensions of hip. Mailer's apocalyptic view, like Clarence Major's more general definition of enlightenment, provides just one frame of what is really an ongoing narrative.

Hip entails a story of America, of the country's passage from an agrarian past to a technological, urban present, from Victorianism into modernism. Though it reverberates abroad in the nouvelle vague films of Jean-Luc Godard or in the studied swagger of Tokyo youth cults, even in these foreign locales—*especially* there—it is the signature American style, the face the New World invented to shake off the Old. America in this transition evolved from an adolescent former colony, beholden to Europe economically and culturally, to a self-regarding player on the world stage. The transition allowed a new blush of national identity to emerge—coarse, robust, resourceful, independent, ruthless, what have you. Yet it also left scars and contradictions, and a population often moving too fast to think about them. These below-the-surface, *subterranean* pressures bubble up in the anxieties of hip: the perplexing gulf of race; the conflict between individualism and the collective good; the roughneck beauty of American colloquial speech.

Hip has flourished in periods when it is needed, always corresponding with wrinkles in the economy and technology. These flash points comprise six convergences of hip. Chapters of this book will discuss each in detail, but a quick chronology might be helpful here. The first hip convergence, in the 19th century, produced black and white Americans' first responses to each other and their lives together: the blackface minstrel show, which looked in one direction, and the blues, which looked in the other. During this period Ralph Waldo Emerson, Henry David Thoreau, Walt Whitman and Herman Melville, in a brief flurry from 1850 to 1855, laid out the formal groundwork for hip. They are hip's O.G.'s, or original gangstas. No skater, raver, indie-rocker, thug, Pabst Blue Ribbon drinker or wi-fi slacker today acts without their permission.

The 1910s and 1920s brought the second hip convergence, as populations moved from country to city. Blacks migrated north, Jews emigrated from Europe, writers split for Paris, and the radio and fledgling record industry brought rhythm to the masses. Hip percolated through a radical, gynocentric bohemia in Greenwich Village, the Harlem Renaissance uptown and the Lost Generation in exile. The third hip convergence, after World War II, saw the parallel emergence of bebop and the Beat generation, two intellectual movements that rejected the mainstream in search of grace and beatitude. This was hip's golden age, and the template for the counterculture of the following decade.

The urban collapse of the 1970s, which hollowed out inner-city neighborhoods like the East Village and the South Bronx, bred the fourth hip convergence, which filled the vacant spaces with do-it-yourself, or DIY, media: punk, hip-hop music, graffiti, break dancing, skateboarding and the zine explosion. The fifth convergence tapped the silicon velocity of the Internet, which moved language, money, information and enlightenment around the world at the click of a mouse. William Gibson's 1984 *Neuromancer* was the founding document; *Wired* magazine was the cheerleading tip sheet. Turntablists and remixers were the rock stars.

The sixth convergence is now.

From our perch in the early 21st century, when multinational corporations hoover anything remotely hip, it is easy to forget how hostile the climate for hip once was. The church, the law, capital and mass opinion all lined up against hip, as against a disease. Voices of authority took pains to be corny. Athletes, celebrities, politicians, war heroes and civic leaders all presented their rectitude—literally, their *squareness*—as a bulwark against hip's sinuous slink. People who smoked a joint or loved out of hetero wedlock were labeled dope fiends or sex fiends; rhythm was considered a threat to civilization. Police narco units of the 1950s specialized in tossing jazz musicians. To be a hipster was to be labeled a hoodlum, hooligan, faggot, nigger-lover, troublemaker, derelict, slut, commie, dropout, freak. When America had a center, hip was outside of it.

Needless to say, this has changed. What used to be radical—putting off marriage, taking drugs to feel better, living by creativity, traveling from town to town, seeking sensory intoxication—now everyone lives that way. The end of the Cold War favored commercial values over ideological ones, and for these, hip simply accelerates the pace of the market. Iggy Pop, William Burroughs and Miles Davis, once scourges of civilization, are now evoked to move merch. Suburban honor students rock full-sleeve *cholo* tattoos and talk like hip-hop gangstas, and global conglomerates fight over the rapper 50 Cent, who boasts a past as a drug dealer and shows off the bullet wounds to prove it. Wearing your jeans a certain way once signaled your rejection of mainstream materialism. Now, Levi's borrows the pants off a Williamsburg lizard named Troy Pierce, worn for a year and washed only twice, so the company can clone his life and sell it. Once opposed to mainstream values, hip now seems merely a step ahead of them. It is taken for granted that what is hip today will be mass tomorrow.

In this environment, who can be hip? Taking the long view, hip is ex-

Deborah Harry

actly what it has always been: an undercurrent of enlightenment, organized around contradictions and anxieties. Hip's trendiness has always been a by-product, not a goal. Hip is not simply the sum of What's Hot Now. In a country that resisted the class hierarchies of Europe, hip offers an alternate status system, independent of money or bloodline. The cultural anxieties that produced it have moved but not diminished. The syntheses now are global rather than local; information is overwhelming rather than pinched. *Hepi* or *hipi,* to see or open one's eyes, is as essential for negotiating 21st-century America as 19th or 20th. If the shelf life for trends or slang has shortened, the premium on knowledge is greater than ever. In a society run on information, hip is all there is.

Hip's evolution, then, continues apace, but for now let us freeze it in the middle, which is to say, in Cleveland. Specifically, in the low-fi Cleveland of Jim Jarmusch's 1984 film, *Stranger Than Paradise.* John Lurie and Richard Edson, veterans of New York's underground music scene, play a couple of petty hustlers from the East Village—card cheats and horseplayers, skinny men who wear suspenders and hats in bed. They drive to Cleveland to see Lurie's cousin Eva, who is fresh from Budapest and already a kindred spirit. With an immigrant's clarity of purpose, she quickly distills her own vision of the American Dream: shoplifting cartons of

Chesterfields and blasting "I Put a Spell on You" by Screamin' Jay Hawkins from a cheap portable cassette player. This is not far from the men's take on America. In the bland sprawl of Cleveland, the three are all wrong angles, outsiders.

Eva takes the two men to see Lake Erie, and it is as if to the abyss. The frozen landscape spreads across the screen, broken only by the three windblown silhouettes. The world around them has gone blank. By most measures, they are figures of no account, all but consumed by the white void. Yet in Jarmusch's frame, their journey taps into a long tradition of vagabond resistance. Instead of falling into the white backdrop, they simply pose stark against it. Pulling back, Eva speaks for them all, in accented understatement: "It's kind of a drag here, really." Against the suck of this landscape, Jarmusch grants them not only immunity, but a kind of grace.

This captures a classic American perspective, which generations have used to create nourishing stories about themselves, and to stake their identities within the country at large. The story of America is among other things about the pursuit of this nobility. Handed down through the centuries, it is an enduring, vital strand in the national romance. For lack of another word, it is the essence of hip.

1

in the beginning there was rhythm

slavery, minstrelsy and the blues

Do you know what a nerd is? A nerd is a human being without enough Africa in him or her.... You know why music was the center of our lives for such a long time? Because it was a way of allowing Africa in.
—BRIAN ENO

Toward the end of 1619, John Rolfe, the first tobacco grower of Virginia, noted the arrival of a new import to the British colonies. Rolfe (1585–1622) is best known as the husband of Pocahontas, and it was his experiments with growing tobacco that saved the Jamestown settlement from ruin. The incoming cargo he noted on this day would change the course of tobacco and the colonies as a whole. "About the last of August," he wrote, "came a Dutch man of war that sold us twenty Negroes."

These slaves, likely looted from a Spanish ship or one of the Spanish colonies to the south, were not the first African slaves in North America. The Spanish explorers Pánfilo de Narváez, Menendéz de Avilés and Coronado had all brought slaves into what is now Florida and New Mexico. Yet the 20 Africans who were brought ashore at modern-day Hampton, Virginia, then carried upriver for sale in Jamestown, formally marked the beginning of what would be 246 years of America's "peculiar institution" of slavery. Five years after their arrival, a 1624 census of Virginia recorded the presence of 22 blacks. Before the country banned new imports in 1808, leaving still the illegal market, around 600,000 to 650,000 Africans were brought to the states in bondage; by 1860, on the eve of the Civil War, there were almost 4 million slaves in the United States, out of a total population of 31 million.

A pressing question in the evolution of hip is, why here? Why did hip as we know it, and as it is emulated around the world, arise as a distinctly American phenomenon? Many of its signature elements existed among the bohemians of the Left Bank in Paris—or, for that matter, among those of Bohemia, now a part of the Czech Republic. The European capitals embraced the romance of scruff at least as early as Henri Murger's 1840s literary sketches, *Scènes de la vie die bohème*, or Giacomo Puccini's 1896 opera based on the sketches, *La Bohème*. Yet it is impossible to imagine Europe producing the blues or the Beats, the Harlem Renaissance or the Factory. What distinguished the United States is both simple and, in its ramifications, maddeningly, insolubly complex. That difference is the presence of Africans, and the coexistence of two very different populations in a new country with undefined boundaries. Without the Africans, there is no hip.

To be finer about it, there is no hip without African Americans and European Americans, inventing new identities for themselves *as Americans* in each other's orbit. These first-generation arrivals, black and white, and their second-, third- and fourth-generation heirs, learned to be Americans together. As a self-conscious idea, America took shape across an improvised chasm of race. Some of the most passionate arguments over slavery were economic rather than moral: Adam Smith argued that it undermined the free market for labor; defenders countered that the peculiar institution was more humane than the "wage slavery" of northern factories. But on a practical level, people on both sides of the divide needed strategies for negotiating the conundrum that held them apart, interdependent but radically segregated.

These strategies are hip's formative processes. While we often think of hip as springing whole into the world in the 1920s or 1950s, its roots go back at least another century. Hipster language, stance and irony begin

Amos 'n' Andy

not in the cool poses of the modern city but on the antebellum plantation, in the interplay of these two populations. For all their difference in
standing, the black and white foreigners taught each other how to talk,
eat, sing, worship and celebrate, each side learning as it was being learned.
Customs passed back and forth. Though history texts talk of Africans becoming Europeanized, or of Europeans stealing the blues, the ways the
two populations dealt with each other were more complicated than that.
Such borrowing is never indiscriminate, nor the copying exact. Like digital samplers, the borrowers pick and choose what works for them, and
shape it to their own ends; the final product comments on both its origins and its manipulations.

    This produced the feedback loop of hip, which centuries later gives us
white kids sporting doo rags. Against the larger story of racial oppression
and animosity, there was also one of creative interplay. The two populations had something to take from each other. In the decades bracketing
the Civil War, when a maturing America began to stage stories about itself, it created two idioms that reflected exactly this unresolved vortex.
The first is the blackface minstrel show, which surfaced in the 1820s and

1830s and is considered America's first popular culture. The second is the blues, which appeared toward the end of the century. These two forms, nurtured on American soil, are the twined root stems of hip. We live among their branches to this day.

If hip is a story of synthesis in the context of division, its origins lie in the unique structure of slavery in America, which pushed the two populations together. In the massive sugar plantations of Brazil and the Caribbean, which accounted for the majority of the transatlantic slave trade, slaves lived in overwhelmingly black worlds. Owners ran these plantations from a distance, working their slaves to death in the tropical climes and then importing huge waves of replacements. African cultures and languages, constantly replenished by new arrivals, survived relatively undiluted, and do to this day. In North America, by contrast, until the invention of the cotton gin in 1793 spurred the growth of big plantations, most farms were small and required few slaves. Owners worked the land, often without overseers between them and the slaves. The races lived together, unequally but intimately. Most white colonists did not even own slaves, and often labored beside them in the fields, either as indentured servants or poor wage earners. Since they were of less value to farmers than slaves, these poor whites commonly got the worst of the dirty work. As Thomas Sowell notes, "slave owners usually hired white workers— typically Irish immigrants—to do work considered too dangerous for slaves."

This closeness did not prevent brutality, especially in the years between the American Revolution and the Civil War. Slave narratives, of which there are more than 6,000, describe merciless beatings, floggings, mutilation, rape and murder of slaves. "They used to tie me down across a cotton bale, and give me 200 or 300 with a leather strap," Tom Wilson, who was born into slavery in 1813, told an interviewer. "I am marked with the whip from the ankle-bone to the crown of my head. . . . [T]hey burned my back with a red hot iron, and my legs with strong turpentine." Even where physical menace was less severe, the psychological violence of slavery is beyond account.

But there was also a level of intimacy, the interplay that fostered what we've come to know as hip. If the relationship of blacks and whites was rigidly defined at its essence—that of master to slave, and vice versa—it was fuzzier around the fringes. Day-to-day interactions involved compromise, subterfuge and imitation as well as force. This book is about the action that began on the fringes, and about its growth ever inward. This action does not refute the power of racism, nor limit it. Racism in America is so intractable precisely because it accommodates conflicting values: devout Christians found piety in the slave trade; racists are nothing if not idealists. But the nation developed its character not just in racial certainty, but in ambivalence. Individuals discovered points of contact in their evolving identities as Americans: nodes of language, religion, song, dance and sex. These would become the expressive channels of hip.

It is tempting to imagine the first slaveholders through the images of modern southerners—Rhett Butler, say, or George Wallace. But the settlers of Jamestown and subsequent slave economies were not recognizable southerners, nor even Americans. Almost as much as their slaves, they were foreigners in a strange and largely hostile land. The colonists in Jamestown, for example, had arrived only in 1607, just 12 years before the first slaves, at which time the climate and the natives nearly wiped them out. They did not learn how to survive until the next decade. They were slave owners first, southerners only much later. You could say that slavery invented the southerner—the sense of gentility and apartness, even the peculiarities of dialect—as much as the other way around. By the same token, the early slaves brought a mixed pedigree, not wholly African. As the historian Ira Berlin has noted, until late in the 17th century, most slaves in North America came not directly from Africa but from sugar plantations in the Caribbean and Brazil, and were often "Atlantic Creoles," bearing mixed legacies of culture and even race. In other words, both populations arrived with unsustainable notions of nationality and identity. The country was new, undefined. Blacks and whites together would give it definition.

The cultural interplay of hip began early, as white owners thrust themselves into every part of their slaves' lives. Sarah Fitzpatrick, who was born into slavery in Alabama in 1847, much later recalled an extraordinary level of meddling, not just in the slaves' labor but in their private affairs as well:

My Mistus use'ta look at my dress an' tell me when hit wuz right. Sometime she make me go back an' put on 'nother one, tell us what to wear,

tell us to go back an' com' our heads. Young "Niggers" f'om sev'ral plan'a-
tions used to git toget'er at one 'er der white fo'ks houses an' have a big
time. White fo'ks lact to git 'round an' watch 'em, make 'em ring up an'
play games an' things lack dat. You see de "Niggers" couldn't write in dem
days an' ef a boy wanted to court a gal he had to git his Marster to write
a letter fer him an' den de gals Mistus had to read de letter to her an' write
de boy back.

Owners prided themselves on their stewardship over their "people." This
paternalism, presented as benevolent, actually served two more self-
interested purposes. It let white slave owners rationalize the institution,
and it encouraged slaves to bond individually with their masters, diluting
their ties to each other. It was effective; mass rebellions were few. It also
immersed white owners in the culture of their slaves, and vice versa.

From the start, younger generations of whites and blacks were more
intimately entwined—closer to the enlightenment of hip—than their
elders. Hip is a culture of the young because they have the least investment in the status quo. Unlike the Caribbean slave colonies, which were
deadly for Africans, the conditions of American slavery produced positive
population growth, more births than deaths. By the Revolution, black
slaves born in America outnumbered those born in Africa four to one.
Children born on American soil, white or black, had progressively weaker
connections to Europe or Africa, and progressively closer ties with one
another. White and black Americans often ate the same poorly balanced
diet; even today the difference between "southern food" and "soul food"
lies largely in the name. Habits and folkways slipped back and forth.
Touring the south in the 1850s, the landscape architect Frederick Law
Olmsted was struck by "the close cohabitation and association of black
and white" on Virginia farms. "Negro women are carrying black and
white babies together in their arms; black and white children are playing
together . . . ; black and white faces are constantly thrust together out of
doors, to see the train go by." The influence they exerted on each other
flowed both ways. The historian Mechal Sobel, no doubt overstating the
case, has argued that by the end of the colonial period in Virginia, "both
blacks and whites held a mix of quasi-English and quasi-African values."
Hip's syntheses flowed from this interaction.

The first of these syntheses, and the first great cultural invention in

America, was black English. For Africans of different backgrounds, English was often their first shared vocabulary. The combination of English and slavery made diverse Yoruba and Akan and Wolof and Bantu and Ewe people into "Africans," just as they helped make English and Irish and Spanish and French people "white." The roots of contemporary hip talk go back to this encounter with language. Centuries before Dizzy Gillespie or Jay-Z, slaves and freedmen worked an early form of verbal jujitsu, imposing African values upon the foreign vocabulary. As the ethnomusicologist and psychotherapist Ernest Borneman has written, "In language, the African tradition aims at circumlocution rather than at exact definition. The direct statement is considered crude and unimaginative; the veiling of all contents in ever-changing paraphrases is considered the criterion of intelligence and personality." Adopting their masters' language, slaves bent it and coded it for their own use. Language brought the two races together and held them apart.

The new argot, besides yielding the word *hip*, was a model of hip synthesis. Slave owners were fascinated by it. Some beat their slaves for speaking "proper" English. Others simply fell into the new rhythms, completing a loop of emulation: blacks learned the English of whites, and whites copied the English of blacks. Words from various African languages entered the olio of the new land, becoming hip, dig, jive, juke, banjo, jazz and honky, this last from the Wolof *honq*, a derogatory word meaning pink man. What we know as the southern accent follows the inflections that generations of African Americans imposed on southern whites' formal British diction. Black English is the beginning of hip talk, rich and deliberately ambiguous. Walt Whitman heard in it an incipient national language, independent of Britain, containing "hints of a future theory of the modification of all words of the English language, for musical purposes, for a native grand opera in America." James Baldwin, writing a century later, called black English a record of "brutal necessity," permitting the nation "its only glimpse of reality, a language without which the nation would be even more *whipped* than it is." By the 1990s, the validity of black English, now called Ebonics, became a food fight for the Oakland Unified School District, which was failing to produce African-American graduates with other demonstrable skills. In the midst of this dustup, one might have noticed the students' white peers, hopped on the latest rap CD's, addressing each other, "What up, nigga."

But for slaves, a virtue of the language lay in its opacity, the shelter it provided from the prying ears of whites. The historian Eugene D. Genovese, noting the way slaves used words like *bad* to mean their opposite, describes their verbal tics as evasive maneuvers.

> The slaves, in effect, learned to communicate with each other in the presence of whites with some measure of safety, and the studied ambiguity of their speech, reinforced by reliance upon tone and gesture, helped immeasurably to prevent informers from having too much to convey to the masters beyond impressions and suspicions. If a slave informer heard a black preacher praise a runaway by calling him a *"ba-ad* nigger," what could he tell his master beyond saying he thought the preacher meant the opposite of what he said? Even slaveholders usually required better evidence.

The word *bad,* of course, has a storied history in hip, and its early appearance illustrates the longevity of hip talk. By using words like *bad* to mean two things at once, black English freed them from their one-to-one connections to the physical world. Words didn't mean one thing or another; they meant what their speaker said they did. This process, which separates words from things, is the beginning of irony and humor. Later hipsters, from Mark Twain to Biggie Smalls, used similar indirection to entwine freedom and sorrow in the same tale.

For slave owners, who worried about what slaves were saying, it was important to try to follow each new coinage; this, in turn, prodded blacks to invent still newer codes. This process goes on today; it is the essence of hip invention. Hip begins with a small circle, whose members push each other to more inventive or extreme forms of expression, then radiates outward in concentric circles. Each circle grabs what it can. By the time the outer circles have caught up, the inner ones have to invent new codes. Hip talk is not simple gamesmanship or sloppy grammar, but a strategy for multiplying meaning. It uses humor and ambiguity to convey one message to its intended recipients, and another to those looking on. The befuddlement of squares, like the confusion of white slave owners, is part of the play; verbal riffing wants an audience that doesn't get it as much as one that does.

Muddy Waters

African Americans worked a similar alchemy on white religion, absorbing a European idea to create something hybrid and new, neither European nor African, but fully both. The cultures of West Africa did not draw lines between the spiritual and secular worlds, and ascribed the actions of deities everywhere, sometimes benevolent, sometimes capricious or spiteful. In the New World, forbidden from practicing their faiths, slaves had a complicated affair with Christianity. Slaveholders were divided about whether to try to convert their charges. Some felt it was their Christian duty; others worried that if slaves were baptized, they would have to be freed. With the evangelical revivals of the 1770s and 1780s—and, more significantly, after Nat Turner's insurrection in 1831, which left 59 people dead and many more panicked—many whites saw the gospel as a useful tool for pacifying slaves. Christianity became a meeting ground for the two populations, a set of core stories shared.

The stories, however, were a starting point, not an end. Slaves added their own shades of meaning and metaphor. Slaves who converted were often taught to read and write, tools otherwise denied them. "Praise houses" on or off plantations became centers of independent black life, where descendants of Africa combined joy and tragedy—what Ralph Ellison called the missing element in white America—in dance and song. Religious practice straddled the two cultures, funneling one through the other. The Christian baptism mirrored West African rituals to river spirits; the "ring shouts," rich in polyphony, carried on the West African tradition of calling spirits down through music. When whites banned dancing, slaves contended that the limber movements of the ring shout weren't dancing, because the practitioners did not cross their legs.

Doctrine changed as well, emphasizing deliverance—and, by implication, escape—rather than Christian obedience. The story of Moses leading his people out of bondage assumed central importance. In 1898, W. E. B. DuBois, a founder of the Pan-Africanist movement and the NAACP, argued that slaves simply used Christian rites as a vessel for African values and mores. The black church, he wrote, is "the only institution of the Negroes which started in the African forest and survived slavery. . . . The communism of the African forests with its political and religious leadership is a living, breathing reality on American soil to-day, even after 250 years of violent change." White southern Christianity, in turn, took on some of the fervor of the black church, becoming vastly more flavorful than the pulpits of New England.

Less discussed is the extent to which the races mixed together in sex. The testimony of former slave women describes an abomination of sexual violence and rape. But records of marriage and long-term relationships suggest as well a range of erotic encounter, from terror to mutual affection—everything, perhaps, but equitable balance of power. Though we think of white plantation owners forcing themselves on their slaves, more children of mixed unions were born in the towns and cities, where there were populations of free blacks, than on the plantations. Nor were the affairs strictly between white men and black women. As the white Georgian artisan J. J. Flournoy insinuated, in an 1858 letter to R. F. W. Allston, the governor of South Carolina, "Do not many of our pretty white girls even now permit illicit Negro embrace at the South?"

Without romanticizing the encounters, it is reasonable to suppose they included a range of mixed feelings. After all, sex is rarely simple. The races became keepers of each other's most intimate secrets. Sex generated webs of complicity among white and black men and women.

Mary Boykin Chesnut, a white woman of Charleston, South Carolina, noted in her diary on March 14, 1861:

> Like the patriarchs of old, our men live all in one house with their wives and their concubines; and the mulattoes one sees in every family partly resemble the white children. Any lady is ready to tell you who is the father of all the mulatto children in everybody's household but her own. Those, she seems to think, drop from the clouds.

The place of cultural exchange, then, was often the pillow. Here, too, people were learning the ambivalent gestures, the coded language, that became America.

The white and black populations also shared folklore, putting their children to bed with each other's stories. In a nation built by mavericks and runaways, Africans absorbed the Western cult of individuality. A shared character was the "trickster," a wily hustler who displayed many of the nascent resources of hip: independence, guile, style and dexterity with the ambiguities of language. As the historian Peter Kolchin has remarked,

> Notably absent from Southern slave folklore are stories depicting heroic behavior—stories of dragon slayers, popular liberators, or people who sacrificed themselves for the good of the whole. Rather, the dominant themes are trickery, subterfuge, and securing as much as possible of a desired item (often food) for oneself. Justice, fair play, and compassion for one's rivals rarely emerge as desirable characteristics. In short, surviving in a heartless world assumes overriding importance.

The trickster, whom I'll discuss in depth in chapter 7, is a central archetype for hip. Descendants of the Greek god Hermes and the Yoruban prankster Esu-Elegbara, tricksters are lone operators, combining the European-American ethic of individualism with its African-American counterpart. Their prominence in slave tales, as the historian Michael Flusche has noted, complicates the image of slave culture as simply unified in the face of white oppression. Tricksters were not united against anything. Their individualism later replicated itself in the solos of jazz and the blues, in which each player competes within the ensemble, while the group pulls together against the outside world. This action became the hew and haw of hip: binding people together as outsiders, pushing them apart as lone rebels. Along the way, what was purely African or European receded into a cycle of mutual influence.

The blackface minstrel show, which hit the American stage in the 1820s and 1830s, was the purest projection of this ambivalence. Minstrelsy provided a model for white curiosity and co-optation of black forms, a superstructure of hip. It is worth pausing to consider the American weirdness of it all. Blacking their faces in burnt cork and performing skits and songs in crude racial stereotype, white minstrels (and less commonly blacks) created the most popular entertainment of the 19th century. Whitman loved the spectacles; Charles Dickens called William Henry Lane, a black man who performed as a minstrel character named Master Juba, the "greatest dancer known." Lane combined African and Irish traditions to invent a form of tap dancing, a typically American hybrid. In mid-century, performers like Thomas Dartmouth "Daddy" Rice, the Christy Minstrels, the Ethiopian Serenaders, the Virginia Minstrels and the Georgia Minstrels (a black group who billed themselves as "the Only Simon Pure Negro Troupe in the World") traveled the country and abroad, performing for mostly working-class white audiences.

The relationship to real African-American culture was always fanciful, but rarely wholly false. Rice, born May 20, 1808, in the rough Five Points neighborhood of lower Manhattan, created his most popular character after a trip to the South on which he said he watched a southern slave "turn around and jump Jim Crow." Dressed in a ragged blue coat and baggy striped trousers, Jim Crow—really a folk character common in the South—was alternatively a trickster and a hayseed, twisting the language into outlandish malapropisms. His minstrel counterpart, popularized by George Washington Dixon, was a citified dandy named Zip Coon who was regularly hoisted by his own pretensions. Performances often featured these two characters—or their rough analogs, Tambo and Bones— along with an "interlocutor," or straight man. The first minstrel characters performed during intermissions of Shakespeare or other drama, gaining popularity until the Christy Minstrels gave the first full minstrel concert in June of 1842 in Buffalo, New York. At the height of its popularity, the standard minstrel show consisted of a first act of songs and "black" countrified humor; a middle section, or "olio," offering dialogues, skits and soliloquies; and a closing set of songs and scenes, generally of the plantation South. Though its themes were southern, minstrel shows were most popular in the North. Some southern cities, not wishing to stir up abolitionists, banned the shows in the 1850s.

If there is a central vein of American popular culture, it proceeds from these crude outpourings of racial fantasy. Consider the defining songs of Stephen Foster, including "Oh! Susanna" and "Camptown Races," which he wrote for minstrel shows. Foster declared his aspiration to become "the best Ethiopian song-writer" in the country, though he never ventured near Ethiopia, or even south of Cincinnati. Before Irving Berlin wrote "God Bless America," he wrote and performed minstrel tunes as a singing waiter in a Manhattan restaurant known as Nigger Mike's, whose swarthy owner was, like Berlin, really a Russian Jew. Or consider the anthem "Dixie," credited to a white Ohioan named Daniel Decatur Emmett (1815–1904), leader of the Virginia Minstrels, though the brothers Dan and Lew Snowden, black performers who lived nearby, disputed this credit. The inscription on their tombstone, near Emmett's in Mount Vernon, Ohio, reads, "They taught 'Dixie' to Dan Emmett." Blues icons William Christopher "W. C." Handy, Gertrude "Ma" Rainey and Bessie Smith all started in minstrel shows. Little Richard, Muddy Waters, Jimmie Rodgers, Roy Acuff, Gene Autry, Bing Crosby and Fred Astaire all worked in or beside blackface. Dizzy Gillespie gave his first public performance, in 1929, in the pit band for a minstrel show at his elementary school.

Nor does the legacy of blackface end at the foot of the minstrel stage, any more than does the shadow of Jim Crow. The minstrel model has continued to function as a white ticket to black innovation. Hemingway argued that "all modern American literature comes from one book by Mark Twain called *Huckleberry Finn*"—which can be seen as a minstrel show on a raft, complete with dialect, ethnic characterization and comic misunderstandings. Blackface played a key role in landmark movies like *Uncle Tom's Cabin* (1903), *The Birth of a Nation* (1915) and *The Jazz Singer* (1927), the first talkie. *Amos 'n' Andy*, which translated minstrelsy for radio, was the most popular program in America in the late 1920s and early 1930s, perhaps the most popular of all time. The medium would not have proliferated as rapidly without it. The television version, canceled in

1960 after protests from the NAACP and others, created the template for the modern sitcom. Even now, a half century after Elvis, the sexual, violent caricatures of gangsta rap—what black music executive Bill Stephney calls "the commodification of nigga culture"—continue the line, selling cartoons of black thuggery to a largely white audience. The white rappers Eminem and Kid Rock repackage the same cartoons, parading their closeness with African Americans as license for their rhymes.

Surely this is a legacy of degradation used to reinforce the rationalizations for slavery. Frederick Douglass in 1848 denounced minstrels as "the filthy scum of white society, who have stolen from us a complexion denied to them by nature, in which to make money, and pander to the corrupt taste of their white fellow citizens." If you view white supremacy as an economic force, as I do, you might also notice that the profits from this entertainment, this conversion of black life into image, went almost entirely into the pockets of white men.

But as offensive as the shows were, the sentiments stirred in minstrel theaters were by nature mixed. Douglass, after watching an African-American troupe called Gavitt's Original Ethiopian Serenaders in 1849, wrote that there "is something gained, when the colored man in any form can appear before a white audience; and we think that even this company . . . may yet be instrumental in removing the prejudice against our race." This suggests a recognition of humanity on the part of the white audience, rather than a ritual negation. The writer and historian James Weldon Johnson, an architect of the Harlem Renaissance of the 1920s, argued for the artistic importance of minstrelsy, recognizing in it "the only completely original contribution America has made to the theatre." More recently Ishmael Reed praised *Amos 'n' Andy* for presenting a broader view of black America than the average 'hood film. "A lot of black people" found the show funny, Reed said. "But you're not supposed to say that to whites. When I was growing up, for black people, that was the favorite show."

Like gangsta rap, minstrel shows invited the white audience to participate vicariously in a world that was both alluring and inaccessible. The stereotypes enacted on stage rippled with sexual potency and license. "The white imagination," as the dancer Josephine Baker later observed, "is sure something when it comes to blacks." White minstrels were "trying on" being black; the working-class audience empathized with the minstrel characters against pompous boss men and snooty aristos. For many white theatergoers, such identification was a short stretch. The depression of 1837 gave the exaggerated shabbiness of the characters—and the downward mobility of the performers—a particular resonance. To put on the black face was to make tangible one's status as outsider. Behind burnt cork and ham fat lay the embryonic sentience of hip.

What made the minstrel shows so combustive, then, was not just the racial mockery, buts its contradictory knotting with empathy, in what the sociologist Eric Lott calls "love and theft." Lott quotes Leslie Fiedler's remarks on how this combination encapsulates the American white male experience: "Born theoretically white, we are permitted to pass our childhood as imaginary Indians, our adolescence as imaginary Negroes, and only then are expected to settle down to being what we really are: white once more." Curious about black life and identity, perhaps threatened by it, white performers and audiences invented their own version of it, nonthreatening and remunerative. African Americans had long enacted their own racial pantomime, putting on a smiling, obedient "black" mask for slave owners, or caricaturing white hauteur in the plantation "cakewalk" dance. Now it was white performers' and their working-class audience's turn to mold the mask of race.

Over the following century and a half, this pattern of love and theft played a vital role in hip, creating cultural currents whose origins were properly not black nor white, but a jumble of the two. As the cultural historian Ann Douglas notes, the way we talk or sing involves not just white caricatures of blacks, but black parodies of whites as well, in an ongoing dialogue. "Blacks imitating and fooling whites, whites imitating and stealing from blacks, blacks reappropriating and transforming what has been stolen, whites making yet another foray on black styles, and on and on: this *is* American popular culture." Nimble performers manipulate the crossover, pushing the audience to rethink the categories of race. Consider the mask Bob Dylan donned in his song "Outlaw Blues." Describing his woman in Jackson, Mississippi, he sings, "She's a brown-skinned woman but I love her just the same." This expression of shade preference only makes sense as an intragroup thing, a black singer addressing a black audience. For the duration of the song, everyone plays a role. This promise of reinvention—that we are not bound by our pasts—is a core current of hip.

•   •   •

T he blues, the other root stem of hip, took on the question of America from the other side. As Amiri Baraka argues, the blues was the first cultural idiom created by blacks as Americans. If ministrelsy was a record—perhaps a *warped* record—of whites' encounters with blacks, the early blues and its antecedents document blacks' encounter with the New World. This encounter, as Baraka notes, involved a transformation in two steps, first from captives to slaves, then from African slaves to a new identity born of America. "When America became important enough to the African to be passed on, in those formal renditions, to the young, those renditions were in some kind of Afro-American language. And finally, when a man looked up in some anonymous field and shouted, 'Oh, Ahm tired a dis mess, / Oh, yes, Ahm so tired a dis mess,' you can be sure he was an American."

This plaint, if it has a home, belongs to the muddy soil of the Mississippi Delta, a 200-mile stretch of rich farmland running south of Memphis, Tennessee, between the Yazoo River on the east and the Mississippi on the west. This is the cradle of the blues. From Highway 61 south of Clarksdale, Mississippi, the fields of scrub wood and swamp today stretch out as they must have at the dawn of the previous century, and the one before that. Writers like to describe the Mississippi Delta as "one of the most beautiful spots on earth," but it has a tumid inertia to it, a reminder that nature's bounty is both ripeness and rot. The Delta has some of the highest rates of poverty and illiteracy in the nation, and draws a steady stream of tourists to see the legacy of this deprivation, meaning the blues. You could feel that time does not move around here, until you see the occasional gaudy mansion among the Delta shacks, evidence that crack cocaine, having run its cycle in the cities of the North, is still chugging in the rural South.

This is a book about an abstraction, but it is worth tracing its outlines through concrete dates. In 1929, Charley Patton (1891–1934), the son of a Mississippi sharecropper and the first epic artist of the Delta blues, recorded his first sides, "Pony Blues" and "High Water Everywhere—Parts 1 and 2." In July 1954, Elvis Aaron Presley of Tupelo, Mississippi, recorded Arthur "Big Boy" Crudup's "That's All Right." If you think the syrup of

Son House

time drips slowly in the Delta, consider the short gap, just 25 years, between these two dates. Patton's sides looked back on the existential dread and high life after the Civil War, and the Great Flood of 1927, which many Mississippians saw as a throwback to biblical tribulation. Presley's record, besides launching his career, looked forward to the modern world as we know it: the outrageous commerce in celebrity and image; the movement of sex from private to public commodity; the explicit play of white and black music; the question of theft. Such is the speed of modernity in the Delta, zooming by when you're not looking. All of this contributed to hip's development. And all of it was prefigured in the formation of the blues.

Slaves on the Delta plantations in the 18th and 19th centuries were heirs to a broad range of African musical traditions. Though Americans often think of "African music" as a single idiom, slaves from different parts of the continent brought widely divergent styles. Robert Palmer, in his book *Deep Blues,* identified three distinct musical traditions that came together on American plantations. Slaves from Senegal and Gambia invoked the plucked string instruments, Arabic intonations and call-and-response songs of the Wolof empire. Men and women from the slave coast—what is now Sierra Leone, Liberia, the Ivory Coast, Ghana, Togo,

Benin, Nigeria and Cameroon—built music around intricate poly-rhythms. Even after slavers banned drums for fear slaves would use them to signal insurrection, this lineage remained highly rhythmic, telling its stories through subtle changes in beat rather than melody. Bantu slaves from farther south in Congo and Angola specialized in complex vocal arrangements. All three groups used music to accompany everyday tasks. Though there were some specialist musicians, in the main everybody participated.

Workers in southern cotton fields mixed all these flavors, adding also elements of the Irish ballad, the hymnal and other European influences. The music they created was an American hybrid, neither African nor European. They sang to synchronize their movements and relieve the monotony. The vocal leader of a work gang would call out a line and the others would respond, often in sprawling polyphony. In the praise houses, singers mixed Western hymns and African elements in the call-and-response of spirituals. While other African cultural practices withered in antebellum America, by force or habit, music thrived and evolved. Even now, black parents who cannot trace family trees pass the heritage of their ancestors to their children through songs. Music bears the weight of collective memory, not just in its lyrics but in its intonations and rhythms. For whites, meanwhile, music was the most accessible part of slave culture; though parents and children, blacks and whites, preachers and sinners have all squabbled for centuries about rhythm, it remains the nearest thing to a universal language. In the slave cultures of early America, it gave away secrets even as it harbored them.

With the end of slavery in 1865, the large work gangs of the plantations broke into smaller units for sharecropping. This changed the structure of song. Organizing themselves in smaller groups, sharecroppers improvised field hollers or arhoolies that could be sung by a few men. Some sang solo. Unlike a slave, who might have no cause to celebrate his situation, a free man could sing his own song, tell his own story. Though the music still served a communal function, it became more personal, less collective or anthemic. Changes in the availability of instruments pushed musicians further in this direction. In the late 19th century, the firms of C. F. Martin and Orville Gibson popularized the guitar, which replaced the African-derived banjo in black music. Mail-order companies like

Sears Roebuck made guitars affordable even to the poor, creating opportunities for footloose combos or solo performers.

Though Sunday services remained the core of black community life, Saturday night began to take on a new significance. Singers developed lambent melodies and language that juxtoposed sorrow and laughter, engaging daily life while providing ironic distance from its hardships. Delta guitar players could capture the slurred sonorities of West Africa by sliding a knife or a bottle neck up and down the strings. Singers and instrumentalists flattened notes for emphasis of feeling, as in African pitch-tone languages like Yoruba and Akan. The humor was that of African-American trickster tales, which reveled in misfortune, often cruelly, as a way to transcend it. The new narratives burst with sorrow and comedy and fear and sex, often all at once. By around 1900, the emerging individualized music had diverged far enough from folk ballads like "John Henry" and "Frankie and Albert" to be its own thing, known as the blues.

The history of the blues seems custom-made for American legend, an act of spontaneous creation by rebel geniuses. Charley Patton, for example, defied his preacher father to pursue a dissolute life of booze, devil music and appreciative women. His early acolyte Tommy Johnson claimed to have sold his soul to the devil in exchange for mastery of the music. The deal was simple, Johnson explained to his brother LeDell: You just go to a crossroads at midnight with your guitar. "A big black man will walk up there and take your guitar, and he'll tune it. And then he'll play a piece and hand it back to you. That's the way I learned how to play anything I want." This story, as Palmer points out, traces back to Yoruban folktales in which a trickster named Legba struck similar deals. Only in Christian retellings did this figure become the devil. Many musicians told a version of the story to explain their skills, most famously Robert Johnson (no relation to Tommy), whose haunted stories and plangent voice made the presence of the devil real in his music. Blues musicians were folk antiheroes in a landscape of their own invention.

Or at least this is how the story came together after the blues eclipsed the other musics of its day. The fibs of history are those told by the winners, and the blues won out as a category. Properly speaking, though, there were few blues singers in the Delta. Itinerant black performers played a mix of minstrel tunes, ballads, folk songs, rags and blues—

roughly the same repertoire as white country singers. Many of these "songsters" were skilled in European classical music, reels, jigs and waltzes. The guitar, more versatile than the banjo, allowed performers to play everything on the same instrument. The singers absorbed and transmitted huge bundles of heritage, only some of it with roots in Africa. They played for white audiences and black. Sam Chatmon, a musician who may have been Charley Patton's half brother, once told an interviewer, "Mighty seldom I played for colored. They didn't have nothing to hire you with." One music blended into another; cultural connections rolled back and forth.

With the advent of recordings in the early 20th century, though, these ambiguities became a liability. Records aspire to markets, and markets like fixed categories; since you can't see the singer, you have to understand him through his genre. Black performers became blues singers in the studio, dropping their other mastery at the door; whites became hillbilly singers. The blues singer, then, was an invention of the studio, and often of white record executives. In the same way that the technology of guitar manufacture changed the music's form, the technology of recording changed the identity and repertoire of the performers. On their own, the musicians had put their stamp on all sorts of music. It was only in the recording process, converting the singer to commodity, that the blues singer came to sing only the blues.

The biography of the blues singer—rather than the well-rounded entertainer whose set list included the blues—added value to the music, as the biographies of Kurt Cobain or Charlie Parker add dimension to their recordings even today. This is how hip works, attaching stories to one thing and not another—usually in accord with unseen needs of the economy. In the pantheon of hip characters, the blues singer was one of the first images concocted *as image* in the service of mass production. The blues emerged as the nation was beginning to move from an agrarian to a manufacturing economy, spreading luxury items (like records) to parts of the population that could barely afford essentials. The blues, too, went from being country music, driven by the Delta, to city music, driven by the urban needs of New York and Chicago. The first "race" recording, Mamie Smith's 1920 "Crazy Blues," recorded in New York, defined blacks for the first time as a consumer group. African Americans who did not have record players bought the record as a signal of a promising black future: industrial, technological, full of luxury goods and time to enjoy them.

The performers sketched the early profile of the hipster. In a society overburdened by toil, they ditched plantation work, living by their wits and ability to transform themselves into image. They developed a layered language that signaled sorrow and transcendence in the same breath. Admired almost as outlaws, they boasted the illicit enlightenment of the crossroads. They were outsiders, cultivating the disdain of proper black society—including Patton's father, who considered secular music the work of the devil. For the next century, many standard-bearers of the black middle class repeated this pattern of disapproval, castigating early jazz, bebop, vernacular poetry and hip-hop, partly for the impression such raw art might make on whites. In each case adventurous white audiences and black bohemians have swept in to embrace the work, not in spite of its elemental roughness but because of it.

Throughout this book, I'll return to this pattern of upright black disapproval as the opening by which white hipsters stake their claim to the culture. The logic runs something like this: If these white hipsters are down with Charley Patton or 50 Cent, while black naysayers feel he has gone too far, the hipsters can imagine that they are part of a cultural vanguard defined by taste or attitude rather than birthright. This is one of hip's central premises. Popular culture becomes a virtual world detached from the thornier realities of race. The white embrace of Charley Patton or 50 Cent perpetuates stereotypes even as it undermines them. When black censors like the Rev. Calvin O. Butts of the Abyssinian Baptist Church in Harlem or C. Delores Tucker of the National Political Congress of Black Women protest rap stereotypes, they energize these stereotypes among white listeners, where historically they have done most harm. Black and white rap audiences, then, share the same stereotypes that in other ways divide them. The value of this sharing is open to debate.

This debate reflects the difference between minstrelsy and the blues. Though they respond to similar absurdities, they are not the same. The minstrel tradition has its origins in the old South, and longs nostalgically for simpler times. It is in love with the myth of the primitive, whom it sees as man before the fall. The blues, which began after emancipation, celebrates escape from the past and believes in a better future. It is a voice of modernism, hurtling ever forward—sometimes scared by what it sees, but unwilling to go back. In minstrelsy, the passage of time separates man farther from Eden; in the blues, it delivers man toward the unknown. Hip time is a synthesis of the two: an isolated present tense, cut off from the past and future, remaking itself in the instant.

The economy that came of age with the blues called for legends and masks more subtle but no less communicative than those of minstrelsy. Both forms worked along the frontiers of race and money, where the needs of popular culture—the curiosities of listeners, the economic exigencies of performers—ran ahead of pedestrian society. They were more impure than the nation knew it was or wanted to be. The mythologies of the blues, like those of minstrelsy, belonged to the sales offices of the entertainment biz as well as to the Delta or the plantation. As an engagement with America, the blues traced a pathway through the brambles of race, surviving tribulations through humor and resilience; minstrelsy plowed its own path through.

The economy made this map available to white audiences as well as black: some secrets shared, some held in reserve. Hip was the point at which, for those who got it, the incomprehensible moved closer to their grasp.

2 the o.g.'s

emerson, thoreau, melville and whitman

Whitman is a rowdy, a New York tough, a loafer, a frequenter of low places, a friend of cab drivers! —JAMES RUSSELL LOWELL

From the start, America offered the promise of reinvention: the erasure of past ties, the chance to create a new identity. This remains the nation's principal fantasy. Whether you are a Yiddish-speaking immigrant on the Lower East Side or a pop singer named Madonna, you can create yourself anew. As recently as 1997, the writer Bharati Mukherjee described America as "a stage for transformation. I felt when I came to Iowa City from Calcutta that suddenly I could be a new person. . . . I could choose to discard that part of my history that I want, and invent a whole new history for myself." In the country's early history, this reinvention had a savage side. White slave owners, stepping out of their own pasts, forced this same condition on their slaves, erasing their names, languages, religions, nationalities, cultures and family lines. As the country grew dynamically in the 18th and 19th centuries, blacks and whites continued to reinvent themselves, concocting new language to contain their new identities. This was the incipient voice of hip: vulgar, fly, wise, self-made, new. Its liberties challenge the boundaries of race. If you can be what you want, unbound by name or past, what does it mean to be black or white?

While the blackface minstrels and blues performers discussed in

Bob Dylan and Joan Baez *(© Daniel Kramer)*

chapter 1 acted out this fluidity of identity, the major writers of the antebellum period—Ralph Waldo Emerson, Henry David Thoreau, Walt
Whitman and Herman Melville—explored the full dimensions of the
paradox. In the 1850s, as the nation lurched toward Civil War, they
produced a body of work that has been dubbed the American Renaissance. The five-year period between 1850 and 1855 saw the publication
of Emerson's *Representative Men,* Melville's *Moby-Dick* and *Pierre,*
Thoreau's *Walden* and the first edition of Whitman's *Leaves of Grass.* (I
skip over Nathaniel Hawthorne, whose great novels, also published in this
period, were too singularly moralizing for our purposes here.) These
writers set down the intellectual framework for hip. Celebrating the individual and the nonconformist, advocating civil disobedience, savoring

the homoerotic, and above all claiming the sensual power of the new, the writers articulated a vision of hip that we now carry everywhere like an internal compass. The hip felicities that have come since—the uncapped solos of bebop and hip-hop, the gnostic blur of the Lost Generation and the Beat generation, the indie purism of Chapel Hill or Olympia, the altered consciousness of the drug culture—all built on the principles they threw down.

Their work reflected the early rumblings of industry and urbanization, and the exuberant hype of the first advertising agencies. Amid this churn, the writers of hip's first convergence sought to invent a literature and identity for a nation whose mandarins still preached the high culture of Europe. Outlawed in their sexual practices, tax habits or literary ideals, they defined civil disobedience, not just in politics but in culture and lifestyle. In the 1855 preface to *Leaves of Grass,* Whitman (1819–1892) prescribed an ethos for poets that can stand as a founding hipster manifesto. His subject was not verse but revolt:

> This is what you shall do: Love the earth and sun and animals, despise riches, give alms to every one that asks, stand up for the stupid and crazy, devote your income and labor to others, hate tyrants, argue not concerning God, have patience and indulgence toward the people, take off your hat to nothing known or unknown or to any man or number of men, go freely with powerful uneducated persons and with the mothers of families, read these leaves in the open air every season of every year of your life, re-examine all you have been told at school or church or in any book, dismiss whatever insults your own soul, and your very flesh shall be a great poem and have the richest fluency not only in its words but in the silent lines of its lips and face and between the lashes of your eyes and in every motion and joint of your body.

In a country without a literature, the major writers outlined a break from both the literary shadow of Europe and the political shadow of their own country: a gospel of nonconformity in prose and verse. They jettisoned the call of the past. Americans did not have the long history that defined European character and discounted the Old World hierarchy of bloodline. The promise of the New World was that the past was not binding, that a pauper today could be a prince tomorrow. In America, old families were mostly just old. As Emerson observed, the new country called for mythologies rather than history. Myth allows the past to speak in the present tense. "Our admiration of the Antique is not admiration of the old," he wrote, "but of the natural. We admire the Greek in an American ploughboy often." Though social mobility in America has always been as much shibboleth as reality, it is a powerful shibboleth. The signature tense of the new land was the mobile present, a voracious gully sucking up the claims of past and future.

In later eras, this oceanic present suited the improvisations of jazz—inventing in the moment, rather than working from a fixed score—or the spontaneous prose of the Beats. Mary McCarthy, writing in 1963 about William S. Burroughs's 1959 *Naked Lunch,* wrote that the novel "has no use for history, which is all 'ancient history'—sloughed-off skin. . . . The oldest memory in *The Naked Lunch* is of jacking-off in boyhood latrines, a memory recaptured through pederasty." This ahistoric voice, shorn of absolutes, indulges contradiction. The American present, heedless of cause or effect, became the tense of hip.

But first it had to be created. The emancipation of the present tense, which now informs every new product or advertisement, is a deceptively radical force. It undermines the authority of work, school, church and family, which all demand that we subordinate the present to the future. The writers who insisted on this tense put themselves outside of society, and paid a price for their rebellion. Hip did not become hip without resistance.

Until the 19th century, the reigning literary form in the country was the sermon. Before America was a country of writers, lawyers, hipsters, geeks, DJs or Starbucks franchises, it was a country of orators. They were the enforcers of community will. Though American schoolchildren learn that the country was founded on religious freedom and tolerance, the New England pilgrims preferred religious conformity and discipline. The Anglican minister Nathaniel Ward, best known for his 1647 treatise *Against Toleration,* articulated the Puritan version of religious freedom, declaring that anyone with different views "shall have free Liberty to keepe away from us, and such as will come to be gone as fast as they can, the sooner the better." The Massachusetts Bay Colony legislated the death penalty for Quakers. Sermons like Jonathan Edwards's fearsome *Sinners in the Hands of an Angry God* (1741), the preeminent American text of its era, defined the role of the individual: to subordinate the self to the doctrine of the community, to conform to the values of the charter. If American religion was weak on theology, it was strong on political dogma and muscle. Its tense was the future: defer now for the kingdom of heaven later.

Hip's evolution begins with individuals breaking this bond, and by the late 1700s, the cultural impulses of the nation were already starting to swing in that direction. The black church, fittingly, was ahead of the shift. African-American preachers like Harry Hoosier and John Jasper brought a roaring, individualistic message to the pulpit. In a country whose churches condoned slavery, they preached a direct individual relationship with God. The self was noble where the high church was not—the outsider, in other words, became sacrosanct. At the same time, itinerant white preachers like Peter Cartwright and Edward Thompson Taylor were starting to blow hot from the pulpit. Such preachers disseminated news and slang from town to town and built audiences through their performance. The Second Great Awakening, which began in the late 18th century, stoked demand for preachers who rocked the house. Especially along the western frontier, where preachers went from church to church, they had to give congregations something to remember them by. The WASP propriety of New England pulpits gave way to a volcanic, frontier individualism, both in the delivery of the preacher and in the substance of the sermon. Taylor (1793–1871), a former sailor, was one of the most dynamic new shouters and a strong influence on the major writers. Like them, he attempted to bridge the gaps in society. An account of an 1845 sermon at Concord observed that "black and white, poet and grocer, contractor and lumberman, Methodist and preachers, joined with the regular congregation in rare union." Taylor maintained a close friendship with Emerson and was likely the model for Melville's Father Mapple, the fulminating minister in *Moby-Dick*. Whitman called Taylor the country's only "essentially perfect orator."

This is not to suggest that the road to Miles Davis runs through the pulpit of Concord. But the changing dynamic of the sermon inspired both the grandiose rhetoric of Whitman and Melville and the gospel of individualism that was central to hipsters to come. The self was turned loose. It was up to the great artists to give it great direction.

Ralph Waldo Emerson (1803–1882) was the first of the major writers to take up this challenge. Born into a family of Boston ministers, he followed his father to Harvard Divinity School, becoming sole pastor of the Second Unitarian Church in Boston in 1830. But he quickly lost faith in the church, as in other institutions. In 1838, his "Address at Divinity College" challenged both the Harvard intelligentsia and what he saw as a sterile church. Tapping the heartier energies of preachers like Taylor, he saw the country's strength in salty vulgarity, declaring, "I embrace the common, I explore and sit at the feet of the familiar, the low." Emerson considered society everywhere to be "in conspiracy against the manhood of every one of its members," and preached a program of self-reliance and nonconformity. In place of obedience he advocated the insolence of youth: "A boy is in the parlor what the pit is in the playhouse; independent, irresponsible, looking out from his corner on such people and facts as pass by, he tries and sentences them on their merits, in the swift, summary way of boys, as good, bad, interesting, silly, eloquent, troublesome." This is the essential play space of hip. The tattoos and piercings of 21st century bohemia are not transgressions against Emerson's legacy but odes to it.

Henry David Thoreau (1817–1862), the son of a shopkeeper and pencil manufacturer, was Emerson's most illustrious pupil. Like his mentor, he refused to support a government that sanctioned slavery or a church that did little to interfere. For his best-known book, *Walden*, he built a crude house in the woods around Walden Pond and removed himself from society, subsisting on his skills in the wild. In July 1846, during a visit into town from Walden, he was arrested and spent a celebrated night in jail for refusing to pay his poll tax for six years. His explanation, eventually published as "Civil Disobedience," celebrated the individualist who does not keep pace with his companions "because he hears a different drummer." In a society of scolds and strivers, Thoreau saw the nation's promise in loafing, not achieving or acquiring, and he argued that "the only true America is that country where you are at liberty to pursue such a mode of life as may enable you to do without" excess stuff. A century later, Kerouac echoed these words in *Visions of Cody*, writing that "[e]verything belongs to me because I am poor."

Like later hipsters, Emerson and Thoreau both explored Eastern spiritual disciplines. Melville, a career sailor, brought Eastern beliefs back from his travels, and Whitman wrote that one of his goals was to make clear "the myths Asiatic, the primitive fables . . . eluding the hold of the known, mounting to heaven!" This pursuit of alternative consciousness or enlightenment has run alongside of hip, from the 19th-century transcendentalists to the 1960s counterculture to the yoga and meditation centers of today. The Harvard historian and philosopher Eugene Taylor calls this lineage America's shadow culture, "a vast unorganized array of discrete individuals who live and think differently from the mainstream but who participate in its daily activities." This culture is neither Eastern nor Western, but like hip itself, exists in the straddle, where it can be more than one thing at once. It thrives in the hyphen. Taylor says the shadow culture "holds exactly the opposite prejudices of the dominant culture. Where the dominant culture tends to overemphasize its Judeo-Christian and Anglo-European roots, the shadow culture embraces world cultures rather than defining itself as separate from them. . . . [V]isionaries of the American shadow culture, in turn, absorb the identity of ethnic subcultures and yet remain within the iconography and mythology of the dominant culture." This altered consciousness, which comes in many forms, allows hip to critique the mainstream from without as well as within.

Emerson and Thoreau's theories played out in the new sprawl of the cities. Hip's signature voice—its jaunty talk and floating layers of meaning—comes together in dense, mixed neighborhoods, and in the 19th century, these neighborhoods were starting to add up. Waves of immigrants, free blacks, drifters, rogues, hustlers, con men, prostitutes and profiteers began to cluster in urban centers. The bucolic charms of the Bouwerie— so named for the pleasant shade of its bowers—gave way to the congested bustle of the Bowery, home to a hale breed of Irish immigrant known as the Bowery b'hoy or g'hal (a transliteration of the Irish accent). Though most Americans still lived and worked on farms, cities grew rapidly in the 19th century. Alexis de Tocqueville, touring the country in 1831 and 1832, wrote, "I look upon the size of certain American cities, and especially on the nature of their population, as a real danger." In the following three decades, the urban population grew by 700 percent.

It was the second part of Tocqueville's observation—the *nature of their population*—that concerned moralists, even as it fostered hip. Cities brought together diverse tribes of immigrants, who were pulled by opportunities on the frontier, or pushed by the potato famines that wracked Ireland in the 1840s. Five million immigrants came to the north between 1820 and 1860. About 60 percent of free blacks lived in cities, compared with about 20 percent of the population as a whole. The new slums bred a mix of styles and languages, sometimes fractious. The historian Paul Boyer notes that between 1834 and 1844, there were more than 200 major gang wars in New York City, "and in other cities the pattern was similar." Right-minded people saw slums like Five Points as a blot on the country.

The quickest route to reinvention in a new land is through fashion. Clothes are part of hip's language, signaling autonomy, desire, ethnicity and sexual come-on. Like the blackface mask, they allow wearers to explore who they want to be, to straddle identities. Hip fashion does not mean having the right clothes, but being able to work the language, which bubbles up from the streets and thrift stores, not down from the design houses. In the 19th century, New York was a hotbed of single working women, whose presence is catnip to any hip scene. An 1855 study found that half of the city's unmarried women lived away from their parents. These women dressed for themselves rather than their families, with a sense of daring and lip. They dressed to walk on the Bowery with girlfriends or dates, not to help with the family chores. Immigrant women entered the country at Castle Garden wearing the peasant threads of Ireland or Italy but quickly transformed themselves in styles that played off the fashions of the rich.

Fashion, like language, was democratized. Women from the needle trades or the new cosmetics trade made mischief with the styles of their social betters. The historians Edwin G. Burrows and Mike Wallace, in their encyclopedic *Gotham: A History of New York City to 1898*, describe an 1850s street parade of "startling color combinations, ornate hats, and elaborate decorations even gaudier than those favored by the wealthy. By recycling fashions of the 1820s, they essayed a retro look." B'hoys had their own look, designed to mix menace with sexual aggressiveness. They loitered with cigars in hand, hair slicked forward with soap. From these early impulses—toward sex, retro chic, class revenge and thug vitality—you can project the history of hip fashion. By 1855 on the Bowery, the ground rules were drawn.

The shift to the city involved a shift in tense. If farmers dwelt on the past and future, living between last season's seeds and next season's harvest, city life existed in the present. People earned wages by the hour, and often drank them at a similar rate. The industrial economy turned work into an abstraction. Workers now left the natural world for a factory or job site, between arbitrary hours, among strangers and rivals, to produce objects of questionable value to themselves. Unlike farmers, who had no boundaries between work and other parts of their lives, industrial laborers had to adopt personae for the duration of the workday, conforming to roles that had little to do with their interests. Their identities became situational, segmented. Farmwork was as consuming as survival itself, but city work ended when the whistle blew. By 1869, 2 million Americans earned their living in factories or small industries; by the end of the century there were nearly 5 million in factories alone. At the end of each workday, they had to reconstruct their identities in the world of leisure. The working world called for an antithesis or escape. Hip germinated in the off hours.

The writers of the American Renaissance reacted to these abstractions, treating identity itself as negotiable. In the famous opening line of *Moby-Dick*, "Call me Ishmael," the narrator doesn't so much identify himself as invite readers to distrust his identity, to consider this "Ishmael" a provisional conceit between themselves and the author. By the time Melville wrote *The Confidence-Man* six years later, he created a nameless protagonist who changed identity from page to page. The character appears as a crippled black man in one chapter and as a white man wearing a weed in his hat in the next. Melville's con man, a trickster, evokes the most famous American of the day, Phineas Taylor Barnum (1810–1891), who opened his American Museum of oddities, freaks and scams on lower Broadway in 1842. Like other tricksters, Melville's confidence man performs for sport as much as for profit. "You two green-horns!" a character upbraids two of the man's serial dupes. "Money, you think, is the sole motive to pains and hazard, deception and devilry, in this world. How much money did the devil make by gulling Eve?" Changing identities on the fly, the protagonist frees himself from the past and the future, making hay in the improvised present.

Where Melville saw the fall in such deceit, Whitman positioned

Walt Whitman

himself to be the bard of the rascally streets. Born in 1819 in West Hills, Long Island, the second of nine children, he moved to Brooklyn four years later, where his father, who came from a family of successful farmers and landowners, hoped to make his fortune building houses. The venture was a flop. Walt left Brooklyn's sole public school to work as an office boy at 11, and apprenticed himself to a printer the following year. New York at the time harbored a chaotic Babel of penny newspapers, many of them very short-lived, and Whitman flitted from one to another, serving as printer, editor, publisher, reporter, poet and diarist. He, too, was crafting his identity. An 1854 daguerreotype shows him with his shirt collar open, a fist on hip, head cocked defiantly, goatee around his full, unsmiling lips. He called himself "one of the roughs" and chronicled the lives of prostitutes and firemen, newsboys and gamblers, promising to give account of "this great, dirty, blustering, glorious, ill-lighted, aristocratic, squalid, rich, wicked, and magnificent metropolis."

In 1855, Charles Pfaff, a portly man of German and Swiss descent, opened a basement beer hall where the riff and raff of Whitman's New York could come together. Pfaff's, at 653 Broadway, north of Bleecker Street, was the first outpost of bohemia in America. The staff of Henry

Clapp's *New York Saturday Press,* the nation's first countercultural news-paper—daring in its radical politics, sexual frankness and blunt humor—did much of their drinking and thinking in this convivial basement. *Bohemia* is an imported word, and it should be remembered here and throughout this book that hip's roots lie in pursuit of knowledge and awareness, not in the anti-intellectual grunt of sitcom hoodlums or the knuckleheaded creed of "keeping it real." Its rejection of conventional wisdom is a reflection on convention, not wisdom.

Clapp's circle included Fitz Hugh Ludlow, whose 1857 bestseller, *The Hasheesh Eater,* introduced the country to one of bohemia's secret plea-sures (by which I mean his subject, not his prose). Though in many ways Pfaff's resembled the European cafés immortalized by Murger and Puc-cini, the carousing swagger of the b'hoys gave it a uniquely local aroma. Whitman held court at his own reserved table, inviting common laborers off the street. The drama critic William Winter described Whitman in his "eccentric garb of rough blue and gray fabric—his hair and beard griz-zled, his keen, steel-blue eyes gazing, with bland tolerance, on the frolick-some lads around him." Whatever other desires Whitman's steel-blue gaze entailed, he cocked an ear for the b'hoys' language, writing in his note-book that "[m]any of slang words among fighting men, gamblers, thieves, prostitutes, are powerful words." This language remains part of hip's leverage on the mainstream.

While modern readers may think of Whitman as a rebel outsider, he saw himself as a patriot. He believed that his poetry could heal the divi-sion between North and South and purify the corrupt government. With an almost blind faith in the present, he pushed his fellow citizens toward the primitive intensity of nature, advocating "Behavior lawless as snow-flakes." Where Emerson and Thoreau preached rigorous contemplation of nature, Whitman, a city boy, went in for simple loafing. In mid-century, because of cycles of economic depression, loafing was an estab-lished franchise among the American working class. The b'hoys were among its devoted practitioners. Though loafers were condemned, like slackers in the following century, Whitman saw in loafing a path to enlightenment, joking even about creating a political party of loafers. "I loafe and invite my soul," he wrote, "I lean and loafe at my ease observing a spear of summer grass." Even in contemplation, though, his subject wasn't so much what was in his gaze as the fact of him gazing. He exalted himself as a means of exalting the general self:

> Walt Whitman, a kosmos, of Manhattan the son,
> Turbulent, fleshy, sensual, eating, drinking and breeding
> No sentimentalist, no stander above men and women or apart from them.

Though he lived very much in public, making a poem of himself, some corners of his biography remain shadowy or unknowable. To the end he denied that he was homosexual; his writings are pansexual, finding carnal ripeness in the soul, in nature, as well as in men and women. In 1841, when Whitman was a teacher in the fishing village of Southold, Long Island, a local minister named the Rev. Ralph Smith accused him of behaving improperly with a male student. The congregation tarred and feathered him before driving him out of town. The school was subsequently nicknamed the Sodom School, an epithet that endured into the 20th century. Whitman, who objected to the cheap sexuality of pulp literature, wove some of the most erotic images in American poetry—many of them, needless to say, homoerotic. In "Song of Myself," he wrote,

> I mind how once we lay such a transparent summer morning,
> How you settled your head athwart my hips and gently turn'd over
>   upon me,
> And parted the shirt from my bosom-bone, and plunged your tongue
>   to my bare-script heart,
> And reach'd till you felt my beard, and reach'd till you held my feet.

The passage is addressed to his soul.

The affinity between gay and hip circles extends throughout this history. Whitman anchors a long line of gay or bisexual men or lesbians who have been essential to hip's course. The line runs through Gertrude Stein and Hart Crane in the Lost Generation, Alain Locke and possibly Langston Hughes in the Harlem Renaissance, Allen Ginsberg, William Burroughs, James Baldwin and Andy Warhol in the postwar era, and on up to post-gays and homo thugs in the new century. Homosexuality, androgyny and sexual outlawry have been part of hip's playground from the beginning. The alliances are natural. As an aesthetic of the hybrid, hip embraces difference and loves experiment. Where divisions exist, as between black and white or gay and straight, it crosses them. It thrives where social norms are relaxed, sex is not taboo, religion is slack and there are enough people to find friends and partners. Gay men and lesbians, among the most mobile people in America, seek the same conditions. For most of this history they have shunned conventional marriage or family life, the inhibitors of hip. Nothing belongs more to the present, denying other tenses, than gay sex, both as an act and an organizing principle. As outsiders, subject to violence, gays have developed coded language and explored provisional identities. In virtually any era, this history would not be the same without them.

The lawlessness that Whitman embraced on the page was a force to be reckoned with in the urban streets. One of the most colorful and deadly outbreaks, a sign of a new populace seeking a new national identity, was the Astor Place Riot of May 10, 1849. The riot, which left 22 dead—four times as many as the Boston Massacre—centered on, of all things, the proper way to stage Shakespeare. The trouble began when an English actor named William Charles Macready was booked to star in *Macbeth* at the recently opened Astor Opera House. In downtown New York at the time, the Astor, located where Broadway crossed the Bowery, played host to the city's patrician swells; the nearby Broadway Theater and the Chatham entertained the b'hoys.

Macready, born in 1793, was the most celebrated British actor of his day, known for his eloquent speech and refined gesture. To the b'hoys, however, he was a symbol of British snobbery. They preferred the American-born Edwin Forrest, a lusty, muscular prole who rocked the rafters even in contemplation. A lithograph of Forrest (1806–1872) in the role of Spartacus shows a human knot of muscle, all scowling brow, jutting chin and straining cables of tendon about his neck. Whitman, who was cool on Macready, praised Forrest for his "massive freshness." Forrest bore a particular grudge against the Brit, blaming him for a poor reception Forrest had received in London in 1846. When Macready booked the Astor, Forrest readied his own production of *Macbeth* for the Broadway, sure that the b'hoys would give him vengeance.

The b'hoys were happy to oblige. Most belonged to the neighborhood's rivalrous fire companies, so they had experience creating organized mayhem. How much more satisfying, though, to visit the pain upon the local aristos and the English. Already there had been riots surrounding the performances of British actors Edmund Kean, Joshua R. Anderson and George P. Farren. On Macready's opening night, May 7, rowdies in the crowd pelted him with rotten eggs, potatoes, coins, even chairs, bringing the performance to a halt. For the next performance, New York mayor Caleb S. Woodhull, in his first week on the job, assigned 150 policemen and 350 troops to keep order. A crowd of 10,000 to 15,000 people gathered outside the theater, some to do mischief, others just to watch the fun. As Macready tried to perform inside, the mob rained rocks and bricks through the windows and dug up paving stones to hurl against the blockaded doors. The 7th Regiment fired their rifles once into the air, and, when this did not quiet the mob, twice into the crowd. Before the smoke cleared, 22 were dead or dying, and more than 150 injured; police arrested 117.

The riot unleashed many of hip's democratic, antihierarchical passions, which in more constructive times bred pulp fiction, bop or punk. While the major writers condemned the lawlessness of the riot, it brought to life much of the vulgar potential they had been preaching. It needed only shaping. Thoreau had advised American writers to reject "imported symbols," and Emerson, writing in 1842, seven years before the riot, had called for an American genius who could see, "in the barbarism and materialism of the times, another carnival of the same gods whose picture he so much admires in Homer. . . . Our log-rolling, our stumps and their politics, our fisheries, our Negroes and Indians . . . are yet unsung. Yet America is a poem in our eyes; its ample geography dazzles the imagination, and it will not wait long for metres."

Barbarism and materialism and negroes and Indians—this was the stuff of America. Disdaining European high culture, the writers sought to tap the raw vitality of the new mob, not to civilize it into submission. They courted what the literary scholar David S. Reynolds calls the "peculiarly American combination of *outward innocence and inner demonism*."

Whitman decried "the enemy, this word culture," meaning art that held itself apart from the common man. Speaking to his friend Horace Traubel, he described *Leaves of Grass* as "a book for the criminal classes," because "the other people do not need a poet." The criminal classes, on the other hand, inspired him with their rugged voice—hearty, profane, visceral.

Within hip's juggernaut is a quest for the real, a belief that enlightenment involves stripping away sophistication, not adding it. This is the wisdom of Mailer's wise primitive, or of Kerouac typing madly at a roll of teletype paper, claiming no revisions. Hip promises truth received, not constructed. It belongs to the gnostic or visionary tradition. Explaining why he removed himself to Walden, Thoreau wrote, "I went to the woods because I wished to live deliberately, to front only the essential facts of life. . . . I wanted to live deep and suck out all the marrow of life, to live so sturdily and Spartan-like as to put to rout all that was not life, to cut a broad swath and shave close, to drive life into a corner, and reduce it to its lowest terms, and, if it proved mean, why then to get the whole and genuine meanness of it, and publish its meanness to the world." Melville, who called his country "civilized in externals but a savage at heart," played to both sides, adding Shakespearean complexity to the common sea adventure in *Moby-Dick*.

This call to primitive experience resists the nation's cult of progress. In place of status or achievement, the writers offered nonmaterial values by which people could define themselves. Their sedition, mild as it seems now, was considerable. The founding fathers had built the country on work, finance, government and the church. Success was a signal of God's favor. The writers opposed these incursions on individual liberty. In the following century, the writers of the Lost Generation and the Beat generation similarly withdrew from the surges of economic and military progress that followed the two world wars. As Alan Watts wrote when hipsters were finding zen in 1958, the alternative was to detach, "to find the significance of life in subjective experience rather than objective achievement." This impetus—repeated by bohemians, beboppers, action painters, hippies, punks, hip-hoppers, etc.—has been remarkably resilient over American history. Though we often think of these as discrete responses to the mainstream, they are really an ongoing part of what makes America American. They are not footnotes; they belong to the story. By our rebellions are we sometimes best known.

Though the mainstream eventually catches up with hip, the process is not always immediate. Whitman was pained that his great poem was not more popular. Four years after Thoreau published his *A Week on the Concord and Merrimack Rivers* (1849), he took possession of the unsold copies, sighing, "I have now a library of nearly nine hundred volumes, over seven hundred of which I wrote myself. Is it not well that the author should behold the fruits of his labor?" The book had sold just 219 copies. Melville enjoyed great success with the simple adventure tales *Typee* (1846) and *Omoo* (1847), but began a rapid decline in sales and reviews with the more adventurous *Moby-Dick* in 1851. Even so, he knew what he was in for, writing to Hawthorne before publication of *Moby-Dick*, "though I have wrote the Gospels in this century, I should die in the gutter." (A century later, Ralph Ellison praised the book as "full of riffs, man; no wonder the book wasn't understood in its own time, not enough moses [African Americans] were able to read it!") Following a string of unappreciated masterworks, including *Pierre* (1852), "Bartleby the Scrivener" (1853), "Benito Cereno" (1856), and the misanthropic jewel *The Confidence-Man* (1857), Melville for the last 34 years of his life published only minor poetry, in editions of as few as 25 copies, leaving behind the posthumous novel *Billy Budd*. At his death in September 1891, the *Press*, a New York newspaper, noted his passing with the headline "Death of a Once Popular Author." A *New York Times* obit mourned the passing of "Henry Melville."

It is significant that the work of these writers coincided with another new voice, the squeal of advertising. The manufacturers who sprouted up in the first half of the 19th century needed to tell people about their goods; the penny newspapers needed a revenue stream. To meet these needs a man named Volney Palmer opened the first American ad agency in Philadelphia in 1841. His trade brought together the hucksterism of P. T. Barnum and Melville's confidence man and the desires of a public that was comfortable with abstraction. Palmer was an overweight, overbearing man who carried a cane with a golden head and pursued rivals with a bitter passion. He proclaimed that "the day will come when a man will as readily think of walking without feet . . . as of success without ad-

vertising." In Palmer's old age, Horace Greeley (1811–1872), the great editor of the *New York Tribune,* gratefully paid someone to care for him. But
Palmer's revolution was in effect. In 1847, 11 million ads appeared in
2,000 American newspapers.

Like hip, ads celebrated the aura around the product, not the thing itself. In the logic of advertising, what matters is not the essence of the
thing, but the perception of it. Advertising reinvented things in the same
way that Americans reinvented themselves. Identity no longer depended
on pedigree like workmanship or materials, which belonged to an object's
past, but was as fungible as the copywriters said it was. Ads did with products what proto-hip Americans were doing with their own identities. The
explosion in hype met a quenchless hunger for the new—the perfect appetite for a country that erased the past.

All of these elements—the rejection of history, the liberation of the
self, the merging of high and low culture, the embrace of paradox and
ambivalence, the shadow flirtation with the East, even the poor fortunes
of the writers—went into the foundation of hip. In the coming century
and a half, writers, musicians and hipsters would apply the same values to
vastly different social conditions, producing archetypes as disparate as
Dashiell Hammett's hard-boiled hero, Sam Spade, or Tupac Shakur's enlightened thug. The questions of identity, individualism and citizenship
that the major writers raised have remained the relevant puzzles of America. To be a sentient American is to tackle these same questions; to be a
hip one is to tackle them with style.

On November 30, 1957, Allen Ginsberg wrote a letter to his father,
Louis, addressing the same conflicts:

> People keep seeing destruction or rebellion in Jack's writing, and *Howl,*
> but that is a very minor element, actually; it only seems to be so to peo-
> ple who have accepted standard American values as permanent. What we
> are saying is that these values are not really standard nor permanent, and
> we are in a sense I think ahead of the times. . . . Whitman long ago com-
> plained that unless the material power of America were leavened by some
> kind of spiritual infusion we would wind up among the "fabled damned."
> It seems we're approaching that state as far as I can see. Only way out is
> individuals taking responsibility and saying what they actually feel—

which is an enormous human achievement in any society. That's just what we as a "group" have been trying to do. To class that as some form of "rebellion" in the kind of college-bred social worker doubletalk . . . misses the huge awful point.

Ann Charters uses these words in her collection *Beat Down to Your Soul: What Was the Beat Generation?* to introduce this post-WWII group of artists and bohemians. But the questions Ginsberg raises, and even the language, could as easily introduce the writers of the American Renaissance a century earlier. For them, the "huge awful point" held the only beauty and horror worth addressing. They engaged the task of being awake, in its full ardor and hellfire. As Emerson wrote, invoking a *law of consciousness*, "If any one imagines that this law is lax, let him keep its commandment one day."

To sustain this consciousness, the writers created a present tense that contained multitudes. It loosened identity, tapping the American capacity for reinvention. This capacity takes in the contradictions of hip: the syntheses and divisions of race, the elusive modernity of the primitive. It suggests commonality across the broadest of gulfs. This enlightenment can be both lustrous and horrific. In *Moby-Dick,* Ishmael saw the individual forever cursed to invent himself on the losing side: "Who ain't a slave?" he asked. "Tell me that." Yet in this same loss, Whitman saw transcendence, enriched by lines of race and identity but not bound by them. He asked: "[Who] need be afraid of the merge?"

my black/white roots

jazz, the lost generation and the harlem renaissance

> It is the glory of the present age that in it one can be young. Our times give no check to the radical tendencies of youth.
>
> —RANDOLPH BOURNE

In a 1973 essay entitled "An Aesthetic of the Cool," Robert Farris Thompson traced the concept of cool, recognizable on any street corner or commuter train platform in America, to origins in Africa. Thompson, a professor of African art at Yale, followed the semantic trail of cool across 36 African languages, tracking it back to a 15th-century king in the Nigerian empire of Benin who was awarded the name *Ewuare,* meaning "it is cool," after bringing peace to a region torn by internecine warfare. Later kings added refinements like *oba ti o tutu bi osun* to signify that they were "cool-and-peaceful-as-the-native-herb-osun," which in any language is pretty cool. Thompson found cool connotations that were uniquely African, including newness, salinity, healing, rebirth, wetness and silence. But across its linguistic range, coolness consistently referred to composure or balance in an individual, or to stability in a group. To be hot-tempered or hotheaded, scalding or intemperate, hot to trot or hot under the collar, is to lose one's cool. Semantically, this cool is not the same as

Gypsy Dancer, 1925

hip, which denotes a state of enlightenment or awareness. Yet the two are related. In its thoughtful repose, cool begins the journey to hip. "In the African sense," Thompson says, "I would argue that cool is the mask of mind itself." Hip, then, is the process beneath the mask.

The chapters of this book so far have looked at how individuals in colonial and antebellum America strove to create a distinct national identity around untutored enlightenment, a kind of proto-hip. In the 1910s and 1920s, as the country became a world power, this identity coalesced as an American iteration of cool. The historian Peter N. Stearns argues in *American Cool: Constructing a Twentieth-Century Emotional Style* (1994) that Americans developed cool as a protective armor during the transition from the Victorian era (roughly 1876–1915) to the more precarious arena of modernism. As the country extended its influence politically and culturally, cool became America's signature style, ideally suited to the new economies of mass production and mass media. Three generations after Whitman and Thoreau had called for a unique national language, that language communicated through jazz, the Lost Generation and the Harlem Renaissance. Riding the growth of radio, recorded music and advertising, American cool was being reproduced, identically, in living rooms from Paducah to Paris. It belonged neither to the elites nor to the masses, but to the dynamic, intuitive marketplace evolving between them. With this voice, America began to produce the popular culture that would stamp the 20th century as profoundly as the great wars.

The story of American popular culture is often told through a simple racial narrative: black innovators, barred from the economic mainstream, draw on their African roots to invent forms like tap dancing, jazz, the Charleston and hip-hop; white performers hijack these idioms for their own rewards; black apostates who get too fancy risk watering down the culture to appease white audiences. These are essentialist formulas, treating certain cultural values as *essentially* black—usually spontaneity, sensuality, raw emotionality—and others, like control and cerebral rigor, as *essentially* white. This reading defines blackface minstrels or the hit parade of pale hip-shakers from Elvis to Justin Timberlake as simply white boys who stole the blues. In turn, black artists like Wynton Marsalis, Will Smith or the Harlem Renaissance novelist Jessie Fauset have all been criticized as not "black" enough, or too "white." There is something therapeutic or faith-based about this reading, as if the existence of a pure black culture, untainted by white influence, would mean that the threads of culture were not really severed during slavery. When Robert Farris Thompson says that "American popular culture is a euphemism for black American culture," or when the defunct rap crew N.W.A. refer to themselves on CD as "real niggaz," they are invoking an essentialist framework.

But the production of culture is rarely so simple. Black and white Americans have honed their artistic impulses in each other's presence and under each other's influence. These impulses are necessarily hybrid. This narrative of intertwined roots, extending from 1619 to the present, is the core of American culture, and it entails much of what I mean by *hip*. Fed from many troughs, the culture is *associative* rather than essential. One cannot make sense of such quintessential American figures as DuBois, Twain, Jelly Roll Morton, George Gershwin, Ethel Waters, Irving Berlin, Ray Charles, Rudolph Valentino, Carson McCullers, Elvis Presley, Lenny Bruce, Miles Davis, Chet Baker, Jimi Hendrix or Michael Jackson without following their claim to all the material within their grasp, whatever it looked or sounded like. To allow them half a world to play in is to deny the import of their range. It is to let semantics rather than genius determine the culture. When the stride pianist James P. Johnson, who in the 1910s helped define ragtime and jazz piano, remarked that "[t]he reason the New York boys became such high-class musicians was because the New York piano was developed by the European method, system and style," he was invoking a framework as rich and mongrel as the country itself.

In the 1910s and 1920s, this hybrid culture spread through new channels of art and commerce. The player piano, radio, movies, the fledgling record business, Broadway and other outlets generated a new, market-friendly mythology of race. Duke Ellington played for white swells at the Cotton Club, and Ethel Barrymore, doyenne of white stage actresses, wore blackface in the show *Scarlet Sister Mary*. Entertainers in Harlem nightclubs run by white gangsters whirled black, white and mixed audiences in a moneyed spree that glossed over the more divisive economic realities. Culture, then as now, ran roughshod ahead of politics. Black performers who could not vote in parts of the United States, or sit in theaters with whites, could command these same theaters from the stage, basking in wealth and admiration. Though quotidian life buckled with racial division and inequality, and lynching surged in the period, the nation sought its purer reflection in a pop culture that was inseparably black and white.

Hip marked the point of exchange. From the bluesy prose of Ernest Hemingway (1899–1961) to the borderless sounds of Louis Armstrong (1901–1971), the culture that emerged in this period owed debts to both Europe and Africa, but could have emerged only from America, where these roots were hopelessly, joyously entangled.

• • •

As a form of enlightenment, hip flourishes during periods of technological or economic change. These changes produce new freedoms and anxieties, and are divisive. Some people reinvent themselves through the new, others cling to the old—they get hip, in other words, or they get corny. Teenagers and young adults, who have the least stake in the old order, tend to move fluidly in the uncertainty of the new. Youth cultures have organized around new machines and media like the phonograph or the car in part because young people grasp the implications of the new better than their elders. They use technology to produce new styles, postures and languages—the vocabulary of hip. For example, old people saw cell phones as mobile versions of wall phones; kids saw them as new ways to communicate using their thumbs. Their identities, in turn, reflect this skill that is theirs alone. One reason hip seems closer to the profiles of ethnic minorities, immigrants or the poor is that these groups have bigger families and so a greater percentage of young people. Hip simmers when these youth cultures begin sharing the knowledge that holds them together.

In the early part of the 20th century, sweeping changes in the economy, technology and demography produced the nation's first important youth culture. In polyglot cities like New York and Chicago, young Americans began to codify the modern hipster: smart, urban, literate and disaffected, colonizing marginal neighborhoods and using popular culture to accomplish what they couldn't through other means. Hip was no longer a literary ideal but a social reality, filling tenement blocks and producing new messages of its own. It grew around new ways of distributing rhythm and information.

This second hip convergence, in which young Americans moved too quickly for the old categories of race and racial purism, created the model for the countercultures of the 1950s and 1960s; and like those eras, it drew its energies from what Whitman called "the merge." Its influence, often considered quaint or sinful at the time, has been profound. Nearly a century later, if you compare the bombs dropped over Europe with the beats dropped in New Orleans or Chicago, it would be hard to tell from today's society which was the diversion and which the main event. In fundamental ways we resemble the nation envisioned by the youth culture more than the one for which the generals fought.

The French writer Charles Péguy proposed in 1913 that "the world has changed less since the time of Jesus Christ than it has in the last thirty years." Nowhere was the pace of change as tumultuous as in the United States. In a little more than a generation, the country moved from the chaos that followed Reconstruction—the nadir of agrarian factionalism—to become an urban, industrial, technological power that decided the course of world war. Old certainties and institutions were receding. New technologies moved people and information at astonishing speeds. The Wright brothers launched the first powered flight at Kitty Hawk in 1903, and Henry Ford introduced the Model T in 1908, selling 27 million "flivvers" before dropping the model in 1927. The huckster brio of P. T. Barnum gave way to the corporate sell of Madison Avenue, where revenues rose to $3 billion by 1929, attracting such talents as Hart Crane and F. Scott Fitzgerald to its mercenary tribe. The town crier yielded to syndicated gossip columnists, relentless in their manufacture of celebrity. The American movie industry, which was jump-started with *The Great Train Robbery* in 1903, was by 1926 the fifth-biggest business in the country. Talkies, which debuted the following year, only increased the medium's clout. All of these were promises of pleasure, beckoning Americans to define themselves outside the institutions of family, church, work and the harvest. They called for new identities and new allegiances; what they got was hip.

The population that consumed this culture, black and white, was racing from farms to cities. New York, which in 1900 strained to accommodate its 3.4 million residents, swelled by another 2.2 million in the next two decades; Chicago grew by 1 million and Detroit by 425,000. The 1920 census found for the first time that more than half of all Americans lived in cities. Much of the growth came from unprecedented immigration, which continued to tilt the composition of the country. More than 17 million immigrants arrived between 1900 and 1917, and by the early 1920s, one-third of all Americans were either first- or second-generation immigrants. As I'll discuss in chapter 15, booms in immigration bring new ideas, skills and identities to dense urban areas, providing essential oxygen for hip. Amid urban squalor, a new American sophistication was taking root in New York and Chicago especially. In the wreckage of the Great War, the cultural capital of the English-speaking world was no longer London but New York. Fitzgerald explained this shift succinctly in a 1921 letter to Edmund Wilson. "Culture," he wrote, "follows money."

Cities provided fertile soil for youth culture and hip. If hip is an awareness, the new cities provided tight clusters of like minds to circulate its codes, defining themselves in the process. Because urban populations were new and often transient, they enjoyed a protective anonymity; unlike in small towns, nobody could tell your parents or spouse or clergyman if you were acting up. Cities' disorder also provided cover for marginal or radical ideas. You could cultivate your iconoclasm and expect to meet other iconoclasts more freely than in the provinces. Density was everything: a book or play that shocked mainstream sensibilities could find a constituency in a city, spark debate and beget even more radical works; in a small town it would just be weird.

The soundtrack to this whirl was jazz. Just as the major writers of the first hip convergence invented a literature for the new country, the major musicians of this era provided a sound. And like the American Renaissance, it grew in the cracks and seams of the culture around it. Like any cultural movement, jazz did not will itself into being overnight, but evolved from other styles over a long period. Yet to the extent that it has an origin—or an origin myth—it is in New Orleans at the turn of the century. Here, the music followed the idiosyncratic racial and class contradictions that animated the city itself. Beginning in slavery days, New Orleans defined Creoles, or free people of mixed race, as a separate racial category. In the years after the Civil War, when brass bands formed throughout the South, Creole musicians prided themselves on their formal training and mastery of European classical music. Many preferred not to mix with blacks or identify with black culture; the music in their parlors and schools was French. The best known of the Creole players, Jelly Roll Morton (1890–1941), who printed business cards declaring himself the father of jazz, often denied any African ancestry and held blacks in haughty disdain.

Morton's racial saga exemplifies the impure lines of hip. He was born Ferdinand Joseph Lamothe in the high pretensions of Creole New Orleans. Raised in the proper French home of his grandmother, where he took up the piano after attending an opera recital, he also partook of other vices in the sporting houses of the city's officially sanctioned red-light district, Storyville, or the District, as most musicians called it. For this low behavior his grandmother ultimately barred him from the house. Morton apprenticed mainly in bordellos that would not hire black musicians, yet he made a point of absorbing the more robust flavors of black New Orleans. Formally, he seems most influenced by the cornetist Charles "Buddy" Bolden (1877–1931), who was said to have picked up *his* sense of form from the Holy Roller Church on Jackson Avenue, not the brothels of the District. Morton was a liar, a braggart, a gambler, a pimp and an exacting musician; according to one legend, which may be apocryphal, when a sideman refused to play a melody the way Morton wanted at a 1920s recording session, Morton laid a pistol on the piano by way of persuasion. The next take, he got what he wanted.

In 1894, the Louisiana Administrative Code began to dismantle the relative privilege of Creoles, forcing the downtown Creole musicians together with the black bands uptown, who played in a hotter, self-taught, more improvised style. Pushed together, the Creole and black musicians shared a mixture of quadrilles, waltzes, ragtime, blues and the looser sounds played at parades and funerals. Idioms flowed back and forth. As Morton said, "If you can't manage to put tinges of Spanish in your tunes, you will never be able to get the right seasoning, I call it, for jazz." Any tune could be fit to any idiom, depending on how it was performed. Morton's signature "King Porter Stomp" and "High Society," for example, began as pieces for cotillions, metamorphosed to ragtime and are now played as jazz standards. Marching bands learned to play songs like "Didn't He Ramble" or "When the Saints Go Marching In" both somber, for the way to the cemetery, and joyously syncopated or "ragged," for the way back. The early New Orleans groups improvised collectively, juggling the melody and the harmony between them. Everybody played rhythm.

As a delivery system for hip, popular culture moves in tandem with technology and media. Technology has a way of making race into an abstraction, because it removes information from its human source. The media are literally *in the middle,* between the author and the audience, beholden to neither. They demand only that the people on either side play their roles—that they produce or consume. Whether they are black or white, young or old, rich or poor, is secondary.

The rise of jazz at the turn of the century paralleled a revolution in the way Americans produced and consumed music. The unprecedentedly diverse population, pushed together in cities that never slept, called for the social lubricants of dance and rhythm. The player piano, patented in 1897 by an American engineer named Edwin Scott Votey (1856–1931), answered this call with ragtime. Like future devices, it was a vehicle for racial exchange, a starter kit for hip. White amateurs who couldn't play the syncopations of ragtime could bring the music home on rolls. The machines neatly split the singer from the song, allowing white Americans to taste black music without engaging black people. The piano rolls of players like James P. Johnson (1894–1955) or Willie "the Lion" Smith (1897–1973) converted race to an abstract category of music. As Gertrude Stein observed, America's machine culture gave its citizens a unique gift for such abstraction. In cities that were becoming increasingly segregated, and rent by racial violence, music created a *virtual* sphere that was pleasantly integrated. Ragtime changed the way Americans danced, replacing the waltz or polka with the rhythmic rocking, swaying and sliding of the foxtrot, bunny hop and other social dances. These were often barely altered descendants of African dances. For example, though most dancers were too busy to notice, the Charleston is little more than a recasting of an Ashanti ancestor dance.

The phonograph similarly stoked the country's romance with rhythm. Invented by Thomas Edison in 1877, the first machines appeared in saloons and drugstores in the 1890s. In 1902, two of the leading manufacturers, Columbia and the Victor Talking Machine Company, shared their patents, improving the sound quality and making the players affordable to the public. Americans bought 27 million records in 1914; in 1921, sales were up to 100 million. The new delivery system needed product; jazz and blues fit the bill. These styles became emblems of progress, as new as the technology that delivered them. This symbolism recurs throughout hip: black or mixed style means new and progressive; white or segregated style, like classical music or high Episcopalianism, means old. For a nation of immigrants, the hybrid was what they were moving toward, the pure what they hoped to leave behind. America's past lay in ethnic separatism; the future could only mean pluralism, the merge. Throughout this book, the yearning for the good old days, which views impurity as decline, recurs as the lament of the square, from Cotton Mather to William Bennett. It runs counter to history, and to the American faith in the new.

The Original Dixieland Jazz Band, five white guys from New Orleans, cut the first jazz record, "Livery Stable Blues," in Victor's New York studios on February 26, 1917. According to jazz lore, Freddie Keppard, a black New Orleans bandleader, turned down the date because he thought people would steal his licks. The record, which included barnyard noises, sold more than a million copies. Instead of playing for a roomful of dancers, records allowed jazz to reach thousands or millions of listeners almost at once. On August 10, 1920, Mamie Smith (1883–1946) brought the blues out of the Harlem cabarets to the recording studio with "Crazy Blues," which sold 75,000 copies in its first month and a million before the first year.

The record business called for marketable personalities who could burst through the impersonal plastic of the medium. Louis Armstrong, the affable and extraordinarily gifted cornetist and trumpeter in Joseph "King" Oliver's Creole Jazz Band, became the first dominant soloist in jazz, breaking the democratic parity of the ensemble. Buoyed by the economic boom, performers cut figures larger than life, often souping up images of white gentility. No show of wealth was too bold. Having shared their improvised music with the world, the players improvised themselves. Jelly Roll Morton sported a diamond in his tooth and a biography woven of myth. Ellington crafted an image of regal sophistication. As James P. Johnson remembered, a performer's work began before the first note.

> [W]hen you came into a place you had a three-way play. You never took your overcoat or hat off until you were at the piano. First you laid your cane on the music rack. Then you took off your overcoat, folded it and put it on the piano, with the lining showing.
>
> You then took off your hat before the audience. Each tickler had his own gesture for removing his hat with a little flourish; that was part of his attitude, too. You took out your silk handkerchief, shook it out and dusted off the piano stool.
>
> Now, with your coat off, the audience could admire your full-back, or box-back, suit, cut with very square shoulders. The pants had about fourteen-inch cuffs and broidered clocks.

These exaggerated characters suited the new record business. In 1926, American record companies, mostly owned and run by white men, released more than 300 gospel and blues recordings; the next year they put out 500. In the pop marketplace, race worked as a consumer category, a reason to buy or not buy a record, not a product of historical forces.

This period was not the golden age of jazz, and most of the recordings of the 1920s now feel antiquated compared to the music Ellington and Armstrong made in the next decade. But the musicians and the new media they supported synched jazz to the consciousness of the century. The music reflected the new speed of the automobile, the percussive textures of the city, the rhythms of the assembly line—in short, the exuberance of American technology and money. But as Robert Farris Thompson says, even at its most American, it harbored a distinctly African aesthetic of the cool. Through improvisation, jazz shifted the creative moment from the past to the present, from the inflexible score to the free inventions of the performance. Like black English, jazz extended meaning through inflection and nuance. A musician like Louis Armstrong or Sidney Bechet (1897–1959), two of the New Orleans greats, could play the same notes as joy or pain, often conjuring one out of the other. The audience completed the conversation, responding with their bodies.

Within the aesthetic of the cool, Thompson notes, this interplay of the musicians and dancers suggests a philosophy of beauty and ethics. Its underlying values are spiritual. Through rhythm and inflection, it signals stability in the social order and composure in the individual, even amid the hottest of blowing. In other words, cool. "Perhaps one reason many American Negroes sing a sad song happy and some whites sing it sad," he writes, "is that the Negro is an heir to an aesthetic of the cool and the latter is not. It is cool to sweeten hurt with song and motion; it is hot to concentrate upon the pain."

Mobility favors the young and footloose, and the youth culture that emerged in the 1910s and 1920s reflected a new identification with speed and change. Young Americans, suddenly, were not lesser members of their families but avatars of the society to come. Their heroism in the war determined the fate of Europe; their dances—the black bottom, the Charleston, the fox-trot, the Lindy Hop—were lewd, vulgar and more exciting than anything the world had seen. Instead of being investments in the future, the young were valuable and influential in the present tense. They were hip, enlightened. Born into the secular uncertainty left by Darwin, Freud and Marx, the generation buttressed itself with the insouciance of cool, and the enlightenment of hip. The radical critic Randolph Bourne (1886–1918), disfigured at birth with a hunchback, predicted in a brash 1913 collection of essays called *Youth and Life* that his generation would whisk away the funk of the past, sweeping the country to a more democratic future. "[T]here was never a time when there were so many radical young people who cared little about that worldly success," he crowed. "The secret of life is then that this fine youthful spirit should never be lost. Out of the turbulence of youth should come this fine precipitate—a sane, strong, aggressive spirit of daring and doing. . . . To keep one's reactions warm and true is to have found the secret of perpetual youth, and perpetual youth is salvation."

Bourne was just one of many young migrants who flocked to the cheap rents and cold-water bonhomie of Greenwich Village in the years before World War I. The Village, formerly known as the 15th Ward, looked out on the radical Jewish community of the Lower East Side and the labor agitation of Union Square, but was slightly removed from either. It was one of the few places a woman could walk unescorted after dark. The neighborhood drew a combustive mix of hoboes and Wobblies; Harvard idealists; Freudians and Jungians; anarchists and tourists; office women and grifters; society types and penniless artists; open gays and lesbians. The weird people from towns too small to accommodate the weird migrated to the Village. For children of the middle classes, the community offered permissive camaraderie and intellectual stimulation, to say nothing of the possibilities for sex. When Prohibition took effect on July 1, 1919, the splayed streets of the Village were among the easiest spots in America to buy a drink.

Fresh arrivals like Bourne, Mabel Dodge, Floyd Dell, Eugene O'Neill, Claude McKay, Max Eastman, Edna St. Vincent Millay, John Reed and others reinvented themselves through alcohol and other Village intoxicants. Forsaking good jobs and better families, the moderns refashioned themselves a "proletariat of the arts," finding shabby gentility in $3-a-week tenement apartments and scrappy journals like *Seven Arts, The Masses* and the *Dial.* Anarchism, socialism, the free love movement and the sexual revolution all mixed with the hard work of literature and self-promotion. The iconoclastic writer Harold Stearns, who rented a basement apartment at 31 Jones Street, was described by a friend as having "a Murger complex," with a drive to "outdo La Vie Boheme in dinginess." Instead, Stearns compiled a searing volume of essays called *Civilization in the United States: An Inquiry by Thirty Americans* (1922), which arrived at the conclusion that the terms *civilization* and *United States* were mutually exclusive. The social order the Villagers formed, which met both curiosity and disapproval from the outside world, was an early model of the hip inner circle.

Hip is an ethos of individualism, but it tends to grow in cliques. It has an epidemiology. In its larval, pre-hip stage, it is a creed without followers, out of rhythm with whatever is hip at the time. Only the abject, isolated or beat down are willing to sign on. In relative isolation, a small group of individuals, forsaking the general trends around them, give each other permission to do something new. They develop their own slang as part of their group identity, and encourage each other's idiosyncrasies as badges of membership. As the inventions become more flamboyant or cohere as a style, a second, slightly broader circle begins to adopt some of the gestures—and in turn to transmit these to a circle slightly broader than itself. With each expansion, something is lost. The smallest group consists of what the sociologist Herbert J. Gans calls *creators* rather than *users*, though in practice they do both. Individuals in close company exchange ideas and push each other to extreme behaviors, either through encouragement or one-upmanship. The successively larger circles, though appreciative and even imitative, are to increasing degrees passive consumers, taking what suits them and shaping it to their own needs.

At each step, the smaller group sets up barricades against the larger group, and feels betrayed when these are inevitably breached. It is a universal complaint that hip ceases being hip the moment it spreads beyond one's own circle. After all, once people fractionally more clueless than yourself are in the club, what is the value of membership? But this is a parochial stinginess, at odds with the circulation of knowledge. It devalues the information it means to esteem, in the same way that record collectors devalue the music for the rarity of the serial numbers. Hip becomes *too hip*—boring, negative, nerdy—when a small group continues to police the barricades after the epidemic has spread beyond. In practice, hip needs this constant exposure to the larger group; if no one is looking it isn't really hip. Like the tape recordings at the beginning of *Mission: Impossible,* which self-destruct after delivering their message, hip communicates best as it is disintegrating by its own hand.

In the decade before World War I, the bohemians of Greenwich Village chose life on the margins in the modernist faith that margins shape the mainstream. The era's technological breakthroughs supported this faith. Information machines like the phonograph, the radio and the car all began as playthings for an elite few, then pushed their way to the center of society. The moderns similarly believed they could break society of its habits by their own example, including their personal lives. They were a movement led by women but joined by men, experimenting with open marriage and preaching contraception, free speech, free love and sexual revolution. I'll discuss this gynocracy more in chapter 11.

The Village moderns were idealists, often naïve. Better educated than their parents, they believed power lay in information, which moves from small groups to large ones, rather than in material resources, which move from large groups to the pockets of the few. To shape society you had to cultivate ideas, and new ideas were by definition on the outside. The bohemians thought they could change the way the country worked, governed and made love simply by setting alternative examples, which would then filter back through the mainstream. They kept their distance to keep their difference.

Rebellion in the Village merged politics, lifestyle and the arts. Margaret Sanger (1883–1966), the birth-control advocate who later founded Planned Parenthood, became a cause celebre in 1914 after she was indicted for sending materials deemed obscene in the mail. Emma Goldman (1869–1940), a homely, lusty émigré from czarist Russia, plotted with her lover Alexander Berkman to assassinate the industrialist Henry Clay Frick in 1892. While Berkman bungled the hit and spent 14 years in prison, Goldman rose to fame on the lecture circuit, blowing as hot about Ibsen or Shaw as about free love. In 1913 the vaudeville promoter Oscar Hammerstein offered her a thousand dollars a week to work the circuit. John Reed (1887–1920), a radical journalist lapsing into dissolution and drink, left the Village to become the most vivid on-scene chronicler of the

Bolshevik Revolution. Such was the Village pastiche of iconoclasm, show-manship and zeal.

But if culture runs ahead of politics, politics periodically catches up. As America entered the war, and the Communists rose in Russia, the Justice Department cracked down on the Village radicals. Goldman and Berkman were put on trial in 1917 for conspiring to obstruct the draft. Two years later they were among 249 radicals deported to Russia on a ship dubbed the *Red Ark*. Culturally, this was a government assault against outsiders, or hip. It removed the cloak of urban anonymity that had allowed hip to foment. In January 1920, A. Mitchell Palmer, the red-baiting attorney general under Woodrow Wilson, ordered the arrest of more than 4,000 alleged communists in 33 cities. More raids followed throughout the year. The lefty arts magazines that once sustained Village bohemia were barred from the mails. Mabel Dodge moved her salon to New Mexico.

Viewed in retrospect, the moderns who filled the Village in the years before World War I formed a hip prototype not just by their liberties but also by their exploitation of their image. Tourists swarmed the neighborhood even before lushes. In *Quill*, an early zine, an article titled "As We Are Reported" parodied the way the mainstream panted over the morals and hygiene habits of downtown women. Mabel Dodge (1879–1962) perfected the art of self-promotion. A refugee from upper-class Buffalo, she opened her spacious white apartment at the foot of Fifth Avenue as a hub of Village intellectual life, and courted renown as energetically as art. She worked bohemia like a DJ, mixing people rather than records. At the 1913 Armory Show, which introduced 70,000 visitors to a circus of modern art, Dodge distributed copies of a profile of herself written by Gertrude Stein. She felt she, too, was a work worthy of appreciation. "I had rapidly become a mythological figure right in my own lifetime," she wrote later.

Max Eastman (1883–1969), editor of the radical magazine *The Masses*, dismissed her as having "neither wit nor beauty, nor is she vivacious or lively-minded or entertaining," but as Dodge saw it, her recessive charms were her greatest asset. She wrote, "The faculty I had for not saying much and yet for being there gave people's imaginations a chance to fabricate their own Mabel Dodge." Though the bohemians protested the materialism of the machine economy, they were its most prescient advertisements, rejecting the old, ever demanding the new. Even where hip overtly opposes the market, its ethos of change becomes a reason to buy.

After the war, a new generation drifted to the Village, replacing the idealism of their predecessors with champagne and broken faith. This was a turn of hip toward a cooler voice, more detached, seeking stimulation and numbness at the same time. Francis Scott Key Fitzgerald (1896–1940), their most empathic chronicler, described his peers as having "grown up to find all Gods dead, all wars fought, all faiths in man shaken." A product of prep schools and Princeton, Fitzgerald missed action in the war but came home from duty in Alabama with the generational mix of self-destructiveness and boredom. "The events of 1919 left us cynical rather than revolutionary," he wrote barely a decade later. "It was characteristic of the Jazz Age that it had no interest in politics at all." By the time Malcolm Cowley (1898–1989) arrived in the Village after spending the war in the French ambulance corps—as had Hemingway, John Dos Passos, E. E. Cummings, William Slater Brown and Harry Crosby—he found a gap not just between the Village and the rest of the country, but between two generations of bohemians.

> The Village in 1919 was like a conquered country. Its inhabitants were discouraged and drank joylessly. "We" came among them with an unexpended store of energy: we had left our youth at home, and for two years it had been accumulating at compound interest; now we were eager to lavish it even on trivial objects.
>
> And what did the older Villagers think of us? . . . Sometimes they were cruel to us in a deliberately thoughtless way. Sometimes they gave us advice which was never taken because it was obviously a form of boasting. I don't believe they thought much about us at all.

For Hemingway, Fitzgerald, Cowley and their peers, the country after the war reeked of failure and hypocrisy. They had neither energy nor will to take up lost battles. Enlightenment lay elsewhere. Gertrude Stein (1874–1946), who was a generation older, had established herself in an apartment at 27 rue de Fleurus on the Left Bank of Paris as early as 1903. Reared in Baltimore and mentored by William James, Stein presided over the Left Bank with a hacksaw laugh and breasts that Hemingway estimated at 10 pounds per. With her partner, Alice B. Toklas, she filled her apartment with paintings by then-unknown friends like Matisse and Picasso, and ultimately with the conversation of expatriates like Hemingway, James Joyce, Ezra Pound, T. S. Eliot, Sherwood Anderson, Cummings, Dos Passos, Archibald MacLeish, William Carlos Williams and others. It was Stein who hipped Hemingway to the violent theater of bullfighting, vital to both his writing and his image. She loved Paris for the license it provided, especially after the Palmer Raids had chilled the United States.

For these new bohemians, too, age mattered; it sparkled. Fitzgerald became a literary icon with *This Side of Paradise* by the age of 24; Hemingway, with *The Sun Also Rises*, by 27. The young writers trumpeted the raw, profane language of their peers, gleefully alienating their elders. Stein, after meeting Hemingway in March 1922, noted that the young Americans all seemed to have the same blush. "It became the period of being twenty-six," she wrote. "During the next two or three years all the young men were twenty-six years old. It was the right age apparently for that time and place. . . . Later on, much later on they were twenty-one and twenty-two." After watching the workers at a French auto shop one day, she decided this age group was a "lost generation."

For the Americans, who kept the city at a cool distance, Paris offered late nights and freedom to publish, as long as you didn't expect much money out of it. Archibald MacLeish, who left a Boston law practice for the literary life of Paris, observed that the Americans there were not so much expatriates as transients whose *patria* was no longer waiting for them. They drifted with the currency exchange rates. They lived in hip's present tense, cut off from past certainties by the violence of the war, which had killed more people, using more violent machinery, than any previous conflict. Hemingway, ever circling the problem of writing, noted in *A Farewell to Arms* (1929): "Abstract words such as glory, honor, courage, or hallow were obscene beside the concrete names of villages, the numbers of roads, the names of rivers, the numbers of regiments and dates."

Without absolutes or country, there was only improvisation, the blind momentum of the Jazz Age. The poet Hart Crane (1899–1932), who went to Paris in 1928 to complete his life's masterpiece, *The Bridge*, wrote home of a city in erotic swirl, all nouns in blurred motion: "Dinners, soirees, poets, erratic millionaires, painters, translations, absinthe, music, promenades, sherry, aspirin, pictures, Sapphic heiresses, editors, books, sailors.

And How!" Needless to say, he made more progress with the absinthe and sailors than with the poem.

The conundrum for the moderns was the evil of banality, the "deracination" of industrial society. The bland, Victorian language they had been taught in schools was inadequate to describe the horrors of the war and the odium of the industrial revolution. Their response was a turn to what they saw as the primitive. In their social lives, this meant the blur of drink and sex; in their psychological lives, the id of Freud; and in their art, a romantic notion of Africa and black America. American jazz and blues filled the Paris clubs. Josephine Baker (1906–1975), naked except for a feathered boa or a skirt of bananas, was a sensation at 19 in *La Revue Nègre,* stimulating the primitive jones of mostly white audiences. "People have done me the honor of believing I'm an animal," she said, in a droll tribute to the white imagination. Hart Crane called for "an idiom for the proper transposition of jazz into words!" The African influence extended beyond music. Picasso and Matisse were already attempting to translate African sculpture into new forms of abstraction. Stein, who was not modest about her accomplishments, announced that she had launched the literature of the 20th century with her portrait of an African-American woman named Melanctha in her 1909 novel, *Three Lives.*

Hemingway, mustering the midwestern bristle of his native Oak Park, Illinois, dismissed his American peers in the same language used today by the hipsters of Wicker Park in Chicago or SoMa in San Francisco to dismiss the hipsters who arrived a minute after they did. Hemingway called his fellow expats "the scum of Greenwich Village . . . skimmed off and deposited in large ladles" in the city he called a "Mecca of bluffers and fakers." But this was at least part bluster, put on for an audience. Eugène Jolas, a Franco-American who founded the avant-garde quarterly *Transition,* observed that Hemingway's assault on affectation was itself affected. In the absence of a past, he, too, was remaking himself in the present. "He usually wore workman's clothes and was always most careful to avoid being taken for a literary man," Jolas wrote of Hemingway in Paris. "He seemed to have a preference for intermingling his vocabulary with strong four-letter words. Frequently, however, these gave the impression of being carefully calculated."

Ralph Ellison saw Hemingway's act as an extension of the minstrel mask, or the mask worn by African Americans to fool white people. It belonged to an American tradition, held together through hip. "Hemingway poses as a non-literary sportsman, Faulkner as a farmer," Ellison wrote. "Here the 'darky' act makes brothers us all. America is a land of masking jokers. We wear the mask for purposes of aggression as for defense, when we are projecting the future and preserving the past. In short, the motives hidden behind the mask are as numerous as the ambiguities the mask conceals."

In *The Sun Also Rises* (1926), Hemingway contrasted the civilized yammer of his social set with the elemental truths of the bullring. At one point he planned to call the book *The Lost Generation*, and said he wrote the novel as a refutation of Stein's diagnosis, which he reprinted as an epigraph. Describing the lethal dance of the matador, he endowed him with a consciousness that expressed itself physically, not verbally: "It was like a course in bull-fighting. All the passes he linked up, all complete, all slow, templed and smooth. There were no tricks and no mystifications. There was no brusqueness. And each pass as it reached the summit gave you a sudden ache inside. The crowd did not want it ever to be finished." As in Robert Farris Thompson's account of African dance, the matador's improvised ballet spells out a philosophy of beauty and ethics. Nestled in a sometimes vindictive roman à clef about his expat set, the writing forged an annealing vision of hip: wise as well as primitive, a performance of enlightenment that became the thing itself.

Though Hemingway could write unflinchingly of physical violence, his most revealing works, like the 1927 short story "The Killers," lingered on the flash of clarity *before* the blows, the present that never becomes the past. Fitzgerald, who persuaded him to drop a long digression at the beginning of *The Sun Also Rises*, considered Hemingway's true forte not physical conflict but the dread underneath it—"his great studies into fear," which Fitzgerald was sure would outlast Freud's. In this novel of the Lost Generation, Hemingway drew this unnamed fear as the mask of cool.

I f their white counterparts were a lost generation, black Americans were eager to get where they were going. At the turn of the century, 90 percent lived in the South, most of them on farms. Booker T. Washington,

Fats Waller and Willie the Lion Smith, May 1937

then at the height of his influence, pronounced that African Americans' future, like their past, lay in the rural South. His constituents did not agree. In the coming decades, half a million blacks left the debt cycle of southern sharecropping for low wages in the industrial North. As the war years crimped European immigration, industrialists in Chicago, Detroit, Pittsburgh and other cities reached out to black workers. The *Chicago Defender,* the leading black newspaper, ran a "Great Northern Drive" in 1917, calling southern readers to the "promised land." In 1920, when the price of cotton in the Mississippi Delta plunged from a dollar a pound to 10 cents a pound, the trickle northward expanded into the Great Migration. African Americans in the North tripled in number during the first three decades of the century, and like other new arrivals, they flocked to cities. Blacks constituted 40 percent of the urban population in 1930, up from 22 percent at the turn of the century.

Black migrants were fleeing the poverty and violence of the South, but as Amiri Baraka has noted, they were also actively choosing their meaning in the emerging industrial nation. It is one thing to be the face of the rural fields, another to be that of the urban block. Prominent blacks in New York eschewed the term *negroes* to call themselves Aframericans, stressing that they were true Americans, with tenure that predated the Pilgrims. Waves of black migrants from the South and Jewish immigrants from eastern Europe, both pariah populations within pariah populations, formed uneasy alliances that have been essential to hip, and that will be discussed in depth in chapter 9.

Black migrants constructed a new identity that was urban, transitional, unrooted. The activist Charles S. Johnson, a former protégé of Booker T. Washington who became the editor of the Urban League's influential monthly, *Opportunity,* contended that by leaving the agrarian South for the urban North, "[i]n ten years Negroes have been actually transported from one culture to another." They aligned themselves with the course of capital and modernity. Alain Locke, one of the architects of the Harlem Renaissance, argued in his pivotal 1925 essay "Enter the New Negro" that "the migrant masses, shifting from countryside to city, hurdle several generations of experience at a leap."

Their arrival brought hip's juxtapositions: urban with rural, hard poverty with high life, blues detachment with a sense of arrival. The masses moved to Detroit to build automobiles, to Pittsburgh to forge steel. They came to New York for the culture. The publishing, entertainment and advertising industries, once scattered around the country, were now concentrated among the new skyscrapers of Manhattan. Blacks within the city continued their own microcosmic migration north, from the Five Points to the Village to the Tenderloin to San Juan Hill and now finally to Harlem. Uptown landlords, discovering that they could squeeze higher rents from black tenants, encouraged the influx of color, whatever their personal prejudices. By the 1910s, the former Dutch settlement, with its cozy thoroughfares and Stanford White mansions, was becoming the capital of black America. As alarmists raised warnings of a dark "invasion," the new residents attracted a class of culturally curious whites, whom Zora Neale Hurston (1903–1960) tartly dubbed "Negrotarians." Their motives were unclear. As Carl Van Vechten, the most dedicated of this species, remarked to H. L. Mencken in 1924, "[j]azz, the blues, Negro spirituals, all stimulate me enormously at the moment. Doubtless, I shall discard them too in time."

Langston Hughes (1902–1967), who became a major poet of the Harlem Renaissance, arrived in Harlem in September 1921, stepping out of the subway at 135th Street and Lenox Avenue into a social swirl unlike any that existed before or since. In his autobiography, he remembered:

> It was a period when almost any Harlem Negro of any social importance at all would be likely to say casually: "As I was remarking the other day to Heywood—," meaning [the columnist] Heywood Broun. Or: "As I said to George—," referring to George Gershwin. It was a period when local and visiting royalty were not at all uncommon in Harlem. . . .
>
> It was a period when every season there was at least one hit play on Broadway acted by a Negro cast. And when books by Negro authors were being published with much greater frequency and much more publicity than ever before or since in history. It was a period when white writers wrote about Negroes more successfully (commercially speaking) than Negroes did about themselves. . . . It was the period when the Negro was in vogue.

Prohibition, enforced less stringently in Harlem than in many neighborhoods downtown, proved a great catalyst for this mix, throwing otherwise disparate people together and making them literally partners in crime. Parties of the day sought epic grandeur. The Harlem hostess A'Lelia Walker, heir to a hair-straightener fortune, gave a party where whites were segregated and served chitterlings and bathtub gin, while black guests enjoyed champagne and caviar. Working people up from the South gathered at rent parties exploding with jazz and blues. In nightspots like Connie's Inn, the Renaissance Ballroom or the grand Savoy Ballroom, which opened on Lenox Avenue between 140th and 141st Streets on March 12, 1926, musicians exaggerated the boom of the age, flaunting wild styles and sexual innuendo. White revelers, drawn by the music, dancing girls and Prohibition booze, treated the neighborhood as a hedonist theme park, as if its locals were unbound by civilization. "You go sort of primitive up there," said Jimmy Durante.

If the Harlem Renaissance had a formal inaugural, it might be a March 21, 1924, dinner symposium organized by Charles S. Johnson at the Civic Club on 12th Street near 5th Avenue, and attended by more than 100 black and white literary figures. The occasion was the publication of *There Is Confusion,* the first novel by Jessie Fauset (1882–1961) and one of just a handful of novels by black authors published since the start of the century. But the real subject was one that had been brewing in black America: the New Negro. Two hundred thousand African Americans had fought in the war, returning with demands for justice and a new archetype of resistance. "The Old Negro goes," declared the *Crusader,* a militant Harlem paper. "His abject crawling and pleading have availed the Cause nothing." St. Louis, Detroit, Chicago, Washington, New York and other cities erupted in riots. At the same time, the anti-Semitism of the 1919 and 1920 Palmer Raids, and the rise of full-service white hate groups, was cementing a unique relationship between the New Negro and liberal Jews. The Civic Club, known for its liberal politics, was the only snooty downtown social organization that allowed Jews, blacks and women.

At the March 21 dinner, leaders from the NAACP and the Urban League mixed with white plutocrats, who became patrons to Harlem's artists and civic organizations. The thrust was an idea long advanced by James Weldon Johnson (1871–1938), the historian, poet, diplomat, songwriter and one of the six "midwives of the Harlem Renaissance," as the historian David Levering Lewis calls them (the others were Fauset, Locke, Charles Johnson, the novelist and society patriarch Walter White, and Casper Holstein, a West Indian hustler who ran the numbers racket uptown). James Weldon Johnson contended that art, not politics or economics, should be the field on which African Americans battled for equality. Though white racism held blacks back in other areas, he argued that culture was wide open. As he wrote in 1922, "The world does not know that a people is great until that people produces great literature and art. . . . And nothing will do more to change the mental attitude and raise his status than a demonstration of intellectual parity by the Negro through the production of literature and art." This is a faith that runs throughout hip— that the values of after-hours recreations will filter down to the way the mainstream behaves in the light of day. An integrated pop culture today, in other words, tokens economic and political change tomorrow.

The crowd at the Civic Club, black and white, was ready to hear this message. Countee Cullen, the prodigy of Harlem, read a poem, and Gwendolyn Bennett offered verses of bland uplift: "We claim no part of racial dearth, / We want to sing the songs of birth!" Carl Van Doren, editor of *Century* magazine, closed the proceedings with a plea for the primitive. "What American literature decidedly needs at this moment is color, music, gusto, the free expression of gay or desperate moods," he said. "If the Negroes are not in a position to contribute these items, I do not know what Americans are." The symposium led to a special Harlem issue of the journal *Survey Graphics,* edited by Locke, and ultimately a book of essays called *The New Negro,* featuring 34 black writers and 4 whites. The *New York Herald Tribune* pronounced the developments a "Negro renaissance." The dinner was a template for the cultural politics of the Harlem Renaissance: black artists and leaders skillfully maneuvering their white benefactors and sympathizers to create publicity that would lure more black artists and white dollars to the community.

But the social wiring of Harlem was more complex than the Civic Club proceedings let on. Harlem hosted diverse, sometimes conflicting factions: patrician elders, rural southerners, bluesmen, literati, white philanthropists, slumming socialites and a silent majority of struggling blue-collar families. In the climate of anonymity and tolerance fostered by the big city, many of the Renaissance's leading lights were gay or gay-identified, including Locke, Van Vechten, Cullen, Wallace Thurman, Bruce Nugent, Claude McKay and Langston Hughes. Some of these men were married and led double lives.

A conservative establishment, following DuBois's belief that the "Talented Tenth" of the black population would lead the way to equality, bemoaned the undignified examples set by their new neighbors, especially those from the lower classes or, worse, the farm. This elite gobbled up stories in the *Amsterdam News* that told of endless progress and firsts, and fretted over the popularity of joyous black musicals like *Shuffle Along* and *Chocolate Dandies,* or the viral spread of jazz and black slang. Their cry, in Zora Neale Hurston's wry accounting, was the same all over: " '[T]hat good-for-nothing, trashy Negro is the one the white people judge us all by. They think we're all just alike. My people! My people!' " Cullen, whose formal, restrained verses won the approval of this faction, argued that black writers had "more to gain from the rich background of English and American poetry than from any rebellious atavistic yearnings towards an African heritage."

More important for our story, the Renaissance gave rise to funkier voices as well, often with the help of white patrons or supporters. The fault lines between these groups created space for hip reinvention, and allowed new hybrids to form, even if people insisted on calling the results black. Wallace Thurman (1902–1934), Hurston and Hughes saw richness in the neighborhood's popular idioms, not its social register. Hurston, apprenticing herself to the German-American anthropologist Franz Boas, combed the rural South for folktales, which she published in the language she heard them, reclaiming the beauty of black English from Joel Chandler Harris and Mark Twain. Hughes, a scion of two prominent families, celebrated the vulgar power of the blues and the characters of the night. Poems like "The Weary Blues" abandoned the ivory tower for the funk of Lenox Avenue: "Droning in a drowsy syncopated tune / Rocking back and forth in a mellow croon / I heard a Negro play." Hughes frankly mocked the idea that blacks could conquer white supremacy through culture. In his withering 1933 short story collection, *The Ways of White Folks,* he filleted the faithful.

> And as for the cultured Negroes who were always saying art would break down color lines, art could save the race and prevent lynchings! "Bunk!" said Oceola. "Ma ma and pa were both artists when it came to making music, and the white folks ran them out of town for being dressed up in Alabama. And look at the Jews! Every other artist in the world's a Jew, and still folks hate them."

Jazz may have seemed an ideal social meeting ground, but it was also a field of contention, creating unstable alliances and divisions among blacks and whites. In many conservative African-American households, blues and jazz were the sound of sin; spirituals filled the air (though truly proper households banned these, too, as uncultured). Mamie Smith's recording of "Crazy Blues" gave secular music a foothold, but the musicians still carried an aroma of disrepute. As the jazz saxophonist Benny Carter said, "We sensed that the black cultural as well as moral leaders looked down on our music as undignified." The new strivers were often even more severe. The stride pianist Willie "the Lion" Smith found that migrant families, struggling for a nut, took an especially hard line on idle pleasures: "Among those who disliked this form of entertainment the most were the Negroes who had recently come up from the South to seek a better life." It is likely that the majority of white Americans shared or surpassed this disdain, but these people did not go to Harlem. The whites who did brought a headful of deluded fraternity, according to Hughes, "thinking the Negroes loved to have them there, and firmly believing that all Harlemites left their houses at sundown to sing and dance in cabarets, because most of the whites saw nothing but the cabarets, not the houses." White money, in turn, was the gasoline that made the engine spin.

This money also pulled in several directions. White publishers wanted a certain flavor of black literature. One publisher rejected Fauset's mannered *There Is Confusion,* explaining, "White readers just don't expect Negroes to be like this." Hip was a dance white culture-mavens expected African Americans to perform. The attention was nurturing but also condescending. Charlotte Mason, one of the rich white patrons who had their own notions of blackness, fretted that Harlem's artists were paling before her eyes, warning that by the time they "finished running their inheritance on this slippery pond of civilization, there will not be any place where the white man has not divided the spoils of primitive African art, African music, all Africa's strengths." In other words, the Harlem Renaissance was running too "civilized," too white for her tastes. The music industry similarly made demands, drawing jazz and blues artists to New York, but imposing its own commercial agenda. Blues, a music cultivated by rural men with instruments, became a platform for urban female singers like the Smiths—Mamie, Clara and Bessie (no relation). Jazz in New York followed the dapper sophistication of Ellington and Fletcher Henderson, who equaled the schematic complexity of European classical music but left some black listeners cold. For musicians, Chicago was the place to blow, New York was the place for dough. Sidney Bechet, watching the Original Dixieland Jazz Band snag the first jazz recording date, lamented the role of industry: "These people who was coming to make records, they was going to turn it into a regular business, and after that it wouldn't be a pleasure music." White money was pushing Harlem writers, musicians, and nightlife toward its own vision of Afrotopia. While whites were absorbing a flawed education about black people, blacks were learning the profitability of living up to white expectations.

Carl Van Vechten with Gertrude Stein and Alice B. Toklas

In the crossover, no figure was as freighted as Carl Van Vechten (1880–1964), a former music critic for the *New York Times* whose ubiquity above 110th Street inspired the Harlem songwriter Andy Razaf to pen the lyric, "Go inspectin' / Like Van Vechten." Born into a wealthy family in Cedar Rapids, Iowa, Van Vechten met the century with open eyes and ears, championing modern artists as far afield as Igor Stravinsky, Arnold Schoenberg, Bessie Smith, Isadora Duncan and Gertrude Stein; his cheerleading helped Americans finally honor Herman Melville. As Harlem began to jump, Van Vechten played tour guide for downtown society. He described his interest in African Americans as "almost an addiction," and commissioned a caricature of himself as a black man, labeled "A Prediction." Though he was married, and affected a heterosexual identity, he collected photographs of nude black men.

Van Vechten was the circuit's most tireless promoter, hounding publishers, philanthropies and the public on behalf of Harlem artists. His parties on West 55th Street were drunken experiments in cultural chemistry, mixing high culture and low, old money and no money. Here Harlem met Tallulah Bankhead or George Gershwin, Alexander Woollcott or Theodore Dreiser. At one legendary bash, Bessie Smith, already drunk and looking for whiskey, collared the opera singer Marguerite

a prediction
to Carl from
COVARRUBIAS.

Carl Van Vechten unbleached, by
Miguel Covarrubias

D'Alvarez, who had just charmed the room with an aria, and advised, "Don't let *nobody* tell you you can't sing."

If he began as a welcome interloper, Van Vechten forfeited much of his goodwill with a 1926 novel called *Nigger Heaven*. The book now seems relatively innocuous, but the title, a reference to the segregated balconies in theaters, offended many blacks. The African-American press denounced him; Small's Paradise banned him. Hughes, James Weldon Johnson and others defended the book specifically and their friend generally. Most telling, *Nigger Heaven* warned of the threat represented by people like Van Vechten himself. A white character in the book berates a black novelist for writing about middle-class life rather than the more picturesque hustlers and gamblers of the neighborhood. "If you young Negro intellectuals don't get busy," the white character lectures, "a new crop of Nordics is going to spring up who will take the trouble to become better informed and will exploit this material before the Negro gets around to it." Of course, with *Nigger Heaven*, Van Vechten was doing just that. A prototype of the white negro, Van Vechten walked the line between good faith and presumption, and he was too perceptive not to know how precarious and thrilling this line was. His ventures profited everyone, including himself.

As the 1920s peaked, there was hip awareness on both sides of the color line, and opportunities for advancement built in. Jessie Fauset and Countee Cullen crossed one way in pursuit of myth while Hart Crane and Hemingway were crossing the other. Figures like Van Vechten or Ellington struck comparable poses of cool amid the chaos. Their art, like their lives, spread its roots widely. All of these figures resisted the idea that ethnicity was destiny; they sampled whatever was in front of them, black and white, and spit it back as hip as they could. When the Depression crashed down around them, revealing the pervasive poverty underneath the glitz, it demonstrated the fragility of this alliance. The joyful hybrids of the 1910s and 1920s gave way to retrenchment. It would take another world war before a group of blacks and whites so openly explored their shared roots.

The period in this chapter began the dominance of American popular culture around the world, and rhythm's dominance within American popular culture. The nation was finding its voice, and that voice was a mixture of black and white vernaculars, what Baraka calls "the picture within a picture within a picture, and so on, on the cereal package." Technology allowed whites and blacks to engage each other through culture without crossing paths in real life. At the same time, popular music, the vessel for this interaction, was becoming more important than ever. Player pianos, phonographs and radio gave music the kind of boost that literature had enjoyed with the invention of the Gutenberg press in the 15th century. Music permeated American homes like never before, and its story lines, to a great extent, spoke of both Europe and Africa. The phonograph was integrated in a way that neighborhoods, churches and schools increasingly were not. It aligned with the dynamism of the country. Nothing represented the new superpower like jazz, the music of the least powerful segment of society. This was not an aberration of the national character so much as a mark of it. America stood for fluidity and change, and this conceit of dynamism at the bottom of the economic ladder was a recipe for upheaval.

But this fantasy had its limits. As Hughes predicted, James Weldon Johnson's faith that breakthroughs in the arts would lead to wider empowerment proved flawed, even as an economic equation. The white dollars flowing into Harlem typically ended in the pockets of white club owners, mobsters, publishers, record companies or landlords. By the end of the decade, the white gangster Dutch Schultz had even taken over the Harlem numbers racket once ruled by Casper Holstein. Slumming, in the end, left mainly slums. Cultural success did not translate into political success: whites simply proved that they were happy to watch blacks sing and dance.

In betting on the arts to influence society, Johnson discounted the influence that society exerts on the arts. As black artists matched or surpassed white ones in popularity, their work began to be described under separate racial rubrics. Record companies segregated the music in black, or "race" departments. What was properly the center of American culture—the music of Ellington and Armstrong, the dances that began at the Savoy—was pushed to the periphery. Dividing lines that had fallen went back up, and new ones rose around them. In the recording industry country blues became separate from hillbilly or folk music—one black, the other two white—even though the people who played one probably played all three. Though the writers of the Lost Generation and Harlem Renaissance often shared the same disillusionment, sexual frankness and raw language, these similarities were considered secondary to the differences of the writers' skin tones. The role whites assigned to black artists was not to join the national culture but to short-circuit it from the outside, to save it from itself. The playwright Eugene O'Neill advised black writers, "Be yourselves! Don't reach out for our stuff which *we* call good!"

The lesson from these syntheses, which went over the heads of the square mainstream, involved a central fact of black life: that America was not monocultural, and that your rewards depended in part on how well you played the other guy's game. The alienation and creative bloom of the post-WWI years were in many ways a dress rehearsal for the alienation and bloom of the post-WWII period, with Armstrong paving the way for Dizzy Gillespie, Hart Crane for Jackson Pollock, and the Beats splitting the difference between the Lost Generation and the Harlem Renaissance. Significantly, in both eras white and black artists fortified themselves overtly from each other's stash. If the crossover was not always wholly enlightening, for now it offers a good, short definition of hip: being able to play the other guy's game. With flavor.

4 would a hipster hit a lady?

pulp fiction, film noir and gangsta rap

> From thirty feet away she looked like a lot of class. From ten feet away she looked like something made up to be seen from thirty feet away. —RAYMOND CHANDLER, The High Window

Visiting the United States in the fall of 1912, the Swiss psychiatrist Carl Jung saw it as a country uncomfortable with its own manhood. In the wake of its conquests, he said, the country had grown prudish and matriarchal, as if embarrassed by the wild, masculine violence that marked its history. As Jung saw it, "whenever the American husband spoke to his wife there was always a little melancholy note in his voice, as though he were not quite free; as though he were a boy talking to an older woman." The Victorian torpor, according to Jung, reflected the sexual frustration of women who needed men in their beds, but had only little boys. Such prudery was "always a cover for brutality," he said: until America faced up to its savage nature, it would never be great. What Jung missed, on his rounds of conferences and dinners, were the countervailing currents of hip.

In a later chapter I will salute hipster women, whose coolness refutes Jung's stereotypes, but for now let us consider the relationship between hip and masculinity. Hip's central romance, the myth of reinvention, is a quintessential male fantasy. It allows birth without a womb. Though women can reinvent themselves as well as men, either scenario knocks a leg from under female authority: if anyone can create identity from scratch, then women are not the only ones who can generate life. Boys and girls alike make this break as adolescents; hip continues the process later in life. When white hipsters reinvent themselves through jive talk or droopy jeans, the process is always sexualized—it is an escape from the feminine, meaning the conditions of one's birth, toward a fantasy of black hypermasculinity. In this fantasy blackness means a primal connection to sex and violence, a big penis and relief from the onus of upward mobility. (White hipsters do not co-opt African Americans' tradition of reverence toward the mother. When Eminem imagines raping and killing his mother in "Kill You," he is at his whitest, going where no rapper, black or white, has ever gone before.) Black culture becomes shorthand for unrepressed masculinity. This projection, which animates Mailer's white negroes, is not necessarily harmless.

Hip's romance of the road, which runs from Huck Finn to Jack Kerouac to the drifters in *Stranger Than Paradise,* also plays out a male escape fantasy. This romance unites the vagabonds, outlaws, minstrels, bluesmen, existentialists and DJs who make up the hip nation. For Twain it was a twisting river; for Kerouac, ping-ponging across the country in *On the Road* (1957), it was wherever Neal Cassady might lead him, its surface "unfurling and flying and hissing at incredible speeds across the groaning continent with that mad Ahab at the wheel. When I closed my eyes all I could see was the road unwinding into me." Muddy Waters taught America and Britain alike about the "Rollin' Stone Blues." Though the road has no destination, it leads away from both work and the feminine. If women's power in the home reduced men to little boys, as Jung thought, the road promised growth and enlightenment. This romance, too, has its casualties. Wherever you find deadbeat dads, you will likely find this rationalization close at hand.

In the decades between the two world wars, hip responded to two pressures on American men: the weight of Jung's smothering matriarch and the increasingly dehumanizing nature of work. These pressures fed each other: guys worked degrading jobs in order to support families—which, Jung said, promptly unburdened them of their manhood. Both crimped their masculinity. As Americans left farms, where men and women had split the labor, the new order organized itself around men earning money

Edward G. Robinson in *Little Caesar*

and women spending it. If this struck some men as a poor deal, they could not improve the terms simply by earning more (nor, for women, by spending more). Writing in 1918, H. L. Mencken, a confirmed bachelor and sometime sage of hip, pitied the poor dupe who would eagerly "yield up his liberty, his property and his soul to the first woman who, in despair of finding better game, turns her appraising eye upon him."

Work itself was also seen as emasculating. The new factories, with their mindless, repetitive tasks, encouraged a "profound national impulse [that] drives the hundred millions steadily toward uniformity," wrote Carl Van Doren in 1926. This anxiety was best captured in *Modern Times*, in which Charlie Chaplin (1889–1977) is literally put through the assembly line. Men's stature was tied to their accomplishments as breadwinners, which no longer involved subduing wild lands or the native population, but pushing paper or tightening widgets. The challenge for hip, then, was to stretch masculinity into the world of urban leisure. This was the new frontier.

In the 1920s and 1930s, these two currents came together in a new avatar of masculine hip, the hard-boiled detective or pulp hero. As drawn by Dashiell Hammett, James M. Cain, Raymond Chandler, Jonathan Latimer, David Goodis and other disciples of the penny-a-word form, the hard-boiled hero was a figure of masculinity unbound: big shoulders, strong chin, smart lip, big pistol and a taut gift of gab. As if in answer to Jung, this hero—Philip Marlowe, Sam Spade, the unnamed Continental Op, Three Gun Terry, Race Williams and others—introduced an all-American style of sex and violence, bordered only by the writers' equally homegrown tools: rhythm, humor, sensationalism, mass production and bald opportunism. The private eye was his own invention, usually an independent operator, unmarried, childless and motherless. He cowed neither to women nor to work. He did not suffer an employer; in many stories he gained the upper hand by walking away from a check. Similarly, he cut a sexual swath but did not have any attachments or obligations; on this front, he gained advantage by walking away from hot nookie. Produced and sold in bulk, he was an early model of mass hip. His lineage, which offered brutality as style and product, has continued in film noir and, since the late 1980s, in the cinematic nihilism of gangsta rap.

In an oft-quoted passage from Hammett's *The Maltese Falcon*, the hero, Sam Spade, tells a story to explain why he does what he does. The tale does not appear in the three movies made from the novel, and is an odd digression for Hammett, whose characters rarely say more than they have to. It concerns a real estate man named Flitcraft, who went to lunch one day and narrowly missed being crushed by a falling construction beam. For Spade as for Flitcraft, this brush with random, meaningless death was a lulu. "He felt like somebody had taken the lid off life and let him look at the works," Spade says. If death was so arbitrary, the man figured, then his attempts to lead a reasonable and orderly life were a sham, putting him "out of step, and not into step, with life." He kept walking, leaving behind his name, his job and his family. When Spade tracked him down a few years later, Flitcraft had rebuilt a life nearly identical to the one he left behind, falling into it with the same inevitability as the beam that had nearly killed him.

Published in 1930, as the bubble of the Jazz Age crashed with the Depression, the passage is as close as Hammett came to defining the mechanics of the pulp universe. Life is random and senseless, the story says; but that does not mean that men are free. Given a chance to reinvent themselves, some, like Flitcraft, will simply take the same walk on the mild side, defined by their jobs or families. But for bolder players like Spade, not content to be what Jung called "a boy talking to an older woman," the same epiphany opens a frontier of possibility. He invents not just himself but the moral order around him. The terms of this order— money, violence, betrayal, sex and ultimately male loyalty—were the stuff of the new urban America. Just as the nation's contribution to the theater was the minstrel show, and its contributions to music were jazz and the blues, its gift to literature was the detective mystery—and, beginning in the 1920s, the genre's dark variant, the hard-boiled story. Like the other forms, hard-boiled fiction was a wholly mongrel creation, blurring the lines between high art and low.

Inherent in hip's evolution so far has been the displacement of rage. In daily life rage is destructive and inarticulate, harmful to both subject and object. But in the artful dodges of hip, it can be productive, articulate and edifying—not repressed but put to use. Slaves encoded their rage in language and art—cool on the surface, hot below. This is an early instance of *signifying,* in the African-American sense of using words to mean more than one thing. Emerson and Thoreau redirected their anger into the oxymoron of civil disobedience; the Lost Generation wove its cynicism into jazzy, saturnine prose. All of these played out as hip detachment. Hard-boiled fiction brought rage closer to the surface. There was no mistaking its presence. Instead of turning away from it, or coding it in a language in which *bad* meant good, the pulp writers packaged violence in choppy, kinetic prose. It was contained rather than masked.

In the speed and violence that followed World War I, the hard-boiled protagonist was at home in these elements and nowhere else, able to cope with anything but boredom and sobriety. The books served up a masculine swinger in action. Equally comfortable with lowlifes or swells, he was detached from both. In the high art of the period, modernism cracked the continuity of narrative. Pulp writers applied this disjunction to sex and violence, rendering them as discontinuous facts, without foreplay or afterglow. The action assumed a slapstick illogic:

> I giggled and socked him. I laid the coil spring on the side of his head and he stumbled forward. I followed him down to his knees. I hit him twice

more. He made a moaning sound. I took the sap out of his limp hand. He whined.

I used my knee on his face. It hurt my knee. He didn't tell me whether it hurt his face. While he was still groaning I knocked him cold with the sap.

In this passage, from Chandler's *Farewell, My Lovely* (1940), the violence is all in the syllables, short and fast, but the rub lies in Chandler's small wisecrack: *He didn't tell me whether it hurt his face.* Even in the midst of this pounding, the narrator distances himself from the violence by converting it to attitude and performance. Violence, then, becomes a kind of language, with its own humor and point of view. Through this device action becomes consciousness.

The first detective stories are generally considered to be Edgar Allan Poe's "The Murders in the Rue Morgue" (1841), "The Mystery of Marie Rogêt" (1842–1843) and "The Purloined Letter" (1845), which introduced a Parisian investigator named C. Auguste Dupin. Like the sleuths who followed in his wake, most notably Sherlock Holmes or Hercule Poirot, Dupin was a man of ratiocination, using deduction to piece together a logistic puzzle. Force was not part of his game. These conventional mysteries pitted gentlemen of sedentary intellect against hearty but doomed criminals. The bad guys were bad, the detectives and citizenry good; the detectives' mission was to root out the evil festering among the innocent. This is the *Masterpiece Theatre* view of crime—once the bad apples are routed, all will be right in the world and PBS can go to the pledge phones. Compared to Poe's gothic stories, in which corruption and evil spread throughout the population, the detective stories treated society as a perpetual virgin in danger of losing its maidenhead. These parlor mysteries lacked the respect for evil that Poe tendered in horror tales like "The Masque of the Red Death," which ended on a less cheery note: "And Darkness and Decay and Death held illimitable dominion over all."

Hard-boiled, by contrast, spread the darkness and decay around.

Nick Tosches has written that there would be no rock and roll without the motivating force of Cadillacs. Similarly, there might be no hard-boiled lit without a cynical grab for cash. After World War I, H. L. Mencken and

George Jean Nathan needed money to float their ornery literary magazine, *Smart Set*. In this period, Henry Louis Mencken (1880–1956) and his dapper, Ivy League literary partner, the drama critic Nathan (1882–1958), slung their withering prejudices across America, skewering hypocrites and the "booboisie." The son of German immigrants, Mencken cultivated a perverse detachment from American society, studying it in the same spirit, he said, that men go to zoos. At *Smart Set* and later the *American Mercury,* Mencken and Nathan published early works of Fitzgerald, O'Neill, Joyce and Dorothy Parker, among others. To pay for this falootin', they also ran a sideline in literary cheese, pandering to low tastes with pulps called *Parisienne* and the erotic *Saucy Stories.* These pulps bore out Mencken's most famous, though oft-misquoted, adage: "No one in this world, so far as I know—and I have researched the records for years, and employed agents to help me—has ever lost money by underestimating the intelligence of the great masses of the plain people."

In April 1920, they added a magazine called *The Black Mask,* printed on the uncoated paper stock that gave pulp fiction its name. They conceived the title, later shortened to simply *Black Mask,* to cover all the exploitation subgenres, but quickly settled on strictly crime stuff. Though they cashed out after just eight months, the magazine went on to launch the careers of Hammett, Chandler, Erle Stanley Gardner, Lester Dent and Cornell Woolrich, among others. Within its mercenary mandate, it was as groundbreaking as *Smart Set.* In May 1923, Carroll John Daly (1889–1955) introduced a detective named Terry Mack who brought a new level of misanthropy and hard-boiled violence to the job. With his follow-up character, a PI named Race Williams, Daly hit a vein the detective story had not explored before. Race Williams was a cliché waiting to be written. His violence, he said, was not some ivory tower abstraction. "[R]ight and wrong are not written on the statues for me, nor do I find my code of morals in the essays of long-winded professors," the PI says. "My ethics are my own." He had a gift for dispensing justice: "I sent him crashing through the gates of hell with my bullet in his brain." Daly's books have fallen out of print, and hold more historic than literary interest. But a few months after Race appeared, a former detective named Samuel Dashiell Hammett began to fill the hard-boiled style with smoke and music and life.

Dashiell Hammett

Hammett (1894–1961) published his first, unremarkable story in *Black Mask* in December 1922, writing under the pseudonym Peter Collinson. The dashing, alcoholic, chronically unfaithful son of a dashing, alcoholic, womanizing father, Hammett came to crime fiction after a stint as an operative for the Pinkerton detective agency. The work left him with no illusions about detectives. On one job, he worked as a strikebreaker at a mine in Butte, Montana, where Pinkertons may have murdered a labor organizer named Frank Little. Hammett's background provided verisimilitude and a sense of the absurd; his cases included one of a man who stole a Ferris wheel. After a handful of forgettable stories, in October 1923 he introduced a nameless character called the Continental Op who operated in a moral universe like Race Williams's, but full of cinematic details and sentences that were nimble enough to keep up with the bullets. Like Daly, Hammett did away with the quaint oppositions of good and evil, freeing the mystery story from its grid of stock saviors and villains. Instead, his detectives are in conflict with themselves—sexual, moral and professional. As a grifter in *The Maltese Falcon* sums up Spade, approvingly, "I made somewhat extensive inquiries about you before taking any action, and was assured that you were far too reasonable to allow other considerations to interfere with profitable business relations." Over the course of the book, Spade will prove this assessment both right and wrong.

Hammett moved crime out of the drawing room of the traditional whodunits and into the alley, where it belonged. As Raymond Chandler wrote in a 1944 essay called "The Simple Art of Murder,"

> Hammett gave murder back to the kind of people that commit it for reasons, not just to provide a corpse; and with the means at hand, not with hand-wrought dueling pistols, curare, and tropical fish. He put these people down on paper as they are, and he made them talk and think in the language they customarily used for these purposes. He had style, but his audience didn't know it, because it was in a language not supposed to be capable of such refinements.

A typical Hammett story began with a tiny drop of corruption, then traced its seep from the top of society to the bottom.

The stories reflected the ethical murk of both Prohibition, which turned genteel living rooms into crime scenes, and the vogue for Freud, which projected unknown capacities for sex and brutality, possibly in tandem, on one's most innocent-looking neighbors. Like Freud, Hammett began with the premise that everyone maintained a false front, and that the truth lay repressed below. "Everybody," as Spade says, "has something to hide." Unlike the virtuous Dupin or Sherlock Holmes, who tried to restore the purity of their communities after a crime, Hammett's investigators made their home amid vice and the strong-arm. Piety, which is essentially matriarchal, had no place in the pulp universe, except as the A-side of hypocrisy. Hammett's detectives tried to influence the action, not stop it. They were as duplicitous as the mob boys and the cops. When Spade accepts a client's patronage at the beginning of *The Maltese Falcon*, he has no illusions that he will be acting on the side of good. "We didn't exactly believe your story," he tells the client, one of the many deadly blondes who ankled through Hammett's novels. "We believed your two hundred dollars."

Though they are called crime fiction, the stories were only incidentally about crime. Often the crimes were the most formulaic element. In *The*

Maltese Falcon, for example, the black bird is a red herring. The work was about work. No art has ever dealt as exhaustingly in the mechanics of earning a living: the solicitation of clients, the interview, the day rate, the expenses, the office furnishings, the secretary. This work, in turn, was not about money. For a Depression readership, pulp treated money as a cheap metaphor or plot point. Money served a literary function. For the bad guys, money was power; in trying to get it, they were ultimately beholden to it. Money locked both cops and criminals into a pecking order of toadies and bosses, which many readers could identify with their own workplace.

By contrast, for the detective money was freedom—arising, paradoxically, from his freedom to reject it. He worked strictly freelance. His claim to hipness began with his independence. When Spade's partner is killed at the opening of *The Maltese Falcon,* he instructs his secretary to remove the partner's name from the door before he considers finding the killer; incorporation, apparently, burdens him more than murder. Chandler was even more explicit about the drag of the nine-to-five. After being slugged, drugged, kidnapped and ambushed, Chandler's detective, Philip Marlowe, still feels "not as sick as I would feel if I had a salaried job." The detective worked hard, but for himself, and never really for the money, which represented too many obligations. By separating work from money, and removing both from matriarchal control, pulp revitalized the masculine archetype that Jung had found in defeat. Marlowe and Spade were just as masculine earning or not earning. And because they were willing to refuse money or sex, they were not diminished when they decided to take a piece.

Hammett restored the evil of Poe's horror stories, planting it in a plush office or a tight skirt. His ops kept it in check with language. Though pulp is a low form, the good writers are as rare as in higher climes, and have the same uncompromising discipline. Hammett loved metaphors and avoided euphemism, trimming words to make his action move ever faster. The sentences glisten. By the time of his first novel, the toxic *Red Harvest* (1929), he could create a fallen world in a few opening sentences: "I first heard Personville called Poisonville by a red-haired mucker named Hickey Dewey in the Big Ship in Butte. He also called his shirt a shoit. I didn't think anything of what he had done to the city's name. . . . A few years later I went to Personville and learned better." Already, as a reader, you are reconsidering any plans to visit. The result is a literature at odds with itself. The narrator's prose creates a world of violence but is helpless to protect him from his creation. Darkness and decay and death, as Poe might have noted, held dominion over all, even the eloquent.

Though detective stories could come from all over, pulp found its fertile crescent in California, through a coterie of writers that included Hammett, Chandler, Horace McCoy and James M. Cain. Like the expatriate writers in Paris, they were far from home, often scorched by their experience in the war, and driven to the edge of the continent in search of something. As Chandler wrote of his military service, "Once you have had to lead a platoon into direct machine-gun fire, nothing is ever the same again." The coast was a place to contemplate the failure of the open road. Playing against the popular image of California as a land of sunshine and opportunity, pulp writers recast the state as a dark, violent place where the outcasts, drifters and grifters dug in after they ran out of room to run.

Hammett, born in rural St. Mary's County, Maryland, landed in San Francisco in 1921, broke, dependent on the penny-a-word rates of East Coast pulps. Chandler (1888–1959), an American educated in English public schools, followed the oil industry to Los Angeles after the war, where he crashed and burned as an executive for the South Basin Oil Company before turning to prose. Cain (1892–1977), a protégé of Mencken and onetime managing editor of *The New Yorker,* moved to Hollywood to write for Paramount in the early years of the Depression. McCoy (1897–1955) left the Nashville area for an MGM screen test, and spent the Depression sleeping in abandoned cars and chasing menial work, ultimately working as a bouncer at a marathon dance contest in Santa Monica (he turned the experience into his bleak 1935 masterpiece, *They Shoot Horses, Don't They?*).

The literature these men produced was a West Coast answer to the Lost Generation and the Greenwich Village moderns: harsh, profane, alienated and geographically dystopian. The pulp hero, the first hip icon that did not rely on the East Coast bohemia or intelligentsia, drew on the character of the western outlaw, but without the tragic fatalism. The detectives were not criminals, but not exactly law-abiding. They were a different mix of the civilized and primitive, able to dip into either when needed. Hammett worked San Francisco, the first metropolis of California; Chandler, who published his first story in *Black Mask* in 1933, a decade after the debut of Hammett's Continental Op, moved the action to the balmier sprawl of Los Angeles. Where the writers in Paris and New York felt stateless, harboring a grudge against the place they left, their California peers described the end of the line, the point where the promise of the West opened up to reveal rot underneath.

The dystopian voice was not limited to detective fiction. California novelists like McCoy, Nathanael West and John Fante overturned similar rocks; Chester Himes honed his voice writing about the California defense industry well before his Harlem crime novels. West (nee Nathan Weinstein, 1903–1940) evoked the fierce bitterness of California's broken dreamers, who "loitered on the corners or stood with their backs to the shop windows and stared at everyone who passed. When their stare was returned, their eyes filled with hatred." His 1939 *The Day of the Locust,* still the definitive Hollywood novel, sets this hatred loose in the racket of cheap hustles, betrayals and broken faith. The book climaxes with the town in flames and a movie audience turned into a lynch mob, ripping apart a loser naïf whose name is Homer Simpson. Working a moral universe like Hammett's, these writers were hard-boiled without the crime.

As a metaphor, the California of pulp brought the intellectual processes of the 19th century to a bad end. The promise of reinvention, so vital to the American Renaissance, unraveled in pulp into a hive of false identity, where no one was what he or she seemed. Similarly, the individualism of Emerson and Thoreau metastasized into a society without a social contract. The detectives themselves lived in an alcoholic Sahara without friendship or love. If, as Hemingway wrote, there were no more absolutes to guide these processes, then they could only lead to ambiguity or deceit. In the defeat of the matriarchy, institutions held little respect. "I used to like this town," says Philip Marlowe in Chandler's *The Little Sister* (1949). "A long time ago. There were trees along Wilshire Boulevard. Beverly Hills was a country town. Westwood was bare hills and lots offering at eleven hundred dollars and no takers. Hollywood was a bunch of frame houses on the interurban line. Los Angeles was just a big dry sunny place with ugly homes and no style, but good-hearted and peaceful."

Idyllic on the surface, Los Angeles was built for pulp disillusionment. Its first building was the jail; its chamber of commerce, created to pump happy stories in the place of history, was the first in the nation. Decades before the movie industry made it official, the city's chief product was fantasy, and its chief subject was the city itself. In the 1880s and 1890s, a group of real estate barons, having bought the land cheaply, invented a heritage for Los Angeles in order to raise property values. One of these barons was Harrison Gray Otis, who owned the *Los Angeles Times*, and one of the ablest boosters was Charles Fletcher Lummis, whom Otis hired as an editor at the paper. The Los Angeles of 1880 was an arid country town, with no water or industry. Its past as a frontier wasteland did little for real estate values. Using the new power of the press, Otis, Lummis and others fabricated a city heritage out of the hulls of Spanish missions that could be seen decaying on every hillside. It was a sales pitch offered as local history. In truth, as the historian Kevin Starr has noted, the Spanish mission era declined when Anglo settlers overran it. Otis and the land barons used their influence to bring them what they needed: water, railroads and people, all in service of their investments. Lummis also played to local nativism, promising that "The ignorant, hopelessly un-American type of foreigner which infests and largely controls Eastern cities is almost unknown here."

Hard-boiled literature replaced Lummis's myths not with the realism of Frank Norris or John Steinbeck, but with violent surrealism. The writers played with the absence of history, presenting the detectives as pure self-invented style. For Chandler, who arrived in 1912, the split between myth and reality was both an irritant and a source of wry amusement. He admired the staying power of its false promises, which beckoned to suckers long past their expiration date. Approaching the old cow town, Marlowe is torn between its luster and decay. "I smelled Los Angeles before I got to it," he says. "It smelled stale and old like a living room that had been closed too long. But the colored lights fooled you. The lights were wonderful. There ought to be a monument to the man who invented neon lights."

Chandler was born in Chicago, the son of an Irish mother and a heavy-drinking father he described as "an utter swine." After his parents divorced, his mother took him to her own mother's home in a respectable but dull suburb south of London. Reared in a house of stern, contentious women and the snooty Dulwich College Preparatory School, he returned to America with nothing but the arrogance of a classical education. He married a woman 18 years his senior, and by the time he did any serious writing, guided by the great *Black Mask* editor Joseph T. "Cap" Shaw, he'd drunk his way to the bottom of the oil industry and run up a record of swinish infidelity all his own.

A committed Anglophile, he devoured American slang as only an outsider could. Often he made up his own; even after decades of parody, nothing is as much fun as Chandler's language. "An hour crawled by like a sick cockroach," he wrote, using up a metaphor the language didn't know it had (not to mention a zippy description of time's slowness). As he explained, "All I wanted when I began was to play with a fascinating new language, and trying, without anybody noticing it, to see what it would do as a means of expression which might remain on the level of unintellectual thinking and yet acquire the power to say things which are usually only said with a literary air." Mixing high-art pretensions with low-art sensationalism, he dismissed the distinction between the two as a product of "parvenu insecurity." Chandler promised access to the private slang of LA's gutter and the private depravity of the manor.

Where Hammett's characters inhabited an arbitrary moral universe, Chandler's proxy, Philip Marlowe, tackled Los Angeles with moral certainty. The city was a mess, and it was his job to clean it up. In "The Simple Art of Murder," Chandler wrote that his hero's "moral and intellectual force is that he gets nothing but his fee, for which he will if he can protect the innocent, guard the helpless and destroy the wicked, and the fact that he must do this while earning a meager living in a corrupt world is what makes him stand out." Fortunately, Marlowe himself never spoke in such prissy terms. "To hell with the rich," he says in Chandler's first novel, *The Big Sleep* (1939). "They make me sick." Within this moral universe, though, the detective's victories are at best provisional. He never actually gets the girl, and the city at the end is just as lousy as before he started.

•   •   •

I n a city without history, hard-boiled detectives did not have mothers, or at least you never read about them. Presumably the heroes invented themselves through chain reactions of cigarette ash and bathtub gin. Nor did they have wives, steady girlfriends or children. It was a cliché of the genre that they had nothing to lose, neither future nor past. Pulp played a trick on readers, asking them to identify with characters who were unwilling or unable to return the favor. No one was more isolated than the detective. Hip was detachment: only disconnect. At the end of *The Maltese Falcon,* when the blonde femme fatale begs Spade to spare her in the name of love, he wavers for only a second. "I won't because all of me wants to— wants to say to hell with the consequences and do it—and because—God damn you—you've counted on that with me the same as you counted on that with the others." When the cops arrive, Spade sends her over.

Male insecurities, brought on by work and home, played out in pulp as a river of misogyny. Sex, the golden elixir of Greenwich Village and Harlem, turned acrid in the California light. In Chandler's *The Long Goodbye* (1953), his best novel, he treats an unnamed woman at a pool as a surrogate for Los Angeles, building to a crescendo of desire and disgust. At a Beverly Hills hotel, Marlowe eyes a luscious figure in a sharkskin swimsuit: "I watched the band of white that showed between the tan of her thighs and the suit. I watched it carnally." A moment later, he observes, "She opened a mouth like a firebucket and laughed. That terminated my interest in her. I couldn't hear the laugh but the hole in her face when she unzipped her teeth was all I needed." Sometimes the rage in pulp is not simply aesthetic. Yet on the whole, pulp objected less to women than to male roles—the drabness of the domestic hubby, or the foolishness of the lover who sacrifices everything for a little action. For the hard-boiled detective, home and hearth seemed as deadening as a corporate career. The threat to hip is not women but domesticity.

James Mallahan Cain, whose protagonists were not lawmen but ordinary saps, made a literature of this threat. In novels like *The Postman Always Rings Twice* (1934), *Double Indemnity* (1936) and *Mildred Pierce* (1941), trouble slithers in as erotic compulsion, taking everyone downward in its wake. In his novels, as the critic Geoffrey O'Brien notes, "desire is all there is." Men wander into the opening chapters, catch a whiff, then plummet into a manhole. Cain makes clear that his characters are not engaged in the higher pursuit of beauty. "Except for the shape, she

Barbara Stanwyck and Fred MacMurray in *Double Indemnity*

really wasn't any raving beauty," says the protagonist of *The Postman Always Rings Twice,* setting eyes on the Wrong Woman. "[B]ut she had a sulky look to her, and her lips stuck out in a way that made me want to mash them in for her." Bodies will hit the sheets; bodies will hit the floor.

Like the work of Chandler and Hammett, Cain's stories came most stylishly to life on the screen. In the 1940s and 1950s, a cohort of German and Austrian émigrés who landed in California after fleeing the Nazis translated pulp's terse prose and subarticulate characters into melodramas of bullets and existential despair. In the hands of Billy Wilder, Fritz Lang, Otto Preminger and others, pulp was an American analog to European expressionist cinema. French critics, connoisseurs of American low culture, called the crime movies film noir, though studios called the cheaper efforts B movies, signifying that they were the lesser acts in double features. The emotional emptiness of the books filled the screen. Like pulp, film noir traded on the hip premise that language means more than it says, and that silence communicates more than words. Most important, pulp action moved shapes and shadows around the screen. Marlowe's droll contempt passed effortlessly to Humphrey Bogart in Howard Hawks's version of *The Big Sleep* (1946). In Bogart's heavy-lidded sensuality, audiences saw "the corpse on reprieve within each of us," wrote the French critic Andre Bazin. With a smoke dangling from his lip, bogarted by the eponym, he appeared to be moving at two speeds—his body inert in the whirlwind of impending violence, his mind racing at the speed of the script's dialog. No combination could have been hipper.

The noir biz double-dipped from the pulp well. William Faulkner, who was toying with hard-boiled tropes in novels like *Sanctuary* (1931) and *The Wild Palms* (1939), cowrote the screenplay to *The Big Sleep*. Jonathan Latimer, whose own pulp novels used exaggerated black humor, wrote the screenplay from Hammett's novel *The Glass Key*. Chandler collaborated with Wilder on *Double Indemnity,* from the novel by Cain, whom Chandler dismissed—unfairly—as "every kind of writer I detest, a faux naïf, a Proust in greasy overalls, . . . the offal of literature." Chandler loathed the movie business, and agreed to write only if the studios marinated him in whiskey. The more scripts he wrote, the more bitterly his novels peeled the facades of Los Angeles. Studio lots were free-for-alls of alcohol and badinage, often presided over by foreigners or the alumni of New York's garment trades or Yiddish theater. Pulp was the first literature written with movies in the foreground, creating characters that were all exterior, expressing thought through motion.

The literature itself evolved in relationship to its genre clichés: it winked at them or undercut them. Jim Thompson (1906–1977) perfected the oeuvre of the untrustworthy narrator. Thompson, the son of a disgraced Oklahoma sheriff, came to pulp writing after a drunken blackout that consumed much of his adult life. Unlike Hammett and Chandler, who told their stories through reliable moral characters like Spade or Marlowe, Thompson experimented with psychopathic narrators who may or may not be telling the truth. If pulp is an aesthetic of hip detachment, Thompson pushed readers to its limits, leaving them no one to identify with. His best book, *The Killer Inside Me* (1952), is narrated by a small-town sheriff named Lou Ford, who talks in bland, have-a-nice-day clichés and kills out of sexual sickness. Ford dares people to call his shtick, piling one cornball saying on another, as if to suck the meaning out of their brains. "Striking at people that way is almost as good as the other, the real way," he says. But of course there will be plenty of the real way as well. The book puts you in bed with a liar and madman; if you think things will work out well, you've been napping. By the murderous conclusion, it is impossible to tell whether the narrative is a lie, a confession, a hallucination or all three. In *Savage Night* (1953), the narrator is a murderer and rapist who over the course of the novel cleaves apart from himself. "You can do that, split yourself in two parts," he says. "It's easier than you'd think. Where it gets tough is when you try to get the parts back together again." By the end of this book, we realize that the narrator is already dead.

Thompson turned out a series of nasty novels that sold astonishingly well and then went out of print. He went to Hollywood, flamed out, then helped write a mean noir sceenplay called *The Killing*, the 1956 breakthrough film for a former *Look* photographer named Stanley Kubrick. Though the two men fell out over credit, they teamed again on Kubrick's 1957 film *Paths of Glory*. For all his ambition and success, Thompson shared Chandler's beef with the movie industry, and his sister later remarked, "Hollywood basically killed him off." It did not bury him, however, before he added his own poison tribute to the Golden State, describing it as "nothing but desert, parched and withered and lifeless, where a dead man walked through eternity."

Though Hollywood loved pulp, its feeding cycle was too voracious, grinding pulp mannerisms into clichés the way beer commercials do the blues. Many of the better hard-boiled heirs, like Elmore Leonard and Carl Hiaasen, write a kind of meta-pulp, winking at the conventions while working their mojo. James Ellroy retrieved the genre from self-parody with a 1987–1992 series he called the Los Angeles Quartet. Set between 1947 and 1959, *The Black Dahlia, The Big Nowhere, L.A. Confidential* and *White Jazz* dipped the city in a gleeful brine of hypocrisy and hustle. Ellroy's Los Angeles was not fallen, like Chandler's world, but actively evil, like Poe's. He tapped the city's uncelebrated history: the 1910 bombing of the antiunion *Los Angeles Times,* which sparked open warfare between labor and paid thugs; the city oligarchs' corrupt play for water (captured in Roman Polanski's *Chinatown*); the 1940s riots between white soldiers and zoot-suited pachucos; the 1957 murder of the starlet Elizabeth Short, nicknamed "the Black Dahlia," whose body was found severed at the waist. Ellroy's goal, he said, was to honor the city with the tribute it deserved—the "biggest, baddest, sickest, ugliest, most sex-saturated, unformulaic, most pervasively evil, profound fucking crime novels of all time."

From childhood he had a close relationship to the city's dark history. He was born March 4, 1948, in the LA neighborhood that is now Koreatown, to an alcoholic, promiscuous mother and a wayward father who claimed to have laid Rita Hayworth. The marriage quickly dissolved. When Ellroy was 10, his mother was found strangled to death in the bushes near a football field. Ellroy became obsessed with the similarities between his mother's murder and the Black Dahlia case, both unsolved. His teens and 20s unreeled in undirected fury: neo-Nazi gestures, petty crime, drug addiction, jail. He broke into apartments and sniffed women's underpants. His father offered advice but not wisdom. His last words to his son were "Try and pick up every waitress that serves you."

When he emerged from his own 12-year-blackout, Ellroy funneled the bile into his fiction. He dispensed with good guys entirely. "If there's one rule I'd like to break, it's the rule that says, 'We need sympathetic characters to engender sympathy with our readers,' " he said in 1996. Instead, he filled his books with a cast he described as "your shakedown artist, your rogue cop, your lowest-level implementer of public policy. I like profiteers. I like soldiers of fortune. I like the racist toadies of the fascist system of 35 years ago. I hate the cheap humanity inherent to the private-eye genre. I hate Raymond Chandler's Philip Marlowe and his 18,000 clones.' " But if Ellroy shunned Marlowe's sanctimony, he fed on the terse precision of Chandler's prose. When his publisher insisted that he cut the manuscript of *L.A. Confidential* from 800 pages to 662, he slashed the language down to what he called a "telegraphic shorthand style," eventually writing the next novel, *White Jazz*, in prose that resembled a violent personal ad: "I drove home, showered, changed—no reporters hovering yet. Downtown, a dress for Meg—I do it every time I kill a man." His 1996 memoir, *My Dark Places*, an investigation of his mother's murder, turned this prose as ruthlessly on himself and the dry mechanics of crime solving.

•　　•　　•

The art of the Lost Generation and the Harlem Renaissance took an essentially liberal view of race. It saw racial diversity as complementary rather than factional. Contact among different peoples, at least within the virtual realm of pop culture, sustained the myth of a common bond. Proximity worked as social agar. This is the benevolent face of hip. The pulp of Los Angeles, like the political turf, held more conservative, apocalyptic views of race. Betrayed by the promises of a utopian future, pulp and film noir had the reactionary zeal of a liberal who has been mugged. The distances of Los Angeles bred more fear than curiosity. For the hard-boiled hero, diversity was warfare; down every pulp street lay a different depravity. His role was to enter the ethnic cauldron so his clients wouldn't have to. Jazz, a soundtrack to good times in New York or Paris, meant danger in the smoky dens of film noir.

The nightmare inversion of the California dream echoes in recent books like Kem Nunn's *Tapping the Source* (1984), Bret Easton Ellis's *Less Than Zero* (1985) and Walter Mosley's Easy Rawlins mysteries. But the dystopian vision of Los Angeles continues most vividly in the rhymes of gangsta rappers like N.W.A., Snoop Dogg and the late Tupac Shakur. Cultivated in the 1970s in the boroughs of New York, with an accent on neighborhood, rap turned unneighborly in the gang turf of southern California in the 1980s. As Max Roach said, "Hip hop lives in the world—not the world of music—that's why it is so revolutionary." New York was hard, and hip-hop was the hardest part of New York; Los Angeles, the prettier coast, proved infinitely more feral.

At the Bronx River public housing project some years back, Afrika Bambaataa told me, "To understand hip-hop, you have to understand the gang structure of the Bronx." Bambaataa, born Kevin Donovan, was one of the early New York pioneers, who graduated from the Black Spades street gang to graffiti to DJ-ing. His adopted name is that of a 19th century Zulu chief and means Chief Affection. New York hip-hop crews, which were often gang-affiliated, tamed some of the gang violence into more sustainable recreations. In Compton, Long Beach and South Central Los Angeles, the music drew on a gang culture that was bigger, tougher, free-spending and self-promoting. It was made for anti-

The Notorious B.I.G.

myth. "We weren't livin' in hiphop culture, hiphop started in NY," re-called Tracey Morrow, a transplanted New Yorker who named himself Ice-T, after Iceberg Slim.

> They had graffiti artists, breakdancers, we didn't have any of that, we had gangs. So when I was in gangs and when I was in the army and shit, I was out here stealin' and gangbangin', and pimpin' women, and hangin' out with drug dealers, so . . . I'm pimpin' and doin' that shit, then I'd go into a club dressed like a breakdancer and tryin' to rap and my boys was like, "Hey man, you gotta rap about what we do, do some of that gangsta shit". . . . I was like, you know, fuck it, if that's what muthafuckas want I can do that, that's easy for me to do that shit. That's my life. It's like if you made eggs every mornin' and one day someone said, hey you should sell these eggs.

The first breakout West Coast rapper, Ice-T spun morality tales with no moral:

> I am a nightmare walking, psychopath talking
> King of my jungle just a gangster stalking

Here was a vision of Los Angeles the country had not seen before, even in the fallen narratives of pulp. Gangsta rap was as corny as noir and as hard to dismiss. Like the pulp writers, the rappers commonly came from homes with absent fathers, and wrought a literature of masculinity on parade, defined by clique loyalties. Like the motherless detectives, rappers were their own invention; in the absence of roots, they invented their own names and surrogate families. They were outsiders' outsiders. Eazy-E, a founding member of N.W.A., who died of AIDS in 1995, caught Chandler's deadpan, self-mythologizing word jazz in the anthem "Boyz-N-the-Hood." The song, written by Ice Cube, collapsed the gap between today's pathology and tomorrow's headline:

> The boy JB was a friend of mine
> Til I caught him in my car tryin to steal my Alpine
> Chased him up the street to call a truce
> The silly motherfucker pull out a deuce-deuce
> Little did he know I had a loaded 12 gauge
> One sucker dead, *LA Times* front page

In just six lines the rapper and JB move through friendship, betrayal, attempted conciliation, rejection, gun competition, murder, media sensationalism and conversion into legend.

Hip-hop on either coast was ripe for outlandish figures. As rock stars abandoned larger-than-life personae in order to become the indie boys next door, rappers like Snoop Dogg or the Notorious B.I.G., Brooklyn's answer to the West Coast, developed characters who were as funny and rich as they were pathological. They combined intense individualism with surreal violence, and converted themselves to myth. As Biggie rhymed, in a song released shortly after he was killed in a 1997 drive-by shooting in Los Angeles, "You're nobody till somebody kills you."

The pulp anti-myth of California came to fulfillment with Tupac Shakur (1971–1996), who was murdered in Las Vegas in September 1996. The son of a Black Panther, Tupac wore his most resonant myths on his heavily tattooed skin; years after his death, the faithful believe he is still alive. "But why be a thug?" an elderly black man once asked him. "Because if I don't, I'll lose everything I have," he answered. "Who else is going to love me but the thugs?" Like the heroes of pulp, he navigated a sea of moral ambiguities, playing both post-Malcolm X hero and victimizer. His Los Angeles was a place "where cowards die and the strong ball." The drumbeat behind all these lyrics is the thud of Flitcraft's falling beam, the sound of a world pulling senselessly apart and of a poised narrator looking at the works.

The loner protagonists of pulp, noir and gangsta rap were weapons of mass production. Conspicuously without mothers or childhood mementos, the detectives are unabashedly *produced,* not born. One differs from another mainly at the level of consumer preference, as Crest differs from Colgate. They represent the hipster as repeatable commodity. Their branding of style as consciousness anticipated the information economy of a few decades later, when hipness would literally be a commodity, adding value to any product.

From its earliest days, this commodity has traveled well. The French, of course, gave film noir its name and most enthusiastic reception. Rebecca West teased Cain that he was "a fool not to be born a Frenchman. The highbrows would have put you with Gide and Mauriac if you had taken this simple precaution." Gide himself declared Hammett's *Red Harvest* "the last word in atrocity, cynicism and horror." Albert Camus said he wrote *The Stranger* after reading *The Postman Always Rings Twice.* Yet if the violence plays universally, the perspective it calls for is distinctly American. This perspective is sometimes lost in translation. The French appreciation for noir is weighted too heavily toward metaphor, missing the low art; they do not appreciate that sometimes a cigar burn is just a cigar burn. Others err the other way. The hip-hop journalist Dream Hampton visited South Africa in 2000 and was dismayed to see gangs naming themselves after Tupac or LA's west side. "They didn't get it," she said. "American culture is all about irony, especially black culture. That's lost on them. They take it literally."

What's lost is the ambivalent voice of the blues, which overlays hardship with transcendence. To feel the blues is to feel both bad and good. N.W.A. captured this dark humor in couplets like "I'm expressing with my full capabilities / And now I'm living in correctional facilities." Pulp, noir and gangsta rap all worked this split message, speaking out of both sides of the mouth. The voice is as serious as cancer, as the rapper Rakim says, but it is also a ride. Hip is not the ability to talk like Marlowe or Ice-T, or to sulk like Bogart. That's what the gangs did in South Africa, missing half the message. Hip is the ability to hear both meanings in their voices, to catch the undertones complicating the plainest prose. In *The Big Sleep*, Marlowe muses,

> What did it matter where you lay once you were dead? In a dirty sump or in a marble tower on top of a high hill? You were dead, you were sleeping the big sleep, you were not bothered by things like that. Oil and water were the same as wind and air to you. You just slept the big sleep, not caring about the nastiness of how you died or where you fell. Me, I was part of the nastiness now. . . .

To read this straight is to see that he has the blues, and it feels so bad. But to read it hip is to recognize the wink and humor. Like the N.W.A. lyric, the passage is both liberating and funny. The speakers have the blues, and it feels so free and good.

5 the golden age of hip, part 1

bebop, cool jazz and the cold war

> The goatee, beret, and window-pane glasses were no accidents....
> [T]hey pointed toward a way of thinking, an emotional and psycho-
> logical resolution of some not so obscure social need or attitude. It
> was the beginning of the Negro's fluency with some of the canons
> of formal Western nonconformity, which was an easy emotional
> analogy to the three hundred years of unintentional nonconformity
> his color constantly reaffirmed.　　—AMIRI BARAKA (LeRoi Jones)

Two dates from the golden age of hip: On a blustery night in the winter of 1948, Miles Davis took the El train up to the Argyle Show Bar on the north side of Chicago. He was 22, the son of a dentist, recently dropped out of Juilliard to play in Charlie Parker's band. And he was broke. Parker arrived at the club in a condition that appeared contrary to one of his rare shared wisdoms: "Never take Seconals and play chromatics." He spent the gig nodding off and lurching back in, catching the right key but the wrong tune. Miles smoldered; Max Roach, the drummer, laughed at the sputter of incoherence and brilliance. Parker staggered off the stage, so wasted that he urinated in a phone booth. The owner fired them without pay. Some months later, Parker and the band returned unruffled, impeccable, *regal*. This time when Bird walked off stage toward the phone booth, he knew what he was doing. Repeating his past indiscretion, he sauntered back, zipping himself up as he went. It was a neat reversal of authority, with black genius asserting itself over white ownership. Parker raised his horn and blew the next day's news over the heads of the crowd.

And so we arrive at the golden age of hip, a Cold War convergence of art, image, dope, clothes, celebrity, intellectual arrogance and rebel grace. In the postnuclear, pre-Selma crush of the 1940s and 1950s, the complementary revolutions of bebop and the Beat generation provided a new answer to the question of what it meant to be an American. Parker, Dizzy Gillespie, Thelonious Monk and a small handful of peers transformed America's music, jazz, from a reflection of national aspirations to an unblinking critique of them. The players were flamboyant in their personal style, often self-destructive in their habits and meticulous in their art. A generation of white writers, led by Jack Kerouac, William S. Burroughs and Allen Ginsberg, could only clock in and follow in kind. The meeting point, Kerouac wrote, was one of defiant affirmation: "[Y]ou'd see hundreds of heads nodding in the smoky dimness, nodding to the [bop] music, 'Yes, yes, yes.' . . . I saw a whole generation nodding yes." These two self-marginalized groups staked out new ways for America to approach art, language, work, sex and identity. Against the chilly climate of the Eisenhower and McCarthy years, they created a model for the mass counterculture of the 1960s, in which rock and roll codified rebellion as personal style. This counterculture, in turn, would leave their revolution behind.

Specifically, the beboppers and the Beats changed the role of music and art in bohemia—and in the process, the relationship between bohemia and the marketplace. Rejecting the role of entertainer, the beboppers held themselves above the tastes of the public. Where American popular songs have celebrated the society that produced them, bop presented itself as the opposition: smarter, harder, colder, purer. It was deliberately difficult for both listeners and players. In venues where audiences had come to expect happy rhythms or cathartic ballads, the musicians fostered a cult of rebellion that spread through the same distribution networks as their music and reputations. If the mainstream was unworthy of their regard, a hip subculture, black and white, could get on board by purchasing the right records or making the right scene.

For this small but virally influential group, the jazz hipster who emerged in the 1940s offered a vision of enlightened self-invention. Draped in high seriousness, quoting both the universities and the streets, he hinted at what America might become, a thing that inspired both fear and admiration. The poet and novelist Gilbert Sorrentino, describing the early bop years in New York, recalled the savor of intellectual superiority:

> Be-bop cut us off completely, to our immense satisfaction. It was even more vehemently decried as "nigger music," but even to the tone-deaf it was apparent that it (the music) didn't care what the hell was thought of it. . . . It was probably, more than at any other time in its history, including the present, absolutely non-popular: and its adherents formed a cult, which perhaps more than any other force in the intellectual life of our time, brought together young people who were tired of the spurious.

What they shared was an ethos of nonconformity in an era of steely gray. As the pianist Hampton Hawes (1928–1977) wrote, "We were the first generation to rebel, playing bebop, trying to be different, going through a lot of changes and getting strung out in the process. *What those crazy niggers doin' playin' that crazy music?* Wild. Out of the jungle. But so long as they're not lootin' no stores or shootin' our asses, leave 'em be. . . . Our rebellion was a form of survival."

Charles "Yardbird" Parker (1920–1955) came out of Kansas City, Missouri, more prolific in his personal dissolution than his early playing. The son of an itinerant entertainer and doting mother, he dropped out of high school and was married at 15; he began using heroin and morphine regularly around that time. After an unpromising start, Parker began to hear music in his head that didn't exist in the world around him. One day in December 1939, he discovered that by raising his solos into the higher intervals of a tune's chord changes, he could free himself from the limits of the original tune. This discovery, and the torrents of deconstructed melody he poured forth, provided the foundation of bebop.

John Birks Gillespie (1917–1993) was born in Cheraw, South Carolina, the last of nine children in a poor, musical family. Dizzy grew up studying

Thelonious Monk

piano, trumpet and other instruments at home and at the Laurinburg Institute, a trade school in North Carolina. He joined Cab Calloway's band, where he battled with the bandleader until finally, during an argument in which Calloway accused him of shooting spitballs onstage, he stabbed Cab in the fanny, thereby ending his unhappy tenure. When he met Parker in Kansas City in 1940, Dizzy recognized a kindred spirit. "[T]he moment I heard Charlie Parker, I said, there is my colleague," he remembered. "Charlie Parker and I were moving in practically the same direction too, but neither of us knew it." Parker called Dizzy the other half of his heartbeat.

Thelious Monk Jr., known as Thelonious (1917–1982), grew up on West 63rd Street in Manhattan's San Juan Hill, the neighborhood where James P. Johnson and Willie "the Lion" Smith laid down the rudiments of stride piano. Monk got his start in traveling gospel bands, and by the time he began working the clubs of Harlem, his playing pitted the past against the future: the rolling pump of his left hand evoked the music of 20 years earlier, while the fractured chords and leaping intervals of his right hand explored the unknown.

Kenneth Spearman Clarke, later known as Liaquat Ali Salaam (1914–1985), studied piano, trombone, drums, vibes and music theory as a high school student in Pittsburgh, and played with Gillespie in the big band led by the saxophonist Teddy Hill. Clarke's asymmetric accents, or "bombs," on the bass drum earned him the onomatopoetic nickname "Klook-mop" or "Klook," and got him fired from Hill's band. All four of these men were born in the flush of the Great Migration, had their childhoods interrupted by the Depression and came of age with the wave of black nationalism that swelled after World War II. By the time they met in New York in the early 1940s, joined by Bud Powell, Max Roach, Miles Davis and a group of fellow conspirators, they were distilling these experiences into something new—nonconformist in sound, look and attitude.

It is a dated word, *nonconformity*. In today's splintered pop culture, it is hard to imagine a norm that anyone might conform to; the very notion is unhip. This marks in part the triumph of hip as a national organizing principle, and in part the inevitable absorption of hip into market demographics. Yet in the 1940s, nonconformism still echoed Emerson and Thoreau. In his essay "Self-Reliance," Emerson prescribed creative individualism against the mediocrity of the masses. "Who so would be a man must be a nonconformist," he wrote. To Emerson, the approval of society was the stamp of the second-rate. "To be great," by contrast, "is to be misunderstood." This is nonconformism as a relinquishing of privilege, opting out of the state in order to shed responsibility for its actions.

The nonconformism of bebop, on the other hand, involved a symbolic *reclamation* of privilege. This was the nonconformism of the group, responding to collective disenfranchisement. Where the Harlem Renaissance had fed on the aspirations of the Great Migration, the fractured sounds of bebop reflected the frustrations that set in as these aspirations remained out of reach. For the bop generation, a new familiarity with white society bred contempt, or at least critique. As Amiri Baraka noted, "To understand that you are black in a society where black is an extreme liability is one thing, but to understand that it is the society that is lacking and is impossibly deformed because of this lack, *and not yourself,* isolates you even more from that society."

These players rained musical, political, sartorial, chemical and attitudinal changes, in different proportions for everybody who encountered them. Gillespie saw bop as evolution, not revolution. Langston Hughes, who was introduced to the music by Ralph Ellison, heard in it the insult of a policeman's nightstick on a black man's head. "Bop comes out of them dark days," he wrote. "That's why real Bop is mad, wild, frantic, crazy—and not to be dug unless you've seen dark days, too. Folks who ain't suffered much cannot play Bop, neither appreciate it. They think Bop is nonsense—like you. They think it's just crazy crazy. They do not know Bop is also MAD crazy, SAD crazy, FRANTIC WILD CRAZY—beat out of somebody's head! That's what Bop is." For white hipsters, who often knew "them dark days" mainly as metaphor, bop posed an abstract test of society: Could America accommodate black expression at its least accommodating? In short, could it embrace its own prosecution? This test recurs throughout hip, attaching white affections to even separatist black culture, not just for the rebel romance but as moral investment. When white fans embrace, say, black nationalist hip-hop, they're acknowledging both the rap and the context of racism that would silence it in their names. If this investment remains at the level of art (or FUBU sportswear), rather than black humanity, such are the limits of hip.

As in earlier hip convergences, there was defiance and rage here, but instead of hiding them behind a cool mask, the bop musicians showed their anger on the surface. Wearing the hauteur of a despised minority, they combined political theater with hustler's put-on. The squares made easy game. Malcolm Little, a Harlem hustler known as Detroit Red, signaled the new day when he appeared at the draft board in 1943. Dressed in his flashiest zoot suit, yellow knob-toe shoes and wildly conked red hair, he confided to the shrink, "Daddy-o, now you and me, we're from up North here, so don't you tell nobody. . . . I want to get sent down South. Organize them nigger soldiers, you dig? Steal us some guns, and kill us crackers!" The draft board deferred him. Years later, when he spun similar riffs under the name Malcolm X, he turned white America's paranoia into his own sport.

The image of the bebopper, like that of the Beat poet, inevitably reeks of cliché. The terms *bebop* and *Beat* turned to corn almost as soon as they were coined. As Max Roach explained, it was white critics who called the music bebop, after the name of a Gillespie tune. "It's another one of those nicknames like boy, nigger and jazz," he said. "In fact, the music which Dizzy, Bird, Monk and people like that created is very difficult to master technically and very difficult to play emotionally. . . . They've been nicknaming our music for a long time, and I resent terms such as jazz and bebop." The jazz hipster was literally a cartoon as early as 1942, when the animator Bob Clampett, a regular at the clubs of Central Avenue in Los Angeles, celebrated jazzbo panache in *The Hep Cat,* the first color Looney Tunes short, now banished as racially insensitive.

Yet this capacity for cartoon or cliché is one way hip spreads its gospel. Though hip often hovers around the arts, it is not quite the same thing. Bebop's musicians, like the Beats who followed closely in their wake, shook the country as much by their public lives as by their work. Jazz historians often try to separate the two, distinguishing the music from the pharmacological flights or jive talk. This does justice to their musical importance but slights their social impact, which was in many ways more profound. Popular culture leaves its truths through folklore and rumor as well as through higher aesthetic accomplishments. The chords and rhythms tell only part of the larger American story.

As a coded signal, hip communicates through the manners of its messengers as well as the contents of their messages. Some people get it, some simply don't. Bop went over the heads of many listeners, and even many older players. Sometimes it talked in jive. Yet it was never simple gamesmanship. "There was a message in our music," said Kenny Clarke. "Whatever you go into, go into it *intelligently.* As simple as that." Though the music was complicated, and the musicians often strung out or high, the seriousness traveled with the music. The drummer Tony Williams, who later played with Miles Davis, was moved as much by bop's demeanor as by its changes:

> Miles and Max Roach were speaking like men, acting like men. I saw them and said, "That's the life I want to live." Miles showed you how to carry yourself. He inspired people to think beyond what they thought they were capable of. . . . [T]his is before anyone knew about King or Muhammad Ali or Malcolm X. Miles was the person people of my generation looked to for those things. So when the sixties came, I didn't need anybody to tell me, "We shall overcome." I was already living it.

With the expansion of media after the war, including a strong jazz press, bop style spread into the culture. It signaled a break from the routine. Few could play the music, but many could dress or talk the part. Slim Gaillard, a singer who claimed to have coined the term *groovy*, invented a language he called "voutie," whose syllables flew around the brain: "Voutie oroony macvoosie ohfoosimo," and so on. In an era that punished political dissent and distrusted new ideas, a little haberdashery went a long way. Billy Eckstine, who hired both Parker and Gillespie in his bands, marketed his own Mr. B shirts with soft-roll collars; Babs Gonzales launched his own line of bow ties. Dizzy, with his beret and goatee, was such a style icon that wannabes used to copy his glasses using windowpane lenses; when he was once photographed unwittingly with his fly low, some hipsters adopted the half-mast look as the acme of correctness. For a price, Fox Bros. Tailors in Chicago offered a complete getup, including bop tie ($1.50), bop cap ($2.00) and a "leopard skin jacket as worn by Dizzy Gillespie" ($39.50). Ads beckoned aspiring cats to "Bop in here and let Fox build you a crazy box!" The come-ons had an inspired silliness:

OO PAPA, DA FOX BROS. suits are gone!
STAY ON IT, Daddy, you'll come on like the dawn.

At the same time, as Mailer said, hip reflected the horrors arising from World War II, both domestic and military. In the war, 900,000 African Americans joined the battle against Aryan racism in Europe, only to experience a local version at home and in the service. At home many responded with new resistance to racial discrimination; abroad there was destruction on a level previously reserved for God. While race riots flared in Harlem, Detroit and other cities, and the civil rights movement raised its formative noises, the bop generation restored the separateness that jazz had given up during the mainstreaming of 1930s swing. Bop demanded its own space; it did not try to represent the collective tastes of the public. Bop was the first jazz idiom in which it was not a commercial advantage to be white, and for which the black inventors enjoyed the spoils. They flaunted values that were opaque to the white mainstream and repugnant to many upwardly mobile blacks. It was one thing for previous jazz musicians to endure the clueless belittlements of the establishment, and quite another for the bop clique to take on the jazz faithful.

While hip in the 1940s assumed the silhouette of the bop iconoclast—say, Thelonious Monk, immaculate in goatee, glasses and angular bravado—it also revealed broader shifts in the society at large. It is a unique quality of hip that it appears both cool in the face of racial roil and agile in the face of racial intransigence—like a subatomic particle, moving and not moving. In the golden age of hip, this paradox of cool and kinesis captured the anxieties of a nation on a racial threshold. Bop was the soundtrack to these anxieties.

The underlying conditions of bop had been gathering since the 1930s. Blacks who came north, leaving behind a safety net of family and community, were often disillusioned with the fruits of white America. When the Depression hit, many found themselves with no property or kin in neighborhoods that were degenerating into slums. Northern poverty was less severe but more isolating than the despair of the South, where at least there was food in the fields and the support networks of church and neighbors. Northerners, by contrast, were surrounded by massive black unemployment and the white society that rejected them. They girded themselves with speed and abstraction: hipster slang, hustler fashion, ferociously novel music and dance. As Max Roach said, "We're not the kind of people who can sit back and say what happened a hundred years ago was great, because what was happening a hundred years ago was shit: slavery. . . . That's why every new generation of black people is obliged to try something new. Every new generation of black folks comes up with a new innovation because we're not satisfied with the way the system is economically, politically and sociologically."

At the same time, a broader trickle of African Americans was entering the middle class, producing what the black journalist Roi Ottley (1906–1960) called "Café au Lait Society," a class of black intellectuals and professionals who were politically more liberal and socially looser than the conservative black elite. This class included people like Miles Davis's father, a middle-class dentist, a Garveyite, an internationalist and a community pillar. Their children grew up with new expectations, reinforced by the media. A daily newspaper from the period might show violent racial strife on the front page, and in the arts pages, the new thing called swing, which captivated blacks and whites alike. These two stories, of social division and cultural crossover, evoke opposite sides of America's drama of race. The hip of the 1940s would take both into account.

The massive industrial buildup to World War II increased both frictions and interdependence. Hitler's aggression in Europe, under a banner of racial purification, sparked debate at home about the meaning of race and racism. In 1938, the Carnegie Corporation commissioned a Swedish economist named Gunnar Myrdal to conduct a broad study of the state of black America, ultimately published in 1944 as *An American Dilemma: The Negro Problem and Modern Democracy.* This marked a new level of white curiosity about black life, which is a step toward hip. While many industries refused to hire African Americans, even though they needed the labor, black activism was both visible and increasingly effective, with an invaluable ally in Eleanor Roosevelt, the first lady. In 1941, Asa Philip Randolph, whom Congressman Arthur Miller of Nebraska once dubbed "the most dangerous Negro in America," threatened a march of 100,000 African Americans on Washington unless Franklin D. Roosevelt banned discrimination in the defense industries. Roosevelt yielded and passed the landmark Executive Order 9902, the first presidential effort since Reconstruction to include blacks in the American Dream. The victory inspired waves of activism that swept through the following decades. Membership in the NAACP multiplied tenfold during the war.

The media, in their role as nursemaids of hip, provided pockets of integration—in the virtual world, if not the real one. Radio broadcasts of Joe Louis's heavyweight fights were among the first media events that united the nation. Blacks and whites were glued to the same drama at the same time. The Brown Bomber naturally meant more to African-American communities, where people cried when he lost. But when he fought the German boxer Max Schmeling in 1936 and 1938, against a backdrop of Aryan aggression, the nation cheered a black man in a symbolic battle for racial supremacy. Black rage, once taboo, became a subject for polite literary conversation. By 1940, Richard Wright's novel *Native Son,* in which a tormented protagonist named Bigger Thomas accidentally kills a white woman, was a Book of the Month Club selection. (Some taboos still held, though: the club censored passages describing the white woman's sexual attraction to Bigger.) This minuet of attraction and revulsion, step and counterstep, presaged the fragmented momentum of bop.

Musically, the preamble to bebop involved a similar churn of race and money. The Depression closed many of the jazz clubs that had thrived in the 1920s, and the repeal of Prohibition in 1933 sunk the speakeasies, which had kept many jazz musicians fed. Record sales fell precipitously after the 1929 stock market crash, from more than 100 million in 1927 to just 6 million in 1932. At the same time, the new medium of radio brought music into people's homes for free. The first commercial radio station, KDKA in Pittsburgh, began broadcasting in November 1920, and by the end of the decade annual sales of receivers topped $850 million. These shifts in economy and technology altered the working relationships among musicians. The scarcity of work depressed wages, making it cheap for bandleaders to put together large ensembles. Bigger bands, in turn, meant more juice for the arrangers, less for the soloists. Publishers, hurt by the declining record industry, made their money selling compositions and arrangements, not performances.

In this economy solos were secondary. The leash for improvisation shortened; the rhythms tightened around steady, danceable beats. Radio sponsors, who became gatekeepers to both money and fame, favored white bands performing in venues frequented by white dancers. The swing era, unofficially inaugurated with Benny Goodman's August 21, 1935, date at the Palomar Ballroom in Los Angeles, created a playing field on which white bands could compete with black bands for an audience that expected only to be entertained. It is no small irony that Goodman won over the Palomar crowd when he stopped playing the bland pop expected of white bands, and unleashed the jazz charts of his black arranger, Fletcher Henderson.

Though often maligned by modernists, the swing era produced magnificent songwriting and crack ensemble work. Goodman, the biggest star of the era, dented barriers with his interracial bands. But for our purposes here, swing's racial cast and eagerness to please worked against it as an incubator of hip. White bandleaders like Goodman and the less-talented Paul Whiteman overshadowed black acts. Swing coddled public preju-

Dizzy Gillespie

dices that regarded even Duke Ellington and Count Basie as simple show-men. When the bebop generation arrived, one of their first targets was jazz showmanship. Gillespie, who revered Louis Armstrong, also chastised him for ingratiating himself to white audiences. "I criticized Louis for . . . his 'plantation image,' " he wrote in his autobiography, faulting Armstrong's obeisance, "handkerchief over his head, grinning in the face of white racism. I never hesitated to say I didn't like it. I didn't want the white man to expect me to allow the same things Louis Armstrong did." The older jazzmen often returned the favor, dismissing the new music as discordant and inaccessible. Cab Calloway famously slagged Gillespie's experiments in his band as "Chinese music," and Armstrong, who made similar objections, complained, "You got no melody to remember and no beat to dance to." But in distancing themselves from public tastes, the moderns also challenged a white arts establishment that denied jazz the respect accorded European classical music.

•   •   •

We often think of hip as a reaction against the mundane, but even at its most *out there,* it is never totally above worldly concerns. At the tail end of the Depression, bop's inner circle came together as it did, and where it did, in part through the most ordinary of considerations: free food.

In 1938, Henry Minton, a former saxophonist and the first black delegate elected to the New York musicians' union Local 802, took over part of the dining area in the Hotel Cecil on West 118th Street in Harlem. He called the place Minton's Playhouse, and in the fall of 1940 hired the reedman and big band leader Teddy Hill to manage it and plan the musical program. The men had two bright ideas. First, they offered free food to musicians on Monday nights. And they opened the bandstand for jam sessions, providing a house combo and an open invitation to musicians from the touring bands encamped at the Savoy, the Apollo and other venues. It was good barter. The guest musicians ate for free, then they entertained for free all night long. Minton's was a scene. Inside, musicians dined on white linens and puzzled over the new math their peers were laying down. Outside, a pair of locals named Baby Laurence and Ground Hog tap-danced for heroin, echoing the 19th-century performers who used to dance for eels at the Catherine Market downtown. Like the musicians inside, Baby and Hog turned their isolation from the mainstream into art, but it was an art of humble ambitions.

The art on the bandstand was a different story. Hill's roots were in the swing era, but at Minton's he offered musicians a freedom they didn't have in their big bands. Though he had only recently fired Kenny Clarke from his band for messing with the foursquare beat, he now hired him to anchor the house band, and brought in Monk to hold down the piano. Clarke was already experimenting with freer rhythms, keeping time on the ride cymbal and saving the bass drum to push the music at odd angles. Monk was a bearish enigma who sometimes went days without talking. He became mentor to Earl "Bud" Powell (1924–1966), another New Yorker, who ultimately disappeared into drug abuse, mental illness and electroshock therapy. Passing few words, Monk and Powell sometimes held hands innocently in public. At Minton's, Monk broke the music into playful but difficult eccentricities. Soloists couldn't know when Monk was going to push them off a cliff or show them up as passé. Nick Fenton and Joe Guy, more conventional support men, filled out the house band on bass and trumpet.

Though the primacy of Minton's as the birthplace of bebop is overstated, the place was a steady home for invention and experiment. The regulars who gathered, including the guitarist Charlie Christian (1916–1942), developed their own private agenda. According to Gillespie, "there were always some cats showing up there who couldn't blow at all but would take six or seven choruses to prove it. So on afternoons before a session, Thelonious Monk and I began to work out some complex variations on chords and the like, and we used them at night to scare away the no-talent guys. After a while, we got more and more interested in what we were doing as music, and, as we began to explore more and more, our music evolved." In truth, Gillespie was rarely at Minton's, and Clarke later denied setting out to embarrass lesser players. But like other cliques, the musicians pushed each other to greater extremes of speed, idiosyncrasy and dissonance. If a visitor to the bandstand couldn't keep up, Monk might school him, "That's not the way we play. We changed all that."

As a vehicle of hip, bop steeped itself in the intellectual world beyond jazz and the hustle of making a living. Like their generation of African Americans as a whole, the bop clique were better educated, more widely read, and more urban than their predecessors. The anarchy onstage or in the musicians' personal lives conspicuously signaled not sloppiness but intellectual curiosity, a rejection of limits. The players often compared their music to abstract expressionism and action painting, which grew around similar circles of artists exiling themselves from tradition, challenging each other to more abstract and difficult work. Like the musicians, the painters were also social and intellectual outsiders, mainly European émigrés driven from their homelands and into each other's drunken company by the rise of Hitler. They, too, worked outside popular taste or institutions, even as they carried on in the public eye.

The bebop pioneers were the first generation of jazz musicians who grew up wholly in the age of jazz recordings, familiar at once with the entire breadth of the music. They were the first who could conceive jazz *as commentary on jazz.* They wore their enlightenment on the outside, sporting the uniform of French intellectuals. Kerouac saw them as 12th-century monks. Even song titles like "Klact-oveeseds-tene" or "Epistrophy" invited incomprehension. Hostile to elements of jazz tradition, they pored over contemporary classical theory and dissected their own work with the same seriousness. The pianist Randy Weston remembered hanging after hours at a Brooklyn luncheonette run by his father, where cats fed coins into a jukebox that played both Stravinsky and Bird. "We were like scientists of sound," Miles Davis said. "If a door squeaked we could call out the exact pitch." Their scientific experiments also ran to drugs, which will be discussed more fully in chapter 12.

The players had all developed their chops in big bands, but together they cultivated the hip of the small clique, using their manners as a buffer between themselves and outsiders. They saw their audience as tainted and their loyalties to each other as paramount. "I wanted to be accepted as a good musician and that didn't call for no grinning, but just being able to play the horn good," Miles Davis said in his autobiography. "Max and Monk felt like that, and J.J. [Johnson, the trombonist] and Bud Powell, too. So that's what brought us close together, this attitude about ourselves and our music." The musicians often declined to announce tunes; they sped the tempos too fast for dancers and expected audiences to listen attentively. Davis famously turned his back to his audience, which critics took as a gesture of arrogance, though he claimed it was just a way to hear his musicians. With some notable exceptions, the white musicians of the swing generation could not keep up with bebop; few older big band musicians, black or white, truly mastered the new idiom. Even after the music moved down to 52nd Street in the late war years, white audiences faced musicians who were self-possessed, inscrutable, wrapped in a dialog that did not include them. Bop was a secret from which it was easy to feel left out.

Gillespie and Parker, the good cop and bad cop of bebop, played this secret from opposite angles. Parker, as Stanley Crouch has written, waged "war with the complicated fact that the Negro was inside and outside at the same time, central to American sensibility and culture but subjected to separate laws and depicted on stage and screen, and in the advertising emblems of the society, as a creature more teeth and popped eyes than man, more high-pitched laugh and wobbling flesh than woman." The year before Hill and Clarke assembled the band at Minton's, a head-wrapped Butterfly McQueen attended to Miss Scarlett in the 1939 film *Gone with the Wind*—a stark reminder that the most lustrous projection of the American psyche, the movies, still saw race relations through the lens of minstrel comedy.

Parker simply blew through this image. In a life lasting just 34 years, he lived in a state of autonomous chaos, beholden for neither his accomplishments nor his spectacular downfalls. Both belonged to him alone. His music was complicated but viscerally communicative. Instead of pandering to audiences, Parker mastered the put-on, adopting a fake English accent and refusing to define his music, describing it only as "trying to play clean and looking for the pretty notes." Peers described him as thoughtful and well read, yet on key dates he might show up not just high but incoherent. Dedicated to his art, he showed little regard for the needs of his audience, his employers or his colleagues. When he needed a fix, he might hock his horn before a gig or a recording session, or stiff the musicians in his band.

Parker scattered the mythologies of the minstrel show by setting standards no one could follow. The minstrel is a figure audiences feel comfortable with because, even in his duplicities, they know what he's about. He's circumscribed by their imagination. Parker, on the other hand, defied measure; personally, musically and chemically, he lived in the uncharted. Though plenty tried, no one could take as many drugs, play as many notes, court disaster as wholeheartedly and then rise from the wreckage with such pure, unpredictable music. It was easier to judge him by his failures—as a colleague, a professional, a husband and father—than to keep up with his accomplishments. Yet these barriers to empathy helped foster a rabid cult among his followers, white and black: If you could hear the man or the music without judgment, you could commend yourself as vicariously inside the loop, hip. This set you apart from the mainstream, which saw only his bad behavior. To accept him was to abandon what Emerson saw as the dull omniscience of the crowd for the enlightenment of the wayward prodigy.

By the time audiences caught up to his early 1940s breakthroughs, Parker had moved on, recording with strings and announcing his desire to study with Edgard Varese (in return, Parker would cook for the composer). Living on 10th Street and Avenue B in the East Village in the early

1950s, Parker listened mostly to classical music and delighted in TV Westerns. He spent his nights gabbing in Ukrainian bars. Like only a few jazz figures, including Armstrong and perhaps Ellington, Parker changed the way musicians approached every instrument. Yet he was detached from the people in his life. A chronic womanizer and absent father, he married four times, the first two times to black women, the last two to whites. In his richest period financially, his daughter Pree died while under the care of a public clinic because Parker did not send enough money for private treatment—in large part because he spent the money on drugs. When he died in 1955, just a few years after his finest recordings, most of the New York newspapers did not even run obituaries, and two papers identified him as Yardbird Parker, not even bothering to learn his age or his first name. The faithful simply kept the faith. The graffito "Bird Lives" began appearing around New York and other jazz towns. Charles Mingus (1922–1979) was among those who insisted that Parker wasn't really dead, just "hiding out somewhere, and he'll be back with some new shit that will scare everyone to death."

Where Parker was personally remote, Gillespie was bop's great communicator, schooling both his peers and the audience at large. Because he chose survival rather than glorious implosion, the Dizzy myth is much less romantic than Parker's. Yet his music was every bit as uncompromising and original, and he pushed his peers to higher heights. "Bird was responsible for the actual playing of it and Dizzy put it down," said Billy Eckstine, who hired both in his pivotal 1944 band. "And that's a point a whole lot of people miss up on. They say, 'Bird was it!' or 'Diz was it!'— but there were two distinct things." Hip needs both of these types. With his affable showmanship and fierce professionalism, Gillespie did more than anyone to bring bop to the jazz public. He happily gave Parker the credit for bebop, but rarely worked with him because Bird was too erratic. Avoiding serious drug abuse, and married to the same woman for half a century, he worked a precarious paradox of his own: having invented the aesthetic that rejected jazz showmanship, he used his own abilities as a showman to sell that unsellable aesthetic. Yet his humor had an edge. It was unpredictable, sometimes sharp. Miles Davis, who criticized Gillespie's stage antics in the same way that Gillespie criticized Armstrong's, remembered that when they first met in New York, Dizzy would "be sticking his tongue out at women on the streets and shit—at white women. I mean, I'm from St. Louis and he's doing that to a white person, a white *woman*. . . . He used to love to ride elevators and make fun at everyone, act crazy, scare white people to death."

His hipster-huckster look and jive brought him celebrity but little in the way of record sales. Gillespie maintained that he wore the beret simply because he could stuff it in his pocket, and the goatee because he didn't like to shave around his lips. But as with Davis's back-turning, mystique spoke louder than facts. Six decades after his first recordings, these two sartorial accidents remain the easiest way into an often difficult body of music.

Gillespie scattered the aura of the minstrel show by casting his music in global terms, with himself as funky ambassador. Early compositions like "A Night in Tunisia," which he debuted with Parker in Earl "Fatha" Hines's band in 1942, referred explicitly to Africa, not just in the title but in the intonations. In 1947, he formed a partnership with a Cuban percussionist named Luciano Pozo y González, better known as Chano Pozo, which ranks among the most visionary in jazz. Chano, who spoke no English, brought West African chants from his Cuban *lucumi* religion into Dizzy's big band. When the band debuted the chants at Boston's Symphony Hall in 1947, even African Americans were not yet ready for his lesson in Afrocentricity. "[T]he black people in the audience were embarrassed by it," said George Russell, who composed "Cubana Be–Cubana Bop" for Pozo and the band. "The cultural snow job had worked so ruthlessly that for the black race in America at the time its native culture was severed from it completely. They were taught to be ashamed of it, and so the black people in the Boston audience were noticeable because they started to laugh when Chano came on stage in his native costume and began." The following year Pozo was killed at the Rio Bar on Lenox Avenue and 111th Street after an argument about a bag of weed, but the Afro-Cuban rhythms he and Gillespie brought to jazz survive today in the syncopations of funk, rock, disco and much of modern jazz.

Gillespie's Pan-African grooves brought a new metaphor to hip. Parker's prolific whir mirrored the urban clamor of the war years; Monk and Miles, who hit their stride in the 1950s and 1960s, captured the nuclear jitters of the Cold War. Gillespie reflected the early stirrings of glob-

Hip for sale

alism, tweaking the language of race as presciently as he had the orthodoxies of jazz. Where European modernists like Picasso had evoked a mythic, primitive Africa, Gillespie restored the continent to the present tense. He aligned modern, urban black Americans with modern Africans, each caught in a political struggle for autonomy. His mercurial humor, sometimes self-effacing, sometimes cutting, can be read as global diplomacy from the African diaspora. This is the opposite of shucking from the plantation. Even in his clowning, Gillespie subtly recast race as a product of history, not biology. Minstrelsy could not work on this stage because its ahistoric notions of black and white did not hold. He was like the term *bebop* itself: a self-effacing, unserious term, in the shape of a minstrel mask, but doing little to hide the intemperate seriousness underneath the fun.

If hip is enlightenment, Gillespie's globalism was as visionary as his percussive bop. While Americans tend to think of World War II's aftermath as nuclear terror and the Cold War, in many ways this has proven a sideshow. The bigger story, as the historian David M. Kennedy argues, has been a realignment of global powers: the gradual triumph of nonwhite revolutionary movements throughout Asia, Africa, Latin America and the Caribbean; borderless trade and debt; the intercontinental transit of disease. By century's end, Kennedy writes, "who can deny that globalization . . . was the signature and lasting international achievement of the postwar era, one likely to overshadow the Cold War in its long-term historical consequences?" In its intensification of both Third World rhythm and First World abstract modernism, Gillespie's music prefigured this international free-for-all. The hip cat was both a player and a product for the coming global marketplace, talking a new Esperanto. Where Stravinsky met Bird, and "Klact-oveeseds-tene" was the word of the day—that was where the world was heading. Bop got there first.

Hip thrives on contradictions, and like other movements in this book, bop fed from conflicting traditions. Its complex polyrhythms and extended scales reclaimed a tie with Africa, and the musicians echoed the black nationalism in the streets and barbershops. But the bop crowd's rejection of their elders, break with tradition and indifference to public tastes owed more to Western modernism. Bop had no interest in being folk art. It rejected African traditions of ancestor worship, functionality and community participation. Where African musics tend to close the gap between performer and audience, inviting everyone to add a line, bop exaggerated this distance. Amateurs were actively discouraged. Bop had it both ways. It was as restless with Africa as with Europe; its legacy was unsettled, dynamic, American.

This internal contradiction reflected the ambiguous interplay of race and jazz. For much of the bebop era, the most popular musician in jazz was not a Minton's alum, but Benny Goodman. As a clarinetist, Goodman was peerless; as a popularizer, he cut just the right corners. As a bandleader, he was a bastard. But American celebrity responds as much to image as to music, and here Goodman led a split existence. For much of the public, he embodied a mint American archetype, the Urchin Who Made Good. One of 12 children born to poor Russian immigrant Jewish parents, he was ethnic, but not too ethnic; disadvantaged, but not victimized; well mannered but not Brahmin; smart but not donnish. He had rags, he had riches—sign him up. Then as political winds shifted, he came to embody another signature American fable, just as iconic: he was the White Boy Who Stole the Blues.

The story of the white boy who stole the blues is one of the central recurring folktales within hip's history. It has featured many lead characters, going back to Twain, Dan Emmett, Irving Berlin, Elvis, and on up through Keith Haring, Tom Waits and Eminem, to name just a few. The story—really a body of stories, some felicitous, some shameful—bears ugly testimony to the discrimination faced by black artists, even from a white public with a jones for their art. As it is generally told, it involves simple thievery, hapless imitation and a public too corrupt or ignorant to know the difference. The story assumes that popular culture begins with Platonic ideal forms, from which descend lesser knockoffs, the least of these being the white rip-off. Bop was in part a reaction to this degenerative process in the swing era, when white skin was an advantage in the marketplace. At Minton's and elsewhere, the bop crowd called the white boy out. As the pianist Mary Lou Williams remembered, Monk told her he wanted "to create something that they can't steal because they can't play it." Though Goodman played at Minton's, and was treated respectfully by the musicians, many did not survive the treatment with their dignity intact. As the drummer and bandleader Art Blakey put it, "the only way the Caucasian musician can swing is from a rope." Where white interlopers changed the music, it is taken for granted that what they added was water, diluting a vital black idiom.

But in practice the musicians, black and white, were more expansive than exclusionary. American music, like hip, resists purism; both thrive in the hybrid. Bop's interests were wide-ranging from the start, European as well as African and Afro-Cuban, and as it evolved, the stew only became more complicated. In 1948, shortly after he left Charlie Parker's band, Miles Davis joined a racially mixed crowd of musicians, composers and arrangers at the 55th Street apartment of a self-taught white Canadian named Gil Evans. Like the circle at Minton's, they wanted to push beyond the music that was playing in clubs, experimenting with different textures and instrumentation. With the older Evans (born Ian Ernest Gilmore Green, 1912–1988), Davis developed a rare empathy. "Here was this tall, thin, white guy from Canada who was hipper than hip," Miles remembered. "Here was Gil on fast 52nd Street with all these super hip black musicians wearing peg legs and zoot suits, and here he was dressed in a cap. Man, he was something else." The rotating nine-piece group that came together in Evans's one-room place was mixed in education and musical background, exploring the possibilities of intricate, precise chamber jazz. The music they came up with, released as 78s and ultimately collected as *Birth of the Cool,* polished the edges of bebop, simplifying the rhythms and slowing the tempos to allow lush spires of elaborate counterpoint. Though the records sold poorly, they gave a name and emotional temperature to a style that fulfilled many of bop's promises while closing some of its aesthetic doors. The school was cool.

In Robert Farris Thompson's study of the aesthetic of the cool, he notes that Africans use the cool mask to cover not just sadness but exuberance as well. Davis wore this as a mask of vigilance across the emotional spectrum, implying depths of feeling while showing none. The cool embodied in those sessions was watchful, expectant. The cool mask suited both the Cold War, which bred fear and secrecy, and the laconic furtiveness of the heroin user, whose numbers, black and white, now filled the jazz world. Cool was both defiant and protective. In a famous photograph from 1957, you can see this mask on 15-year-old Elizabeth Eckford, one of nine black students who integrated Little Rock's Central High School, as she walked through an angry white mob armored only in her sunglasses and poise. "What bothered them," recalled Minnijean Brown Trickey, another of the Little Rock Nine, speaking of the white students, "was that we were as arrogant as they were."

Cool, though, came with unexpected consequences in the jazz world. Unlike bop's first circle, the cool crowd was largely white, including Gerry Mulligan, Lee Konitz, Stan Getz, Lenny Tristano, Dave Brubeck and Paul Desmond, among others. Where bop's radicals had made a virtue of their outsider status, these musicians—sometimes known as the West Coast school, though few actually lived there—had access to audiences and monies that eluded their black peers. The jazz press hyped an East Coast/

West Coast rivalry, as the hip-hop press would do four decades later. Cool was complicated but not confrontational, flattering to the generation of men who flooded colleges through the GI Bill. Suiting the new managerial class who made their living with their brains, not their bodies, the music was more cerebral than visceral. By the time it reached the phonographs of the new suburbs, its signature trumpet player and crooner was a white *homme fatal* named Chet Baker (1929–1988), who seemed to use his prolific flaws to hide his talent, rather than the other way around. Cool players like Dave Brubeck, who made the cover of *Time* in 1954, enjoyed popular success that eclipsed Parker's, while bop's great pianists, Monk and Powell, struggled with the cabaret laws and mental illness, respectively. Davis's record company, noting this white boho market, graced the jacket of his 1957 *Miles Ahead* album with a blonde model, to which he responded, "Why'd you put that white bitch on there?" The new audience expected the music in its own likeness. As Miles saw things, "it was the same old story, black shit was being ripped off all over again."

But the story of the white boy who stole the blues is never as simple as his critics would have it. American pop culture begins in the mongrel, not the Platonic. This is hip's central story. What we call black or white styles are really hopelessly hybrid. The bebop of Minton's, for example, brought African and European impulses to a music that already traced its lineage to both continents. Even in the name of purity it was impure, and richer for it. By the same token Goodman, Twain, Berlin, Elvis and Eminem all stand out more for what is uniquely theirs, not the vehicle they borrowed. In a pluralistic cultural marketplace, it makes more sense to think of pop evolution as additive rather than derivative—every change adds something, even if just through the accidents of faulty copying.

In his autobiography, Miles attributes the *Birth of the Cool* sessions to pure black musical sources: "We were trying to sound like [the white bandleader] Claude Thornhill, but he had gotten his shit from Duke Ellington and Fletcher Henderson." But this is like saying a rock band has pure white sources because it borrows from the Rolling Stones. Ellington and Henderson themselves adapted ideas from European classical music and African musics as well as jazz. And so on. In American culture, there are no pure black or white sources to tap. When the West Coast musicians took on East Coast bop, they similarly put it through the filter of their own influences and abilities, changing it in the process. If the results were less overtly tied to New Orleans, and more reflective of the car culture and television images of the late 1950s and early 1960s, this was less a dilution than an evolutionary mutation. Cool was the aloofness of bebop taken literally.

Significantly, it built on bebop's embrace of nonconformity *as an ethos of success.* Unlike Thoreau, the masters of cool and bop did not drop out of society, but practiced their art in places of public debate. They competed in jazz polls and led the sexual lives of royalty. The jazz press, which grew throughout the 1940s and 1950s, conferred success beyond the judgment of the marketplace, affirming the marginal as valuable art. To be out was to be original; to be original was a measure of success, even if you didn't necessarily get rich. Bop musicians, who held their own tastes above those of the public, insisted that this was the true success. As the commercial record business boomed around them, lifted by the postwar economy, theirs was a music of transition, relinquishing jazz's hold on the mainstream of American popular music. That mainstream, which swing had helped create, would soon move elsewhere. Jazz was becoming more like classical music, a taste for an elite minority. Cool told the story of this transition.

Hip would have to move elsewhere as well.

In the popular imagination, ideas like bop or cool travel according to the needs of the people who receive them. Among the cult, they communicate as divine revelations, to be dissected with Talmudic care. Each transmission is wholly new, unlike any that came before. To the broader public, they communicate as familiar image and genre. The bigger the audience, the fewer nuances come through. The difference between the two can be little more than time lag. One reason confrontational art does not topple its targets is that by the time it reaches them, it does so in comfortably familiar form. For example, Kurt Cobain's nemeses, the frat boys and jocks, ultimately made up much of his audience because they heard the specifics of his indictments as generic wail.

Yet even stripped of their complexities, the ideas can still take root. Bop communicated on both of these levels, as invention and romance. Without the truly breakthrough ideas, it would have passed as simple fad.

But without the broader mystique of the bop hipster, which trickled to parts of the culture that the music alone could never reach, its impact would have been limited to the jazz universe, which even then was shrinking. The triumph of hip requires these two operations working in tandem—the cultist and then the universal, each delivering the right drug to the right habit.

The bop musicians' cerebral music, hieroglyphic lingo and rambling habits all posed the argument that alienation could be a deliberate choice—a position of critical distance, not a condition imposed from above. Parker once said that bebop was not an extension of jazz tradition, but "something entirely separate and apart." Instead of explaining themselves to the mainstream, they cultivated its incomprehension. As the bassist Coleridge Goode recalled, "It was the bebop tradition to freeze out strangers." In the tradition of the Greenwich Village moderns, bop was a performance of countermobility, moving *out,* not *up.* To be marginal, or *far out,* was to claim the moral high ground.

The myth of Minton's, however oversimplified, has survived because it helps us understand where the music came from. It was local, elitist and artisanal—a proudly marginal culture developed against the postwar incipience of mass culture. But as radical as the changes were on the bandstand at Minton's, the audience was undergoing an even more sweeping transformation. Radio, which became indispensable during the war, brought jazz rhythm to more people than ever before, in a format that ran counter to the elitism of bebop. The transistor radio, invented in 1947 by Walter Brattain and Robert Gibney, made sets portable and cheap, well suited to the budding car culture. They let young people take their music away from the supervision of adults. Radio broadcasts served different needs than nightclubs. They had to entertain and stimulate audiences, not challenge them; to flatter, not provoke. These media craved repetition and novelty more than intricacy and ambiguity. Television's rise in the 1950s created the first true mass culture in America. Unlike the crowd at a nightclub or a local church, TV audiences were not differentiated by taste or background, and might have little in common with each other or the entertainers. They did not pay to get in, and so did not demand to get their money's worth; instead, they needed to be held, buttered up for the commercial messages.

This mass audience called for more elemental pleasures: simpler rhythms, simpler sexuality, emotions that resonated throughout the population. Where bop moved toward baroque complexity, the growing audience beyond Minton's wanted a strong beat, some blues humor and an echo of its newfound mobility and wealth. Though the musicians continued to make important recordings throughout the 1960s, and Monk made the cover of *Time* magazine in 1964, two more dates stand out from the golden age of hip: On November 20, 1955, eight months after Charlie Parker died, a New York disc jockey named Tommy "Dr. Jive" Smalls brought his rhythm review, featuring Bo Diddley, LaVern Baker, the Five Keys and Willis "Gator Tail" Jackson, to *The Ed Sullivan Show*. They played strong, simple rhythms with an immediate sex appeal—just the sort of things bop had steered around. The idiom was perfect for television; it jumped off the screen. Nine months later came a Mississippi kid named Elvis Presley. He was the urchin who made good, the white boy who stole the blues, the purest practitioner of nonconformity as an ethos of gaudy success. He was all the stories wrapped up in one libidinal yearn. The other stuff didn't have a chance.

the golden age of hip, part 2

the beats

[It's] a story of many restless travelings and at the same time an imaginative survey of a new generation known as the "Hip" (The Knowing), with emphasis on their problems in the mid-century 50s and their historical relationship with preceding generations.... This new generation has a conviction that it alone has known everything, or been "hip," in the history of the world.   —JACK KEROUAC

The critic Richard Meltzer lined up the affinities of postwar hip this way: Kerouac was Charlie Parker—the meteoric alpha soloist, a fuckup and ingrate, blowing chorus after chorus of his personal asymmetries into art that was neither happy nor sad, but contained excesses of both. Ginsberg was Dizzy Gillespie—the articulator of principles, self-promoter, persevering while his peers flamed out, deceptively brilliant underneath the showman's spiel. William Burroughs was the sphinxlike Thelonious Monk, deconstructing paragraphs rather than chords—opaque and uncompromising, wary of all group identity, cult or mass. Coming together in the same years as the bop musicians, the writers formed a parallel subculture that was just as self-mythologizing, exploratory and defiantly young, refusing the era's most insistent de-mand: that they grow up and out of such curiosities. Both groups made exile a lifestyle choice. These six writers and musicians are all gone now, many at an early age, but their life-affirming refusal has held sway ever since.

For the purposes of this book I've tried to distinguish hip from simple trendiness or consumer choice. Though the latter are often part of the bargain, hip and *hepi* preceded them, and tell us more about who we are or want to be. When people talk about "hip" hotels or restaurants, or how demolition derby or Mexican wrestling have become hip, this usage signals currency but not necessarily meaning. This currency is a boon to marketers and lifestyle magazines, which bathe it in the narcotic pleasures of buying and flaunting. But currency by itself can be exhausting, and produces mainly a lot of future trivia. Aficionados of the Von Dutch trucker hat or amateur burlesque, which were in vogue at the time of writing, should bear in mind that we know such quaint expressions as *pet rock* or *dookie rope* because somewhere, somehow, enough people once thought these were hip. Today's Red Bull cocktails are tomorrow's Rob Roys or sidecars.

For the bop and Beat generations, who have endured periodic bouts of trendiness, speed and transience served a more liberating function. Beyond its trend value, speed protects behavior or ideas from the public eye. It is a license to ill. For example, the language developed by antebellum slaves protected the speakers' meaning from nosy whites. The bohemians of Greenwich Village or the hipsters of the Harlem Renaissance used the speed of innovation to keep their critics a step behind. This protection, or grace, is a kind of forgiveness claimed in advance. Under its umbrella, hip becomes not sumptuary correctness—the right shoes or the right flip of the lip—but a state of forgiveness for being *incorrect*. The hipster, who is by nature out of step with the society that would judge him, lives within this grace; we admire him not for his perfection but for the blamelessness of his flaws. We should all have his or her capacity for error.

This connection between meaning and transience involves a perpetual reinvention of the *now*. It lives in the present. For the Wolof slaves who brought the word *hip* to America, the past provided sustenance but little autonomy. The future, in turn, was simply contingent. Instead of looking back in longing or forward to the justice of the next world, hip offered a way of rationing time into microfine slices of the present. Sub-

sequent hipsters, from the major writers of the 1850s to the existentialists manqué of pulp, sought grace in the imperfections of the present.
Walt Whitman, patron saint of the chapter at hand, saw this quest as an
inevitable turn inward, opening the self to absorb the flaws and contradictions of the society around him. To live wholly in the present, he understood, was to be as bad as it was. Being better than your times is for
saints and prisses, who live for future rewards. "I am not the poet of
goodness only, I do not decline to be the poet of wickedness also," he
wrote, adding, "Great is Wickedness—I find I often admire it, just as
much as I admire goodness / Do you call that a paradox? It certainly is a
great paradox." Though the paradox is always the same, at any instant
hip requires that its terms be written anew.

From different angles, the musicians and writers of hip's golden age
shared each other's isolation and intent. Not since the 1920s did a group
of white writers and their peers identify the best of themselves in such
specifically African-American terms. "It's all bop," Ginsberg wrote in a
1956 letter to his mentor, the Columbia professor Mark Van Doren, describing his recent work and that of his peers. "Unworried wild poetry,
full of perception, that's the lillipop." For both groups, the Great Depression of their childhood crimped their use of the past tense, and the

Jack Kerouac

atomic bomb made burlesque of the future. If the future could be erased at the turn of a key, it didn't make sense to sacrifice the present for its rewards. For the white hipsters of the Beat generation, no one seemed to live more wholly in the present, with less regard for the past or future, than their African-American counterparts. The pursuit of the present, as Kerouac envisioned it in *On the Road* (1957), looked explicitly across the gulf of race: "At lilac evening I walked with every muscle aching among the lights of 27th and Whelton in the Denver colored section, wishing I were a Negro, feeling that the best the white world had offered was not enough for me, not enough life, joy, kicks, darkness, music, not enough night."

In an era that saw the reasoned devastation of Hiroshima and Nagasaki, the bebop musicians and Beat writers produced art that was unreasonable. Instead of rendering polished works, they celebrated the jagged moment of experience, which is intuitive rather than rational; it moves on as soon as reason catches up. This was the virtue of improvisation, distinct from the perfections of composition. Following the lead of the musicians, who rejected swing's tight arrangements, the writers put themselves in the same tense as their audience, working things out on the fly—"wild, undisciplined, pure, coming in from under, crazier the better," as Kerouac put it, releasing "unspeakable visions of the individual." Spitting their words or notes headlong, they perfected an aesthetic of imperfection. For this they earned a mixture of public condemnation and discipleship. The word *bebopper* became a code word for juvenile delinquent, and Herbert Hoover declared the Beat generation one of the three most dangerous groups in America, along with communists and "eggheads." Within his lifetime, the six generational avatars named above each saw his legacy reduced to a caricature and a commercial imitation; all but Parker lived to see it expand to massive social upheaval, by which I mean the extension of the now.

Encounters between the two groups were rarely substantive, but there are at least two worth mentioning. In 1958, after a gig at the Five Spot on St. Mark's Place, Ginsberg gave Monk a copy of *Howl*, the book that thrust the Beats' raw prolixity on the public ("Moloch! Solitude! Filth! Ugliness! Ashcans and unobtainable dollars! Children screaming under the stairways! Boys sobbing in armies! Old men weeping in the parks!").

The taciturn Monk nodded: "Makes sense." Two years later, after scoring psilocybin from Timothy Leary, Ginsberg passed some to Gillespie and Monk, hoping to start a revolution of the mind. Monk was unimpressed. "Got anything stronger?" he asked.

Of these six innovators, all born between 1914 and 1926, none survived to the new century. Parker never saw 35, and Kerouac never saw 50, and in truth both men had diligently corroded their talents well before their early deaths. Just 12 years after the publication of *On the Road* made Kerouac an emblem for a generation, granting him a celebrity he found unbearable, fewer than 300 people came to his funeral. Many of their peers also raced toward early deaths. Jackson Pollock (1912–1956), who splashed bop rhythms across his enormous canvases, silenced his demons in a car accident on Long Island before he turned 45; James Dean (1931–1955), bearer of the Beat shrug, lost control of his racing car at 24; Lenny Bruce (1925–1966) OD'd at 41; Neal Cassady (1926–1968), Kerouac's tour guide to the American night, surrendered to the elements at age 41. (Early death, as a public romance, is the ultimate renunciation of the future tense.) Had they lived, what turns they might have seen. Within a generation of their deaths, their transgressions had fallen to greater outrage, perpetrated not in back alleys but in big-money ad campaigns. Burroughs in his lifetime made a commercial for Nike, while Kerouac and James Dean, like Miles Davis and Chet Baker, appeared posthumously in ads for the Gap. No longer controversial quasi-criminals, they became hip avatars of casual Fridays. Except for Gillespie, all lived with depression, addiction or other psychiatric disturbance, and this emotional weather— this overbearing *now*—figured prominently in both their work and their public image.

What the two groups left, besides their music and writing, were the sands of their own erasure. Bebop marked the transitional spasm of jazz as a popular music, replaced by the more elemental, marketable sounds of rhythm and blues. The Beats, similarly, marked the last fling of poetry as the chief delivery system for the poetic. When future bards wanted a vehicle for sentiments like "Go fuck yourself with your atom bomb," an icebreaker from Ginsberg's poem "America," they could turn to the more elemental, marketable medium of rock and roll. Rock made absurdism easy. A verbal non sequitur like Ginsberg's "hydrogen jukebox," which begged heavy lifting on the page, simply kept the beat in a rock song, and provided material for late-night stoned discussion. (The aspiring poets who called themselves the Beatles, spelled I-think-you-know-why, were just one example.) It is impossible now to imagine an America enthralled and threatened by the habits of, say, Wynton Marsalis and the recent poet laureate Billy Collins, and not just because these two men go light on thrall and threat. As jazz and poetry have receded into publicly funded respectability, the lasting impact of bop and Beat now plays on a bigger, louder stage.

Ginsberg, who had a remarkable gift for embracing and blessing future movements, saw his generation's legacy as the invention of a new baseline. "[I]t went beyond anything we 'planned,'" he told the writer Bruce Cook. "It was a visionary experience in 1948, when we started. Now everybody sees and understands these things." The generations bop and Beat stood at the precipice of this 1960s counterculture, shaping its foundations and then falling back as the media phenomenon moved on without them. Though they were called the Beat generation, as Hettie Cohen once said, they could have all fit in her living room. They were radical individualists overtaken by a narrative of the collective. Their truest heirs—let's say Muhammad Ali for Parker, Bob Dylan for Ginsberg—were those who could persuade the public that their narcissism was an instrument of generational catharsis, not private need.

J ack Kerouac, Allen Ginsberg and William Burroughs converged at Columbia University in 1944, arriving by different paths. Jean-Louis Kerouac (1922–1969), a football star from the French-Canadian part of Lowell, Massachusetts, came to New York on an athletic scholarship to attend Horace Mann high school and then Columbia. English was his second language. He arrived in love with jazz and the movies, passions that even in his bitter years never deserted him. Kerouac was constitutionally the most conservative of the group, imprinted by his Catholic upbringing and blue-collar roots. He married early and enlisted in the Navy, but lacked the capacity for subordination that makes for success in war or marriage. After a series of petty rebellions, he told a Navy shrink that the only thing he believed in was "absolute personal freedom at all times."

The service deemed him a schizoid personality with "angel tendencies" and granted an honorable discharge for indifferent character. Neither of his two marriages lasted much longer than his military career. The son of a printer, Kerouac returned to New York from the Navy with the intention he had expressed since the age of 10, to become a writer. By the time he met his future comrades, he had a novel under his belt (the still-unpublished "The Sea Is My Brother," about his maritime adventures) and the seeds of a lasting and little-remarked friendship with a fellow Horace Mann alum named William F. Buckley, on whose television program he later renounced much of what the Beats held dear.

Irwin Allen Ginsberg (1926–1997), four years younger than Kerouac, arrived at Columbia from Paterson, New Jersey, in 1943, aided by a $200 scholarship from the union offices of the CIO in New Jersey. His father, Louis, was a modestly successful poet and high school English teacher. His mother, Naomi, a Russian immigrant, spent most of her adult life in and out of mental institutions, where she received insulin shock and other ungentle therapies. As a child, Allen often stayed home to read to her, seeking a bond that would offset the painful impressions of his mother, naked and raving. When she was in the hospital, he said later, he sometimes sought comfort beside his sleeping father, rubbing his erect penis against Louis in the night. Ginsberg went to Columbia with the idea of becoming a lawyer, not a poet. He met Kerouac in the spring of 1944 through a handsome mutual friend named Lucien Carr (later the father of Caleb Carr). Within a few hours, he was in love. The school expelled him the following year after he was discovered in his dorm bed with Kerouac (not sexually, as it happened) and for smudging an obscenity on his grimy window (a lovely metaphor for the career to come).

William Seward Burroughs II (1914–1997), the oldest of the group, carried the burden of two prominent American bloodlines. His mother descended from Robert E. Lee; his paternal grandfather built and perfected the modern adding machine, starting the company that still bears the family name. By the time of Bill's delinquent youth, both family lines had diminished to middle class respectability in suburban St. Louis. At Columbia, he played literary mentor to his younger friends, encouraging them to devour the moderns and pushing them to read Oswald Spengler's withering *The Decline of the West* (1926–1928), which described a culture in its last days, mirroring the fall of classical Greece. Amiri Baraka, one of the few African Americans among the Beats, saw Spengler's vision of decadence, in which artists no longer catered to mainstream society, as a unifying model for the generation. "Burroughs's addicts, Kerouac's mobile young voyeurs, my own Negroes, are literally not included in the mainstream of American life," wrote Baraka, who published many of the Beats in the zines *Yugen* and the *Floating Bear*. "These characters are people whom Spengler called *Fellaheen,* people living on the ruins of a civilization. They are Americans no character in a John Updike novel would be happy to meet, but they are nonetheless Americans, formed out of the conspicuously tragic evolution of modern American life."

Burroughs introduced the others to the criminal and queer byways of Times Square. His guide was the thief and raconteur Herbert Huncke (1915–1996), who had a complexion "the spectralized color of blue cheese" and an untutored literary voice that Ginsberg heard as the "sensitive vehicle for a veritable new consciousness." Huncke initially helped Burroughs fence a stolen gun and some morphine styrettes. These two species of contraband, drugs and guns, became twin obsessions in Burroughs's life and fiction, the former exerting totalitarian control over individuals, the latter a last defense against it. Burroughs was the bridge between the Ivy League and this other world, with a cold eye for either. He had a zoological detachment from the specimens that wandered through his writing: "Subway Mike had a large, pale face and long teeth. He looked like some specialized kind of underground animal that preys on the animals of the surface." Where his friends were drunk with words, Burroughs understood language also as an instrument of state ideology, and eventually began cutting up and reassembling his manuscripts to interrupt any unbidden agenda sneaking into the lines.

Neal Cassady, a reformatory kid from Denver's skid row, arrived in December 1946 after exchanging letters with Kerouac's friend Hal Chase. Cassady, immortalized in *On the Road* as Dean Moriarty and as the title character of Kerouac's more experimental *Visions of Cody,* was the straw that stirred the drink, all fast talk, hyperactive energy and cowboy myth— "a wild yea-saying overburst of American joy," as the narrator, Sal Paradise, describes Dean in *On the Road*. By the time he turned 21, Neal said he had stolen 500 cars and spent 15 months in reform schools. He came

Neal Cassady

to New York asking Kerouac to teach him to write. Prolifically unfaithful and irresponsible, unburdened by guilt, Cassady entranced his new friends. Ginsberg had an affair with Cassady; Kerouac had an open affair with Neal's wife, Carolyn Cassady. "What got Kerouac and Ginsberg about Cassady was the energy of the archetypal West, the energy of the frontier, still coming down," said the West Coast poet Gary Snyder, who appears as Japhy Ryder in Kerouac's *The Dharma Bums*. "Cassady is the cowboy crashing."

But more than that, Kerouac saw Cassady as the untamed primitive in a body that looked uncannily like his own. To the orderly Kerouac, who lived with his mother between adventures, Cassady stood for the freedom and failure that whirled just beyond his own capacity for disorder. He admired Neal and joined in his holy goofs, but always returned to "Memere" to write. Cassady wrote voluminous, hilarious, profane, stream-of-consciousness letters. In December 1950, Kerouac was struggling with a novel when he received a rambling 40-page letter from Cassady, stuffed with philosophical musings and erotic adventure. It was as if a mind had disgorged its contents all at once, uninhibited by propriety or the cavils of form and grammar. For Kerouac, it was a light. "I have renounced fiction and fear," he wrote Cassady in response. "There is nothing to do but write the truth." Hooking his typewriter to a 120-foot roll of teletype paper, he banged out *On the Road*—one paragraph, single spaced—in three flurried weeks.

The assembled writers looked on an America in the throes of sweeping change. "The Cold War," as Ginsberg diagnosed it, "is the imposition of a vast mental barrier on everybody, a vast antinatural psyche. A hardening, a shutting off of the perception of desire and tenderness. . . . So let's say shyness. Fear. Fear of total feeling, really, total being is what it is." For all the gauzy nostalgia that engulfs it now, World War II sent men home complicit in a new level of civilized barbarity. "What kind of war do civilians suppose we fought, anyway?" asked the war correspondent Edgar Jones in the *Atlantic Monthly*. "We shot prisoners in cold blood, wiped out hospitals, strafed lifeboats, killed or mistreated enemy civilians, finished off the enemy wounded, tossed the dying into a hole with the dead, and in the Pacific boiled the flesh off enemy skulls to make table ornaments for sweethearts, or carved their bones into letter openers." American firebomb raids killed as many as 100,000 civilians in a night. The atomic bomb, dropped on Hiroshima and Nagasaki on August 6 and 9, 1945, gave human beings the destructive power of gods, which in turn elevated the rebellions of individuals to serious threats. The Cold War redefined the enemy not as a country but as a belief system, which could replicate anywhere. The reaction was Ginsberg's "vast mental barrier," a vigilant intolerance to new or different ideas.

The rational world, it seemed to the Beats, had turned on itself. As John Clellon Holmes, a Columbia peer who published the first recognized Beat novel, *Go,* in 1952, noted, "The burden of my generation was the knowledge that something rational had caused all this (the feeling that something had gotten dreadfully, dangerously out of hand . . .) and that nothing rational could end it." At the same time, the prosperity that shaped the nation at peace was equally sweeping, providing unprecedented pleasures even as it made unprecedented demands. It defied perspective. Thanks to the industrial buildup before the country entered the war, America at the end had half the world's manufacturing capacity, two-thirds of its gold stocks and half its money. It produced twice as much oil as the rest of the world combined. This dynamism was less a respite from the war mentality than an extension of it. Examined in books like David Riesman's *The Lonely Crowd* (1950) and William H. Whyte's *The Organization Man* (1956), the corporate bonanza locked its winners in cycles of earning and spending that negated the liberties it was supposed to provide. For a small but growing part of the population, the antidote was radical individualism, a luxury afforded by the same economic forces that channeled most Americans the other way. The country's growth product was the middle class, which by 1960 included two-thirds of all Americans. The refugees from this class, stepping out on comforts they didn't have to earn, became the nodding multitudes of hip.

The adjective *beat*, used to describe a human condition, goes back more than a century. Ann Charters, quoting an 1888 book called *Hardtack and Coffee*, traces it back at least to the Civil War, when it denoted "a lazy man or a shirk who would by hook or by crook get rid of all military or fatigue duty that he could." Herbert Huncke, who introduced the word to the group, used it in the sense of the drug underworld, as in beat down, ragged, whipped, outside the game. In the fall of 1948, Kerouac and John Clellon Holmes were comparing their postwar circle with the Lost Generation, which had come together out of similar dissatisfaction after the previous war. Gertrude Stein had christened the Lost Generation after watching the directionless men at an auto shop. As Holmes remembered, Kerouac saw as emblematic the wary hipsters in Times Square:

> "It's a sort of furtiveness," [Kerouac] said. "Like we were a generation of furtives. You know, with an inner knowledge there's no use flaunting on that level, the level of the 'public,' a kind of beatness—I mean, being right down to it, to ourselves, because we all really know where we are—and a weariness with all the forms, all the conventions of the world. . . . It's something like that. So I guess you might say we're a *beat* generation," and he laughed a conspiratorial, the-Shadow-knows kind of laugh at his own words and at the look on my face.

For a group of intellectuals who considered themselves a despised minority, or fellaheen, "beat" had many of the original connotations of *hepi* or hip. It was the light at the bottom of the tunnel. Kerouac later said that the word's signifiance came to him in the church of Ste. Jeanne d'Arc in Lowell, where he prayed before a statue of the Virgin Mary and was answered with a vision of beat as *beatific.* Especially after Norman Mailer's "White Negro" essay connected the hipster with violent pathologies, Kerouac went out of his way to stress the gentle, pacifist leanings in beat. In *The Dharma Bums,* he quotes Japhy Ryder, the Gary Snyder character, climbing high on the granola mountaintop to declaim "a vision of a great rucksack revolution, thousands or even millions of young Americans wandering around with rucksacks, going up to mountains to pray, making children laugh and old men glad. . . ." (The rest of the book is not this fatuous, I promise.) After publishing *Go* in 1952, John Holmes wrote an essay for the *New York Times* titled "This Is the Beat Generation" that explained beat as a spiritual quest, a *"will* to believe," despite "the valueless abyss of modern life." Michael McClure, the San Francisco poet, placed the Beats in equally uncontroversial light, as the "literary wing of the environmental movement."

It didn't matter. One indisputable fact about the Beats is that they were a divisive force, and however benign or inoffensive the language they wrapped around themselves, the truth—"Go fuck yourself with your atom bomb"—was more exciting, more threatening and more commercially viable. Through their writings, often about themselves, they promulgated the hip promise that society's margins held more of its life than the mainstream. They were the circus that some children ran away to join, others wished they had the nerve, and even more parents feared lest their children run next. Dislodging themselves from the complacency of the Eisenhower era, the Beats indulged the horror, sadism, sexuality or unbridled irresponsibility that lay just outside the average Joe's grasp. "Ever see a hot shot hit, kid?" a doper raconteur asks a post–Ivy League patsy in Burroughs's 1959 novel *Naked Lunch.* "I saw the Gimp catch one in Philly. We rigged his room with a one-way whorehouse mirror and charged a sawski to watch it. He never got the needle out of his arm. They don't if the shot is right. That's the way they find them, dropper full of clotted blood hanging out of a blue arm. The look in his eyes when it hit—Kid, it was tasty. . . ."

In the Republican decorum of the 1950s the writers talked about

cocks and drugs and negroes—*negro cocks,* even—in language that inti-
mated that they knew whereof they spoke. How awful; how liberating.
Drugs helped. The Beat poet Diane di Prima, one of the few women who
held her own with the men, later explained to her daughter: " 'Honey, you
see, we all thought *experience itself was good. Any experience.* That it could
only be good to experience as much as possible.' . . . [A]nything that took
us *outside*—that gave us the dimensions of the box we were caught in, an
aerial view, as it were—showed us the exact arrangement of the maze we
were walking, was a blessing. A small *satori.* Because we knew we were
caught. . . ." Processing this experience, the Beats broadcast their intimate
secrets, defying an era that suspected secrets and intimacy more than anything. Though as a movement they were not overtly political, they combined what the feminist writer Barbara Ehrenreich identified as two
deeper currents of American rebellion. In the Beats, she noted, "the two
strands of male protest—one directed against the white-collar work
world and the other against the suburbanized family life that work was
supposed to support—come together into the first all-out critique of
American consumer culture." In place of work and family, which link to
the past and future, they chose the immediacy of pleasure and motion.

Their enlightenment, which they often saw in Buddhist terms, was
not gentle. In the summer of 1948, Ginsberg had what he called "the only
really genuine experience I feel I've had," shortly after the traumatic experience of authorizing a lobotomy of his mother (since his parents were
divorced, Allen or his brother Eugene had to sign the papers). He was
reading William Blake and masturbating in his apartment in Spanish
Harlem when the voice of Blake entered the room, telling him to "cultivate the terror, get right into it." The following year, after being arrested
in connection with one of Huncke's robbery schemes, he was committed
to Columbia Presbyterian Psychiatric Institute for eight months. The two
experiences enabled the breakthrough of "Howl" in 1955, a poem that
had the long lines and messianic ambitions of Whitman, wearing all its
emotional raw spots on the surface. When Ginsberg performed it for the
first time at the Six Gallery in San Francisco that October, at a legendary
reading that united the East Coast Beats with their West Coast counterparts, McClure recognized that "a human voice and body had been
hurled against the harsh wall of America." The poem's dedication, "For

Carl Solomon," referred to a patient Ginsberg had befriended in the in-
stitution, and the poem equated the oppressive therapies inside the hos-
pital with those on the outside. He assured his friend, "I'm with you in
Rockland where fifty more shocks will never return your soul to its body."
(Solomon, a mercurial Beat figure, later worked at the publisher Ace
Books, where he signed the manuscript to Burroughs's *Junky* but rejected
On the Road.)

The Beat circus, as followed by the public, also included an aura of violence. In the summer of 1944, shortly after the principal characters met
at Columbia, Lucien Carr fatally stabbed a former teacher named David
Kammerer who had stalked him around the country. Burroughs advised
Carr to turn himself in; Carr turned instead to Kerouac, who helped him
dispose of the knife and was eventually arrested as a material witness. Because Carr belonged to a prominent St. Louis family, the killing was
front-page news. The headline in the *New York Times* ran: "Columbia
Student Kills Friend and Sinks Body in Hudson River." Seven years later,
in the Mexico apartment of a friend named John Healy, Burroughs fatally
shot his wife, Joan, in a wasted game of William Tell using a champagne
glass and a .45. Charged with criminal imprudence, he jumped bail on
the advice of his lawyer and went into mobile exile, eventually settling in
a male whorehouse in Tangier.

Amid this personal chaos, the Beats found direction in the rhythmic
bleat of jazz, and by extension in a romance of black identity. Three
decades after Carl Van Vechten and the Negrotarians of the 1920s sought
release in the nightclubs of Harlem, the Beats updated the romance of the
primitive. Instead of admiring black culture from the spectator box, they
saw themselves as one with it. Where the Negrotarians had engaged black
culture as third-party consumers, the Beats wanted to be active participants, blowing their own jazz and living their own marginal existence, as
alienated from white America's attentions as the narrator of Ellison's *Invisible Man*. Their role models were the studious iconoclasts of bop. "[We] felt
like blacks caught in a square world that wasn't enough for us," John
Holmes wrote. They were pursuing the same questions of America, and
were equally dissatisfied with the official answers. Ginsberg described
"Howl" as a "jazz mass" and likened its effulgent syntax to "the myth of
Lester Young, as described by Kerouac, blowing eighty-nine choruses of

'Lady Be Good.'" Kerouac had similar aspirations: "I want to be considered a jazz poet blowing a long blues in an afternoon jam session on Sunday."

Kerouac's interest in jazz was long-standing and intimate. At Horace Mann high school, he hit the Harlem nightclubs with a classmate named Seymour Wyse, and started a jazz column in the school paper. Having lost his virginity to a midtown hooker, he took his teen pleasures with the prostitutes who worked the uptown jazz circuit. He saw himself as a soloist careering between these bandstands, improvising phrases on end: "Yes, jazz and bop," he told the poet Ted Berrigan, who interviewed him in 1968 for the *Paris Review*, "in a sense of a, say, a tenor man drawing a breath and blowing a phrase on his saxophone, till he runs out of breath, and when he does, his sentence, his statement's been made. . . . That's how I therefore separate my sentences, as breath separations of the mind. . . . Then there's the raciness and freedom and humor of jazz instead of all that dreary analysis. . . ." His speed-writing aspired to bop improvisation, which he saw, naïvely, as an unfiltered gush of the musical subconscious.

Where the white intellectuals and hipsters of the Harlem Renaissance looked to blacks to regenerate the *center* of American culture, the Beats romanticized black life at the margins, imagining it as spontaneous and uncorrupted, liberated from both the war legacy and the economy. It was their ticket away from the center. To be beat in the full scope of the word, beat down and beatified, was to approach a primitive state of grace. In his *Mexico City Blues*, written shortly after Charlie Parker's death, Kerouac beseeched Bird's spirit to "lay the bane, / off me, and everybody," as if Parker's marginal status was worth whatever hardships came with it. Needless to say, this is a distinctly white romance. As the Supreme Court struck down formal segregation in 1954, easing some of the barriers to black access, the Beats made a fetish of black disenfranchisement. The white negro, whether in Kerouac's sense or Mailer's, aspired to a life unburdened by aspiration—to be, as Sal Paradise dreams, "anything but what I was so drearily, a 'white man' disillusioned . . . wishing I could exchange worlds with the happy, true-hearted Negroes of America." Those African Americans who would have exchanged their "happy" poverty for the opportunities the Beats were so eager to renounce were unrecognized in Kerouac's cosmos.

The Beats' racial romance served the writers' needs better than their subjects'. Like bronzing a child's shoes, it exalted them but also treated them as trophies. Except for Mardou, the crush-his-soul love interest of *The Subterraneans,* black characters in Kerouac's work appear mainly as footmen to the white protagonists' liberation. They remain white fantasies of blackness. Kerouac's fancies of improvisation, similarly, ignored the discipline that underlies the freest blowing. The poet Kenneth Rexroth, detecting the aroma of minstrelsy, said that Kerouac "has exactly the attitude toward the American Negro that any redneck gallus-snapping Southern chauvinist has. . . . The Beat novelist just likes them that way. Mailer was right when he said that the hipster was a white Negro—but he neglected to point out that the Negro model the hipster imitates is the product of white imaginations."

But at their least patronizing, the writers invoked the lacunae of jazz to suggest something beyond articulation, a momentary window of empathy:

> Bird Parker who is only 18 year old has a crew cut of Africa looks impossible has perfect eyes and composures of a king when suddenly you stop and look at him in the subway and you can't believe that bop is here to stay—that it is real, Negroes in America are just like us, we must look at them understanding the exact racial counterpart of what the man is— and figure it with histories and lost kings of immemorial tribes in jungle and Fellaheen town and otherwise. . . . And educated judges in horn-rimmed glasses reading the Amsterdam News.

Carl Hancock Rux, writing more recently about Eminem, notes that in the 21st century, "the new White Negro has not *arrived* at black culture . . . he was born into it. He has *arrived* at white culture with an authentic performance of whiteness." For Kerouac and company, this patrimony was still beyond reach. They were peering through cigarette haze across a racial divide, looking for equivalencies and deliverance—seduced by the spectacle, as Robert Farris Thompson says, of people singing a sad song happy where some whites might sing it sad.

•   •   •

Response to the Beats followed in predictable symmetry. Government officials seized copies of *Howl* and *Naked Lunch,* unsuccessfully prosecuting their authors or distributors for obscenity—the nearest thing to a surefire marketing campaign, especially for such difficult, noncommercial texts. As if in counterpoint, tribes of correctly dressed bohemians began to appear in San Francisco and New York. Some were there before the Beats; others learned the way from their writing. The critic Robert Brustein pinned them as "conformists masquerading as rebels," but it was Herb Caen, cranky columnist for the *San Francisco Chronicle,* who cut them down to "beatniks." Beat became a catchall for anything vaguely black-turtleneck. Rexroth, who had championed the Beats at the Six Gallery reading, grew disaffected, in part because he believed Kerouac had brokered an affair between Rexroth's wife, Marthe, and the poet Robert Creeley. After *Life* magazine ran a sensationalistic look at beatniks and their lifestyles, Rexroth dismissed the Beat phenomenon as an invention of the Luce magazine empire.

One of hip's paradoxes is that even as it professes antipathy to the market, it takes the shape the economy needs it to. For all their critique of American consumer culture, the Beats filled a Darwinian market niche. Their popularity complemented the postwar buildup in production capacity. American industry was turning out new stuff; the Beats prescribed an ethos of lifestyle change. Malcolm Cowley, who championed and eventually edited *On the Road,* against Kerouac's wishes, had observed this phenomenon among his own Lost Generation. Bohemianism, he remarked wryly, serves late capitalism by promoting a *"consumption ethic."* Writing about an earlier bohemian moment, he noted that all of its individualist or anti-establishment tendencies were also grounds for spending: *"[S]elf-expression* and *paganism* encouraged a demand for all sorts of products—modern furniture, beach pajamas, cosmetics, colored bathrooms with toilet paper to match. *Living for the moment* meant buying an automobile, radio or house, using it now and paying for it tomorrow. *Female equality"*—not exactly a major Beat concern, but still—"was capable of doubling the consumption of products—cigarettes, for example—that had formerly been used by men alone."

The consumer culture saw possibilities in the new huddled masses. If they rejected the old way of living, why not sell them a new one, with accessories to match? Like bebop, the Beats suggested a whole range of product lines. *Playboy,* which launched in 1953 with its own version of the revolution, ran an ad offering swell goods: "Join the beat generation! Buy a beat generation tieclasp! A beat generation sweatshirt! A beat generation ring!" After the September 1957 publication of *On the Road,* Atlantic Records placed an ad in the *Village Voice* trumpeting, "Atlantic is the label in tune with the BEAT generation. We produce the music with the BEAT for you. Write for free catalogue." You might notice the absence of references to spiritual revelation in these ads (to say nothing of the delirium of black cocks). This is how hip moves from the inner circle to the masses, losing something of itself at each step.

The new tribes gathered in forsaken joints like the San Remo in Greenwich Village, which had a long boho history. Ronald Sukenick, who landed there from Midwood, Brooklyn, in 1948, wrote that for refugees of his generation, even those who only traveled by subway, "You were headed for the Remo, where you'd try to look old enough to be in an actual Village-Bohemian-literary-artistic-underground-mafioso-pinko-revolutionary-subversive-intellectual-existentialist-anti-bourgeois café. Real life at last." The bar mixed cheap drinks and interesting people: writers and artists, gays, interracial couples, hoodlums, Italian toughs, wannabes, voyeurs. Among the patrons were Miles Davis, James Agee, Tennessee Williams, John Cage, Gore Vidal, Bob Dylan, Gregory Corso, James Baldwin, Kerouac and Maxwell Bodenheim. Judith Malina, co-founder of the Living Theatre, called the bar the Sans Remorse in her diaries. Kerouac fictionalized it in *The Subterraneans,* and Chandler Brossard wrote about it in his semi-Beat, pretty hip roman à clef *Who Walk in Darkness* (1952). Mary McCarthy memorialized it in the *New York Post,* attracting the attention of curiosity seekers and tourists. Until her 1950 article, according to Anatole Broyard, a regular, the place didn't have so much as a dirty word on the men's room walls; the gawkers who came subsequently to see picturesque squalor, he noted, did what regulars would not, decorating its surfaces with "the images of their disappointment."

For Kerouac, success and its handmaiden, fame, spoiled everything. He wrote 10 books in the time it took to get *On the Road* published, and by his lights they were all after the fall. Embittered by both celebrity and its limits—specifically the failed efforts to make a movie of *On the Road*—he vented his inner conservative on the unwashed tribes who claimed him as their tour guide. "In actuality," he wrote,

> there was only a handful of real hip swinging cats and what there was vanished mighty swiftly during the Korean War when (and after) a sinister new kind of efficiency appeared in America, maybe it was the result of the universalization of Television and nothing else (the Polite Total Police Control of Dragnet's "peace" officers) but the beat characters after 1950 vanished into jails and madhouses, or were shamed into silent conformity, the generation itself was shortlived and small in number.

By 1959, America's premier beatnik was the protagonist of *The Many Loves of Dobie Gillis,* played with goatee and bongos by Bob Denver.

The heretical truth is that in the broader public imagination, it was Maynard G. Krebs, not the by-then vanishing Kerouac, who led the revolution. Kerouac and Ginsberg made Krebs possible, but it was Krebs whose televised presence connected the isolated dissenters or grumblers, enabling the broad rebellions of the next decade.

H ip entails an acceptance of the imperfect—the low-fi, uncombed or unpolished. Such is the license of living in the present tense: you don't have to worry about mistakes, because their consequences are off in the future. At its most problematic, this devolves into hip's fetish for failure and self-destruction. Hip is imperfect in the sense of being incomplete, transitional. More than any movement in this history so far, the Beats trumpeted their imperfections, trying to redeem America's flaws after its virtues had led it so disastrously astray.

The enlightenment sought by the Beats—and this applies to their relationship with squares, each other, the economy and their mothers—involved an assumption of forgiveness. By this I mean not absolution but a hard acceptance of themselves *as unacceptable.* This is the innocence that Whitman claimed, more multitudinous than being without sin. Their unfiltered writings about themselves served both to validate their existence and to reconcile its flaws with the broad, ugly sweep of the culture.

Allen Ginsberg

Against the perfections of the nuclear bomb, the Nazi death camps and the corporate matrix, the Beats wore their flaws on the outside, offering them as strengths rather than weaknesses. They followed the improvisational license of bop. "Make a mistake," Monk advised his peers. "Play what you want and let the public pick up."

It is significant that the best minds of Ginsberg's generation, though famously "destroyed by madness, starving hysterical naked / Dragging themselves through the negro streets at dawn looking for an angry fix," remained nonetheless just that to the author—the best minds of all. "Howl" portrays a new priesthood educated by its injuries, not debilitated by them. The damage that overruns the next 126 long lines is part of their collective resumé. Its violence—"the absolute heart of the poem of life butchered out of their own bodies good to eat a thousand years"—is the beginning of enlightenment.

The embrace of unpolished, spontaneous writing meant that there were no best or wrong words, just what Kerouac called a "jewel center of interest in subject of image at *moment* of writing." He had his own version of Monk's advice: *"no revisions."* (This commandment was somewhat disingenuous: he filled his notebooks with drafts of scenes for *On the Road* long before his three-week typing spree, and he continued to revise thereafter.) The Beats were prolifically inconsistent, leaving it up to readers to sort the stinkers. In their lives and work they related in detail their unsuitability to polite society. Kerouac envied Cassady the freedom of his unsupervised id, only hinting at the inner life that most readers missed altogether. As Carolyn Cassady said, readers took away a self-serving portrait of her husband: "[W]hatever it is that Neal represented for them, like freedom and fearlessness, Neal was fearless but he wasn't free. Neal wanted to die. So he was utterly fearless as far as chances went because he was asking for it all the time. I kept thinking that the imitators never knew and don't know how miserable these men were, they think they were having marvelous times—joy, joy, joy—and they weren't at all." In February 1968, Cassady lay down beside a railroad track in San Miguel de Allende, Mexico, and froze to death. He was a few days shy of 42. Kerouac finished drinking a hole through himself the following year. He was 47.

The writers were as openly flawed in their personal lives as in their art, placing themselves not above criticism but beneath its pretensions. Ginsberg followed his mother into psychiatric confinement—"always trying to justify ma's madness," as Kerouac put it, "against the logical, sober but hateful society." Both Kerouac and Burroughs abandoned their children. Burroughs vandalized his own texts, wielding scissors against his intentions; this from a man—a *writer*—who once lopped off the end joint of one finger with chicken shears. (He landed in a psychiatric hospital for a month.) His gun accident and junk addiction were always a part of his reptilian allure. Like Miles Davis, he embraced his persona as prince of darkness, asking only that others see themselves in the same unsparing light. In a mock review of *Naked Lunch,* he promised readers an engagement with their worst: "This book is a must for anyone who would understand the sick soul, sick unto death, of the atomic age."

Buddhism provided a useful framework for both righteousness and imperfection. Ginsberg, Kerouac and Gary Snyder, among others, conceived their journeys as quests for satori, or awakening. Their acceptance of all experience or insight sometimes made for dopey literature—writers, after all, have to sort and filter and draw conclusions. But it also brought the writers into harmony with the flawed mainstream of Cold

War America, not above it but *of* it. Alan Watts, in an influential 1958 essay titled "Beat Zen, Square Zen, and Zen," quoted a saying from the Taoist scholar Chuang-tzu: "Those who would have good government without its correlative misrule, and right without its correlative wrong, do not understand the principles of the universe." The Beats took this wisdom to heart, living it out in the public eye. As much as their literary accomplishments, their acceptance of misrule as a constructive force stands as their lasting contribution to the culture.

This creative misrule echoed Whitman's paradoxical claim of being "not the poet of goodness only," but "the poet of wickedness also." Ginsberg invoked Whitman as "the first great American poet to take action in recognizing his individuality, forgiving and accepting *Him Self,* and automatically extending that recognition and acceptance to all—and defining his Democracy as that. . . . Without this truth there is only the impersonal Moloch and self-hatred of others." The challenge for the Beats and their peers was not to disengage from the impersonal Moloch, but to implicate themselves in it—to make it *personal.* In the same way, Whitman had taken upon himself the worst of America before the Civil War:

> I am the poet of slaves, and of the masters of slaves. . . .
> I am the poet of sin,
> For I do not believe in sin.

When Whitman sang of containing multitudes, he did not mean they were all admirable.

Yet they were all implicitly forgiven. To live in the present tense is to claim forgiveness as you go, making peace with your flaws even as you erupt in new ones. It is to live outside of judgment—and to allow others the same grace. There are no wounds left by one's flaws, only new flaws to replace the old ones. In this forgiveness hip can be both noble and ennobling. This is a difference between hip and simple outlaw nihilism. The outlaw is a romantic figure because his violence puts him on the outside of society. He is cathartic but ultimately illusory: you can't get rid of evil so easily. The hipster as romantic figure—the angelheaded, yea-saying overburst of American joy—opens society's eyes, or hips it, to the violence within. Though hip is often belittled as adolescent rebellion, it is bigger than what critics like Robert Brustein say it opposes, and more free than rebellion. Hip works more broadly than simple opposition to someone else's agenda. It surrounds and envelops. Even if you never read past "Howl" and maybe "Kaddish," Allen Ginsberg probably shapes your life more than Dwight D. Eisenhower.

There is another way to look at the Beat avatars and their prototypes. As much as Kerouac was Charlie Parker, he was also Herman Melville, the restless seafarer who traded static clarity for the blur of the quest. The car was his ship, and Cassady his captain. Like Melville, he wrote the gospels in this century and died, if not in the gutter, in self-destructive bitterness, no longer speaking, as he once claimed, for the "solitary Bartlebies staring out the dead wall window of our civilization." When these Bartlebies did not thank him for showing them the road, Kerouac marinated in his disappointment. He wrote to Ginsberg: "I discovered a new Beat Generation a long time ago, I hitchhiked and starved, for art, and that makes me the Fool of the Beatniks with a crown of shit. Thanks, America."

Ginsberg was Walt Whitman, a curious patriot who endeavored to heal a ruptured society through the gape of his own vanity. "It occurs to me that I am America," Ginsberg wrote, and but for the disingenuousness of the first four words—*It occurs to me*—the line might have belonged to Whitman. And in his vigilance toward all systems of control, chemical and otherwise, Burroughs was a coruscating heir to Thoreau, living in voluntary exile, echoing Thoreau's sense of life as civil disobedience: "I quietly declare war with the State, after my fashion, though I will still make what use and get what advantage of her I can, as is usual in such cases." (That's Thoreau, by the way, not Burroughs.)

The critic George W. S. Trow has argued that the retrospective inevitability of the post-Beat counterculture, which is recounted as meeting only cardboard resistance, hides the full magnitude of the Beats' disruption. The 1960s, Trow wrote,

> are presented as mostly motivated by an urge to get Rosa Parks to the front of the bus, on the one hand, and to stop the Vietnam War, on the other. Missing from the story, primarily because the story's never been told from the top down, because that mode of storytelling had simply fallen into disrepute, was that death to the Eisenhower empire. This had

been prefigured in *Howl* by Ginsberg: "America, fuck you and your atom bomb [*sic*]." That effort was now taken to the streets, and this caesura was, first of all, very remarkable in that the Eisenhower empire was the empire. It was the control system that produced our money, our dominance, our unique position in the world, and it was remarkable how little it took to kill it.

By these lights the Beats and their bebop peers, in their echoes of Whitman and Thoreau, represent an enduring constant in the American fabric, not newer than the Eisenhower empire but older. It is always current. Each generation needs its Whitman; each Whitman redeems his peers by allowing them to forgive him. Hip's revolutions begin each time in the humanizing promise with which Sal Paradise begins *On the Road:* "And this was really the way that my whole road experience began, and the things that were to come are too fantastic not to tell." And they remain bound to Sal's flash of enlightenment and absolution: "Somewhere along the line I knew there'd be girls, visions, everything; somewhere along the line the pearl would be handed to me."

the tricksters

signifying monkeys and other hip engines of progress

> The biggest difference between us and white people is that we know when we're playing.
>
> —ALBERTA ROBERTS, quoted in
> Drylongso: A Self-Portrait of Black America,
> by John Langston Gwaltney

In the 1960s, Dick Gregory used to tell a joke to mostly white audiences. "You know the definition of a Southern moderate?" he'd ask. "That's a cat that'll lynch you from a low tree." It was a joke about his audience and himself, and about the ways they were and were not connected. The line was absurd on its face—who could find humor in lynching? Yet it was more absurd in context. If anything divided Gregory from his white audience, blocking the empathy that is essential for humor, it was their relationships to the violence described in the joke. The audience could only be on one side of it, Gregory on the other. The joke depended on these positions; if a white person told it to a black audience, it would mean something entirely different. But the joke also picked at the positions, calling attention to *their* absurdity. The black comedian and white audience shared a laugh not despite the racial divide, but *within* it. The categories of white and black, which are inviolable within the joke, became muddled in its telling.

This was not an escape from reality, but rather, as Clive James said of Mark Twain's humor, an escape from *un*reality, from the greater absurdities that define race in America. Gregory played overtly with the boundaries of this unreality. "Wouldn't it be a hell of a thing," he teased, "if all this was burnt cork and you people were being tolerant for nothing?" By tweaking both the lines that allowed his audience to connect with him and those that kept them apart, he slid himself and the audience into territory where the points of guilt and race begin to shift. This terrain belongs to tricksters.

Tricksters are hip's animating agents: the con men and hustlers, the fools and rascals, whom the culture invents to undermine its own rules. They work the gray areas between moral certainties, pulling the nation along in their wake. Lewis Hyde, in his masterful book *Trickster Makes This World: Mischief, Myth and Art* (1998), notes that tricksters operate in the joints and seams of a culture, where established ideas come imperfectly together. They are always "on the road," he says, the "lords of the in-between." America, a country of immigrants, is all joints and seams.

Like hip itself, the trickster has a long and varied family tree. P. T. Barnum, Abbie Hoffman, Richard Hell—these are the tricksters of doublespeak, edifying the public not with certainty but with the enlightenment that comes of doubt. Their hoax was as good as their truth, and in the end more truthful. Miles Davis, Muhammad Ali and Bob Dylan are the shape-shifting tricksters: now you see 'em, now you don't. They teased the culture into battle lines according to their personae, then redrew their own masks. When I interviewed Ali in 1999, he performed magic tricks and teased, in a voice slowed by Parkinson's disease, "Am I an international figure—or an international nigger?" Mark Twain, Lenny Bruce, Terry Southern and Richard Pryor were the unmerry pranksters, gravely serious as they played atrocity for laughs. Working the gap between words and their meaning, they captured the suspended joy and pain of America's tragicomic form, the blues. As Twain wrote, "The secret source of humor itself is not joy, but sorrow. There is no humor in heaven." Bugs Bunny, whose roots lie in African-American folktales, was the trickster/hipster as national icon. (More on him in chapter 8.)

Tricksters advance hip by crossing and recrossing the lines that hem it in. Their tools are not ideals like justice or valor but humor, wit, wile and

Bob Dylan

self-interest. Nontrickster heroes help societies distinguish between right and wrong; tricksters violate the boundary between the two. In a nation artificially divided into black and white, inside and outside, tricksters open channels of exchange. Often creatures of the spiritual world, tricksters in modern America have flourished among the secular realms of entertainment and business, opening the way for the nation's dominance in these areas. Hip, which validates troublemakers, is an engine of this progress. The hipster emblems of any era—say, the sloth music and matted hair of contemporary Williamsburg—are not just signs of decadent affluence, but catalysts that make that affluence possible. Like mutant strands of DNA, they loosen society's grip on the certainties that prevent it from evolving.

As culture heroes, tricksters work the cracks between more conventional schools of heroism. "Look, up in the sky!" yelled Richard Pryor in a 1977 routine. "It's a crow! It's a bat. No, it's Super Nigger! . . . With X-ray vision that enables him to see through everything except Whitey." Tricksters tell small lies to reveal bigger ones. I said earlier that hip was the ability to play the other guy's game; tricksters undermine all the positions on the board. Chapters of this book so far have described how hip grows among cliques, which bond together through private language. Tricksters, on the other hand, work alone. Instead of the private language of the clique, they use the public language of humor, which signifies as it deceives. You can admire and learn from them, but they don't belong to a circle you might want to join. They are hip's presiding soloists, poking at the myths that hold such circles together.

The first myth in this book is that race is an impasse: that different skin colors denote separate categories of beings. This is among America's founding fables. It allowed European settlers to treat nonwhite natives or Africans as something other than human, or at least something less than European. The second, contradictory myth is that race is infinitely permeable: that when white people or black people look across the divide, they can understand each other through their own experience and language. Kerouac invoked this myth in the previous chapter when he longed to "exchange worlds with the happy, true-hearted Negroes of America," perceiving black culture as an uncorrupted, primitive analog of white. The first myth takes a historical difference and explains it as biology. The second explains it as style. In both cases race is a *process of reading*, to be shaped by whoever has the power to explain things in the marketplace.

Hip operates in the gaps between these two fictions. The myths of race, which serve parts of the population, are both unlivable for many others and stagnating for the whole. They commit great energies to diminishing the nation's cultural resources, by pretending either that some voices don't exist or that they are just echoes of others. The myths also require even weirder contrivances to prop them up, like the "one-drop rule," by which anyone with a drop of African blood is deemed black. I call them myths not because they are untrue, but because their impact does not depend on whether they are true or not. Like the terms *white* and *black*, they carry weight according to who believes in them and how they are used to organize thought. Over time, black and white elites have each upheld both versions. The 1980s quip, "It's a black thing, you wouldn't understand," is a variant on the first myth played against the second. More recently, when people debate the Eminem question—*where does the white boy get off?*—they are engaging both myths without necessarily challenging either.

Such myths are inherently conservative. They arise to hold a society in place, not push it forward. Even at their most benign, they can be stultifying. As James Baldwin once said, "As long as you think you're white, I have to think I'm black." (If the races were called "more lighter" and "more darker," it might be easier to see them as historically *different* and *interdependent,* rather than through lies like *separate but equal.*) Because myths answer to whoever has the power to define ideas, they tend to support established ideas, adding to what is called the conventional wisdom or public consensus, though it is rarely either. This conservative tendency, in turn, is in conflict with the noise of new ideas. In the short term, the old school can win this conflict: they have the guns or the movie studios. But the longer, Darwinian saga favors contradiction and disruption. A society that can close itself off to contradictory ideas is stagnant. One that cultivates contradictions will evolve faster, develop more technologies and have more fun.

Though folklores are broad and varied, the typical trickster tale is of a weaker character, such as Brer Rabbit, who uses superior wit and deceit to prevail over a stronger one, like Brer Fox. The tales may have morals, but their purpose is not to teach what you'd call model behavior. A quick look at two tales will show what I mean. In the European, nontrickster tale of the tortoise and the hare, the tortoise wins the race through his humble, steadfast virtue. He's a good Joe. In a similar African-American slave tale of a race between the terrapin and the deer, the trickster terrapin wins the race by positioning look-alike relatives at different parts of the course, and himself at the finish line. Every time the deer thinks he has the race won, he sees the terrapin *again* up ahead. The deer is done in by his narrow belief system. In the first tale, the tortoise wins by being the dutiful square; in the second, the terrapin is a model of hip, using one word *(terrapin)* to represent more than one meaning (in this case a whole family of terrapins).

A healthy society has use for both of these messages. The first message, of the virtuous tortoise, helps establish order; the second, of the wily terrapin, encourages creativity. The gallery of hipsters in this chapter, from Barnum to Richard Hell, all worked the confidence game of the terrapin, inventing stories and then shifting the meaning of the terms. And like the terrapin, they played most inventively with the public's perception of themselves. Their real essence lay in the manipulation of imagery, not in any one of the images (in contrast to less changeable hipsters like Chet Baker or Snoop Dogg, for whom the image makes the man). Any time you thought you could get a step on Miles or Dylan, or Twain or Ali, there was always another incarnation up ahead, taunting. As Dylan sang, donning one of many masks of dialect: "Don't ask me nuthin' about nuthin' / I just might tell you the truth." You learned from their mercurial inconstancy, not their temporarily fixed bearings.

What tricksters bring is enlightenment, not of absolutes but of the alleys around them. The Greek trickster Hermes, who stole Apollo's cattle, also devised the practice of sacrifice, which opened communication between mortals and the gods. The Yoruban trickster Esu-Elegbara—also known as Eshu, Legba and Papa La Bas—brought mortals the gift of divination, or access to the truths of the gods. In slightly altered form, he ultimately taught Robert Johnson and other musicians to play the blues. Hermes and Esu both used deceit to bring knowledge. Henry Louis Gates Jr., tracing Esu's transit through the Middle Passage, lists among his attributes "individuality, satire, parody, irony, magic, indeterminacy, openendedness, ambiguity, sexuality, chance, uncertainty, disruption and reconciliation, betrayal and loyalty, closure and disclosure, encasement and rupture"—a hit list of hip, even before you get to Esu's prodigious phallus. Through hip, the tricksters' revelations circulate first among an enlightened few, who can use them to their own advantage, then gradually to a broader public. When Allen Ginsberg said that Beat "was a visionary experience in 1948," but that now "everybody sees and understands these things," he was talking about the way tricksters change the center from the fringe.

The main playground for tricksters is language. Their range of mischief, both playful and malicious, can be seen in the semantic spray of the word *nigger*. No word has more meanings, and all of the meanings are present in every usage, if not out front then singing backup. As a synonym for *black*, it begins in the false opposition of black and white (which really refer to overlapping ranges of brown), and spirals outward from this original lie. The word respects no limits. It might seem to mean one thing coming from the white detective Mark Fuhrman during the O. J. trial and another from Method Man, but really it means everything coming from both. This is its power. Like tricksters, the word speaks all the seams and contradictions in the national silence on race. Dick Gregory, who called his life story *Nigger: An Autobiography*, dedicated the book to his mother, writing, "Wherever you are, if you ever hear the word 'nigger' again, remember they are advertising my book." The meaning changes not merely with context or inflection, but according to who is speaking, hearing or overhearing, and who is profiting. The word *nigger* on a blank page is deafening but impenetrable. It could signal love, hate or anything in between. It defies definition not because it lacks meaning but because it has too much.

Tricksters carry similarly loaded messages, bearing information across borders. Zora Neale Hurston, who collected oral tales in the rural South, met a woman named Aunt Shady Ann Sutton who told her that the trickster High John de Conquer "had done teached the black folks so they knowed 100 years ahead of time that freedom was coming." High John had the gift of laughter, which always signals chaos or disorder, even under oppressed conditions. To Aunt Shady this gift, with its momentary loss of control, signaled future freedom, when control would be lost altogether. The trickster's gift reveals the limits of oppression. Where societies try to establish meaning through order, tricksters, like the word *nigger*, reveal the greater abundance of meaning in chaos. This chaos is an equalizer, putting the powerless above the powerful. Gregory's comedy routine about lynching works the same reversal. Both articulate the meaning that order is supposed to hide.

Hip follows from this blurring of boundaries. It hides and reveals at the same time. Mark Twain (1835–1910), who immersed himself in the storytelling of blacks in Missouri, recognized the humorous story as arising from the unique indirection of the American language, which in turn arose from the unique encounter of the African with the European. In his essay "How To Tell a Story," he elaborated: "The humorous story is American, the comic story is English, the witty story is French. The humorous story depends for its effect on the manner of the telling; the comic story and the witty story upon the matter. . . . The humorous story is told gravely; the teller does his best to conceal the fact that he even dimly suspects that there is anything funny about it. . . ." In other words, the humorous story does not mean only what it says, but also the opposite. It creates more than one meaning from the same words. The joke depends on the distance between the two meanings and the artfulness with which they are juxtaposed. In good hands, the chaos becomes a higher, more democratic form of order. The process is by definition liberating: if I can control the meaning of words, and those words constitute my relationship with others, then I control that relationship. As the Freudian critic Ernst Kris wrote, such humor is "a form of rebellion against fate."

Black English works similar ambiguities, saying one thing but meaning another. In 1988, I talked with Chuck D of Public Enemy about what white audiences don't get about hip-hop. "A lot of things are said with words or body language or things meaning something else," he said. "It's like, if you go up to somebody and he says, 'nigga bugging,' he's saying a lot of things besides nigga bugging. It's felt. And I could understand it. Some white person with a middle-class background or little contact with black people won't understand that shit at all. There's a lot of people in Creedmore [State Psychiatric Hospital] that people can't understand."

This confusion lends itself to humor. A traveler in Constance Rourke's classic *American Humor: A Study of the National Character* (1931) noted as early as 1795, "The blacks are the great humorists of the nation." Humor is a conduit of meaning that runs from definition; once you try to define it, it is gone. As a form of control, humor imposes its duplicities on other forms, which rely on words meaning what they say. As DuBois wrote in 1940, when the Depression was wreaking its worst miseries on black communities, "If you will hear men laugh, go to Guinea, 'Black Bottom,' 'Niggertown,' Harlem. If you want to feel humor too exquisite and too subtle for translation, sit invisibly among a gang of Negro workers. . . . We are the supermen who sit idly by and laugh and look at civilization."

Here humor works in two directions, creating order and disorder. It allowed the workers to impose order on their chaotic lives, and at the same time to inject chaos—the possibility of change—into the orderly distribution of poverty, which followed racial lines. It cut both ways. Central to the humor, DuBois wrote, was the wile of the trickster: "the dry mockery of the pretensions of white folk. . . . Many is the time that a truculent white man has been wholly disarmed before the apparently innocent and really sophisticated joke of the Negro, whom he meant to be-rate." This is how the trickster's play reverses certainties: the self-regarding white man, once "truculent," becomes "disarmed"; the joke, seemingly "innocent," reveals a "sophistication" that the white man thought was his alone. Nobody is hurt, but no one is the same.

Sometimes, of course, the confrontation is more direct. The African-American trickster character known as the Signifying Monkey does his battle openly, and never misses the opportunity to mock his victims. An American incarnation of Esu-Elegbara, the Signifying Monkey has en-dured through slave folk tales to the scandalous rhymes of Rudy Ray Moore's blaxploitation classic *Dolemite* (1975). The Monkey's hilariously profane misadventures, usually involving his nemesis the Lion, are often racial allegories:

> Down in the jungle near a dried-up creek
> The signifying monkey hadn't slept for a week
> Remembering the ass-kicking that he got in the past
> He had to find somebody to kick the lion's ass.

In most tellings, the Signifying Monkey uses guile and wordplay to tri-umph over the more powerful Lion. Like DuBois's idle supermen, he is a contradiction in terms, strong in his weakness. He controls the meaning of language. Taken at face value, much of the humor seems cruel, mock-ing the misfortune of others. Tricksters pick on the weak as well as the strong. But their gift, the control of language, is gentler and more gener-ous. Even as it laughs at affliction, the humor provides this tool for disas-sembling it—quite useful for a population steeped in hardship.

This gift, which we see most clearly in the blues, snakes up through Barnum and all the tricksters, changing with each turn. It is a confidence game in which the audience is willingly duped, submitting to the trick in order to experience the conjuring of joy out of pain, and vice versa. It is the cool mask that hides the enlightenment of hip.

In the criminal underworld, which is one trickster realm, there are overlords and underlings, kingpins and masterminds, but only the confidence man is an artist. The con artist is a trickster who blurs the categories of villain and victim, crime and commerce. He plies his craft not by taking but by giving, by inventing a story for his marks. A well-constructed con job entertains, flatters and teases; it invites the mark to fill in gaps in the story. It only works if the sucker's avarice, rather than the con artist's, sets the con in motion. The con artist's greed is wholly controlled and channeled; the mark's is in conflict with itself, ultimately doing him in. It is the mark's identifying mark. Where most criminals try to leave no evidence, the con artist builds a monument to his creativity and wit. The better the story he leaves, the better the con.

The main business of the con artist is not looting but creating belief. He makes the mark believe that the language means one thing, when the confidence man knows it means two. When he pulls the string on that belief, what remains are the loss suffered by the victim and the story of the con itself. The story is more valuable than whatever the victim lost. He could turn around and use it to recoup all losses and more. In fact, this is the essence of modern business, to create value through language. In the information economy, the play of language *is* value: if you buy a pair of jeans or a Hummer, what you're really buying is a story about yourself. After all the con artist's lying, what is left is truth—most recognizably, the truth of the mark's greed; more subtly, the truth that ambiguities are all around us, and that people who say that language means only one thing are probably trying to deceive us. This is the truth of the trickster, who brings enlightenment where more noble citizens might prefer dark.

In the spirit of this confidence, the first true American celebrity was Phineas Taylor Barnum (1810–1891). Born in small-town Bethel, Connecticut, Barnum became the most popular road attraction in the country before he settled down and opened his American Museum at Broadway and 10th Street in 1842. Though fraud and hokum were an established part of the business world in Barnum's time, he brought a unique understanding of the value provided by the commercial trickster. His first great hoax, which he perpetrated in July 1835, involved an elderly black woman named Joice Heth, whom he claimed was the 161-year-old nurse of George Washington. Heth had been a minor attraction for another sideshow operator. Barnum recognized a better way to milk the stunt. He hyped her mightily, then planted tips in newspapers that she was really a lifeless automaton made of India rubber and whalebone, operated by a ventriloquist.

With two frauds in the air at the same time—that she was a robot and that she was 161 years old—Barnum was selling the delight of fraud itself, the intimation that the world around us is not what it seems. At least one of the explanations had to be bogus. And what made this appealing was that, like Dick Gregory's routine or the laughter of DuBois's idle supermen, it revealed some truth. Barnum let the audience in on a secret they already sensed. Even if Joice Heth had been Washington's ancient nurse, the public could only have seen her through their own racial preconceptions, which treated African Americans as an undifferentiated mass. In other words, they would have seen only their stereotype of an old black woman, which they had long ago fabricated from sources no more trustworthy than Barnum. He simply brought the process of self-deception into the foreground. His freaks and oddities—the Fejee Mermaid, the Wooly Horse—might be real, bogus or a mixture of the two. The treat was in the way Barnum bent the lines between these categories. Like all tricksters, he was anti-idealist, and the first ideal he tweaked was the impregnability of truth. "The public," he noted, "appears to be amused even when they are conscious of being deceived." Barnum sullied simple truths to make complicated ones, filled with internal contradiction.

A century and a half later, in the same neck of Manhattan, Richard Meyers and Tom Miller, better known as Richard Hell and Tom Verlaine, perpetrated a similar hoax on a smaller scale, merging their photographic images to create a poet named Theresa Stern and writing a body of poems in her name. "Like myself," she claimed, "my poetry is so alive it stinks." Meyers and Miller were at the time just developing their false identities, and they used them to create an even falser one, calling attention to the scam. "For me it was a liberation to lose myself, to not feel I had to do something to represent me," Hell said in 2003, thumbing a book of Theresa Stern's poems in his East Village apartment. "You could just let the poem be the thing you cared about, rather than this hyper awareness that it was going to be *your* expression."

If Verlaine was punk's shadowy enigma, Hell was its prankster, goading the circus while keeping an ironic distance from it. Born in 1949 in Lexington, Kentucky, Hell came to New York in 1966 in search of poetry. As an original member of Television, he designed the notorious T-shirt stenciled with the words "Please Kill Me." It was a wry comment on punk nihilism that was also an invitation to the thing itself. Hell was too smart to wear it, but he put the guitarist Richard Lloyd up to it. "I think I made it for Richard," he says now. After a Television gig at Max's Kansas City, Lloyd got into a conversation with some fans while wearing the shirt. They "looked as deep into my eyes as they possibly could—and said, 'Are you serious?' " he remembered. "Then they said, 'If that's what you want, we'll be glad to oblige because we're such big fans!' " The shirt did and did not mean what it said. At that time New York was seen as ungovernable, and punk grew from the economic chaos of the East Village. The shirt was a hip evasion that functioned as its own mask, calling attention to punk's theatrical violence as it acknowledged the real violence around the edges.

What both Barnum and Hell were doing, as their black contemporaries would have recognized, was signifying, or using language to mean two things. "The Black concept of *signifying*," notes the linguist Claudia Mitchell-Kernan, "incorporates essentially a folk notion that dictionary entries for words are not always sufficient for interpreting meanings or messages, or that meaning goes beyond such interpretations." In broad strokes, signifying is the use of parody, misdirection, allusion and code to make one word convey multiple meanings. It can be funny, but like many forms of humor, it is no joke. "Signifying," as the novelist John Edgar Wideman defined it, "is verbal play—serious play that serves as instruction, entertainment, mental exercise, preparation for interacting with friend and foe in the social arena. In black vernacular, Signifying is a sign that words cannot be trusted, that even the most literal utterance allows room for interpretation, that language is both carnival and minefield." Richard Lloyd's encounter with the fans at Max's shows how precarious this minefield can get.

In his 1988 book *The Signifying Monkey: A Theory of African-American Literary Criticism*, Henry Louis Gates placed the oral tradition of signifying within hip's natural turf, in the imperfect seam that connects and divides two cultures: "at a sort of crossroads, a discursive crossroads at which two languages meet, be these languages Yoruba and English, or Spanish and French, or even (perhaps especially) the black vernacular and standard English." The action is not limited to words; when musicians "ragged" a pop song or abstracted its changes on the way to bop, they were signifying on it.

The Olympics of signifying is the dozens, an African-American sport of ritual insult. Like signifying, the dozens showcases the limber grace of black English. The civil rights activist H. "Rap" Brown (Jamil Abdullah Al-Amin), who was convicted in 2002 of killing a police officer, remembered doing the dozens as a schoolboy in Baton Rouge, Louisiana in the 1950s:

> I fucked your mama
> Till she went blind.
> Her breath smells bad,
> But she sure can grind.

The dozens, also known as woofing, sounding or joning, were Brown's higher ed, the source of his nickname. As he recalled in his 1969 autobiography, *Die Nigger Die!*, the dozens demanded standards of excellence higher than any found in the classroom. "And the teacher expected me to sit up in class and study poetry after I could run down shit like that. If anybody needed to study poetry, she needed to study mine. We played the Dozens for recreation, like white folks play Scrabble."

Derived from the archaic English verb "to dozen," meaning to stun, stupefy or daze, the dozens matches wordplay with wordplay, wit with greater wit. It provided Muhammad Ali's first escape from the role of dutiful, "primitive" black athlete. Ali signaled his independence in rhyme: "The crowd did not dream when they laid down their money / That they would see a total eclipse of the Sonny." As a form of high-wire rhetoric, the dozens provided a model for cutting contests in jazz, in which two musicians spin each other's phrases, trading fours, eights or twelves, and later for rap's verbal battles. Though the dozens is built on fighting words, the spell is broken, and the game is lost, if one contestant gets hurt or wants to fight. Like signifying, the dozens is a system of control and chaos. Where signifying adds layers of meaning to language, the dozens releases language from meaning. Insults directed at your mama aren't really; the dozens is pure performance, in which the performers triumph over meaning.

Yet the subject matter—your dignity, your mama—is not entirely arbitrary. As Rap Brown noted above, the dozens packs a lesson. How can

Muhammad Ali *(Hulton Archive/ Getty Images)*

it mean defeat for a contestant to fight for the things most worth fighting for? In a society that considers these subjects sacred, a game that treats them as mere pieces on a chessboard plays with the nature of language itself. It works the seam between words and meaning. The game dares you to take its terms literally, then cuts you for taking the dare. The loser is the one who lets the culture define the meaning of the words; the winner puts the game itself above the words used to play it—even these holiest of words. The essence of hip talk, the game says, lies not in its vocabulary or syntax but in its ability to continually make these anew. This is a constant of hip: it lies in the process of invention, not the products. For example, to dress hip means to play coherently with the language of fashion, not to wear the correct black jeans or turtlenecks. To dress square, or be a fashion victim, is to mistake the means for the ends.

Samuel L. Clemens absorbed the strategies of signifying and the dozens growing up among slave children in Hannibal and Florida, Missouri. "I was playmate to all the niggers," he said, "preferring their society to that of the elect." As a child, he watched a local overseer kill a slave with a hunk of iron ore just for performing a task awkwardly, and watched his neighbors sympathize not with the dead man's family but with his owner. Such experiences left Sam ambivalent toward slavery but alive to the way whole communities bent themselves around the conceit of race. He later pulled at these contortions, writing, "All I care to know is that a man is a human being, that is enough for me; he can't be any worse."

Mark Twain, as he was known, took his pseudonym from the call used by riverboat pilots to signal that water was two fathoms deep. On his uncle John Quarles's farm, Twain learned much about concealment—about how signifying can mislead as it informs—from the African Americans whose stories he listened to "as one who receives a revelation." In one of his major pre-Huck stories, an early experiment in dialect called "A True Story, Repeated Word for Word as I Heard It" (1874), he transcribed a tale told him by a family cook named Mary Ann Cord, who had been violently separated from her husband and children during slavery. For the tale he changed her name to Aunt Rachel. When the narrator asks her, preposterously, "Aunt Rachel, how is it that you've lived sixty years and never had any trouble?" she schools him to the ways of signifying. Of course she had had woes, she explains. Her light manner simply signified more than it let on. If you were hip to its signifying, you could hear the hardship in the gentlest syntax. This lesson—in blues invention more than accent or dialect—set Twain free to begin *The Adventures of Huckleberry Finn* two years later.

The voice that Twain developed, in part through his exposure to African-American storytellers, marks a beginning of American literature. Without "the spoken idiom of Negro Americans," Ralph Ellison declared, Twain could not have had the language for *Huck Finn,* for the shifting racial consciousness that twists with the river. "No Huck and Jim," Ellison wrote, "no American novel as we know it." Ellison counted himself among the writers to whom the novel gave a voice. The book engaged the great American subjects, race and progress, and forced readers into the knots that entangle the two. Twain saw *Huck Finn* as an internal collision between "a sound heart and a deformed conscience," in which "conscience suffers defeat." The conscience, in this case, is that of the conventional wisdom, which afflicts poor Huck as an illness. He suffers pangs of guilt for the "sin" of helping Jim escape and depriving Miss Watson of her property, before finally deciding, "All right, then, I'll go to hell." Huck is the victim of this conscience, not the author, but he is also responsible for anything he does in its name. Over the course of the novel, he learns to question his received absolutes, and the language for his questioning is that of the trickster. Because his words do not always mean what they say, they force us to view Huck from both inside and outside, but never omnisciently: whenever an easy answer to his moral dilemmas presents itself, it quickly slithers out of reach.

The book has remained controversial. Critics still disagree about its ending, in which Huck and Tom tarry rather than helping Jim to freedom. Originally banned from some libraries for its vulgarity, it is now banned at others for its use of the word *nigger*. Every year another library or school system adds it or drops it. But these are the objections that rise up in response to many things hip. They arise less from the book than from the very racial myths it engaged; the word *nigger,* which apologists excuse as just the language of the period, was loaded then, and remains loaded today. People who expect language to mean one thing won't find it in *Huckleberry Finn.* The book might have been more comforting if Twain had sent Huck on a simple moral quest of right against wrong, rather than twisting the two, but it would not have been as rich.

Twain's heirs, including Lenny Bruce, Terry Southern and Richard Pryor, used similar indirection to pry at the orthodoxies of post-WWII America. Bruce, born Leonard Alfred Schneider in 1925, grew up basking in the hypocrisies of mid-century America, attending Times Square strip clubs with his mother, who sometimes performed a stand-up act under the name Boots Malloy. In the late 1950s, when Jewish comedians presented themselves as compliant cogs in the entertainment racket, Bruce insisted on telling the truth about sex, religion and violence, and making it funny. Like Twain and like the Signifying Monkey, he pulled at the meanings beneath the surfaces of words. The role of comedy, as he saw it, was to drag these meanings into the public eye. He held words like *kike* or *come* up for examination in order to break their spells. Instead of telling jokes, he riffed on themes like a jazz improviser, crossing wires between sexual prohibitions and ethnic stereotypes: "A lot of people say to me, 'Why did you kill Christ?' " he asked in one routine. " 'I dunno . . . it was one of those parties, got out of hand, you know.'

Lenny Bruce

We killed him because he didn't want to become a doctor, that's why we killed him."

Though he had fun with the middle-class phonies in the new suburbs, and the would-be hipsters who visited the strip joints and later comedy clubs where he worked, he saved his sharpest satire for showbiz itself. Flooding his routines with Yiddish and smarm, he exploded the bland euphemisms of the biz. In routines like "How to Relax Your Colored Friends at Parties," he poked at the racist sentiments behind with-it liberal banter. In the routine, a white character meets a black stranger at a party. "That Bojangles," he says, apropos of nothing. "Christ, could he tap-dance! You tap-dance a little yourself?" In a later routine, Bruce imagined two Jewish agents at MCA (Mein Campf Arises) auditioning leaders for the Third Reich, inventing the Führer in a frenzy of hype. "Adolf, my friend," says one agent, "tomorrow we will be going on the road, my friend, as soon as you sign on the paper right there."

Also like Twain and the Signifying Monkey, Bruce suffered for his words. First arrested for obscenity in 1961, he spent much of his final years performing the transcripts of his trials. No bits could be more absurd; nothing he could say about the constraints on language could be as damning as the actual court proceedings. Yet the shows were a drag, and Bruce, strung out on dope, seemed defeated by the words that were once his. When he died of a morphine overdose in his bathroom in Los Angeles in August 1966, police let news crews photograph his swollen body beside the toilet. It was their revenge, the final exposure of a man who insisted on performing naked.

Southern (1924–1995) was a Zelig of Cold War hip, appearing on the cover of *Sgt. Pepper,* writing movies like *Dr. Strangelove* and *Easy Rider,* and turning up amid various Beats, Beatles, Stones, drugs and sexual malfeasances. Born in Alvarado, Texas, and reared in the Parisian high porn of Maurice Girodias's Olympia Press, Southern played with the gonzo, sensationalist riffs of New Journalism popularized by Hunter S. Thompson and Tom Wolfe. But his specialty was satire, a dish he preferred to serve hot. He spelled out his m.o. (Southern abbreviated anything he could get away with; for example, referring to the gentleman writer of Oxford, Mississippi, as Big Bill Faulk) in a 1964 interview. "The important thing in writing," he said, "is the capacity to astonish. Not shock—shock is a worn-out word—but astonish. The world has no grounds whatever for complacency. The Titanic couldn't sink, but it did. Where you find smugness, you find something worth blasting. I want to blast it."

Southern delighted in sex and pretension—frolicking happily in the first, mocking the second, and finding the subversive humor in their intersection. He seemed to love the immense depravity of the world he satirized, whether the nuclear brinkmanship of *Strangelove* or the baroque sexuality of the Rolling Stones' aptly named "Cocksucker Blues" tour, on which he was the official recorder. Even at his most lubricious, he dressed his language in mock formality. Luc Sante, one of many admirers, captured the timbre nicely as a "breezy compound of street jive and Madison Avenue knowingness woven around an arch pedantic formality that stands like the ruins of the square world." Though Southern wrote a couple of hipster classics—*The Magic Christian* (1959) and the short story collection *Red-Dirt Marijuana and Other Tastes* (1967)—he managed to appear anti-productive, hip for who he was (or who he was with) more than what he did. His greatest literary invention was an ingénue named Candy, a nubile update of Candide created with a heroin addict named

Mason Hoffenberg. In their semiporn *Candy*, written for Girodias and initially published only in France, she offers her body to a psychotic hunchback, cooing, "Give me your hump!," and rides him to an orgasm of insane prolixity, screaming, "Cunt! Cock! Crap! Prick! Kike! Nigger! Wop! Hump! HUMP!" In a career that tapered to premature inconsequence, this is what you'd call a heck of a climax.

Richard Franklin Lennox Thomas Pryor, born in 1940, arrived after the comedy revolution of the late 1950s and early 1960s, in which comics like Bruce and Mort Sahl weaponized the gentle joking of their forbears. Pryor played more subversively in the role of the trickster. "I was a nigger for 23 years," he once joked. "I gave it up—no room for advancement." Where Southern and Bruce ridiculed the hypocrisy of the ruling classes, Pryor, like Twain, humbled audiences by making them try on the humanity of the despised. Raised in a whorehouse in Peoria, Illinois, the son of a prostitute, he created characters of the drunks, winos, hillbillies and hustlers he encountered. Even more than Bruce, he did not so much tell jokes as share perspectives. His best character was himself: naked, scared, angry, smart, cursed, in love with white women. "Art is the ability to tell the truth," he said, "especially about oneself." He outed the word *nigger*, putting it in the mouths of white and black characters, which stripped white audiences of their sense of entitlement. Like the bop musicians, he challenged white Americans to accept a worldview in which they were neither central nor exemplary. As Mel Watkins noted in *On the Real Side*, a comprehensive survey of African-American humor, Pryor was "the first African-American stand-up comedian to speak candidly and successfully to integrated audiences the way black people joked among themselves when most critical of America."

Pryor's own life, severely limited since the 1990s by multiple sclerosis, has been as chaotic as his comedy. His struggles with poverty and wealth both made it into his routines, as did his drug addiction. His work reflected the pain of a man who tried to take his own life by dousing himself in ether and lighting a match, which he initially pretended was a freebasing accident. Yet he recognized that the pain was not his alone. "Pryor belongs to the sassing tradition of the trickster," said Ishmael Reed, who befriended Pryor when the comedian moved to the Bay Area in 1970, and who along with Cecil Brown helped Pryor channel his radical side. In the manner of tricksters, Reed said, Pryor used his comedy to illuminate absurdity. "The trickster goes on anybody's side. As long as he can get sex and gain, that's where he'll go. But [Pryor] gets away with it because he's very vulnerable." Pryor was insider and outsider at the same time, passing knowledge from one realm to the other. He did so with both bravado and humility, and with the trickster wisdom that lay between the two. As Reed said, "Tricksters are important as scavengers. We go through all the dead weight, clean it up. We serve a purpose. We pick up stuff from every culture, every form, every discipline. We're in business forever."

n 1987, toward the end of his life, Miles Davis (1926–1991) was invited to a White House dinner hosted by Ronald Reagan. Ray Charles was receiving a Lifetime Achievement Award. Miles wore black leather pants, two vests and black tails with a red snake on the back, trimmed in white sequins. By this point Miles loomed as a national historic figure, an elder trickster in a jazz world that had few provocations left up its sleeve. One of his dinner companions, a Washington matron, asked him what he had done that was so special. Miles sized her up. "Well, I've changed music five or six times," he said. "Now tell me, what have you done of any importance other than be white?" Abrasive and compact, the remark was classic Miles: a slip of truth-telling in an envelope of talking shit. The truth was that he *had* changed music several times, often for the worse, but that his profile grew more from the skins he sloughed off than the new ones he took on. It took a special man to turn his back on *Kind of Blue*.

Baptized in the early waters of bebop, he built his career by successively walking away from public affections. At the height of bop he blew cool; at the apogee of cool he went hot; in the retrenchment of classic jazz he used drum machines. He seemed to accrue identities, each one hip by association. Looking at Miles in a 1970s dashiki, playing in an electric band, you still heard the cold edges of 1940s Brooks Brothers blowing past. (The late-period leathers and designer sequins are forgiven for this reason.) In a society that assigned black men roles, Miles was a whole cast of his own devising, indifferent to the audience's applause. The conventional wisdom—the body of ideas that hold a society and its members in place—was his lollipop. He spent half a century licking it. Playing against expectations and commercial taste, he forced the past into the present tense: for all his changes, when you heard 1969's *Bitches Brew,* for example, you also heard echoes of 1954's *'Round About Midnight.*

From our perspective now, when the Woodstock era runs in rotation on VH1, it is sometimes difficult to see how hip figured into the 1960s, except in holdovers from the decade before. The surges of Miles or Monk, who appeared on the cover of *Time* magazine in 1964, were really echoes of the 1940s and 1950s, vestiges of a coolness that was on its way out. Bob Dylan seemed to triumph not with the 1960s but at their expense. His stature as hipster icon begins when he rejected the folk revival, one of the decade's defining movements. He lurched forward, instead, into an echo of 1950s rock and roll—exactly what folk had sought to replace. Muhammad Ali, similarly, seemed to jump from Kennedy-era Cassius Clay to 1970s-style black power without passing through the integration rhetoric and anthems of the 1960s civil rights movement. Like Miles, both seemed out of time.

But really Dylan and Ali embodied the energy of the decade, the promise of change. To the reinventions and nonconformity of the Beats and beboppers, the 1960s added hope and the numerical strength of the baby boom. Dylan and Ali, appropriately, emerged as tricksters of the shape-shift. Like Miles, they turned their backs not on their era but on themselves. Born less than a year apart (Zimmerman in May 1941, Clay in January 1942), they belonged to the first generation to experience itself through the mass electronic media, which built possibilities for reinvention into the circuitry. The province of tricksters is disruption, and the electronic media, which could broadcast images of Watts or My Lai across the country in the same instant, disrupted everything that went through them. The war and the hydrogen bomb portended monstrous change imposed from the top down. Tricksters like Dylan and Ali suggested the possibility of reinvention from the bottom up.

I have said that tricksters teach through their deceptions, but they also learn from them. The lies of Hermes on Mount Olympus or the Signifying Monkey down in the jungle begin in awareness of the difference between things and words. This is the root of humor, in which one word or image stands for two or more things. Tricksters teach this awareness even to their adversaries, often the hard way. In the ongoing battles between the Signifying Monkey and the Lion, sometimes the Monkey wins, and sometimes the Lion gets hip. They are locked in a kind of intellectual arms race, getting wiser with each version of the tale. This is how cultures grow from disorder. (In the same way, the people seeking ways to download free music will always be hipper than the people trying to stop them; readers of the Signifying Monkey canon will bet on the sharers, not the leonine labels, to prevail.) Their battles, then, are places of learning and growth. Hip circulates the lessons of these disruptions.

Ali and Dylan arrived in a pop world that considered mass spectacle to be of a low order, and through their darting intelligence they flipped the script. The son of a middle-class sign painter in Louisville, Kentucky, Cassius Marcellus Clay was born into an era when black athletes fit themselves to nonthreatening roles. Joe Louis, the heavyweight champion, made a point not to stand over his white victims or be photographed with white women. Jackie Robinson, a proud warrior of a man, swallowed untold insult and physical abuse after joining the Brooklyn Dodgers in 1947. For his perseverance, Malcolm X belittled Robinson as "the white man's hero," but when many Americans, white and black, turned against a newly christened Muhammad Ali in 1964, Robinson urged the country to celebrate the champion and accept his religion. Robinson and Joe Louis had loosened racial myths through their steadfast virtue; the next step of learning required a trickster.

Ali changed roles and taunted the public to keep up. He played the dozens and sported with white reporters, many of whom did not approve. In a sport that celebrated pure brawn, he was a mind game. After his shocking 1964 upset of Sonny Liston, he explained to Alex Haley that Liston was cooked "before he ever got in the ring with me." His conversion to the Nation of Islam after the fight put Ali outside the mainstream of black American faith but deeper into the psychic heart. Boxing's stakes were no longer defined by the purses of white promoters. His bouts were morality plays addressing higher issues. When he refused the draft for the Vietnam War, Ali lined up his contradictions: he was a paid punisher refusing the violence of war; a beautiful face in an arena that mauled beauty; a lively mind in a sport that hid mind behind muscle. Ali played in the seams of racial myth, rejecting first the nonviolent civil rights movement and later the Nation of Islam itself. He continued to change, disturbing the expectations by which white supremacy held itself up. As Cassius Clay once said, before he became Muhammad Ali, "If the fans think I can do everything I say I can do, then they're crazier than I am." Like the magicians of the blues, he had a sense of humor that inspired dead seriousness. Ali never resolved these paradoxes. Their fullness was his trickster gift to the world.

Robert Allen Zimmerman, from Hibbing, Minnesota, worked the trickster's changes from the other side. The son of an appliance merchant, he hit the folk revival of the early 1960s like a self-made wastrel. Like Ali, he was smarter and funnier than his peers, faster with the put-down or put-on, and more ambitious. He wanted things no one could have known existed. The folk revival, which grew on college campuses and coffee shops, was a romantic movement against the commercialism that rock and roll embodied. It introduced young baby boomers to the ideas of the new left and to the blues. Its mission, articulated through countless authentic Child ballads and genuine cotton peasant blouses, was a return to authenticity, away from the pop music machinery. Dylan saw the movement as a means to self-invention, the most personal form of artifice. Romantic and ambitious, in a scene where these two values were bad chemistry, he remade himself first in the Minneapolis neighborhood of Dinkytown and then, starting in 1961, in the folk clubs of Greenwich Village.

He absorbed the folk myths too well, plucking from their authentic archetypes a series of inauthentic identities. He told people he was a hobo, a drifter, a motherless child, a carny tramp—any version of the *real deal*. Like tricksters past, he played with the difference between the word and the thing, saying one thing and doing another. He stole albums from the folk collector Jon Pankake in Minneapolis and borrowed tunes and arrangements from elders in Greenwich Village. When the folksinger Jean Ritchie sought credit for the melody to "Masters of War," which she said he had lifted from one of her arrangements, his lawyers instead paid her $5,000 and kept Dylan's reputation intact. Even as recently as his 2001 *Love and Theft* album, Dylanologists found a dozen passages that (harmlessly) mirrored lines from a Japanese gangster book, *Confessions of a Yakuza*.

Yet in his masks there has been genius and humor, a sense of the possible. He has consistently improved whatever he stole, and his lies have been more revealing than the truth. Dylan came to the public as a vortex of selfishness with a carefully hidden self. He freed the characters of archaic America—Sweet Marie, the Jack of Hearts, Mrs. Henry, Napoleon in rags—into the screech of rock and roll, deepening both in the process. As Emerson said, he captured the ancient in the modern, singing the past in the hip present tense. His cons had history; they bore more meaning than the pious verities of folk music or the vainglorious inventions of rock and roll. Long after famously shocking the easily shocked by playing electric at Newport in 1965, he has continued to confound expectations, evolving through various religious conversions and guises. He now sings a layered ballad of mortality and adult love. As ever, the truth you can trust is not in his words but in his astringent voice, which always means more than it says.

A robust society produces ideas contrary to its own wisdom, because only by these can it learn and grow. It tweaks its own authority. The tricksters in this chapter, who all seemed like monkey wrenches in the gears of American progress, in reality helped make the machine go. Middle Eastern scholars like Bernard Lewis argue that the Islamic world, once a leader in art and technology, lost its edge when it repressed contradictory ideas, particularly those of women. It shut itself off from the outside. The United States, by contrast, thrived because of its cacophony of ideas—not a melting pot but an unmelted melee. Its noise is the sound of growth.

Like humor or the blues, hip is a system of order that incorporates chaos. It refutes purity. It calls out the African element in the pale man, and the unseen European in his darker neighbor. If the result is chaos, it is also intellectual growth. As children, we are taught to learn from our mistakes, meaning that once we suffer the consequences we won't make the same error again. But for societies, the errors *are* the learning: having confounded the conventional wisdom, we learn that it was flawed to begin with. Organisms evolve through accidents, or dissonance in the DNA; societies evolve through dissonance in the public imagination. Often frowned upon by the gods or elders, tricksters upset the ideologies by which cultures bog.

The role of tricksters is to introduce contradiction. Hip's role is to circulate this contradiction and validate its authors—hip is the incentive for making trouble. In *Trickster Makes This World,* Hyde argues that this learning, which incorporates the chaos of outside ideas, is a true escape from unreality—not toward misrule but toward truer order. "[M]aybe it is not the trickster who is unruly; maybe our own rules and need for order are the true authors of misrule and cruelty," he writes. "The prophetic trickster points toward what is actually happening: the muddiness, the ambiguity, the noise. They are part of the real, not something to be filtered out." Tricksters chase away the naïveté that believes in life without ambiguity. The people who built America had a word for this stripping of illusion. The word was *hepi* or *hipi,* to see or open one's eyes. It is the beginning and end of hip.

8 hip has three fingers

the miseducation of bugs bunny

> People have a reluctant admiration for those that don't obey the rules and do so gracefully. And Bugs is graceful. —CHUCK JONES

In 1938, a group of animators working in an infested bungalow they dubbed Termite Terrace created a frisky icon of wiseass urban cool. Named for one of his first designers, Ben "Bugs" Hardaway, the new character was part Brooklyn hipster, part Groucho manqué, part animal trickster. And, of course, he was all wascally wabbit. In a genre where characters defined themselves in blinding action, Bugs was pure consciousness. He made his debut in circumstances of grave danger, calmly seeking enlightenment, as any hipster would. Staring down the barrel of a gun, he uttered his first words: "Eh, what's up, doc?"

The animated cartoon, which took root in the American imagination in the same years as the first blues and jazz recordings, was a vehicle for hip like no other. Everybody saw them; they were the folklore of 20th-century America. And what they communicated, in deceptively simple form, was a poetics of hip. For millions, they were the first taste of hip as a national, unifying set of directions. They made sassing authority a sport. Cartoons posed a universe organized around misrule, an unreality that provided escape from the unreality around them. Conceived in parallel with the Jazz Age and Harlem Renaissance, early cartoons drew together the sexual propulsion of jazz, the humor of the blues and the deadpan cynicism of pulp, in ways that would have been impermissible in live action or print, to say nothing of real life. They were relentlessly modern, as new as the celluloid they were drawn on. And their voice was that of the wise primitive. "It's preliterate thinking," says the comic artist Art Spiegelman, whose graphic novel *Maus* recast his father's experience during the Holocaust. "As much as philosophers would like to think otherwise, we think in cartoons. We're all kids that way. This makes the cartoon seem charged and dangerous, and it is. That just means you have to treat it with respect."

Created as adjuncts to movies or vaudeville revues, early cartoons began in primal misbehavior. They were not for kids. The six- or seven-minute outbursts played with hip's underlying anxieties: the unreal lines of race, class, sex, ethnicity, power, righteousness and the hep-daddy zest of jazz. Felix the Cat, created in 1919 by Otto Mesmer, got drunk, chased white females, danced to jazz and bent the rules of physics. Cartoons speak the unspeakable. Time, space, gravity, solidity, and essence all yield to the needs of rhythm. Cats cavort with dogs, eyeballs spring like erections at the sight of curvy rodents, men turn into hounds salivating after Betty's boop. Everything is negotiable, a hustle. By their nature cartoons are against nature.

For a country that liked to erase its past, cartoons explored the absurdity of an untethered present. If someone thwacked Sylvester the Cat on the noggin with a frying pan, he might assume the shape of the skillet, but he would not carry the trauma into years of therapy, or even into the next violent scene. The past does not continue into the present. Cartoons connect physical non sequiturs as they sever time. Popeye can become a propeller or a ton of bricks, but he cannot develop as a character. This discontinuity is essentially amoral; if even catastrophic injuries are fleeting, so must be the values we apply to them. These values run counter to ruling institutions, which stand on continuity. Instead, cartoons play out the nonhierarchical rule of rhythm. They give rhythm a look and meaning. The square hand-wringing over cause and effect, vital to courtrooms and other halls of governance, gets left behind by cartoons' manic sprint. Rhythm, after all, starts anew—innocent, free—with each repeating downbeat. It is the cause or effect only of itself.

In place of character growth, animation cast its lot with another essential strain of the American character, the one that led out of Puritanism and into hip. The hipster hero, from Huck Finn to Snoop Dogg, is a comic rebel. His laughter is serious business. Max Eastman, the Village bohemian and critic, noted that Americans had from the start conceived their myths as a goof. The new nation's folk legends, like Paul Bunyan, Davy Crockett and Pecos Bill, had none of the gravitas of their counterparts on Olympus, but they had far better comic timing. They were cartoons waiting for someone to hand them a frying pan. "All mythical heroes have been exaggerations, but they have been serious ones," Eastman wrote. "America came too late for that. Her demigods were born in laughter; they are consciously preposterous; they are cockalorum demigods. That is the natively American thing—not that her primitive humor is exaggerative, but that her primitive exaggerations were humorous." When the nation looked into a mirror, the reflection it saw was the funhouse face of a trickster.

Cartoons fulfilled this lore, creating an America of uncivil disobedience. In a 1920s culture buffeted by mechanization, urbanization and war, cartoons treated mayhem and discontinuity as entertainment. Since order could no longer keep up with the speed of life, animation made speed itself a principle of order, and made disorder the status quo. Anxiety was the medium's putty. Before regulators clamped down on sex and later violence, animators projected their polymorphous perversities across the screen. Sex—interracial, interspecies, what have you—rippled through the action. Seamus Culhane, who worked on Betty Boop in the 1920s, recalled the array of vice that went into the pert, no-necked vixen. On Saturdays, he wrote, the animators

> gathered for a weekly bout of sex, drinking and bridge with a bevy of whores from a local bordello. Monday mornings were always the time for box scores of the previous weekend's exploits—alcoholic, sexual, and bridge playing—with an extra fillip of stories about the seamy side of Harlem. . . . When women were thought of in terms like "quiff," "snatch," and "gash," a la Studs Lonigan, there was no possibility of a story being written where Betty Boop used her charms in a light, flirtatious manner.

Betty was a "good" girl with a hymen like a boiler plate, and her sex life would never be more than a series of attacks on that virginity by unpleasant characters with heavy hands.

All of this mischief came to a head in Bugs Bunny. He set the principled rebellion of Emerson and Thoreau in a landscape of outrageous violence, shaped by a theology of humor and payback. "The only god I ever relied on was Mark Twain," Chuck Jones, who directed many of the great Bugs shorts, told me in 2001, about a year before his death. "I read *Huckleberry Finn* every year for 80 years. If you do that you're either a fool or you're going to learn something about morality. But yet today people are still harping about that." Bugs was all sentience and performance, talking back to the animators or speaking directly to his audience, playing with the frame of the cartoon. He had an unlimited vocabulary of revenge, often gratuitous. In the 1946 short *The Big Snooze*, for example, after doping Elmer Fudd with sleeping pills, he swallowed a dose so he could torment Elmer in his dreams. In other cartoons, he became female to tease his pursuers sexually. A primer for hipsters, the Bugs cartoons made style a metaphor for mind. Bugs himself navigated the gulfs between high culture and low, male and female, power and

Betty Boop

sass, ultimately unseating Disney's more domesticated, less jazzy mouse as the face of America around the world. At its most populist, American hip circulated at the end of a carrot, in the rebellious, stylized, blue-collar vowels of a bunny who thought the base after second was toid.

Though he lived in the country, Bugs was unmistakably a creature of the modern city. He was scrappy, wise, ethnic. The accent and the action around him reflected the jitters and jump of an urbanizing society. Beneath the play of cutely drawn animals, cartoons explored the meaning of race and ethnicity from angles other media could not. In a world without certainties, identity and its contents were up for grabs.

I began this history with the year 1619, when Africans and Europeans came together on unfamiliar soil and started to remake themselves as Americans. This collision forms the basis of hip, the story hip has to tell. It is a story of synthesis in the context of separation. Though whites and blacks have borrowed from each other, the dance is by no means symmetrical. In part, the tilt follows from the inequities of slavery. But it also reflects a deeper cultural difference. Cultures borrow and process differently. Ishmael Reed described the difference in a 1984 interview: "The thing about the [African] voodoo aesthetic," he said, "is that it's multicultural and can absorb, while the [Euro] settler thing is monotheistic and nonabsorptive. In other words, if you're not on my side, I can do anything I want to do with you." The distinction can be seen in the difference between minstrelsy and the blues, hip's twined root stems. In minstrel shows, white performers and audiences kept blackness at a distance— something to be ogled or painted on, but not mixed with other parts of their lives. Minstrel performance did not reveal the man behind the mask, and it washed off with the burnt cork. In the blues, black performers integrated Western instruments and language into something wholly their own and new, which both revealed and empowered the men playing it. Minstrelsy longed for a past in which racial categories were unambiguous; the blues created a present in which they were blurred.

Hip's history follows in the path of this asymmetry. Jack Kerouac's wish to step inside black skin in order to find "enough life, joy, kicks, darkness, music, . . . enough night," highlights the limits of cultural borrowing, at least in one direction. He felt he had to go outside himself to make an authentic connection. The white boys who stole the blues, from Al Jolson to Eminem, similarly straddle black and white traditions like unconnected continents, lacking a framework to fold one into the other. Eminem dramatizes the tensions between the two, rhyming about his white trash roots and the commercial advantages of his white skin. He is fascinating in his internal jostle. Jolson, a Jewish immigrant who dominated the minstrel stage in the 1910s and 1920s, did not develop a self behind the mask, and when real black faces pushed him off the stage, he had no other face to show the public. Where Ellington or Miles Davis seamlessly incorporated elements from all over, Jolson needed cork to feel at home in the blues.

Early cartoons, created almost exclusively by white animators, rewrote the rules for cultural borrowing. In the crazed illogic of the seven-minute short, everything was up for grabs. As swelling cities of the 1920s pushed together blacks with whites, and waves of immigrants from all over, the new medium gobbled up whatever came its way, bending all to its own plastic needs. It was absorptive and polytheistic, full of sprites and tricksters, endlessly shifting shape. If it was not smoothly integrative like spirituals or the blues, it was kitchen-sink inclusive like digital sampling. Cartoons did not respect the boundaries of identity; they thrived on discontinuities. Like young Irving Berlin and the other singing waiters at Nigger Mike's, who flipped from one ethnic caricature to another, early cartoons treated ethnicity as a playground that was navigable and elastic, and always part of the human performance. Not all stereotypes were equal. During World War II, animators filled their cartoons with the most hateful caricatures of Japanese. Black stereotypes ranged from demeaning Sambo figures to frankly admiring (if ill-informed) portraits of urban hipsters. They reinforced stereotypes even as they bent them literally out of shape.

Race and ethnicity were perfect material for animation: they were real and unreal, as thin and contingent as a veneer of greasepaint. The first American animated short, James Stuart Blackton's *Humorous Phases of a Funny Face* (1906), ends with the words "Cohen" and "Coon" morphing into Jewish and African-American caricatures. The medium had a certain racial play built into it. In the early days, black characters were simply easier to animate than white ones. Mickey Mouse, created in 1928, was a

solid black mass, accessorized with the white gloves of a minstrel performer. Early cartoons rippled with minstrel connections. When Mickey made his debut in *Steamboat Willie,* the first synchronized sound cartoon, it was to the minstrel anthem "Turkey in the Straw," also known as "Zip Coon." Leon Schlesinger, the producer of Merrie Melodies and Looney Tunes, had his own tie to minstrelsy. After he invested in the 1927 Warner Brothers film *The Jazz Singer,* which starred Jolson in and out of blackface, Jack Warner agreed to distribute Schlesinger's cartoons, putting them in all of Warner's theaters. In exchange, Schlesinger agreed to use the cartoons to plug songs from the Warner musicals. The animators' first lead character was a slow-witted minstrel figure named Bosko. By his second short, *Congo Jazz* (1930), Bosko was in the jungle, discovering the primitive roots of jazz.

It goes without saying that much of the stereotyping was degrading, even where putatively affectionate. An early instruction manual for animators advised that "the colored people are good subjects for action pictures: They are natural born humorists and will often assume ridiculous attitudes or say side-splitting things with no apparent intention of being funny. . . . The cartoonist usually plays on the colored man's love of loud clothes, watermelon, crap shooting, fear of ghosts, etc." In many cartoons blacks carried razors, dice and libidos the size of automobiles. Even if they were not intended to be malicious, these stereotypes are the gentle kiss of white supremacy. As Henry Louis Gates Jr. has written, "Afro-American history is full of examples of 'racist' benevolence, paternalism and sexual attraction which are not always, or only, dependent upon contempt or aggression. . . . 'Skip, sing me one of those old Negro spirituals that you people love so dear,' or 'You people sure can *dance*. . . .' These are racist statements, certainly, which can have rather little to do with aggression or contempt in *intent*, even if the effect is contemptible (but often 'well intentioned')." Hip is not above this patronizing racism.

But like other outlets for racial fantasy and anxiety, cartoons carried more than just derision. As Chuck Jones counseled, to be a good animator, "You must love what you caricature." Hip requires the possibility of self-invention, a rebellion against the idea of fate. Cartoons made ethnicity a term of this rebellion. Without continuity of time, cartoon characters are essentially unstable. They can change shape at the drop of a frying pan. Animators relied on ethnicity to hold identity at least partly in place. The idea is that a wily coyote might turn into a rocket, but the meaning of, say, *black* was constant. Animators piled on ethnicity to define their characters from scene to scene. Early Betty Boop cartoons draped the heroine in Jewish imagery—for example, her speedometer reads in Hebrew—as she defended her maidenhood in a world of horny Cab Calloway hipsters. The effect was not just to fix the characters but, in the other direction, to turn ethnicity loose, *signifying* on the fixed myths of race. When the characters changed shape, even the most ossified racial templates were forced to change with them. Inbred hicks, violent micks, oleaginous wops, Old World hebes, outer borough sharpies and an erotomaniacal French skunk named Pepe LePew all played out the frenetic anxieties of a new urban society.

Within this tangle of ethnicity lay an animated ideal of hip. Much of this book has followed the evolution of jazz and blues, from field hollers to the birth of the cool, along with the parallel evolution of hip. But hip and music are not the same. Wynton Marsalis, who can blow circles around most jazzmen, past or present, is no one's model hipster; Miles

Davis even in his awful periods had hip to spare. Hip works at one re-move. It is enlightenment set to rhythm, not rhythm itself. You cannot capture hip in time signatures or modal scales. It is an attitude within music that can then be applied *musically* toward the rest of life. Ditto with fashion and literature. Living in rhythm—sonic, visual, intellectual, philosophical—is an essential promise of hip. In the 1920s and 1930s, as animation was finding its stride, jazz was blossoming as the sound of American urban modernism. Jazz splintered time into discontinuous fragments, beginning it anew with each rhythmic return. Cartoons frol-icked with the shards. They were not jazz but outlets for a jazz attitude; they defined their worlds by this attitude. Jazz meant freedom, smarts, ur-banity and elasticity. As long as the director Bob Clampett felt the way he did about jazz, Elmer Fudd would never get the better of Bugs.

Like many hip phenomena, the collision of jazz and animation grew as an unintended consequence of new technology. As a manifestation of newness, hip leaps on technological change and shapes itself to the new dope. In the silent era, feature films relied heavily on music. Count Basie and Fats Waller, for example, began their careers playing piano or organ at movie houses. The arrival of recorded dialog in *The Jazz Singer* pushed musicians out of movie theaters, where they were suddenly in the way. Cartoons took up the slack. Early audiences found cartoon di-alog distracting; music suited the action better. Even the first color talk-ing cartoon, Walter Lantz's animated opening to the 1930 feature film *The King of Jazz,* was mostly musical. It featured Paul Whiteman as a great white hunter coaxing jazz syncopations out of an African jungle. Appropriately, a signifying monkey brains him in the head with a co-conut—proof that the world needs more tricksters, not fewer. But the monkey's victory is fleeting. The lump from the coconut swells up in the shape of a crown, allowing Whiteman to convert the trickster's creativ-ity and derision to his own glory, which is pretty much what happened offscreen as well.

Though Schlesinger's studio in particular plugged songs, cartoons did not content themselves with *presenting* music. Like hip, they projected an attitude toward it, then wrapped the action around this attitude. The snark of Bugs Bunny is inseparable from the stylistic leaps of Carl Stalling's jazz-inflected scores. Dialog could be spare or nonexistent.

Compare the musical numbers in a Bowery Boys movie with the crazed jump of a short like *Betty Boop's Snow White* (1933), in which a roto-scoped Cab Calloway turns his body inside out while singing "St. James Infirmary" as ghouls shoot craps. He ultimately becomes a $20 gold piece, a transubstantiation into bling bling. In the Bowery Boys films, every-thing stopped awkwardly for the musical numbers. In the Boop cartoon, Cab's song drives the action. It provides an entire aesthetic of hip: fast, urban, irreverent and racially hotwired.

This value system divided the hip from the square. Hip thrives when it has a nemesis, and for the animators who watched the rise of Walter Elias Disney in the late 1920s, that nemesis was Walt. Ever shaped by his upbringing in Kansas City, Disney steered his studio toward heartland values. The humor was rural, the stories family-friendly, especially once the studio became dependent on royalties from Mickey Mouse products in the 1930s. The technical skills were awesome. But as a cat, the mouse did not swing. Where animators like the Fleischer brothers, who created Popeye and Betty Boop, improvised a lot of their story lines, shadowing the jazz improvisers who powered their films, Disney standardized its methods to remove all room for wiggle. Disney animators wrote every line of dialog in advance, then drew the animation to the script. It was a top-down organization. The Fleischers used a more unpredictable, chaotic system known as post-synching, or drawing the action first, then writing dialog to fit. Like a jazz soloist, they could improvise whatever ac-tion they wanted. The two studios offered competing visions of America, with rhythm as one term in the competition. Disney was as American as the heartland; the Fleischers, five sons of an immigrant Jewish tailor, were as American as jazz.

Fitting for a company that would not hire blacks or Jews, the play of ethnicity in Disney cartoons was circumscribed. It lacked the imaginative freedom that animators had at other studios. When Disney got ethnic, as in the blackface sequences of *Fantasia* and the long-withdrawn *Song of the South,* or in rabid anti-Japanese propaganda during World War II, the fantasies were flat and harsh, without the ambivalence that runs through-out this book. This was stereotyping without curiosity, theft without love; Disney's ethnic stereotypes silenced ethnicity.

Schlesinger's crew at Termite Terrace, forced to work on much tighter budgets than their Disney rivals, defined themselves as the anti-Disney. Where Disney budgets could reach as high as $100,000 in the 1930s, Warner shorts came in at around $9,000, including Schlesinger's cut. As Jones said, "Disney was making Rolls Royces, we were making Model T Fords." But oh, what fun you could have in a Model T. The Warner characters drank booze and fired guns. Bugs changed genders. His attitude reflected the animators' bungalow, of which Schlesinger once remarked, "I wouldn't work in a shit-hole like this." Carl Stalling, a Kansas City native who got his start with Disney, composed scores to mirror the twisted logic of the action, moving from jazz to popular tunes at the speed of a roadrunner. The animators—including Jones, Clampett, Fred "Tex" Avery and Isidore "Friz" Freleng—drew from their grievances with Schlesinger, whom they regarded as a venal skinflint. "We never previewed [ideas] for Schlesinger because he wouldn't have understood them," said Jones, 89 at the time. "And he didn't want to, anyway, because he would have had to buy us dinner." The wisecrack was everything, not just in the cartoons but in the workplace. Jones once described Schlesinger as "a snazzily dressed Gila monster in a Panama hat," and approvingly quoted a colleague's description of later nemesis Eddie Seltzer as a "man who makes his way through life like an untipped waiter." Schlesinger, for his part, returned the compliment, greeting any new production with the invocation "Roll the garbage!"

From the start, hip put the needle in the relationship between workers and bosses. The Looney Tunes and Merrie Melodies animators fed their class antagonisms onto the screen, creating a hip alternative to the dutiful Walt-ism of Disney. Like pulp lit, the Warner cartoons had a problem with authority. Rebellion came with the medium, for both the animators and the audience. Characters talked back to their creators on-screen. Studio executives, including Schlesinger, appeared in cartoon cameos as craven philistines, anticipating the jibes the Simpsons would later poke at their Fox benefactors. The animators who created Daffy Duck endowed him with a lisp that brazenly resembled Schlesinger's. As they waited to be fired for their insolence, the boss only remarked, "Jeethus Cristh, that's a funny voithe! Where'd you get that voithe?"

The baldest rebuke to Disney, and one of the most controversial, is

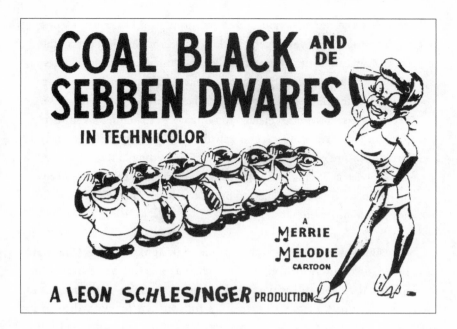

Bob Clampett's *Coal Black and de Sebben Dwarfs* (1943), an all-black parody of Disney's hugely successful 1937 feature film, *Snow White and the Seven Dwarfs,* frenetically set to a jumping jazz score. Though it has long since been removed from circulation as racially insensitive, its name resurfaces any time animators are asked to list the best cartoons ever. No cartoon could be less Disney or more devoted to the urbanity of hip. Like all hip fare, *Coal Black* teases at a submerged truth, one everyone knows and does not know: that *Snow White,* too, was a tale of ethnicity and racial purity.

Clampett was a jazz hound, and he recognized that like God, hip is in the details. To get the right feel, he took his animators to the jazz clubs of Los Angeles's Central Avenue, the heart of the black downtown. Though the West Coast jazz scene really got its due in the 1950s and 1960s with the cool school, Central Avenue had been an extraordinarily rich jazz mecca much earlier. New Orleans stalwarts King Oliver, Jelly Roll Morton and Freddie Keppard went to the West Coast even before they went to Chicago. Central Avenue was a petri dish of hip. The reed player and guitarist Jack Kelson remembered the Dunbar Hotel as "the hippest, most intimate" spot for all the sportsmen on the strip.

I've never seen more glamour anywhere in the world than in that one spot. Because, even if you weren't working and if you were just part of the group, it was almost mandatory that you were sharp. Beautiful clothes, tailor-made clothes, beautiful suits and socks. And that was the day when men had their hair gassed or processed, whatever word you want to use. Everybody was just immaculately, you might say, splendiferous in their appearance. . . . There was Stepin Fetchit with his long white Auburn-Cord or Packard or whatever it was, with a lion sitting in the back. That wasn't far-fetched. That was just one of the things that you were lucky enough to see if you happened to be on the street when he decided to drive down the street.

Such sights were manna to the animated imagination. On Clampett's club crawl, the animator Virgil Ross watched a loose-limbed dancer swing his leg over the head of his partner. Ross used the man as the model for Coal Black's suitor, Prince Chawmin', a full-on hepster with dice in his teeth and a zoot suit for days. This was far from the countrified loll of minstrelsy. Dorothy Dandridge's sister Vivian provided the sex kitten voice of Coal Black, and Louis Armstrong expressed interest in the part of the jitterbugging Prince Chawmin', according to Bob Clampett Jr. When Armstrong's schedule conflicted, the actor Zoot Watson did the honors. Brilliantly paced and syncopated, the cartoon is a whirl of rhythm and sex. When one of the dwarves kisses the heroine, her pigtails explode in orgasmic fireworks.

Coal Black represented animation at its most animated, but it could not last. When cartoons moved from theaters to television in the 1950s, their meaning changed. Now they were for children, harmless sugar for the developing imagination. On television, advertisers held sway. Walter Lantz, who created Woody Woodpecker, complained that he was forced to delete all references to black characters, booze and a lot of the violence. Often cartoons that were made for the big screen ran on television with key scenes removed, replacing their careful suspension of logic with a sloppy, haphazard one.

Yet it was as children's fare that cartoons did most of their damage. The history of hip is one of unsought collisions, and few held more wild cards than that of cartoons and kids. Earlier I compared cartoons to folklore—or, as Art Spiegelman said, to preliterate thinking—and on the retinas of children this became literally the case. Children who could not name the nation's founding fathers could map the conflicts of Sylvester and Tweety, Popeye and Bluto, Red Hot Riding Hood and the zoot-suited wolf. The sexual, violent and racial fantasies of adults, perpetrated in a medium that defied morality, became the province of children. How marvelously inappropriate. In the same way that children on a plantation lived in a culturally richer, less circumscribed world than their parents, cartoons let children in on the secrets their parents could not speak. They prepared a generation to receive the enlightenment of hip.

A t the heart of this enlightenment is the sense that all is not licit, that viewers are seeing something they should not. It is not nice to fool with nature. This sense of the illicit is one of hip's connecting strands. It links Woody Woodpecker with Charlie Parker (who used to mimic Woody's laugh on the sax), or Bullwinkle with James Ellroy. And it allows later cartoons like Ralph Bakshi's *Mighty Mouse, The Simpsons* or *South Park* to carry a charge that the rest of sitcom television does not have. They are hip because they open your eyes, because they give license to play among what is otherwise forbidden or impossible.

In the 1980s, in a somewhat deeper foray into the illicit, I testified for the defense in two obscenity trials involving the 2 Live Crew. The group, authors of such hit records as "Me So Horny" and "Dick Almighty," had an iffy claim to hip. But the trials made for brassy theater, showing the fate of even the marginally hip when it falls into the court of the square world. As jurors dutifully listened to lyrics like "Bring that pussy over here, dear," prosecutors and family-values types charged that such rhymes could only have a bad influence on society. The defense argued that the lyrics just reiterated what society was already talking about. Beneath the charges was a subtext of race anxiety: what had once been contained within black communities was seeping into white ones. Hip white kids didn't need to cross the tracks for it anymore; the 'hood came to them, rhymed over tracks of a different sort.

These competing arguments—that society follows art and that art follows society—snake through hip's history, from the ongoing battles over

Huckleberry Finn through the obscenity trials of Ginsberg, Burroughs and Lenny Bruce, and on up to the huffing that surrounds gangsta rap. Cartoons provided steady grist for both sides. Did Bugs (or Bart Simpson) lead his audience into bad behavior, or was he just a reflection of their bad parts? Neither side of the debate is wholly satisfying. If antisocial cartoons or music simply told people what they already knew—that is, if they just regurgitated public tastes—they wouldn't serve much purpose. Artists would be mere stenographers. Conversely, if the work didn't reveal something of the world around it, or ring true to its audience's experiences or desires, it would be purely idiosyncratic. The public would be reduced to a passive host. Either scenario makes one of the parties a nonplayer.

Really the parties conspire together, in a loop that gives each permission to acknowledge the private truths that more decorous art might rise above. Works like *Coal Black* or Lenny Bruce's "To Is a Preposition, Come Is a Verb" resonate not because they mirror society's self-image, but because they poke behind it, picking at appetites the public likes to disavow. This is why the forbidden is alluring. The offending works and the offended public are in cahoots. Where they meet, their interaction does not so much reveal truth as release it.

This conspiracy, which evaporates in the courtroom, flourishes within hip. Moralists have policed much of the sex and violence out of cartoons, but the medium's essential wantonness—defying the boundaries of shape or color—remains untouched. It is vital to our story here. One meaning of hip is *connected,* or aware of what's going on outside your immediate circle. Hip connects inner circles with outer ones; for example, connecting the bop clique with the immediate cult faithful, and the cult with the broader goatee nation. This process involves a romance of the marginal, an acceptance of the unacceptable—not because these are strange, but because they are familiar. They complete the circuit that allows the culture to move forward, unhampered by its nicer beliefs.

Like the mischief of tricksters, the play of the profane imagination, which is really what we are talking about here, works as an engine of growth. The square world could not hit the high notes without it. In the same way that cultures create tricksters to undermine their entrenched values, they also need to create psychic space for the energies that these values repress. The romance of the trickster or the outlaw, which I will discuss in chapter 10, serves as a safe bin for America to keep its baser lusts, which are unacceptable within proper society but essential to that society's formation and growth. The 2 Live Crew or the Warner cartoons of the golden age occupied a similar outsider space, conjured by the public not to repeat its conversations but to animate its silences.

Cartoons provided a uniquely hospitable playground for these transgressions. Animation lives by and for the profane imagination. In the feedback loop between the work and the audience, cartoons take profane license and give it right back. Looked at in period context, cartoons appear to have arisen as an outlet for the anxieties of modernization. Race, ethnicity and machine-age conformity all play out in cartoons. But throughout this story, hip also serves a broader function, distributing values. Cartoons did not stay in period. They were prescient; they looked ahead. Seen broadly by the moviegoing public, they taught skills that were essential to push American society forward: rebellion against authority, distrust of simple stock myths, fluidity of identity, the possibility of reinvention. Like tricksters, cartoons chipped away at the myths and values the society erected to hold it in place. The spirit of change involved both defiance and inquiry. That is, it forever asked the salient question, What's up, doc?

9

the world is a ghetto

blacks, jews and blues

> To me, if you live in New York or any other big city, you are Jewish.
> It doesn't matter even if you're Catholic; if you live in New York
> you're Jewish. If you live in Butte, Montana, you're going to be goy-
> ish even if you're Jewish....
>
> Negroes are all Jews. Italians are all Jews. Irishmen who have
> rejected their religion are Jews. Mouths are very Jewish. And
> bosoms. Baton-twirling is very goyish. Georgie Jessel and Danny
> Thomas are Christians, because if you look closely on their bodies
> you'll find a boil somewhere.   —LENNY BRUCE

> I wanna be black.   —LOU REED

In early 2002 a group of postcollegiate New Yorkers published the first
issue of a magazine called *Heeb: The New Jew Review.* The title was meant
to be mildly confrontational—a twist on what its editors politely called
the N-word, but pulled back a step, beyond real offense. The articles
waxed knowingly about ethnic tropes in the post-*Seinfeld* era, from jew-
fros to kosher lust. But more striking was the cover. The back showed a
white woman cradling a 40-ounce bottle of Olde English malt liquor, one
of her lacquered nails flashing the letters HEEB. On the front cover the

hands of a black DJ worked a turntable, scratching a piece of matzoh instead of a record. The imagery was recognizably African-American, but recast as the stuff of modern Jewish identity.

Discussing the covers a year later, the magazine's publisher, Joshua Neuman, said they "might have been a little minstrel," but that their intent was irony rather than exploitation. He was in a stylish East Village café with *Heeb*'s creative director, Nancy Schwartzman, who ordered a BLT on challah bread—a sandwich in the ethnic spirit of the magazine. Schwartzman, a photographer, was also the model in the 40-ounce photo. As she saw it, the malt liquor and the DJ deck were ethnic chips to be played with, liberated from their accustomed context. The point was not the origins of the imagery but the wit and connectivity of the play. "We had to grab onto what people recognize as cool, which is white people playing on black culture and hip-hop iconography," she said. "We put our spin on it. It worked."

If hip is a story of outsiders, nowhere has its course been richer or more precarious than in the relationship between the country's quintessential outsider groups, African Americans and Jews. Their collisions in the early 20th century, when black migrants from the South poured into the same cities as Jewish immigrants from eastern Europe, defined the American city as a hip hive of ethnicity and back talk. Their exchanges delivered hip to the nation at large. Both were apostles of the hyphen, grafting idioms to create something new and double-jointed, like Yiddish or the blues. Thrown together in ways that have benefited them unequally, and over which they have had unequal say, they brought many of the same hip impulses, including the drive for reinvention, hustle, and a gift for the vernacular. What they didn't share they borrowed. Like the Europeans and Africans who forged America's identity in the 17th and 18th centuries, sharing the word *hipi*, these urban newcomers established their meaning in America through each other in the 20th. They met in another shared word, *ghetto*.

Significant for our story, each arrived in the new urban century as a second-class population within a second-class population, denigrated both by the mainstream and by the establishment of their own ethnic group. The eastern European immigrants were darker, poorer and less educated than the German Jews who came before them. Sharecroppers from the South were scandalous to Harlem society. Both came as outsiders, raw and poor. Their symbioses, often uneasy, opened the channels by which America learned to understand ethnicity and itself: ragtime, blues, jazz, street literature and on up to gangsta rap. Jewish minstrels from this wave of immigrants took over the blackface tradition, working a low hybrid of black culture, and Jewish composers like George Gershwin and Harold Arlen created highbrow (or as the Gershwins said, *Hebrow*) hybrids of jazz. Barred from the high avenues of culture and finance, which looked askance at ethnicity, the two groups established black culture as an engine of identity and profit, and the civil rights movement as the nation's moral conscience.

The forces that drove them together bred a dynamic that has been essential to hip. Theirs was an alliance of the pariah, both within the nation at large and within African-American and Jewish communities. Because of discrimination, talent in either group did not naturally leave the underclass or the waters of low culture. Instead it concentrated there. I don't suggest that racism and anti-Semitism are identical or equal, or that either is impermeable; but they press in the same directions, both downward and inward. Where gifted WASPs from poor families might have been welcomed into the conservatory, the university, the brokerage house and finally into social circles that had little contact with the low or poor, talented African Americans or Jewish immigrants remained in ethnic communities, undesirable businesses and vernacular arts. This downward pressure bred hipness, concentrating it in cacophonous enclaves and in the points where they came together. In these communities, street slang, thug fashion, grimy music and bootstrap hustle—the vehicles of hip—attracted not just the least-gifted members but the most. Against the elites of their own new communities, these groups established low culture and business as the robust, vibrant, ethnically impure home of hip.

Why these two groups, this fraught two-step? What accounts for a 100-year tradition that produced the rag syncopations of Irving Berlin; the "coon" stylings of Al Jolson, Sophie Tucker, Eddie Cantor or Fanny Brice; the jazz hybrids of Arlen and Gershwin, or the purism of Benny Goodman; the rhythm-crazy cartoons of the Fleischer brothers; the blues and soul hustle of Leonard and Phil Chess, Jerry Wexler, Syd Nathan, Art Rupe, Herman Lubinsky and Morris Levy; the classic soul songwriting of

Jerry Wexler and Aretha Franklin

Doc Pomus or Jerry Leiber and Mike Stoller; the "bop kaballah" of Allen Ginsberg or bop comedy of Lenny Bruce; the rap empire building of Rick Rubin, Lyor Cohen, Tom Silverman, Barry Weiss, Steve Rifkind or Bryan Turner; the hip-hop pastiche of the Beastie Boys or Beck?* Wherefore the cross-cultural whammy of the jewfro?

Nor has the influence been all one way. It is a common perception that African Americans created this culture and Jewish middlemen sold it, but the crossovers—the African-American marketing genius and Jewish cre-

---

*Jolson, Tucker, Cantor and Brice were the leading minstrel performers of the 1910s and 1920s; the Chess brothers launched the careers of Muddy Waters, Bo Diddley, Chuck Berry and others on their Chess label; Wexler produced soul hits for Ray Charles, Aretha Franklin and others; Nathan ran King Records, home of James Brown and Hank Ballard; Rupe (nee Arthur Goldberg) introduced the Soul Stirrers (a young Sam Cooke's gospel quartet) and Little Richard on his Specialty Records; Lubinsky recorded Charlie Parker, Dexter Gordon, Fats Navarro and others on his Savoy label; Levy, a gangland character, ran Birdland on 52nd Street and cut jazz and blues on his Roulette label; Pomus (nee Jerome Felder) wrote "Save the Last Dance for Me" and "Lonely Avenue," among others; Leiber and Stoller wrote "Hound Dog" for Big Mama Thornton, plus soul hits for the Coasters, Robins and others; Rubin started Def Jam in his NYU dorm room; Cohen later ran it; Silverman was the eponym of Tommy Boy, home of Afrika Bambaataa, Queen Latifah and others; Weiss launched Jive, home to KRS-One, the Fresh Prince and later Backstreet Boys; Rifkind started Loud Records, home of Wu-Tang Clan; Turner runs Priority, whose acts include Ice Cube, Snoop Dogg and N.W.A.

ative input—loomed larger than is acknowledged. Jackie Wilson idolized Al Jolson and even recorded a tribute album to him. Willie "the Lion" Smith, a founding pillar of jazz piano, peppered his act with Yiddish and said he was part Jewish. Louis Armstrong, who was virtually adopted by a family of Lithuanian Jewish junk peddlers named Karnoffsky, was said to have modeled scat singing—in the song "Heebie Jeebies," no less— after his exposure to Jewish davening. Bop musicians feasted on Gershwin tunes like "I Got Rhythm." George Clinton built his funk epic "Flashlight" on a chant he heard at a bar mitzvah, and Harry Belafonte rarely gives a concert without "Hava Nagila." As he explained, "Life is not worthwhile without it. Most Jews in America learned that song from me." Richard Pryor built on Lenny Bruce's outrageousness, and Spike Lee and Chris Rock inherited the smart, quirky, New Yorky mojo of Woody Allen. And what to say of the recent downtown klezmer revival, sparked by the dreadlocked Don Byron?

Cornel West has linked the two tribes as "the most modern of modern people," joined by persecution and stories of exodus, bearing "tragicomic dispositions toward reality that put sadness, sorrow, and suffering at the center of their plights and predicaments." In its purest form, this shared tragicomic character produced the allegiances of the civil rights movement, in which Jewish and African-American martyrs like Michael Schwerner, Andrew Goodman and James Chaney met the worst of America at each other's side. Jewish activists and philanthropists like Arthur and Joel Springarn and Julius Rosenwald at the turn of the century helped establish the NAACP and National Urban League, and funded more than 5,000 black schools in the South.

But it is the impure syntheses that interest us here. If the story of hip is the triumph of black vernacular—of rhythm as personal code—it cannot be told without accounting for the agencies of hip Jews. Though their role is often simplified to midwife or profiteer, Jews have played a more complicated and creative part in the transit of blackness across American mass culture. When Henry Ford, notorious racist and anti-Semite, denounced his era's "[m]onkey talk, jungle squeals, grunts and squeaks and gasps suggestive of calf love"—in other words, jazz—as "a Jewish creation," he was not wholly wrong. From ragtime to hip-hop, or the Harlem Renaissance to Black Hollywood, Jewish artists and businessmen have had a hand in the look, sound, texture and economies of African-American *getting over*. Some reinvented themselves in the image of their affections. "We thought that we were black," said Mike Stoller, who with Jerry Leiber wrote classic rhythm and blues songs for the Coasters, Big Mama Thornton and others. "We were sometimes disappointed when we passed a mirror."

The journeys of African Americans and Jews share the clash of the city and the fertile self-inventions of hip. Their borrowings could swing as mellifluous as the jazzbo slang word *copasetic* (echoing the Hebrew *kol b'tzedek* or *hakol b'seder,* for "all is justice" or "all is in order"), or as salty as the mouth on the Chicago blues entrepreneur Phil Chess, who with his brother Leonard recorded Muddy Waters, Howlin' Wolf, Chuck Berry, Bo Diddley and others. A Polish Jew who built his business from a liquor store on the black South Side, Phil Chess cussed with a zeal that led one customer to ask, "Is you black or is you white?"

These connections repeat throughout hip's history, suggesting affinities that lie deeper than the surface frictions. When the hip-hop entrepreneur Aaron Fuchs, who founded Tuff City Records, first saw Jackie Wilson at the Apollo Theater in the early 1960s, many of Wilson's moves were already familiar to him from watching his father, a cantor. But more than the moves, the spiritual yearning crossed gaps. "It was the concept of performance as a spiritual thing," Fuchs said. "This wasn't Broadway song and dance. This was really howling at God or the moon, whatever your preference was."

Bigots have historically been only too happy to lump the two minorities together. Voltaire, for example, wrote, "One regards the Jews the same way as one regards the Negroes, as a species of inferior humanity." Their intramural dealings have erupted in charges of black anti-Semitism or Jewish racism, as if bigotry needed such qualifiers. A joke told by African Americans in the early 20th century singled out Jews as the barrier to black progress. At the dawn of creation, the joke went, God was dispensing gifts to representatives from each of the world's races. The Anglo-Saxon asked for political power. The Native American wanted a hunting ground, while the Chinese sought inner peace. The African American asked for a million dollars. Finally God asked the Jew what he wanted. "The address of the Negro you gave the million dollars," he said.

The other part of this connection, the knot of complicity and debt, is harder to talk about. When asked about the Jewish role in rhythm and blues, Jerry Wexler, who produced legendary albums with Aretha Franklin, Ray Charles and countless soul acts, demurred, "That gets very hairy and I'd rather not get into that." Wexler was once hung in effigy at a black music conference, and believes that there was a plot to kill him to protest white control of the music business. Born in New York City to German and Polish Jewish parents, Wexler has gone public about his marital infidelities, his daughter's drug abuse and the reach of payola in the music business. But on the relationship of African Americans and Jews he would not bite. "It opens up too many questionable areas, and I'm not going to fuck with that," he said. "Just stay away."

Of course, it is much neater to view Berlin or the Chess brothers simply as immigrants made good, or hip-hop as the unmediated voice of the inner city. But really the connections and debts go much deeper than these one-dimensional fables. The nuances are more felicitous, and have fed the spread of hip. Bill Adler, a Jewish publicist who worked with Run-D.M.C., Public Enemy, the Beastie Boys and others, found that compared to the white rock world, which was competitive and monocultural, hip-hop was comfortable in its ethnic sprawl. Working for the black hip-hop impresario Russell Simmons, he watched Simmons form partnerships with Jews in his record label (Def Jam) and clothing lines (Phat Farm), often after wealthy African Americans or mainstream corporations had declined. Adler, whom Henry Louis Gates Jr. once called the blackest white man in New York, steered away from the stereotype of Jews as middlemen. "Are black folks saving nerdy Jews with their hipness?" he asked. "Sure. They can save *anyone*. But sometimes I think Jews have a tribal genius for appreciating what blacks have to offer. Of course, some Jews— like some blacks—refuse to tune in. What can you do? They're just constitutionally square." The story that Wexler shies from began before his birth; its syncopations run through hip's long history.

Hip's evolution follows definitions of race, which are subject to shift and reappraisal. These definitions divide people into categories like black or white, in or out. Though the terms seem self-evident, there is nothing natural or fixed about them; they reflect the interests of whoever controls them at a given time. As the African-American radio host Chuck Nice noted in 2002, racial lines can move like the stock market. "Italians," he said, "are niggaz with short memories." In the late 19th and early 20th centuries, changes in immigration and migration within the United States opened the definitions of race in ways that had profound consequences for popular culture and for hip. The catalyst was the arrival of a new contingent of Jews.

The first Jews arrived in America in 1654, just 35 years after the first African slaves. For most of the next two-and-a-half centuries the two populations had little impact on each other's lives. Some Jews owned slaves, but in no greater proportion than other whites; nor were Jews especially prominent in the abolition movement. The first trickle of Jewish immigrants, mostly from Germany and other parts of western Europe, assimilated into American city life. The Jews who began moving to Harlem in the 1870s, for example, were largely middle class, conservative, analogous to the African-American professionals who later inherited the neighborhood's tonier districts.

This mix changed in the next decades. The assassination of Czar Alexander II in 1881 set off pogroms throughout eastern Europe and Russia, and sent a flood of refugees into the newly established Ellis Island. Between 1880 and 1930, about 2.5 million Jews arrived in the United States, mostly from Russia and eastern Europe. Unlike earlier Jewish immigrants, whose numbers they quickly dwarfed, the newcomers were often extremely poor, uneducated, carrying more embattled tribal identities and new ideas of Marxism and socialism. The Village bohemians of the 1910s and 1920s drew heavily from these arrivals. These immigrants settled in northern cities that were being flooded by another refugee population, southern blacks. Neither was entirely welcome.

For the establishments of both ethnic groups, the newcomers presented an image problem. An 1894 article in *American Hebrew* described the new immigrants as "miserable darkened Hebrews" who were "in a stage of development pitifully low." These immigrants, the article continued, were "almost as peculiar among Jews generally as the race is singular among mankind." Both their numbers and their complexions set the new Jewish immigrants apart. Often swarthy and dark-haired, they were neither as white as the "Nordic" ideal favored by pseudoscience of the era nor as dark as the Africans or Native Americans who preceded them. Like the rural African-American migrants, who brought their country manners to the city, the eastern European Jews were a despised cohort within a despised cohort, a complication in the fault lines of race.

With some willful obtuseness, I've discussed race in this book in terms of black and white, though of course it is more complicated than that, and the country far richer for it. Hip flows through the holes in these false categories. In the early years of mass Jewish immigration, it was unclear how Jews fit into the racial matrix. Were they a race? A subset of white people? Of nonwhites? In Europe they had been persecuted as a race. For Jewish immigrants at the turn of the century, popular entertainment was ripe for negotiating these questions. Minstrel shows, performed by black and white acts, still held the stage. In New Orleans, Creole musicians, who were themselves a racial hybrid, were mixing musical genres to create the early sounds of jazz. Southern musicians borrowed brass instruments from across the Mexican border, changing the timbre of social music. The son of a former slave, Scott Joplin (ca. 1867–1917), redirected the classical lessons of his German-born piano teacher into ragtime. Mixture was the signature of modernity, and Jewish entertainers, publishers and impresarios established an identity as masters of the mix.

The story of hip flows from the conjunctions of the city, which provide both protective anonymity and a stage to perform. For young Jewish arrivals around the turn of the century, the route to becoming American—no longer defined by their past or their parents—led through the culture of the city's most modern citizens, African Americans. Typical of the newcomers was Israel Baline, better known as Irving Berlin (1888–1989), who arrived in New York from the Russian Pale of Settlement in 1893. He brought only one lasting memory of his native Mohilev, that of the family home being burned to the ground by anti-Semitic marauders. His father, Moses Baline, a cantor, told immigration officials that he was a kosher butcher in order to appear more employable. In the ethnic hothouse of the Lower East Side, young Izzy fled the family's cramped tenement for the streets, where he heard the varied sounds of the American ghetto, including the new rhythms of ragtime and "coon" songs, which were essentially hybrids of ragtime and minstrelsy.

At 14, Berlin left home to sing for nickels and dimes, finding a special affinity for these coon songs. In the flophouses that became his homes, he often signed his name Cooney, and by the time he landed as a singing waiter at Mike Salter's Pelham Café, popularly known as Nigger Mike's, coon songs were just one shade of his ethnic palette. His first composition, "Marie From Sunny Italy," was in an Italian dialect. But it was his coon songs and rags—written on what he called "the nigger keys" of the piano—that made his reputation, prompting accusations that he kept "a little colored boy" in the basement to feed him tunes.

Berlin's experiences and background were far from unique. Asa Yoelson and Hyman (or Chiam) Arluck, better known as Al Jolson and Harold Arlen, were also the children of cantors. Isidore Itzkowitz, who made his rep in burnt cork, did so under the stage name Eddie Cantor, linking the two traditions through his pseudonym. Arlen (1905–1986), whom Ethel Waters once dubbed the "Negro-ist" white man she ever worked with, traced his interest in ragtime and jazz to the cantorial music of his home. Like Aaron Fuchs, the rap executive, Arlen recalled "improvisations of my father's that are just like Louis Armstrong's. . . . He knew nothing about jazz, but there was something in his style that's in the style of jazz musicians." One time Arlen took an Armstrong recording home to his father to get his reaction. "And my father looked at me, and he was stunned," Arlen said. Hearing the black jazzman's phrasing and blue notes, Cantor Arluck asked in Yiddish, "Where did *he* get it?"

By the 1910s this new wave of Jewish immigrants, barred from many businesses and professions, had found an identity through the innovations of African Americans. Jewish performers replaced Irishmen as the leading blackface minstrels. Jewish songwriters, publishers, transcribers and song pluggers established Tin Pan Alley, a clamorous stretch of 28th Street between 5th Avenue and Broadway, on the strength of rags and minstrel songs. At least one house, M. Witmark & Sons, even had a minstrel department that provided gags and blackface makeup along with its sheet music. In an era of racial upheaval and riots, these Jewish appropriations were for many Americans the most accessible windows on black life, however distorting. Jewish performers or middlemen were translators between the races, making virtue of their own ambiguous status. Samson Raphaelson, who wrote the stage version of *The Jazz Singer,* which was a hit before the movie, argued that the Jewish pupils had surpassed their masters. "Jazz is Irving Berlin, Al Jolson, George Gershwin, Sophie Tucker," Raphaelson wrote in 1925. "Jews are determining the nature and scope of jazz more than any other race—more than the Negroes, from whom they have stolen jazz and given it new color and meaning." As Americans debated whether the "miserable darkened Hebrews" were or were not white, these Jewish performers made themselves valuable to the national mainstream as interpreters of blackness. Randolph Bourne in this era called America "not a nationality, but a trans-nationality," and no one embodied this more than the Jewish blackface minstrel. There is of course an asymmetry here. African Americans had little say in these appropriations, nor could they have gained as much by performing in the cantorial tradition.

In his 1988 book, *An Empire of Their Own: How the Jews Invented Hollywood,* Neal Gabler describes how in this same period a clutch of eastern European Jews—the Warner brothers, Adolph Zukor, Marcus Loew, William Fox, Louis B. Mayer—reinvented themselves in the opposite direction, without the weight of ethnicity. In California they traded ethnic identities for whiteface. The myths they created were those of a blandly homogeneous America that embraced them as native sons. "If the Jews were proscribed from entering the real corridors of gentility and status in America, the movies offered an ingenious option," Gabler wrote. "Within the studios and on the screen, the Jews could simply create a new country—an empire of their own, so to speak—one where they would not only be admitted, but would govern as well. They would fabricate their empire in the image of America as they would fabricate themselves in the image of prosperous Americans. . . . Ultimately, by creating their idealized America on the screen, the Jews reinvented the country in the image of their fiction."

Where the Hollywood moguls invented an America without history and ethnicity, Jews in the music world leveraged precisely these fields. Race was not a barrier to their arrival as Americans but an accessory to it. The road to Berlin's "God Bless America" and "White Christmas," in other words, ran through Nigger Mike's and coon songs like "Alexander's Ragtime Band" (the name Alexander was understood to signal a comically pretentious African American). This route represented the hipness of

America's future—an ability to negotiate one's ethnicity or tribe, which for so many Americans was simply the drag of the past. For a nation of immigrants, ethnicity as a fixed quantity represented the old country, the past; ethnicity as a negotiable property represented the future. As the cultural historian Jeffrey Melnick notes, "One reason why ragtime, jazz, and blues came to hold so much cultural energy in the early decades of the twentieth century is that they could incorporate these images of mixture." In identifying with African Americans, and at the same time aligning African-American culture with northern, urban lifestyles, Jews cast themselves as symbolic midwives of American progress.

T his is a curious route to the American Dream. Why would Jews, whether in the music world or the civil rights movement, cast their lots with what James Baldwin called a "minority even more unloved" than themselves? Part of the motivation was money, of course. There was gold in the coon songs. Also, as Cornel West notes, the two groups were bound by a biblical sense of purpose, a literature based on the deliverance of their slave ancestors. And as Arlen observed, there were the shared musical sonorities.

But none of these factors explains the unique involvement of Jews in African American politics and popular culture. Other immigrant groups arrived with blue notes and stories of persecution and oppression. Yet only Jewish immigrants found a route to American acculturation—being accepted, respected and paid—through blackness. The historian Hasia R. Diner argues that for Jews in the early 20th century, taking up African American social causes "not only proved their credentials as Americans, conversant with the imagery of American ideals, but also provided them with a way of showing how useful Judaism could be in America." Even this, however, does not go far enough to account for *Rhapsody in Blue*, let alone the Beastie Boys. Irving Howe suggests an explanation much closer to hip's parameters. When they took over blackface from Irish immigrants, he wrote, "the Jewish performers transformed it into something emotionally richer and more humane. Black became a mask for Jewish expressiveness, with one woe speaking through the voice of another. . . . Blacking their faces seems to have enabled the Jewish performers to reach

Al Jolson *(Hulton Archive/Getty Images)*

a spontaneity and assertiveness in the declaration of their Jewish selves."
The stereotypes, however, remained the same, and it is possible that Jewish involvement prolonged minstrelsy's reign.

Howe's argument is that as a persecuted minority, Jews used their access to African-American idioms not so much to express blackness as to
transmit full-blown Jewish identity within America. This is where the
story of Jews and African Americans meets the arc of hip, where language
means more than it says and the mask reveals as it hides. Howe's reading
of blackface as a channel for Jewish self-expression, rather than a put-on,
applies beyond the minstrel stage to artifacts like Mezz Mezzrow's hipster
memoir, *Really the Blues* (1946), or Beck's 1996 "Where It's At," in which
he raps about "two turntables and a microphone." Like the city itself,
blackface provided cover of anonymity, a chance to express traditional
tribal emotions and still be au courant, hip. According to Howe, the burnt

cork was a code, as cryptic and expressive as urban slang. Its message lay not in the root material but, as with the *Heeb* magazine cover, in the audacity of the play. Jewish immigrants—"rootless cosmopolitans" for whom change was a staple of continuity—could find true tribal expression in the straddle.

This negotiation plays out most vividly in Alan Crosland's 1927 film *The Jazz Singer*. Viewed now, the movie is a revelation. The plot is straightforward ethnic melodrama: In an Orthodox home on the Lower East Side, Jakie Rabinowitz falls in love with the American sounds of ragtime. His father, a cantor, disapproves, and expects Jakie to follow him in the synagogue. After a violent confrontation, Jakie runs away to California, where he sheds his past, changing his name to Jack Robin and taking a shiksa girlfriend. But as he becomes a successful "jazz singer"—actually he sings coon songs—he misses the cathartic power of his father's cantorial music. Though it represents a tradition Jack finds oppressive, this music is more soulful than his shallow stage tunes. When Cantor Rabinowitz falls ill before Yom Kippur, Jack/Jakie has to choose between taking his father's place and pursuing his big break in show biz. The choice is between the past and the future, Judaism and America. After agonizing, he gives a wrenching performance of "Kol Nidre" in the synagogue, then—in a coda added for the movie version—blacks up for an equally histrionic performance of the coon song "Mammy" in the theater.

The movie is now known for its two blackface scenes, which do not come until the end. It is shocking to see Jolson at the dressing room mirror, blithely transforming himself with greasepaint and wig. But the dramatic tension in the movie is about Jews in America, not blackness. It spends more time in Orthodox synagogues, listening to Hebrew worship, than a mainstream movie could today. As represented by Jakie's father, Jewish identity is Old World, oppressive, primitive. It isolates its tribe from America. In a literal sense it is unhip: it resists enlightenment outside its own texts. For Jolson and for the film, this means duty without pleasure. Yet at the same time he would not wholly relinquish it. Its sonorities enrich him even when he sings coon songs. The finale, "Mammy," is a song of yearning for a lost southern homeland, and you can hear Jolson (who was in real life the son of a cantor) reaching for both Alabama and his own native Lithuania.

Forced to choose between America and Judaism, he chooses black-face, which, as Howe wrote, lets him have both. In greasepaint he can finally move forward without sacrificing the soulfulness of his Jewish roots. Ethnicity is not destiny. What's black in the performance is also, in the movie's value system, what is Jewish: the process of improvising race, freeing it from essentialist definitions. In the end he uses blackface to enter modern America without being assimilated into it. He can have his "Kol Nidre" and his "Mammy," too.

Jewish involvement with African-American culture, then, is not only a matter of playing middlemen; in a society divided artificially into myths of black and white, this involvement plays with the *nature* of middle. The middle ground it clears is not blandly diluted, as in the nightmare of assimilation. Instead it offers freedom to move between identities, adopting the most useful aspects of each. It is less clear what African Americans got from this unsought bargain, except perhaps that the alternative was complete invisibility. The *Amsterdam News,* a black-owned Harlem paper, wrote of Jolson that "every colored performer is proud of him," but he was also the nation's most prominent carpetbagger.

For the Jewish interlopers, middle ground allowed negotiation, play-acting, reinvention. This state of in-between, with access to two bodies of knowledge, is the turf of hip enlightenment. Jerry Leiber, whose first language was Yiddish, described his involvement with African-American culture as a narrative of personal fulfillment. "I never felt that I was renting the blues," he said in 2002. "I always felt the blues was my language and my field and my poetry as much as Yiddish. And sometimes even more, because Yiddish was fading and the blues was getting stronger." Where the Hollywood moguls shed ethnic difference, their musical counterparts seized ethnicity as a *process.* It is no accident that American popular music has been more ethnic, and so hipper than movies.

The split consciousness in music's ethnic play is a running element in hip. It is at once presumptuous and self-knowing. "The idea of hip," as Jerry Wexler says, "is that you set yourself apart in terms of discrimination, intelligence and awareness from the rest of the people. But if you don't do it with a certain leavening of irony, you're going to be a preening asshole. You have to have some objectivity. If you start wearing a beret, dark glasses and goatee, and you're serious about it, too bad for you. You have to be tongue-in-cheek and kidding on the square." In the decades after *The Jazz Singer,* as Jewish immigrants were succeeded by their Americanized children, the same drama played out through Jewish closeness to jazz, soul and hip hop. With or without blackface, this process of ethnic self-invention remained vital to the fabric of hip. As Mike Stoller said, referring to a time long after Jolson had become a bad joke, "We felt we were authentic. We were hip. We could be whatever we wanted culturally. We could adopt any culture that we felt was superior."

This logic links knowledge with license: if you're hip enough to get an aesthetic, you can claim it for your own. It is a precursor to digital sampling, which allows users to command sounds by virtue of curiosity, not expertise. In both cases the folks who were sampled have cried foul.

I n the 1950s, a few years after his first hits, Muddy Waters gave an interview to the African-American newspaper *Louisville Defender* in which he counted his blessings. "The first was that a friendship developed between Leonard Chess and myself for which I wouldn't take a million dollars," he said. "[W]e became more than business associates, real intimate friends." Years later, talking to the journalist Robert Palmer, Muddy again praised Leonard, adding, "I didn't even sign no contract with him, no nothing. It was just 'I belongs to the Chess family.' " The first remark is a story about the drive of modernity, the way hip's combination of aesthetics and ambition crosses lines of race. A poor immigrant Jew and a poorer Delta field hand conspired to unleash music that was electric and primal, urban and country, as absorbent as the men who released it. The product was hip, and spread the gospel around the country; the process, which combined the enlightenment of two despised minority groups, was even hipper. The conspirators completed each other.

The second remark, about belonging to the Chess family, is a throwback to the relationships of the plantation, a reminder that past injustices are not safely in the past. Instead they repeat. These inequities haunt hip's conceit of a continuous present tense, which feigns to overlook history. They fester in the semiregulated zones of the minority music business. The complaints against the Chess brothers were legendary but also common in the industry. When Waters sued the label and its publishing company and regained the rights to his songs, he was one of several artists to do so.

The story of Jews and the blues is inseparable from the shadow of exploitation. If hip begins in an asymmetric encounter between Africans and Europeans, it continues in this asymmetry. The enlightenment passed back and forth is powerful and valuable, unequally for the two sides. While music put money in the musicians' pockets, the business often still separated them from the real fruits of their labor. As early as 1898, the African-American composer Will Marion Cook accused the Witmarks, who were Jewish, of cheating him on his publishing royalties. Alan Freed hoovered partial writing credit on Chuck Berry's "Maybelline," and Morris Levy listed himself as cowriter of Frankie Lymon and the Teenagers' "Why Do Fools Fall in Love?" Artists' complaints often met with sour condescension. Hy Weiss of the doo-wop label Olde Town (whose son Barry Weiss later launched the hip-hop and pop label Jive), once said of his roster, "Those illiterates . . . would have ended up eating from pails in Delancey Street if it weren't for us."

Jewish executives have often felt betrayed when African-American musicians questioned their motives. When activists hanged Wexler in effigy at a Miami music conference in 1968, shortly after the assassination of Dr. Martin Luther King Jr., Wexler was taken aback: "As a Jew, I didn't think I identified with the underclass; I *was* the underclass." Hip-hop, which progressed from black-owned to mostly Jewish-owned indie labels, raised the volume for charges of Jewish exploitation. In a 1991 song called "No Vaseline," Ice Cube laid out the argument. Chiding his former N.W.A. colleagues about their manager, Jerry Heller, he rhymed, *"get rid of that devil real simple, put a bullet in his temple / 'Cause you can't be the Nigga 4 Life crew / With a white Jew telling you what to do."*

The history of hip is rife with such heated codependencies. Because hip looks forward, it values the people who can add to an idea as much as the originators. For this reason it thrives on difference and crossover. As a business proposition, African Americans and Jews came together due to circumstances of neither group's choosing. Jewish entrepreneurs were able to make headway in ragtime, blues, jazz, soul, rock and hip-hop in large part because more established money didn't want to. In the years before major labels and radio accepted hip-hop, Aaron Fuchs recalled his days as an early rap mogul this way: "I thought, wow, one of these days, if I play my cards right, me and [Tom] Silverman and Cory Robbins"—

the founders of Tommy Boy and Profile Records—"we're all going to be sitting at a B'nai B'rith meeting carving up the country into territories, as indie labels did then."

The black middle class, like the white corporations, was slower to see its future in the music. Consider the brief history of Black Swan Records, the first significant black-owned record company, started in 1921 by a music publisher and insurance executive named Harry Herbert Pace. The company's board, which included W. E. B. DuBois, saw the label as a showcase for operatic ballads that would appeal to the neighborhood gentry and generate the "positive images" favored by the NAACP. Like James Weldon Johnson, they believed that such artistry would force whites to acknowledge the humanity of African Americans. Pace turned down Bessie Smith as too raw. Only when the label's first records failed did he face the funk, recording blues songs by the cabaret singer Ethel Waters. Though Waters temporarily saved the company, by the end of 1923 it went bankrupt.

Conversely, when dirt-poor Jewish immigrants like Leonard and Phil Chess thrust themselves into the record business, they turned not to the sophisticated musicians of Chicago but to a former sharecropper like Waters, whose Delta crudeness was precisely the image the city's black elite were trying to put behind. The Chess brothers did their business in the South Side of Chicago because it was where they could afford to live, and where they were welcome to do business. Their success did not begin as a story of big capital ripping off labor, but of mutual hustle.

Yet there is a hipper story percolating through this relationship, of knowledge passed back and forth or experienced through the other party. Years after his success, Leonard Chess used to empty the change from his pockets when he entered a studio to remind him of his penniless days. This ritual acknowledged that his successes derived from poverty—not his artists', but his own. This poverty led him to the wealth of the blues; his friendship with Muddy Waters was part of this wealth. Similarly, Redd Foxx acknowledged that Lenny Bruce's genius began in his desperate sacrifices. "Lenny paved the way for all of us," Foxx said in the 1960s, calling Bruce a hero. "But you got to remember one thing. Heroes ain't born; they're cornered."

Though it was rooted in deprivation, the alliance between African

Teddy Bunn, Mezz Mezzrow and Hugues Panassie, 1939

Americans and Jews is a metaphor for progress, and in America progress is a metaphor for wealth. If you listen to Muddy Waters's "I Can't Be Satisfied" or follow the story of Leonard Chess and his loose change, both tell of wealth in the context of poverty. Both are stories of suffering and deliverance, not in sequence but at the same time. It is this simultaneity, or twoness, that informs black English or the blues, and that marks the curiosities of bebop or the Beats—"desirous," as Kerouac wrote, "of everything at the same time." Mezz Mezzrow (1899–1972), a Jewish clarinetist who came to believe he was African American, described the commotion on the Lower East Side the day a Jewish burlesque house played jazz records on the PA system outside. Suddenly, business was booming. "Man, those records caused a traffic jam for blocks around," he recalled. "All day long the lobby was packed tight with little old bearded grandpas in long black pongee frock-coats and cupcake-shaped yomelkehs, rubbing their hands behind their backs and shaking their heads sadly at Louis [Armstrong]'s moans, like they understood everything he had to say. . . . I got my kicks from the way the Lower East Side took the colored man's music to its heart." In the catharsis of bad times was a model for the accelerated commerce of good.

Presumably these bearded grandpas did not think they were black, nor, since their reaction was unfamiliar, that they were listening to music they had heard in shul. What they heard, perhaps, was the articulation of Jewishness *as American*. This is what Jolson found in coon songs, or Howe heard in the Jewish minstrels. This awareness belongs to hip's essence: the knowledge of connection even in the context of separation. Bill Adler, the hip-hop publicist, said that when he started working around African-American colleagues and artists, "I just felt so much more at ease, so much more welcome. And it was in contrast to the freeze-out I felt from white folks in the rock business." This is not to make light of the legitimate tensions, but to note that they exist in the presence of equally genuine bonds.

Through Jewish songwriters, publishers and hustlers, the nation could likewise hear blackness *as American*—not assimilated, but made powerful by ethnic specificity. Nothing was more American than Gershwin or Leiber and Stoller, and nothing more in love with blackness as the future. The same pattern repeated through rock, soul, hip-hop and gangsta rap, even the funkier corners of the publishing business. All would have been stillborn without Jewish interlopers who heard magic where many middle-class African Americans heard only regression. Jewish coconspirators bet that African-American creativity could rule the market, without being diluted for the mainstream. "They open industries for us that we wouldn't normally be in," said Russell Simmons, who has had Jewish partners in both his music and fashion lines. "The clothing business? There were no Blacks at all. None. Zero. Now if you go to a clothing convention it is like a Hip-Hop convention. . . . [T]he gains that we made in these communications industries—clothing, advertising, publishing, even—all of these kinds of gains are gains in Black-Jewish partnerships."

At its hippest, the dance offers self-revelation. The anguish that Armstrong's moans convey to Mezzrow's grandpas is not Louis's but their own, seen through somebody else's prism. This is a gift of outsider-dom, an opportunity to be outside even your own experience, as the grandpas listening to Armstrong are outside their own. The relationship between the two tribes is often described in essentialist terms, as if there were an *essential* creative impulse among African Americans and an *essential* business acumen among Jews. But hip's history argues against such essentialist boxes. They stifle noisy intelligence and tell lies. The division is never so clean. The outsider's position breeds irony, self-criticism and reinvention, all of which undermine such simple dichotomies.

The damage of racial stereotypes is not that they are false, but that they eliminate context. Too often the stereotype of the greedy Jew or shiftless negro becomes the only Jew or African American you see, not a member of a broader community. The empathies between Jews and the blues open lanes of context that go beyond these stereotypes. Looked at more closely, the partnerships are less complementary than symbiotic, fueled not by the division of labors but by the merging of them. In the most creative artists, African American or otherwise, we see the art of creative business hustle. In the savviest hustler, Jewish or otherwise, we see the soul of an artist. The arts racket, after all, is its own tribe, cutting against ethnicity. Within the tribe, each side lets the other be on the outside looking in. The knowledge gained is the enlightenment of hip.

10

criminally hip

outlaws, gangsters, players, hustlers

> [T]he roots of the counterculture as a defiant revolutionary way of
> life lay not so much in the sources that the kids were proud to
> show…but rather in that culture that had always been most antag-
> onistic to conventional values and codes of behavior, the culture that
> had always acted out the most basic fantasies of the American psy-
> che and created the whole underground world of drugs, violence,
> street argot and antisocial defiance: the criminal culture.
>
> —ALBERT GOLDMAN

In 1926, as a young adolescent, William S. Burroughs discovered a
book called *You Can't Win,* by Jack Black, and it opened his world. Black
belonged to the nameless swarms of Americans who followed the railroads west around the turn of the century and never took root again,
except in the continuous motion of vice. *You Can't Win* recounted his
criminal adventures along the way—the hop joints and second-story
jobs, the yegg loyalties and penitentiary time. For the young Burroughs,
restless in what he called "a malignant matriarchal society" in suburban
St. Louis, the book was a beacon, summoning him toward literary
characters with names like Salt Chunk Mary or the Sanctimonious Kid,
and toward thrills not so easily named. He bought a gun and began

accruing his own adventures, reinventing himself through the images in Black's pages. As an adult he lifted characters and scenes for his own fiction. "It sounded good to me," he remembered later, "compared with the dullness of a Midwest suburb where all contact with life was shut out."

In the evolution of hip, few characters have been as influential as the outlaw. For many of us, outlaws are the first figures we encounter who reject mainstream society and are celebrated for it. They are hip's miscreant uncles, figures who give us permission to adopt our own code, go our own way. In a society directed toward work, outlaws create the leisure space in which the nation's countercultures, from the colonial rebels to the 1990s gangstas, gather their numbers. Shunned by the law-abiding mainstream—placed literally *outside the law*—they inhabit a country within a country, inventing their own language, economy, values and folklore. These cross back over through hip.

In broad caricature, outlaws embody the mythologies of the American Renaissance: the lives of unfettered freedom and pleasure, of rebellion and primitive violence. Like the bad men of the blues, outlaws convert life into myth and image. Hip in turn shuttles ideas and language between the criminal underworld and aboveground society. It translates crime as an aesthetic: the black leather jacket, the droop-ass jean, the gangster lean. It borrows the hustle of the hustler, the stroll of the pimp. Like outlaws, hipsters spur a mixture of fear and attraction, projecting society's fears back to it as style. The hipster, viewed coolly, is the outlaw as metaphor.

The criminal classes, as Whitman called them, are often considered regressive elements, but really they form a social vanguard. To the extent that laws exist to hold a society in place, outlaws are a creative force. In a Darwinian sense, society produces its outlaws for the same reason it produces hip: to foment noise and conflict, the engines of evolution. Many of the hipsters in this book were perceived first as delinquents, subversives or pornographers, and only later as cultural icons. The whorehouses in New Orleans fostered the development of jazz. Colonial rebels, runaway slaves, homosexuals, Mormons and trade unionists all began as outlaws. Yesterday's crime has consistently proven to be tomorrow's recreation. In between it is hip. To a nation addicted to the new, crime provides a glimpse of future liberties, a primitive look at the next incarnation of the modern.

Outlaw language, similarly, gives purpose to hip talk. It is by nature furtive and communicative. The compilers of the *Dictionary of American Underworld Lingo* (1950), who wrote from various niches in the penal system, noted that criminal slang "constitutes an implicit criticism of traditional mores, particularly with respect to those aspects of the social code which most concern the criminal population—the legal system, standards of group loyalty, and standards of sexual morality." For hipsters living within the law, to sling the slang is to echo its implicit criticism.

Burroughs's epiphany, an early crossroads in his slink toward hip, is just one link in a chain of criminal seductions. *You Can't Win* describes Black's own similar conversion in 1882, when he came across newspaper accounts of the death of Jesse James, betrayed for the reward money by his former accomplice Robert Ford. "Looking back now," Black wrote, "I can plainly see the influence the James boys and similar characters had in turning my thoughts to adventure and later to crime." Modern readers of Burroughs, then, can read through him to Black to Jesse James—and through James to John Newman Edwards, the *Kansas City Times* editor who more than anyone shaped the James legend, likening him to Robin Hood (whose own legend, to carry the regression back, likely owes to Robert Hod, a 13th-century rogue who made his way into song and story). Such links swing forward as well as back. Spin the same associations forward and you might arrive at Bob Dylan, an admirer of Burroughs, insinuating himself into the same genealogy. "I might look like Robert Ford / But I feel just like Jesse James," he sang, playing both the outlaw and his betrayer. This is how myth allows the past to speak in the present tense.

Outlaws hold an elevated position in a nation founded by rebels and runaways. If America lacks the kings and queens of European legend, it has invented its own icons, in the likeness of its own savage heart: Billy the Kid and Jesse James, John Dillinger and Al Capone; and later, through the fictions of mass media, Humphrey Bogart and James Cagney, the Outlaws of country music and the Outlawz of rap. Through hip, the romance of the outlaw poured life into American literature and movies, and

Billy the Kid

in turn sustained itself through these media. The romance flourished not so much in our prisons as in the popular culture it helped create. Its chroniclers are both ambivalent and joyous:

> I began to view the American criminal as a breed apart from the criminals of other countries. The American genus began to emerge as one striving for his own criminal identity in a society that considered him integral with something called the Frontier Spirit; a society that knew the criminal outwardly, condemned him as being against the common good,

yet marked him for special recognition in a pioneer category aligned with obsessive types such as carnival freaks, daredevils, and wilderness adventurers who came with the bark on. The criminal became, in many respects, an extension of all of these—the loudest, the gaudiest. He was noise! He was public! And he was ours!

Like Mailer's wise primitive, the outlaw is a simple way of understanding a complicated story.

At an elemental level, the hipster is a vicarious form of the outlaw. Hipsters are criminals once removed, intimations of crime without the thing itself. In a nation of laws, the romance of the outlaw lies mainly in the potential, isolated from the seamier reality of its results. Americans may love the swagger of the gunslinger riding into town, but they do not like to clean up afterward. Hip freezes this potential in slang and posture. In the instant before impact, the bullet of a criminal or the notes of a Miles Davis solo can have the same promise. Both see themselves as outside the law. Hip captures this moment of anticipation, a present tense that never becomes the done deal of the past. Hip is to crime what gangsta rap is to real gangbanging: the attitude and the lingo are the same, but the music is all implied potential, the real thing all grisly result. Hip is the frisson of the bullet or blue note still in the air, dangerous but remote. Its alternative is the romance of work, and that's no romance at all.

The folklore of the outlaw extends back well before the colonization of the Americas. Among tribal societies of northern Europe in the 5th and 6th centuries, the Old English word *lagu,* or Old Icelandic *log,* the precursor of our own word *law,* referred to the value a free individual held within the society. A person's *lagu,* as the crime historian Frank Richard Prassel has written, included both his material possessions and his rights within the laws of the community. This *lagu* could be forfeited. If a person stole or killed, the victim's family or clan was entitled to compensation, in the form of property or the life of the offender. If the killer escaped, and there could be no proper compensation, then he was considered to have relinquished his *lagu.* He had no claim to the society's wealth or the protection of its laws. He was *utlaga,* an outlaw.

It is not surprising that members of a society would embrace their outlaws. Robert Wright, in his book *Non-Zero: The Logic of Human Destiny* (2000), makes the case that all societies evolve toward more complicated forms, and a society that hangs onto its outlaws preserves an extra wrinkle. Compensation is a zero-sum equation, enriching one party while depleting the other. To embrace outlaws, even symbolically, creates what Wright calls a non-zero-sum game, where one party gains without the other party losing. By the late Middle Ages, the peasants of England saw in this math a fable of class revenge, spinning ever more elaborate tales of the robber they called Robin Hood. After a few centuries the tale took on the twist that Robin stole from the rich and gave to the poor—a way of justifying a romance that preceded such justification.

In America the criminal took on a special significance. The first problem facing landowners in the New World was a vast shortage of manpower. One solution was to import African slaves. Another was to use convicts. The British crown, eager to export its thieves and villains, paid their way to the New World as bound labor. Virginia planters got their land grants from the king based on the number of servants they had, which stimulated a brisk market in convicts. Though they worked in the same fields as slaves and white freemen, convicts constituted their own temporary class, subject to brutal exploitation. In the decades before the Revolution, around 50,000 English prisoners passed into servitude in the New World. France supplied the feminine enticements that America lacked, exporting more than 1,200 women prisoners over a five-year span, mostly to the brothels of New Orleans. In the capital of American pleasure, then, the most basic pleasure began in crime. Criminals were a constructive force in the new country, outsiders on whom the inside relied. In the coming eras, as America developed a celebrity of crime, hip flowed from the possibilities they represented.

The story of Jesse James, the first modern outlaw, might properly begin with Robin Hood, to whom his admirers compared him, or with the bullet of Robert Ford, who snuck up behind Jesse in a rented house in St. Joseph, Missouri, on April 3, 1882, shooting him in the back as he straightened a picture. Or it might begin with the rise of the American press, and of editors like John Edwards, who endowed James and his brothers with a "halo of medieval chivalry," turning them from pathological hoodlums to early models of hipster contradiction. Any of these makes an appropriate starting point, because as fiercely as Jesse determined to be his own invention, he was as much Robin Hood's or Bob Ford's, or John Edwards's. Without these three, he would have been just a poor man who did bad. When he started to invent his own legend in the newspapers of the Great Plains, the door to hip was open.

Jesse Woodson James was born in Clay County, Missouri, on September 5, 1847, the second son of a farmer and itinerant minister. Before Jesse was four, his father headed west with the California gold rush, only to die from a fever just 18 days after his arrival. The boys' mother, Zarelda, raised them with fierce clannish loyalties and a penchant for violence. As the nation headed into Civil War, Jesse and his older brother, Frank, joined the bands of Confederate raiders who skirmished with the Jayhawkers and the Redlegs, Union militiamen roaming the border states of Missouri and Kansas. Accounts of Jesse as an adult describe him as just under six feet, slender but sturdy, with cavernous blue eyes, thin lips and long lashes. He was missing the tip of the middle finger on his left hand after a childhood gun mishap. The entry marks of a musket ball and a bullet, taken just nine months apart in 1864 and 1865, scarred the right side of his chest.

The James brothers and their associates, the Youngers, invented the modern American outlaw not in the field of crime, but in the new furnaces of the media. Their rise coincided with that of the most powerful popular press the world had ever known. From the time they robbed their first bank, on Valentine's Day, 1866, they cultivated their image through journalists like Edwards, granting interviews and explaining their deeds in letters to the regional press. After one train robbery, they left their victim a note, to be passed to the local editor, providing "an exact account of this hold-up. We prefer this to be published instead of the exaggerated account that usually appears in the newspapers after such an event." Since southern readers considered the banks and railroads as Yankee institutions, they were happy to side with the perpetrators, not the victims. Edwards put the muscle of the press into building a story. He described Jesse, who was by other accounts an indifferent gunslinger, as the fastest gun in the West, and bathed the gang's jobs, in which innocent men lost their lives over minor sums of money, in the honey of epic. Edwards portrayed their acts as feats of daring, not the desperate toil of poor men. His editorials treated their crimes as pure style. For the James Gang, he wrote, "booty is but the second thought; the wild drama of adventure first." Jesse appreciated the attention, naming his son Jesse Edwards James.

This third-party perspective, which transformed violence into image and story, opened the connection to hip. Centuries earlier, the legend of Robin Hood had required that he give his booty to the poor; Jesse James only had to be daring and sexy, a criminal rock star on perpetual tour. Like Melville's confidence man, the mythic Jesse seemed to be in it for the grace, not the workingman's payday. Modern biographers like T. J. Stiles, author of *Jesse James: The Last Rebel of the Civil War,* have begun to unravel the myths of the James Gang, but for Edwards and his readers, the outlaws were paragons of shady nobility. The public bought in. After Jesse's death, his landlord sold bloody splinters from the floorboards for a quarter apiece. When all the splinters sold out, the landlord soaked new floorboards in ox blood and kept the business rolling.

Yet there were better ways to tell the story, and hip's history is one of technological opportunism. In 1903, through the auspices of Thomas Edison, Edwin S. Porter made the first modern film, a 12-minute crime sequence called *The Great Train Robbery.* The new medium portrayed crime as pure action, a ballet of violence moving across a silent screen. The menace of the criminal, removed from any association with real life and real victims, became a visual vocabulary of stance, swagger and gesture. Audiences could take these home with them, repeating them as the postures of hip.

It was only fitting that both Jesse James Jr. and Emmett Dalton (1871–1937), a member of the Dalton Gang, slid from crime to the movie business, making myths in celluloid rather than dust and blood. Dalton, who watched his brothers Robert and Grattan die in an 1892 bank job, turned their deaths into the 1912 movie *The Last Stand of the Dalton Boys.* He played the public's ambivalence toward bad men like a fiddle. "Why has the free-running reprobate always been so extolled?" he wrote, in a passage that gracefully shifts scale from the grandiose to the petty. "Is it because he symbolizes the undying anarchy in the heart of almost every man? Because he has the rude courage of his desires? . . . He becomes our fighting vicar against aristocracy, against power, against law, against the

John Dillinger

upstart, the pretender, the smugly virtuous, and the pompously successful person or corporation whom we envy. He becomes a hero of democracy."

Law enforcement agencies joined the coronation, creating the honorific Public Enemy Number One, as if celebrating a sports legend or a Hollywood star. Who wouldn't want to be number one? John Dillinger (1903–1934), a Prohibition-era bank robber, was the first to earn the title, and he cultivated an image as a gentleman Robin Hood. Newspapers covered his acts like the deeds of movie characters, and he punctuated his crimes with the wisecracks and asides that were becoming the conventions of film. When a bank customer moved to hand over his cash during a robbery, Dillinger refused it, explaining that he took money only from banks; on another job, when the gang had to take hostages, Dillinger gave them carfare home, certain that such deeds would play big in the papers.

They did. When he died, shot down outside the Biograph Theater in Chicago on July 22, 1934, women dipped their hems in his blood on the sidewalk. Five thousand people attended his funeral. Even his sexual apparatus has remained a topic of urban myth. To this day, visitors to the National Museum of Health and Medicine in Washington, D.C., ask to see his preserved member, rumored to be residing in a jar somewhere in the museum's vaults. One reckoning estimated its size to be anywhere from 13 to 28 inches—literally larger than life.

In its rhetoric, hip looks down on the drudgery of making a living. But as a broad force, hip shapes itself to economic needs. It forms a kind of consumer avant-garde, not necessarily the first to buy the new product but the first to shape the desire. The romance of the outlaw, similarly, has evolved according to the needs of the economy. The myths of the Wild West stimulated the expansion of the frontier. By the 1920s, as a maturing industrial economy began to produce luxury goods as well as necessities, the romance shifted to leisure criminals, urban figures renowned for their corporate organization and louche glamour. Chicago mobsters like Alphonse "Scarface" Capone, Charles "Pretty Boy" Floyd, Lester Gillis (aka Baby Face Nelson) and George "Machine Gun" Kelly helped coax the nation from the fiscal austerity of temperance to the more profitable model of sin. Their joints, venues for the evolution of jazz, hummed with the possibilities of sex and death, the alpha and omega of hip enlightenment. They spent freely, lived lavishly and invited civilians to do the same. Though crime actually dropped in the 1930s, a rarity in American history, the public fascination with these media-savvy gangsters created the impression of lawless anarchy. Decades later, gangsta rap wove the same illusion, overshadowing the drop in real crime during the 1990s.

As the economy changed, so did the romantic profile of the gangster. Four decades after the Chicago mobsters, the Harlem heroin kingpin Leroy "Nicky" Barnes melded the outlaw archetype to the new corporate paradigms of the 1970s. Barnes's sleek, efficient heroin operation was not so much contrary to the national agenda as an apotheosis of it: a hypercapitalist inferno, with no bureaucracy or internal corruption to cool it down. Barnes was the CEO with a killer instinct, anticipating the cowboy capitalism of Reaganomics. Portrayed in the press as "Mr. Untouchable," as if he were a TV character perpetrating entertainment rather than crime, he made crime a performance. He played Robin Hood of Harlem, giving Christmas turkeys to the poor, and publicly thumbed his nose at authority. When he went on trial for possession of guns and hashish in 1976, Barnes found himself in the courthouse washroom with two narcotics cops. "I need a handkerchief," he said, loudly enough to get their attention. He stuck his hand in his pocket and pulled out a fat roll of bills, more money than a cop made in a month. "Let's see, is this a handkerchief?" Then he patted the other side pocket and pulled out another fat roll, waving it in front of the cops. "Now, that isn't a handkerchief either, is it?" Satisfied that he had made his point, he smiled at the narcs and walked out.

As the Romans used to say, hip fugit. Barnes became a police informant, and is now hiding out under the witness protection program. But he earns a place here not just for his retro flamboyance—copied most overtly by the rapper Notorious B.I.G.—but also for the creativity that flourished on his natty coattails. In the mid-1970s, through a front, he bought the Apollo Theater on 125th Street in Harlem. If Barnes was laissez-faire in his business practices, he was downright negligent in his stewardship of the Apollo. Yet as in the extralegal zone of Storyville in New Orleans, which nurtured the early sounds of jazz, the chaos was fertile. Between acts, a neighborhood youth who called himself DJ Hollywood spun records and kept up a rhyming patter over them. "To the hip, hop, the hibby, the hibby," he began, chanting the name for the unnamed music that was then surging in the parks of Harlem and the Bronx and would soon rule the rhythm nation.

By the turn of the century, the outlaw romance had settled on the padded shoulders of the black pimp, a retro figure who tweaked both the ridiculous and the archaic in the American Dream. Rappers like Snoop Dogg and Too Short played out fantasies from *The Mack;* teenagers declared themselves sneaker pimps, gorilla pimps, or any of the other 52 officially recognized varieties. Pimps had the virtue of believing their own myth—the myth came first, the game second. They were also the consummate lifestyle capitalists, treating the most basic human act as a branded financial transaction. They took the brand logo to absurd limits: one of the most arresting photographs in the recent book *Pimpnosis,* taken by Tracy Funches, shows a topless woman drinking out of a martini glass, her left breast tattooed with the words *Kenny's Bitch*.

T he crossover between hipsters and outlaws has been fluid. Marlon Brando in *The Wild One* (1954) demonstrated the classic straddle, planting one leather boot in each camp. Riding into a square, sleepy town with an unconvincing cast of biker goons, Brando is all sexy brood and bad intent, chewing wads of hokey dialog. When a local famously asks him, "What're you rebelling against, Johnny?" the proper answer might have been, "The script." As hipster and outlaw, he ducked the orderly life by which the townspeople measured a person's worth. That the same middle-class society actually willed this rebellion—and would have created men to perform it, had the population not proven so accommodating—only makes the outlaw story more quintessentially American, and more illuminating to hip's evolution. In reconciling society's fears and attractions, hip serves its critics as well as its adherents.

Like the bluesmen who sold their souls to the devil, outlaws promised

Iceberg Slim

access to forbidden knowledge. They had a code of sangfroid, an essential *cool*. In his autobiography, *Pimp: The Story of My Life* (1969), Iceberg Slim recounts a lesson from his first jail bid: "Always remember whether you be a sucker or hustler in the world out there, you've got that vital edge if you can iron-clad your feelings." The myth of outlaws was that they were ready to kill, ready to die; emotionally steeled. A commonly repeated story about Billy the Kid (William Bonney or William McCarty, ca. 1859–1881) had him killing a band of Mexicans "just to see them kick." Though the story was unsupported, it circulated as gosepl, along with other conjectures regarding this man about whom little is known, and little of that likely to pass a good sniff test.

This cool dispassion, however mythologized, runs throughout the hip canon. In hip circles it signifies emotional intensity, not a void: the notes not played say as much as the ones that are. Hemingway worked it into parched, masculine prose, anticipating the hard-boiled writings of Raymond Chandler, Jim Thompson and James Ellroy. The same chill blew through the heroin-dipped trumpets of Miles Davis and Chet Baker in the cool jazz of the 1950s, and through the aloof postures of James Dean, the Velvet Underground or Snoop Dogg—a river running from one end of hip to the other.

Outlaws and gangsters also provided a model for treating style as identity. Like the major writers of the American Renaissance, the modern outlaw emerged just after the birth of advertising, which freed images from their subjects. A deliciously fanciful account of Billy the Kid decks him in a

> blue dragoon jacket of the finest broadcloth, heavily loaded down with gold embroidery, buckskin pants, dyed jet black, with small tinkling bells sewed down the sides. . . . Underneath this garment were his drawers of fine scarlet broadcloth, extending clear down to the ankle and over his feet, encasing them like stockings. . . . And [his] whole structure of a hat was covered with gold and jewels until it sparkled and shone in a dazzling and blinding manner when one looked upon it.

This seems an unlikely getup for the baked frontier of Lincoln County, New Mexico, but never mind. Iceberg Slim himself could not have been more pimping. Which is not to say he didn't try. In a chapter entitled "A

Degree in Pimping," he writes: "I would see myself gigantic and powerful like God Almighty. . . . My suits were spun-gold shot through with precious stones. My shoes would be dazzling silver. The toes were as sharp as daggers. Beautiful whores with piteous eyes groveled at my feet." (The piteous eyes, you will agree, are the killer touch.) In a suit like that, you wear your outsider status for all to see.

Even the sobriquet *beat*, applied to a generation, was the contribution of the thief and addict Herbert Huncke, who became a friend and inspiration to Kerouac, Ginsberg and Burroughs. He was their connection to a world that would never be wholly theirs. For Huncke, *beat* was drugworld slang for defeated, a condition beyond "the insult of rehabilitation," as Ann Douglas called it—it meant you've fallen and you can't get up. Kerouac called Huncke "the greatest storyteller I know, an actual genius at it, in my mind," and immortalized him in three novels, including *On the Road*, in which he is Elmo Hassel, the seedy savant of Times Square.

Myths are rarely without an agenda. Like hip, the romance of the outlaw serves a broader cultural purpose. America from the start preached Puritan austerity yet thrived by its hungers for sex, conquest and material wealth. Unwilling to acknowledge these compulsions, and unable to give them up, we project them on our outlaws in grandiose excess. If these lusts are essential to the nation's good times, then let them exist outside proper society. Outlaws show the public what its desires would look like with the brakes off. Though reality is often more prosaic, in legend the bad men kill without remorse, stack fortunes beyond taste, fuck like animals. "I shot a man in Reno," Johnny Cash sang, slinging the myth, "just to watch him die," and even in this obvious fabrication there was a gem of truth, not just for the Man in Black (1932–2003), but for listeners as well. As the critic Robert Warshow wrote, criminals embody both "what we want to be and what we are afraid we might become." This threat, or invitation, is the other side of the public's fascination with outlaws—not because they are unfathomable, but because they are us. The features of the criminal, Warshow added, are inseparable from the nicer faces Americans see in the mirror: "The gangster is the 'no' to that great American 'yes' which is stamped so big over our official culture and yet has so little to do with the way we really feel about our lives." The outlaws cannot really be pushed outside the law because their passions haunt the inner life of the community, circulating madly through the fantasies of the populace.

I n such places as Greenwich Village, a ménage-a-trois was completed— the bohemian and the juvenile delinquent came face-to-face with the Negro, and the hipster was a fact in American life." That's how Mailer saw hip's genesis in 1957, but of course the associations were much older, and this sudden confluence, like Burroughs's epiphany on reading Jack Black, was really just one in a longer series of cultural exchanges. The affinity of hipsters for criminals begins in the original self-consciousness of the outlaw, the moment at which the criminal and the artist could converge.

Yet outlaws are not the same as hipsters, different in both motive and what they produce. Burroughs's epiphany, like Black's, led him not just to crime but to prose, where he used the myth to tell broader stories about freedom and dominance. Stealing alone wasn't interesting enough. Though Herbert Huncke introduced the others to a rogues' gallery of larcenous characters, it was Huncke himself, a writer and storyteller, who captured their imagination.

John Clellon Holmes, in a 1958 essay titled "The Philosophy of the Beat Generation," acknowledged the freedoms of the outlaw as a starting point for the Beats, but saw crime as a spiritual cul-de-sac.

> What differentiated the characters in *On the Road* from the slum-bred petty criminals and icon-smashing Bohemians which have been something of a staple in modern American fiction—what made them *beat*— was something which seemed to irritate critics most of all. It was Kerouac's insistence that actually they were on a quest, and that the specific object of their quest was spiritual.

The outlaws represented a more primal enlightenment, a congress with death itself.

Ultimately, though, outlaws are not in control of their own myth. They do not create it and cannot defend it. It owes its currency to the public, and the public can crack it back upon them. A crime reporter laid out the rules at the turn of the previous century:

In case a crime has been committed which incenses the public mind, if the accused is able to divide the public sentiment, then take the sympathetic side of the case; but if the accused has few or no friends, then jump onto him with both feet and stamp him out of existence, for in so doing you will satisfy the mind of the public and close the incident.

The freedom of the mythic outlaw is thus contingent, illusory.

The logic of the romance ultimately requires that the outlaws die for it, preferably in a blaze of glory. Living represents a kind of failure. Theirs is literally a dead end. For all their crossover with hipsters, outlaws are more often transitional figures on the way to hip, guides to the American atavism that hip channels. If they are figures of attraction and repulsion to the straight world, to the hip they are raw material. The division between hipsters and squares repeats that between the criminal world and the straight one. Without outlaws, without the abyss they imply, hip would not have the same power to excite and repel. But where the outlaws can succeed only as tragedy, hip thrives in the continuities of living.

11 where the ladies at?

rebel girls, riot grrrls and the revenge on the mother

> That whole obsession with hip is like collecting records or whatever.
> It's more of a male thing.   —KIM GORDON

Any tradition that romanticizes a man for killing his wife in a drunken game of William Tell will never be exactly correct on the Woman Question. The sexual history of hip reached a low-water mark on September 6, 1951, in the Mexico City apartment of John Healy, where Joan Vollmer Adams and her common-law husband, William Burroughs, had gone to drink gin and to sell a gun. By this time both were in bad shape. Burroughs was adrift in the city's reservoirs of boys, cheap heroin and tequila; Vollmer had polio and her teeth were turning black from too much Benzedrine. What most hipsters know of her life passed in those few minutes above the Bounty bar. Balancing a water glass on her head for Burroughs to shoot, she faced away, telling him, "I can't watch this. You know I can't stand the sight of blood." The words were her last. The guilt from the accident ultimately jolted Burroughs to write his first books, but it is the apparent guiltlessness of it—the surreal violence of the act, the near indifference of the law—that continues to feed his legend. Joan, who was 27, became a footnote in a darkly romantic male tale.

The history of hip, as this incident illustrates, often rides hard over the women who help make it go. Joan Vollmer, born in 1924, was as willful and transgressive as the men around her, and like other women who came of age in the 1940s and 1950s, she faced heavier consequences for her actions. The daughter of a factory manager in upstate New York, she chafed against her family's middle-class expectations before leaving for Barnard College, where she married a law student named Paul Adams, more out of rebellion than passion. Joan was five-foot-six, pretty, with a jutting chin, a voracious appetite for literature and an aloofness that reminded Edie Parker, a Barnard friend and roommate, of Greta Garbo. She liked to spend days in the bathtub, reading or holding court. The string of apartments Joan and Edie took together in the early 1940s became ground zero for the meetings of Kerouac, Ginsberg, Lucien Carr, Hal Chase and—on their visits up from Times Square—Herbert Huncke and William Burroughs. A prostitute named Vickie Russell showed the group how to make lozenges or tea from the papers in over-the-counter Benzedrine inhalers. Edie dated and soon married Kerouac. Joan gravitated to the bennies and to Burroughs. When she was found hallucinating and incoherent in Times Square, and landed in the psych ward at Bellevue, it was Bill who saw to her release.

Though Burroughs was avowedly homosexual, he and Joan lived together in Texas, New Orleans and finally south of the border, and had a son, Billy Jr., whom Burroughs failed almost as catastrophically as he did his wife (Billy had his own affinity for drugs and died in 1981, at age 34, after a liver transplant failed). As for Edie Parker, whose 1944 marriage to Kerouac lasted less than a year, she had to content herself with her own unpublished memoirs and the tang of Kerouac's posthumous *Visions of Cody* (1972), in which he said of his paramours: "Her cunt is sweet, you get to it via white lace panties, and she be fine. This is almost all I can say about almost all girls." Like Vollmer, she gets little more than a marginal note in most Beat accounts.

Where, then, are all the ladies at? The chronicles of hip, as told by men, often play like T. E. Lawrence's adventures in Arabia, in which the only female characters were the camels, or like Miles Davis's autobiography, which could be a how-to manual for aspiring misogynists. In Hip 101 classics like *Huck Finn, On the Road,* Chandler's *The Long Goodbye,*

Sister Rosetta Tharpe at Café Society, December 11, 1940

Dylan's "Like a Rolling Stone" or Iceberg Slim's *Pimp,* women appear either as reproving matriarchs like Twain's Widow Douglas, or as Kerouac's interchangeable bearers of sweet cunts—either the apron strings from which male hipness takes flight or the enticements it consumes along the road. "Hip definitely seems like a male term," said Kim Gordon, bass player in Sonic Youth, who came on the scene after the wave of female musicians in the punk era. "Granted, a lot of it is gay. But when I think of hip I think of the Beat generation, that whole rockster toddler male machismo thing."

Yet there is another side to this story, left out of the male accounts. The line that runs from Zora Neale Hurston to Deborah Harry, or Dawn Powell to Missy Elliott, traces a legacy of self-invention as provocative as its male equivalent. Hip would be incomplete without the withering retort of Dorothy Parker or Laurie Anderson, or the electric gospel of Sister Rosetta Tharpe, who cranked her guitar for the Lord. From the Greenwich Village women who shaped American bohemia at the start of the 20th century to the postfeminist grrrls and ghetto-fabulous divas who revitalized it at the end, female hipsters have withstood a double standard that celebrated men who rebelled as rakish and romantic, but condemned women who did so as slatternly, immoral, irresponsible or bad mothers.

When the Beat poet Gregory Corso was asked about the male club-house of 1950s bohemia, he said the problem was not that women were less adventurous. "There were women, they were there, I knew them, their families put them in institutions, they were given electric shock. In the '50s if you were male you could be a rebel, but if you were female your families had you locked up." Many faced the scorn of their communities, bore interracial or out-of-wedlock children and flouted a social order where even in postwar times, as Diane di Prima put it, "a woman without a man didn't exist at all; a mother without a husband was more than in-visible: she was a kind of negative force-field, a bit of antimatter." Yet still the women have come.

Despite this imbalance, if hip has a gender, it is female—or, like hip's racial play, hybrid. In the African societies where Robert Farris Thomp-son studied the origins of cool, including the Bakongo, source of most African culture in America, he found that cool had a distinctly feminine cast. While men were the great warriors, women were associated with peace, and therefore with cool. The 15th-century king Ewuare, with whom Thompson's linguistic genealogy begins, earned his title by bring-ing this feminine condition. Hip follows a similar symbolic arc. By its metaphors it is more feminine than masculine. Hip is a process in cycli-cal rhythm, like a menstrual cycle, rather than an event, like a male ejac-ulation. It performs for an audience; it only has meaning if it is watched. From the beginning of minstrelsy or the blues, hip has worn a mask. It belongs to the less powerful, to the trickster, who keeps secrets, seduces and communicates ideas through coded image. All of these belong to the mythology of the feminine.

Like what used to be called the feminine mystique, hip is most allur-ing and complete when idle. It is sexualized, objectified. It only becomes newsworthy when men cross toward it, often in feminine habiliments like long hair, sensitive verse or the preening of the cock rocker—or, as we shall see, when women combine the feminine mask with male symbols of power or license. For better and worse, to be female in America is to see yourself from inside and outside, as subject and object. This double perspective, like the double meaning of hip language, defines hip awareness. To open one's eyes, or to see, is to know oneself from both angles. If women get less notice in hip's chronicles, it is in part because they have been there all along.

One way to read the sexual history of hip is as a riff on roles in the American family, which for millions have little to do with real life. The blues, with its twin longings for motion and home, arose from families that had been ripped apart during slavery. The rootlessness of bebop and the Beats echoed men's sense of dislocation after World War II, when community life reoriented around suburban motherhood and the baby boom. In the mid-1970s, hip-hop spoke for a cohort of urban teenagers without fathers, and spread to white kids as the suburbs began to fill with single mothers. Each of these tribes defined itself against the myth of the nuclear family, and particularly the male role of the breadwinner in an economy that trapped both sexes in what Kerouac described as a domestic cycle of "work, produce, consume, work, produce, consume." Hip's reactions against conformity and materialism, from Emerson to the annual Burning Man festival, begin by resisting this cycle.

This resistance often plays out as hostility to women. For men in motion, Kerouac wrote, " 'Pretty girls make graves,' was my saying." (Recently a coed group of feminist punks from Seattle adopted this line as their band name, mocking it as they claimed its edge.) When Huck Finn resists being "sivilized," it means yielding to the authority of Miss Watson and the Widow Douglas. Yet more often the target of this hostility is not women per se but domesticity. Hip's archetypes—outlaws, gangsters, vagabonds, hard-boiled detectives, itinerant musicians, nightcrawlers, slackers, bohemians, drug users—all ramble conspicuously away from the hearth. Gay men, who have been a driving force in hip, represent the most dramatic break from gender roles. Hip's romance of the road turns the pursuit of sexual happiness upside down: though surveys show married men have more sex and a greater sense of well-being, hip rates the domestic cocoon as sexless and square, and the road as erotic adventure.

For many women, especially those with children, the price of this adventure is too high. Instead of reinventing themselves on the road, they have reinvented the home and the parameters of hip within it.

•   •   •

Modern American bohemia, tellingly, begins on the shoulders of women. In the early years of the 20th century, while Gertrude Stein was settling in Paris, the radical women of Greenwich Village created the space, both geographical and intellectual, for one of America's great social experiments. The last generation to come of age in the Victorian era, women like Margaret Sanger, Emma Goldman, Mabel Dodge, Louise Bryant and Edna St. Vincent Millay left home to invent new identities as artists, activists and lovers. "When the world began to change," wrote the journalist Hutchins Hapgood, the first chronicler of this downtown scene, "the restlessness of women was the main cause of the development called Greenwich Village, which existed not only in New York but all over the country." The magazines of the day, on the make for anything saucy, named the new type Bohemian Girls, New Women or Rebel Girls—the last from the title of a radical labor anthem by Joe Hill of the Wobblies.

What they produced was the prototype of the alternative scene, an American modernism that replaced the severity of the European model with a Whitmanesque belief in the unbounded self. Professions like journalism, medicine and the law were opening to women for the first time, providing alternatives to the sweatshops or the marital kitchen. "Life was ready to take a new form of some kind and many people felt a common urge to shape it," wrote Mabel Dodge, who opened her apartment on lower Fifth Avenue for social and literary experiments. "The most that anyone knew was the old ways were about over and the new ways all to create. The city was teeming with potentialities."

The first order of business was to unseat the Victorian matriarchy. Hip needs a foil, and the Victorian matriarch—stout, humorless and moralistic—was made to order. The men and women who poured into New York after the turn of the century had grown up under the granite bosoms of reformers like the temperance leader Frances E. Willard, who declared women "trained by the essence of our nature to deeds of moral elevation, education and the work of God." The New Women had another view. They wanted a revolution they could dance to, as Emma Goldman famously said. In the tradition of male hipsters, this meant breaking with their families, remaking themselves as their own invention. "My people

Billie Holliday, Commodore session, April 20, 1939

are in no way a part of me," wrote the journalist Louise Bryant, a middle-class refugee whose incandescent marriage with John Reed was rivaled only by her affair with Eugene O'Neill.

The women found the city a place to pursue lives of creativity, sex and work, not to re-create the hearths of their mothers. As the illustrator Mary Heaton Vorse put it, women of her generation set "out to hurt their mother" in order to clear room for their own lives. "More and more and more of us are coming all the time, and more of us will come until the sum of us will change the customs of the world." They did not come to be breeders. Of the women who enlivened New York in the early decades of the century, Millay, Djuna Barnes, Jessie Fauset, Nella Larsen, Zora Neale Hurston, Dorothy Parker, Sara Teasdale, Katherine Anne Porter, Marianne Moore and Anita Loos were among those who did not have children.

With a cohort of feminist men, the New Women established many of hip's future channels, beginning with a low-rent salon culture and a potent underground press. Margaret Sanger, the birth-control advocate, started a magazine in 1915 appropriately called *The Woman Rebel*, which called for a rethinking of Victorian sex roles. In what might be the first manifesto of female hip, she declared it the duty of modern women to "look the whole world in the face with a go-to-hell look in the eyes, to have an ideal, to speak and act in defiance of convention." On behalf of her readers, she claimed "[t]he right to be lazy. The right to be an unmarried mother. The right to destroy. The right to create. The right [to live. The right to love." Such small-press magazines, often coed, worked like the concentric circles of bop a generation later: the inner circle pushed each other to more radical ideas, then circulated these to a sympathetic cult audience, and from there to the semi-mainstream. As precursors to the zines and blogs of recent vintage, the offset magazines formed a neutral turf where men and women could speak freely in a way no previous generation had. Before the rise of mass media they flourished; in the early 1910s there were more than 300 socialist journals in America, some with circulations of more than 100,000, plus numerous periodicals devoted to art, literature, labor, modernist social theory and anarchy.

Through their publications and their home lives, the moderns reimagined the family, seeking to free men by liberating women. The new division of labor, and the cycle of working and spending, had bred an asymmetry that limited the freedoms for both sexes. Outside the Village, the bohemians campaigned selflessly for the labor movement. At home, with an innocence born of the prewar boom, they hoped to change society by changing their own personal relationships. Sanger promoted contraception as a way to sexual freedom. Couples like Neith Boyce and Hutchins Hapgood experimented with open marriage. Crystal Eastman, the sister of Max Eastman, proposed that spouses take separate residences in order to keep the sexual fires fresh. Goldman railed against the market framework of marriage. In a lecture titled "The Traffic in Women," she argued that "the wife who married for money, compared with the prostitute, is the true scab. She is paid less, gives much more in return in labor and care, and is absolutely bound to her master."

For many men, Goldman's analogy mirrored their own dissatisfaction with the obligations of marriage. H. L. Mencken, writing in 1918, argued that in the surplus economy of the industrial era, which expected men to work harder to bring home the new consumer goods, men were putting more into the marriage bargain and getting less in return. "[U]nder the contract of marriage," he wrote, "all duties lie upon the man and all the privileges appertain to the woman." The women around such a man could not help but *signify* on him, Mencken believed: "whatever their outward show of respect for his merit and authority, [they] always regard him secretly as an ass and with something akin to pity." The Village bohemians brought these two rebellions—Mencken's and Goldman's—under the same roof. For the men, liberated women seemed like protection from the embalmed life of the breadwinner. Floyd Dell predicted in the lefty publication *The Masses*, "Feminism is going to make it possible for the first time for men to be free."

As it happened, the experiments in free love, open contraception and sexual collaboration did not last. After the war, the New Women's utopianism yielded to more market-friendly expressions of female independence, typified by the urbane, skeptical wit of Dorothy Parker, Dawn Powell and Mae West. Theirs was a different city, pierced by different media. They spun it knowingly back on its homilies. "Gratitude," quipped Parker—"the meanest and most sniveling attribute in the world." By the 1920s, with the first golden age of advertising, the frank sexuality of the prewar bohemians had softened into commercial substitutes like the naughtiness of flappers or the canned candor of the new romance magazines. As an experiment in gynocentric bohemia, the moderns were eclipsed by the more dynamic, masculine hip of the decade that followed. The gap between the sexes resurged as market segmentation.

B y the next hip convergence, the Cold War tandem of bebop and the Beats, from a feminist perspective men were revolting in more ways than one. As Barbara Ehrenreich notes in *The Hearts of Men: American Dreams and the Flight from Commitment* (1983), the economic expansion of two world wars bred two streams of male rebellion. The first, which Hugh Hefner captured in 1953 with *Playboy* magazine, imagined a maverick world of pleasure and connoisseurship, for which family was an impediment. Getting married meant fewer consumer options, both in bed and at the MG dealership. In a booming economy, this was a timely message: the magazine's circulation hit a million by 1956, the year before *On the Road* came out. The *Playboy* mythos was a blend of corporate aspiration and rebellion, as Hefner encouraged readers to "expend greater effort in their work, develop their capabilities further and climb higher on the ladder of success." Rebellion, for the *Playboy* man, was against whatever might prevent him from enjoying the airbrushed nipples on the page or the new goodies flowing into stores. He was a square with a sporty wardrobe and a hard-on, congratulated by a magazine that told him this was hip.

The men who met in the Columbia apartments of Edie Parker and Joan Vollmer in the 1940s nursed a deeper disaffection. While *Playboy* promised better loving through upward mobility, the Beat men opted out of the game. Refugees from good colleges, they lionized petty thieves like Huncke and Cassady or what they imagined as the liberating poverty of African Americans. They took occasional work on the docks or for the railroads. Even Ginsberg, who worked briefly in market research in an effort to go straight, did not last. Their resistence was less to women than to consumerism itself, and the domestic cycle of working too hard and spending too much. In practice, though, this often amounted to running away from women and, inevitably, their children. The Beat men chose the path of poverty and experience—romantic as a solo flight, poor as a family plan.

This raised the bar for bohemian women like Parker or Vollmer to participate fully. The lifestyle of hitchhiking around the country, sleeping wherever your last ride let off, seemed unsafe to many women. Nor could they rebel in the same way against the rat race, because they were never in it. Instead, rebellion and independence meant taking jobs to support themselves and often their children. This meant opting *in*. Edie Parker, who earned $27.50 a week as a cigarette girl, shared this sum with Kerouac, keeping him afloat between his stays with his beloved mother, his other safety net. For the men, gender roles had been flipped. Supported by their spouses, they wrote poetry, talked about their feelings and accessed their sensual side. Presenting themselves as sexual objects, in part because of the mixed orientation of their group, they took on everything but the responsibilities of homemaking and child rearing. This was a makeover the women could not match. Where the bohemian women of the 1910s had been at the artistic and political center of a movement for class uplift, Beat women were saddled with feeding downwardly mobile men whose rebellion meant shedding any return obligations.

For this privilege, the women faced the full censure of the 1950s. Joyce Johnson, who took up with Kerouac in 1957 after Ginsberg fixed them up on a blind date (she paid), said she knew only that "I wanted the life of an outlaw rather than the kind of life my mother had had." In a 1996 panel of Beat women writers, Johnson said she and her peers put up with the sexism of Beat men because the rest of society was worse. "In the late fifties, it was an enormous thing for a young woman who wasn't married to leave home, support herself, have her own apartment, have a sex life," she said. "It wasn't the moment *then* to try to transform relationships with men."

The poet Anne Waldman, who was a few years younger than the first Beat generation, later inventoried the damage the women endured from both their families and their partners:

> I knew interesting creative women who became junkies for their boyfriends, who stole for their boyfriends, who concealed their poetry and artistic aspirations, who slept around to be popular, who had serious eating disorders, who concealed their unwanted pregnancies raising money for abortions on their own or who put the child up for adoption. Who never felt they owned or could appreciate their own bodies. I knew women living secret or double lives because love and sexual desire for another woman was anathema. I knew women in daily therapy because their fathers abused them, or women who got sent away to mental hospitals or special schools because they'd taken a black lover. Some ran away from home. Some committed suicide. There were casualties among the men as well, but not, in my experience, as legion.

Though many of these women were writing, often they could not find publishers, or subordinated their ambitions to their partners'. Bonnie Bremser (nee Brenda Frazer), wife of the Beat poet Ray Bremser, endured his physical abuse and turned tricks to support him. In her eyes, he was "surely poetry's representative in the flesh." Finally, on a disastrous trip through Mexico, she abandoned their baby daughter to escape him. Elise Cowen, a Barnard rebel who had the misfortune to fall in love with Ginsberg, was unpublished in her lifetime, but became widely known through a photo of her naked, ironing a shirt. She battled with mental illness and the era's harsh psychotherapies for women who did not fit in. In February 1962 she leapt to her death from a window of her parents' Washington Heights living room.

Like Kerouac and Cassady, many of the women expressed themselves most lucidly in memoirs or journals, which got attention only much later. At the time, the sexual dynamics of the day rendered their knowledge a species of gossip or dish, and the men's musings the hip gospel. Hip history would look much different if this pecking order were reversed. Hettie Cohen helped her lover and future husband LeRoi Jones (Amiri Baraka) run the Beat journal *Yugen* and a publishing imprint called Totem Press, and supported the couple on her small salary from the *Partisan Review*. When later women asked her if she'd really been just a typist, she reminded them that without typists, nothing would have gotten done. But of her Beat days she recalled, "Many, myself included, wanted far more of ourselves than we ever produced. I've been asked how women in that group got published, and the answer, with some notable exceptions, is 'if men wanted to include them.' "

The exception was Diane di Prima. Raised in Brooklyn by conservative Italian-American parents and anarchist grandparents, di Prima dropped out of Swarthmore College in 1953 to become a writer. When she set eyes on "Howl" in 1957, she interrupted a meal she was cooking for friends so she could be alone with the poem. "I sensed that Allen was only, could only be, the vanguard of a much larger thing," she wrote. "All the people who, like me, had hidden and skulked, writing down what they knew for a small handful of friends . . . waiting with only a slight bitterness for the thing to end, for man's era to draw to a close in a blaze of radiation—all these would now step forward and say their piece. Not many would hear them, but they would, finally, hear each other."

Supporting herself with the odd nude modeling gig and by writing the lubricious *Memoirs of a Beatnik* (1969), a cult classic for its Beat orgies and blow jobs, she moved through the downtown worlds of art, literature, dance and music in a man's shirt, Levi's and cropped red hair, often with a baby or two in tow. She considered the archetype of the father as simply an anachronistic myth. When she left a gathering one night at Ginsberg's in order to take care of her children, Kerouac remonstrated: "Di Prima, unless you forget about your babysitter, you're never going to be a writer." Yet she was already there, and no one now would consider Kerouac's scold a message of liberation. She launched the journal *Floating Bear* with LeRoi Jones in 1961, bore a child with him (after his split with Hettie Jones), helped him beat an obscenity charge, and wrote some of the *Bear*'s most significant poems. More than most Beat men or women, she managed to juggle independence and a family, perching both on the far fringe of the economy. The male rebellion was her rebellion as well.

Recognition for other Beat women came only in the 1980s and 1990s. Now their stories had currency: they were valuable precisely because they had been overlooked, never commercialized or consumed. While the male legacy of Kerouac and Cassady resurfaced in jazzy Gap ads, the mature reflections of Beat women provided a new perspective on both past and present. Joyce Johnson, who had become a successful book editor and was responsible for getting *Visions of Cody* published in 1972, won a 1983 National Book Critics' Circle Award for her memoir, *Minor Characters*. Hettie Jones's 1990 memoir, *How I Became Hettie Jones,* examined the Beat era through the lens of family life, and cut through some of the racial sentimentality that still hangs over the period. Two anthologies, *Women of the Beat Generation* (1996) and *A Different Beat: Writings By Women of the Beat Generation* (1997), published some of the writers for the first time.

The juggernaut of rock and roll, which adopted many of the Beats' precepts, moved their rebellions into the commercial marketplace, just as the Jazz Age had commercialized the rebellions of the Greenwich Village moderns. Between rock and roll and the birth-control pill, which was introduced in 1960, entire swaths of American life were suddenly doomed to oblivion, soon to be as remote as gothic romance. America would no longer lock up its independent young women, who had become mainstays of the office economy. By mid-decade it was men's sexual identity, now draped in androgynous long hair, that got the nation in a lather.

The early rock years packaged women and sex as tightly as the 1920s had, serving up mostly man-made sirens or folkie earth mothers. In the new marketplace of the image, women were still commodities, not the ends toward which commodities were shaped. Pop divas served male songwriters or producers; folkies and sexy rock mamas alike played out narrow stereotypes. Where women tampered with the package, their hip gestures were subtle and coded. Ronnie Spector (nee Veronica Bennett) took beatings in her Spanish Harlem high school for her big hair, but as lead singer of the multiracial Ronettes, she flaunted it as a symbol of Aqua Net rebellion. In the prim early 1960s, she recalled, "we didn't do like the Supremes. Our hair would be up in these big beehives with intentions for it to fall down during the show. I always made sure the pin wasn't tight. I loved getting *messy*. Now, my eyes are a little Chinese. I wanted them ALL the way out. The three of us would sit in the mirror and see whose eyes would get out the longest with the eyeliner."

But it was Phil Spector, her domineering husband and producer, who made all the decisions, at home and in her act. This was typical. In the Velvet Underground, Warhol and Paul Morrissey, who managed the band, felt that Lou Reed was not a compelling front man, so they made the group take on a female lead singer. Icy, blonde, a former fashion model, Nico (nee Christa Päffgen, 1938–1988) had trouble with pitch and rhythm, but looked great under the barrage of Warhol's lighting effects. Despite her formidable junkie cool, she was mainly a pretty front, never a full member. She could sing about being Lou's mirror, but he was always the viewer and main object. Ultimately Lou threw her out of the band. (She did not leave before showing the sharpness of her glass, however; after a romantic spat with Reed, she announced to the band at practice, "I cannot make love to Jews anymore.")

When women's economic opportunities changed, hip's subject matter changed with them. No longer was their knowledge denigrated as gossip. By the 1970s and 1980s, women had far greater latitude as protagonists in their own stories. At CBGB, for instance, the loudest sound was often that of female critique. "The only people who had any money, unless you had a trust fund, were the strippers," said the photographer Roberta Bayley, who worked the door at CBGB and later lived with Richard Hell. "The musicians didn't have any money. This was when apartments cost $100 and you still couldn't make your rent. The girls had the money and the moxie and great apartments." A chart posted in the club's ladies room rated the sexual prowess of the male musicians, with spaces for women to dish what they knew.

The stage was also unprecedentedly coed. Because punk began outside the record industry, it didn't have the same male superstructure as mainstream rock; even now, the indie scene is far more female than the corporate labels. Punk women like Patti Smith, Deborah Harry, Lydia Lunch and the Bush Tetras played with female stereotypes, pushing toward butch androgyny or pulling toward Blondie's feminine mask. Unlike the Beat women, they were as autonomous as the men. "I was always Flash Gordon, not his old lady," Patti Smith explained in 1973. Her idols were Keith Richards and Rimbaud, not Patti Page or Emily Dickinson; her idea of hip was Dylan and Bobby Neuwirth in D. A. Pennebaker's documentary *Don't Look Back.* "I never identified with any female at all," she said. "When I had a baby [at 19, as a college student in Glassboro, New Jersey], I was forced to look at myself as a female, although only physically, not intellectually. I gave it away because I had to assert myself as an artist, in a body of work."

In addition to the front women, punk's amateurism opened doors for support players like Tina Weymouth of Talking Heads or Poison Ivy Rorschach of the Cramps, who were simply part of the band. By the generation after the Ramones, groups of boys with guitars seemed figures of male confusion. More captivating acts, especially in the indie scene, were either female or mixed—ESG, Sonic Youth, the Pixies, the Breeders, Hole, P. J. Harvey, Shonen Knife—or else, like Nirvana, Fugazi and Pavement, they slipped far enough from masculinity to goad it from the outside. The future of rock, as Kurt Cobain said, belonged to women.

Simultaneous with punk, hip-hop was inventing its own dialog between men and women. In 1978, the year before the Sugarhill Gang's "Rapper's Delight" became the first rap single, the census reported for the first time that more African-American children were living with one parent than two. The father was disappearing. Hip-hop reflected this. Born out of family disintegration, hip-hop evolved as a wordwise subculture in which parental authority—especially *paternal* presence—was spectral. No culture has been less interested in the past, except as something to be scratched and remixed. The crews of rappers, graffiti writers and break-

Patti Smith

dancers were alternate families, even supplying members with new names. Like nuclear families, many were dysfunctional. Without fathers, graffiti artists proved their existence by writing their names, constructing roots on the side of subway cars or buildings. This was a twist on hip's promise of reinvention: it explored birth without paternity. And as a mostly male way of getting over, it was symbolically feminine, constructing identities in paint and image.

Though hip-hop parties were largely run by men, and often flagrantly sexist, women like the Mercedes Ladies, Sha-Rock, Sequence and the graffiti writer Lady Pink broke through, first as novelties, then as the sexual balance the scene needed; Sylvia Robinson at Sugarhill Records and Monica Lynch at Tommy Boy, the two most important labels, created a hip matriarchy for the new business. Since nothing ended a party like a shoot-out, the scene's masculine energies were always on the verge of tearing it apart—in part because men were adjusting to being both images and producers. It was not enough to act hard, one had to be hard. By the 1990s, as male rappers beat the tired horse of gangsta masculinity, the hippest voices belonged to women like Missy Elliott, Erykah Badu, Eve and Mary J. Blige. If gangsta is the shutting down of a second internal voice, one that could critique the thug pose, female rappers examined their images from all angles. Instead of threats or bluster, they played with topics of seeing and being seen. As Missy rapped, mocking some fans' speculation on her weight loss, "Girl, I heard she eats one cracker a day."

Like the men who rejected male roles, punk and hip-hop women played with sexual identity. Diane di Prima had been a provocation in the 1950s, running the city in a man's shirt and jeans; two decades later, Patti Smith, photographed in a man's shirt and skinny tie by her friend Robert Mapplethorpe for the cover of *Horses* (1975), was an instant rock icon. Smith in her early days railed against feminists, whom she felt missed the power of hip swagger. "Hung-up women," she told Nick Tosches in 1976, "can't produce anything but mediocre art, and there ain't no room for mediocre art. . . . Every time I say the word *pussy* at a poetry reading, some idiot broad rises and has a fit. 'What's your definition of *pussy*, sister?' I dunno, it's a slang term. If I wanna say *pussy*, I'll say *pussy*. If I wanna say *nigger*, I'll say *nigger*. If somebody wants to call me a cracker bitch, that's cool. It's all part of being American. But all these tight-assed movements are fucking up our slang, and that eats it." By the time she withdrew from music in 1979, choosing domestic life in Detroit with her husband, Fred "Sonic" Smith, such an embrace of domesticity was more controversial than any language she might use in her poetry.

As women raised their value in the commercial marketplace, hip circles, even anticommercial ones, began to claim traditionally female qualities as valuable. A group of bands labeled "foxcore" by Thurston Moore of Sonic Youth—Babes in Toyland, Hole, L7—made waves just by wearing girly dresses. Young feminists calling themselves riot grrrls reclaimed traits that had been buried by their elders. Kathleen Hanna of the riot grrrl group Bikini Kill, writing in her zine *Girl Power* in 1991, proposed a new, girl-centric orientation of cool that was the opposite of Patti Smith's:

> For the most part, cool attributes have been claimed by our society as "male." This means that the only way a person brought up GIRL (and thus the opposite of what is cool) can be "truly" cool is to assimilate into male culture via toughness.
>
> By claiming "dork" as cool we can confuse and disrupt this whole

process. The idea is that not only have we decided that being a dork (not repressing our supposedly feminine qualities like niceness and telling people how we feel) is cool and thus, valuable to us BUT also that we are not willing to accept claims that how we are is wrong, undeveloped, bad or . . . . . uncool.

Men played, too, though not always well: by the end of the 1990s, the antimachismo of Kurt Cobain or Pavement gave way to the whine of emo and Coldplay.

A role model for this school of cool has been Kim Gordon of Sonic Youth, who has now survived more than two decades on the indie or alt circuit, along with marriage and motherhood. Riot grrrls, new folkies, singer songwriters, chick rockers, punk dykes and conventional rock women cite her as inspiration or hip godmother, even when their work bears no similarity to Sonic Youth's. Born in West Los Angeles in 1953, she grew up mostly in southern California in the Manson years, flying up to San Francisco to see bands at the Fillmore. "The Beach Boys were still singing these happy songs, but people were starting to see that LA was actually a little sleazy," she said. Like Raymond Chandler, she made this dissonance her métier. Moving to New York after art school in 1980, she discovered the small no wave scene, an art-school response to punk's glorious filth. No wavers rejected punk for being too conventional. As the drummer Jim Sclavunos, who played briefly in Sonic Youth, told the writer Alec Foege, punk "just seemed like a very easy scene for a bunch of losers. And we were determined to be bigger losers, I guess." Gordon didn't play an instrument, so at first she became a critic. One of the first groups that inspired her was a guitar ensemble hopped up on amyl nitrate. "They'd take a big hit and then do the guitar trio thing," she said.

But it was the curious ritual of male bonding that most interested her. "I thought if I really wanted to learn about it, I needed to get in the middle of it," she said. "So I really came as a voyeur." She picked up the bass and ended up in Sonic Youth. As she mused in a 1987 tour diary called "Boys Are Smelly," which was published in the *Village Voice,* "What would it be like to be right at the pinnacle of energy, beneath two guys crossing their guitars, two thunderfoxes in the throes of self-love and male bonding? How sick, but what desire could be more ordinary? How many grannies once wanted to rub their faces in Elvis's crotch, and how many boys want to be whipped by Steve Albini's guitar."

In tight pants or miniskirts, Gordon plays with sexual imagery on-stage, but at a distance. She is as aloof from her husband, guitarist Thurston Moore, as from the audience. She can always step outside the image and comment on it. Some of her best masks are male, uttering creepy lines like "Hey fox, come here / Hey beautiful, come here, sugar . . . Let's go for a ride somewhere / I won't hurt you." As the center of atten-tion, strapped into a phallic guitar, she is a woman playing a man playing a woman, and setting each role aside in quotation marks. Even now, she said, "when people say, what's it like to be a woman in rock, I still think that you have to look at what it's like to be a man in rock. There's some-thing about being tied into electricity and being able to exert lots of sound, that if you do the moves you can feel what it's like to be a man in rock. But I think it's the same thing for guys, who get a sense of what it's like to be the sexualized idea of what a woman is."

As a rejection of roles like good husband or dutiful daughter, hip has pushed steadily toward androgyny or sexual ambiguity. The male re-volt, whatever its hostilities to women, has done its most lasting damage to the borders of masculinity. Nothing is cornier than a dumbly mascu-line jock, frat boy, company man or golf buddy. Male hip has played against these types, celebrating sensitive Beat poets, long-haired hippies, homoerotic motorcycle boys, New York Dolls and grunge rockers in dresses. Hip women, from Bessie Smith to Patti Smith, have picked at the lines of femininity. In gender as in race, hip thrives in the hybrid, the hy-phen. It requires the enlightenment of a second voice: the female within the male, the black within the white, or vice versa. In a society that has devalued women and blacks, hip embraces the feminine and the African.

It is by now a meaningless exercise to single out the women in hip. That's who is there. If you find yourself in the exclusive company of men, and you are not at a YMCA or a gay bar, it probably means you have fallen into in a room full of record nerds, car guys, sweat lodgers or train-spotters. Though MTV, VH1 and *Rolling Stone* still churn out specials on women in rock, these are mainly programming stunts. Zines like

Chicklit, Bitch and *Bust,* which are constitutionally hipper, by now should consider sympathy coverage for boys. The masculine pursuits that have resurged in the 21st century—*Maxim,* drag racing, mud bogging, street ball, demolition derby, extreme fighting—come as either self-conscious kitsch, like the 1990s cocktail culture, or escapist diversions, like the rides at theme parks. They put *masculinity* in quotation marks, something to be explored from the outside, not claimed from within. Their hippest participants are not men but women, who don the requisite wife-beater tops, aviator sunglasses and tattoos, adding a layer of knowingness to the proceedings. These hip pursuits are less a quest for Kerouac's "jewel center of interest" than an ironic celebration of novelty: *the men in hip.* Imagine.

At the same time, domesticity has lost some of its bad odor. A generation after the 1969 Stonewall riots, which began the gay liberation movement after a police raid on the Stonewall Inn in Greenwich Village, the battle lines of gay culture now focus on marriage and parenthood. Baby boomers, who prided themselves on inventing youth culture in the 1960s, invested the same energies in parenthood in the 1980s and 1990s. Their children in turn took domestic hints from shows like MTV's *Cribs,* in which rappers and rockers showed off pads more stylish and inventive than most of their music. It was no longer clear that the jewel center of interest lay on the road and not at home.

The economy of the late 20th century changed from a model that is traditionally masculine—building things—to a traditionally female one, which sells images. The old model favored male hipsters; the new one does not. In the 1990s, the most mesmerizing male figures—Kurt Cobain, Tupac Shakur, the Notorious B.I.G.—all died violent deaths. Tupac and Biggie were killed in drive-by shootings in 1996 and 1997; Cobain killed himself in the garage apartment of his Seattle home in April 1994. Biggie and Kurt both left behind young children. Unlike past hipster tragedies such as James Dean or Lenny Bruce, the three died in conflict not with a disapproving outside world, but with their mostly male peers or fans. Where Kim Gordon or Deborah Harry made careers of providing both image and commentary, the three men were held by audiences that did not want them to step out from behind the mask to dissect it. Yet even after their deaths, their male fans measure themselves by the performers' "realness." Male hip did not prepare men for this economy that expects them to be both real and unreal.

If women are hipper, and if domesticity has lost some of its square taint, it is in part because both move beyond this self-destruction. Women have long manipulated myth and image, playing with the space between image and reality. They are rarely destroyed when the two are not the same. This is a trickster move, using image to mean two things. The stories of women like Gordon, Sofia Coppola, Missy Elliott, Zadie Smith, Meg White, Lauryn Hill, Macy Gray, Danzy Senna, Eve, Erykah Badu and the rest take image and myths as beginnings, not ends. They restore the second internal voice—not the confusion, but the commentary on the confusion. This second voice, wise and unruffled, speaks the secrets of hip.

12

behind the music

the drug connection

> Heroin was our badge. Hipsters used heroin. Squares didn't. Heroin gave us membership in a unique club, and for this membership we gave up everything else in the world. Every ambition. Every desire. Everything.
> —RED RODNEY

In 1964, Paul Krassner, founder of the underground magazine the *Realist,* asked Terry Southern to define hipness. Southern's screenplay to *Dr. Strangelove* was then in theaters, and his meta-smutty novel *Candy,* written with Mason Hoffenberg, was on the bestseller list. In the interview, which was conducted by mail, Southern (1924–1995) wrote the way he talked, in *italics* and . . . ellipses.

"Well," he began, "in the strictest sense of the word, I'd say . . . a certain *death* of something near the center."

How does this develop? Krassner asked.

"Obviously it begins with an *awareness* far beyond the ordinary and a kind of emotional hypersensitiveness, or empathy, so acute that it's unbearably painful and has to be anesthetized—so what is left in the end is 'iron in the soul' . . . awareness but total insulation from emotion. The big trick, of course—and I don't know that it's ever really been done—is to eliminate all the negative emotion and retain the positive."

He cut to the chase: "About the hippest anyone has gotten so far, I suppose, is to be permanently on the nod."

The romance of self-destruction, to which Southern had given much thought, has been a troubling constant throughout hip history. From the moonshine of Delta juke joints to the heroin despair of Kurt Cobain, every circle of hip can be identified by its intoxicants and casualties, and each would be lonely without them. The cliché of the hipster, wearing sunglasses that hide his pupils and talking slang that covers his intent, is the profile of a junkie. Some drug historians propose that the colloquial use of *hip* began with early opium smokers, who reclined on one hip to smoke; people who "laid the hip" could spot fellow travelers by their telltale bruises. In less archaic times, Mailer wrote that the hipster attitudes of his white negroes "to a certain extent come out of drug-taking," in the belief that "the drug-taker is probably receiving something from God. Love perhaps." In the ménage-à-trois that Mailer postulated among bohemians, hoodlums and African Americans, "[i]f marijuana was the wedding ring, the child was the language of Hip."

The connections between hip and drugs run deep. Like hip, drugs turn outsiders into insiders, forming what Amiri Baraka called "the most securely self-assured in-group extant in the society." Writing specifically about bop and heroin, which in the 1950s were nearly synonymous, Baraka argued that dope transformed "the Negro's normal separation from the mainstream of the society into an advantage (which, I have been saying, I think it is anyway)." The drug fraternity, which includes all races and ethnicities, is both elite and self-sustaining, with its own language, hours, morality, technical skills and economy. As the narrator of Gus Van Sant's 1989 film *Drugstore Cowboy* put it, dope (from the Dutch *doop,* or "sauce") cuts through all other measures of social status. You're either in or out. "See, most people, they don't know how they're going to feel from one moment to the next," he said. "But the dope fiend has a pretty good idea. All you gotta do is look at the labels on the little bottles." Mezz Mezzrow, the white negro who brought his quality grass, known simply as Mezz, to Harlem in 1930, repeated hip's line in his sales pitch. "Light up," he'd say, "and be somebody."

One way to look at the relationship between drugs and hip is as a business arrangement. Drugs are the product, hip is the marketing plan.

Decades before the advent of lifestyle advertising, hip linked drug use to a lifestyle that is sexy, rebellious and streetwise. Americans spent $64 billion on illegal drugs in 2000, according to the federal Office of National Drug Control Policy—eight times what they spent on movies that year, and more than four times what they spent on recorded music. Drugs open trade routes, sustain political careers, destabilize nations and reinforce the unequal relationship between the developed world and its suppliers. In this traffic, hip exists because narco-dollars need it to.

Though most people take drugs for pleasure, hip clings more to the downside: the furtiveness of copping, the risk of harm, the compulsions of the addict. Without consequences drugs have no meaning. Chippers, sippers, dabblers and moderate hobbyists—in other words, the vast majority of drug users—do not make the pantheon. As Lou Reed wrote in the liner notes to his 1975 *Metal Machine Music,* "no sniffers please." For this reason there is no such thing as an anti-drug movie. Even the most sordid depiction of drug use, such as *Trainspotting* (1995), in which Ewan McGregor literally dives into the toilet for a fix, works as an unwitting advertisement for the drug, because hip finds enlightenment at the bottom of the dive, not the top.

Dee Dee Ramone (1952–2002) recalled a similarly ripe adventure with Sid Vicious (1957–1979) during one of the Ramones' early European tours. They were at a party on King's Road in London, deprived of chemicals, when a German man offered Dee Dee some speed. He didn't know what to do with it at first, he recalled.

> Then, with Sid trailing along behind me, we headed to the toilet to figure it out. There was vomit everywhere. On the floor, in the sink, and overflowing from the toilet bowls. . . . I hadn't seen anything yet, though, not until Sid produced a horrible syringe with old blood caked around the needle. I gave Sid some of the speed and he tapped it into the syringe to load it up for a hit. Then he stuck the needle into the toilet and drew up water from the bowl into the hypo so he could coldshake the speed that was in the outfit. The water had vomit, piss, and snot in it. Sid didn't seem to think that this was in any way out of the ordinary. His main concern seemed to be to shoot up and was prepared to put up with any amount of discomfort for the rush. *Now I've seen it all,* I thought.

As gamy as it is, this story nestles into hip lore beside the chemical misadventures of Charlie Parker, William Burroughs, Miles, Kerouac, Lou Reed and any number of subsequent hipsters. Its indifference is part of its allure. As Southern said, there is something beatific about the nod. If hip is the ability to put one's empathy at a distance, to insulate the self from pain, then drugs provide a concrete measure of how much it hurts. Like the money shot in a porn movie, which provides visible proof of the actor's pleasure, drugs act as tangible proof of the users' pain—and therefore their sensitivity. They render feelings as a commodity, to be measured in grams or grains. The more damaging the treatment, the more intense the feelings must be.

What does it mean, then, that reasonable people get off on such unreasonable behavior? The question rarely elicits more than *Beavis and Butt-head* tautology: drugs are cool because they're cool. There is a circular logic to the relationship, like the chicken and the egg. Hipsters mimic the junkie shuffle, and drugs soak up hip's rebel mystique. In a nation addicted to progress, hip and drugs both break the cycle. To be hip or high is to be outside the authority of church, state, work, school and the law. This resignation is the one facet of hip that the mainstream cannot co-opt and still be the mainstream. It is the elitism of last resort.

The substances themselves are neutral, of course, neither hip nor unhip. Nothing in the pharmacology of the opium poppy foreshadows the music of Miles Davis or Stan Getz, or the lucid prose of Denis Johnson or William Burroughs. Kerouac, who liked to write on Benzedrine, found it compatible with his flow. He once asked Donald Allen, one of his editors, to score for him, pleading, "With good white benny tablets I can rattle off amazing chapters and be *interested* in them as I go along." But if the substances are neutral, the prohibitions against them lend all drugs an aura of forbidden knowledge. For upwards of half the population, that innocuous first joint, which ends not in reefer madness but in munchies and *Dark Side of the Moon,* provides an early clue that what their school, parents or government tells them is suspect, and that enlightenment lies elsewhere. Drug epiphanies can be dopey, but this revelation is both clear and profound, and essential to our story here.

Timothy Leary used to distinguish between life drugs, like pot and psychedelics, and death drugs, like heroin and coke. The romance of hip attaches mostly to the latter. At its purest, this story is about heroin. A semisynthetic derivative of opium poppies, diacetylmorphine, as it is chemically known, was first synthesized in 1874 by the English chemist C. R. Wright, as a nonaddictive alternative to morphine. Its first manufacturer, the German pharmaceutical company Friedrich Bayer, christened their product Heroin to suggest the German adjective *heroisch*, or heroic. Such corporate hype has preceded hip approval for all drugs, according to the historian David T. Courtwright, author of *Forces of Habit: Drugs and the Making of the Modern World* (2001). Sometimes the hype has come from manufacturers, sometimes from doctors, who also profit from the product. "Only drugs that were widely used in western societies became global commodities," Courtwright noted, and these only after they had been embraced and promoted by the medical profession.

Charlie Parker, of course, was the alpha heroin user. Born in 1920, Parker began using as a teenager in Kansas City, Missouri. At the time, the city's corrupt mayor, Boss Tom Pendergast, ran the town as his own lucrative vice den, flooding the streets with jazz, booze, prostitution, gambling and drugs. The young Parker, who as a teen showed little promise on the horn, was a natural in this other river of temptation and profit. For Parker, heroin cured what nothing else could; it was both disease and remedy in one neat package. That's why it is called a fix. As he explained to the pianist Walter Bishop Jr., who played with him in the 1950s, "I go to this heart specialist and he treats me but it don't do no good. I go to this ulcer man and give him seventy-five dollars to cool my ulcers out and it don't do no good. There's a little cat in a dark alley and I give him five dollars for a bag of shit—my ulcer's gone, my heart trouble is gone. Everything is gone."

At his peak, when younger acolytes like Sonny Rollins, Chet Baker, Jackie McLean and Frank Morgan followed him to the needle, he used to lecture them against the drug's ravages. But he was less than convincing; the more ragged he was, the more they associated raggedness with his art. Besides, at the end of his lectures, he often asked these followers to help him cop. By 1955, three years after his daughter died of pneumonia, he staggered through the audience at a New York club where Dizzy Gillespie

Chet Baker

was playing and pleaded, "Diz, why don't you save me?" Gillespie couldn't. Parker died that March at the age of 34; the coroner who examined his body guessed his age to be between 50 and 60.

To peel the onion a little, there are hipsters who happen to use junk; people who use it to be hip; and people who live vicariously through the dope use of others. Chet Baker (1929–1988) drifted through several of these categories. Born in Oklahoma just after the 1929 stock market crash, Baker grew up under an abusive, alcoholic father who played jazz guitar and smoked weed. Chet started using heroin around 1951, the year after the great trumpeter Fats Navarro died from tuberculosis and chronic heroin use. Baker, who had only average chops, built a huge audience with his combination of matinee idol beauty, emotionally remote performances and well-publicized drug habit. Until his looks failed him he was a figure of untouchable narcotic glamour. During a rough patch in 1963 he posed for a British tabloid preparing to shoot up. "It wasn't for cheap thrills that I took heroin and cocaine," he rationalized. "Hadn't

Charlie 'Bird' Parker, one of the greatest jazz talents America had ever produced, been an addict? Couldn't I, too, be a genius with the intravenal aid of narcotics?"

What dope offers, and what unites these disparate types, is a suspension of responsibility, a fuckup's version of grace. Heroin is a kind of self-administered fate. The white saxophonist Art Pepper, in his unsparing autobiography, *Straight Life,* described dope as a release from the indignity of personal options. He snorted his first taste in 1950 with a singer named Sheila Harris, about whom he observed, "When you looked at her you just saw your cock in her mouth." As the dope hit him, he said, he no longer worried about what to do or why.

> I said, "This is it. This is the only answer for me. If this is what it takes, then this is what I'm going to do, whatever dues I have to pay. . . ." And I *knew* that I would get busted and I *knew* that I would go to prison and that I wouldn't be weak; I wouldn't be an informer like all the phonies, the no-account, the nonreal, the zero people that roam around, the scum that slither out from under rocks, the people that destroyed music, that destroyed this country, that destroyed the world. . . .
>
> All I can say is, at that moment I saw that I'd found peace of mind. Synthetically produced, but after what I'd been through and all the things I'd done, to trade that misery for total happiness—that was it, you know, that was it.

In his 1974 study, *Popular Culture and High Culture,* the sociologist Herbert J. Gans distinguished between total cultures, "which seek to exist apart from mainstream or straight society," and partial cultures, which "are practiced by people who still 'belong' to mainstream society." Heroin is a total culture. Though it is not a loquacious or social drug, it creates its own fraternity. "Junk," Burroughs wrote, "is not, like alcohol or weed, a means to increased enjoyment of life. Junk is not a kick. It is a way of life." As the top of the drug ladder, heroin is a perfect commodity, exhausting the resources of its users while eliminating the need for other commodities. Users reinvent themselves in its image; after all, what is an addict but someone who has become an adjunct to his product, rather than the other way around? As a metaphor, dope captures the hip universe in a glassine packet, branded to find its target market: Body Bag, Hellraiser, Homicide, Poison, No Way Out.

What hip shares with drugs, as Burroughs hints at above, is a capacity for organizing time, removing it from the forward thrust of the straight world. Both shape it to their own rhythm. Though psychoactive substances have been around for millennia, what we refer to as the drug culture and hip both arise in response to the modern problem of time. The electric light made time something that needed to be managed. Ann Marlowe, an East Village music critic who spent seven years snorting dope, described the experience as a way to stop the clock. "Nonusers wonder why junkies with serious habits don't see the absurdity of arranging their whole day around their need for heroin," she wrote. "[B]ut they've got it the wrong way around. One reason people become junkies is to find some compelling way of arranging their lives on an hour-to-hour basis."

Or as Burroughs put it, "Junkies run on junk time and junk metabolism. They are subject to junk climate. They are warmed and chilled by junk. The kick of junk is living under junk conditions." This rhythm, neatly expressed in the name of the East Village band Cop Shoot Cop, shields users from any concerns outside itself. A goal of hip, then, is to approximate this relationship with time—which becomes, by extension, a relationship with time's one inescapable consequence. Namely, death.

Lou Reed used to wonder that people thought the Velvet Underground song "Heroin," in which the narrator sings about the decision "to nullify my life," glamorized the drug. Novelists had long written about heroin, sometimes in a cautionary way, sometimes naturalistically. Reed said he wrote the song as a neutral exploration, to "exorcise the darkness, or the self-destructive element in me." He hoped other people would take it the same way. It was not meant to be fun. " 'Heroin' is very close to the feeling you get from smack," he said. "It starts on a certain level, it's deceptive. You think you're enjoying it. But by the time it hits you, it's too late. You don't have any choice. It comes at you harder and faster and keeps on coming. The song is everything that the real thing is doing to you."

Recorded in 1966 and released the following year, "Heroin" is a model of the flow between hip, drugs and the romance of self-destruction. No

Velvet Underground. Lou Reed, Sterling Morrison, and John Cale at Rhode Island School of Design, Providence, RI, March 1967

cultural artifact has accrued more hip cachet than the first Velvet Underground album, with "Heroin" as its centerpiece. As Brian Eno famously quipped, hardly anyone bought that first album, but everyone who did started a band. Formed in New York in 1965, the band forged the template for the city's rock underground, drawing from avant-garde film, experimental music, street poetry, free jazz, decaying real estate and the budding urban pharmacopoeia. The gallery of New York indie heroes, from the Dolls to Sonic Youth to the Strokes, followed in the Velvets' wake. For Reed, drugs were a protection that allowed him to work. "I take drugs just because in the twentieth century in a technological age, living in the city, there are certain drugs you can take just to keep yourself normal like a caveman," he said. "Not just to bring yourself up and down, but to attain equilibrium you need to take certain drugs. They don't get you high, even, they just get you normal." In an era when musicians made coy references to weed or acid, "Heroin" introduced a starker vocabulary: the spike going in the vein, the blood shooting up the dropper's neck—the latter a reference to the "register" that tells a user he's in a vein.

Reed wrote "Heroin" as a student at Syracuse University, during what he called a very "negative, strung-out, violent, aggressive" period in his life. Born in 1942 in Brooklyn, the son of an accountant who changed the family's name from Rabinowitz, Lewis Alan Reed grew up in the middle-class suburb of Freeport, Long Island, struggling with his sexuality and the smother of home life. His best work, John Cale believed, came from his hostility to his parents. "I think he might start writing some good songs again, were he to go back and live with his parents," Cale snipped, years after the Velvets' breakup. In 1959, the year before Lou went to Syracuse, his parents sent him to Creedmore State Psychiatric Hospital for electric shock treatments to curb his homosexual tendencies. After these treatments, Reed said, "You can't read a book because you get to page seventeen and you have to go right back to page one again. Or if you put the book down for an hour and went back to pick up where you started, you didn't remember the pages you read. You had to start over." It may be a coincidence, but the Velvets' music often moved in this same rhythm: there is a statement, then confusion, then sludgy movement back toward clarity.

"Heroin" begins with single strokes on the guitar, not quite marking time. Reed's voice enters before the full band, stating the problem, which is not drugs but life: "I don't know just where I'm going." As the first verse gathers momentum, the music rises around the words, cranking and stopping on the screech of Cale's viola and Maureen Tucker's no-brakes tom-toms. The sound grows denser as it accelerates, compressing time into ever-shorter measures. The verbs are gerunds, arrested in mid-action. Lou is "rushing on my run"; he's "closing in on death." From any point in the song, you sense that things are only going to get worse. Then, rather than build this rush to a crescendo—closing *all the way* in on death—the musicians abruptly stop, leaving the hangover of feedback and disordered time. Part of its slurry effect was an accident of the studio, where Maureen Tucker couldn't hear the other musicians. Finally the noise was too much, she said. "I stopped, and being a little wacky, they just kept going, and that's the one we took."

The result calls to mind the use of stop-time in jazz, in which the rhythm section drops out and a soloist keeps flying. Reed was a big fan of Ornette Coleman, and even as a student traveled to New York to see him, often using the trips as occasions to buy drugs. But the effect of "Heroin" is wholly different. Jazz stop-time calls attention to the underlying pulse, which holds the music together even without anyone playing it. It's just there. The stops in "Heroin," on the other hand, show how unmoored time has been all along. Like Twain's river or Kerouac's open road, which restart the action at each bend, "Heroin" interrupts the sequence of cause and effect, building to climaxes that never come. When Lou starts to look backward, wishing he "was born a thousand years ago," sailing "in a great big clipper ship," wearing a "sailor's suit and cap," the lyrics don't register; they're part of the distortion and feedback, like random noise. (And as images they're a little silly, unless you want to market a Maritime Lou action figure.)

Ignored upon its release, the song became the seminal "no" that launched a thousand indie bands, and in its message the "yes" that launched a thousand nods. Elliott Murphy, writing the liner notes to *1969: Velvet Underground Live,* wondered, "What goes through a mother's mind when she asks her fifteen-year-old daughter, 'What's the name of that song you're listening to?' and her daughter replies, 'Heroin'?" Reed honored the Velvets' legacy in the manner of hipsters before him, not by milking it but by squandering it in self-parody, shaving an iron cross in his peroxide hair and pretending to shoot up onstage. The great critic Lester Bangs, who had his own history of drug abuse, called Reed "the guy that gave dignity and poetry and rock 'n' roll to smack, speed, homosexuality, sadomasochism, murder, misogyny, stumblebum passivity, and suicide, and then proceeded to belie all his achievements and return to the mire by turning the whole thing into a monumental bad joke with himself as the woozily insistent Henny Youngman in the center ring, mumbling punch lines that kept losing their punch." Even so, in the same essay Bangs added that Lou Reed was his hero "principally because he stands for all the most fucked up things that I could ever possibly conceive of. Which probably only shows the limits of my imagination."

Like other circus spectacles, Reed outgrew his past, holding himself above it as he did his fans and critics. Removed from its encompassing present tense, the Velvets' music still sounds freshly scornful, but it feels less threatening or deviant than foundational. If suburban garage bands cover it, it literally can't be the end of the world. The shock of the old is nothing if not comfortingly familiar. Honda used Reed's "Walk on the

Wild Side," about East Village transvestites, to sell scooters, and his *Metal Machine Music,* long considered unlistenable, was performed in Berlin in 2002 by a German new music ensemble called Zeitkratzer, with Reed joining onstage opening night. In another demonstration of how time accommodates hip, he played "Sweet Jane" at the White House, and brought former Czech Republic president Vaclav Havel and U.S. secretary of state Madeleine Albright to the New York club the Knitting Factory. In 2003, he even officiated at a wedding ceremony in upstate New York.

But "Heroin," written by an unhappy postadolescent during the Lyndon Johnson administration, will outlast all these incarnations. Though he no longer plays it or even discusses it, it remains his claim to a kind of plainspoken, unspeakable truth. In the suspended animation of the band rushing on its run, closing in on death, it comes as close as a pop song can to the full awareness of life. As Cale said, about hearing it for the first time, "There was commitment there. That was the powerful advantage that all of Lou's lyrics had. All Bob Dylan was singing was questions—How many miles? and all that. I didn't want to hear any more questions. Give me some tough social situations and show that answers are possible. And sure enough, 'Heroin' was one of them. It wasn't sorry for itself."

So what about this is hip?

When we talk about America's drug culture, we are really talking about a history of drug cultures. The opium poppy was first cultivated in lower Mesopotamia around 3400 B.C. The Sumerians called it *hul gil,* or "joy plant." It awaited the maladies of urban societies, such as anxiety, boredom, pain, insomnia and diarrhea. Cocaine, a derivative of the coca plant, which goes back about as far, was a perfect complement, promising energy, stamina and relief from moodiness. America's first drug epidemic began in the late 19th century when the shipping industry and pharmaceutical business, a mostly unregulated market filled with patent medicines, combined to make cocaine and morphine, an opium derivative, widely available. By the start of the 20th century, America had about 250,000 opiate addicts and 200,000 cocaine addicts. In a population of about 75 million, the drug historian Jill Jonnes surmises from these numbers that about 1 in 200 Americans was strung out on coke or morphine, allowing that some were addicted to both.

Yet these addicts have little bearing on the history of hip. They were mostly middle-class women, operating within the law—unless they became prostitutes to support their habits—taking the drugs under medical auspices, however vaguely (and self-servingly) defined. After Congress passed the Harrison Narcotic Act in 1914, regulating opiates and cocaine, these medical addicts gave way to a new type of user, drawn to drugs for pleasure. These new users were mainly working-class men, operating outside the law, without the cover of medical sanction. They were outsiders, bohemians, marginal figures, whose habits threw them into contact with other marginal circles, specifically those of crime and the creative arts. As Burroughs said, altered consciousness is the artist's stock in trade—if he can't provide it, what good is he? In these two eras the same drugs, used for roughly the same effects, produced entirely different cultures. It is this latter group, with its confluence of crime, drugs, pleasure and art, that attached hip to drug use.

We often think of hip as marking geographic space. Every city has a hip neighborhood, and every hip neighborhood has a hot spot or two: maybe a bar or a shooting gallery or a congenial apartment. These spaces are essential to bohemia, allowing people to exchange ideas, hook up or just validate their existence outside the mainstream. As the sociologist Randall Collins notes in *The Sociology of Philosophies: A Global Theory of Intellectual Change,* the history of ideas is the history of these small cliques and the "emotional energy and cultural capital" transmitted between them. The cliques can be both nurturing and competitive. Members push each other to wilder ideas or styles. They produce zines, record labels, design studios, black market businesses, which then expand the networks of hip. The radicalism of the Greenwich Village moderns, the intellectual dap of bebop or the woolly growl of punk—all would not have come together without physical spaces where people could link their ideas.

Within these bohemian spaces, drugs operate as catalysts, bringing together people from different corners of the social matrix. One of the titles Mezz Mezzrow claimed was the Man Who Linked the Races (admittedly, this was not as colorful as another sobriquet, the Man with the Righteous Bush). The Harlem Renaissance would not have blossomed without Prohibition, which drew white people uptown, then dissolved the social barriers in bootleg hooch. The bonds of the 1960s youth culture formed in the places kids could get high; the smell of weed signaled that everyday prohibitions had been suspended. In most cities in America, the most democratic institution is the needle exchange or the illegal drug market, where college kids fraternize with homeless vets, blacks with whites, turbo capitalists with slum anarchists.

Perched, like hip itself, in neighborhoods not yet coveted by the gentry, the drug market glosses distinctions of class or race for the egalitarian immediacies of need. In other words, if you deal it, they will come. The myth of a beautiful mosaic, which rings hollow in much of the straight world, comes to life in the democracy of addiction. In this sense the dope spot is a cash-only distillation of America at its most naked. When the last crack house becomes a yoga center, and private courier services replace street markets for the middle class, offering employee benefits that in some cases already include Christmas bonuses and health insurance, the nation will have lost a pitiless X-ray of its reptilian self.

But as much as hip organizes space, it also organizes time. A recurrent theme of this book is that hip produces a continuous present tense, cut loose from past and future. Whitman and the 19th century transcendentalists accomplished this through intense contemplation, which stilled the clock; the Beats and beboppers got there by fetishizing the moment of improvisation; hip hoppers by inventing their names and personae, severing the continuities of family and bloodline. All of these suspend time. When Southern in his definition of hipness described an "awareness but total insulation from emotion," he meant a disruption of time; in this insulated state we see causes but do not undergo effects. The vapor time of "Heroin," similarly, interrupts the change of tense. The song's kick is not that it braves the consequences of dope, but that it creates a logical system where there can be no consequences, because one thing does not follow from the next. Lou doesn't know where he's going because he isn't going anywhere. The song has freed him from that obligation.

In the same way that hipsters move into unwanted neighborhoods, creating value in their wake, hip colonizes unvalued time, imbuing it with worth. The metaphor of the open road is so central to hip because it suspends time in the present tense. The point of origin or destination (i.e., the past or the future), is secondary to the adventures of the road itself. As Kerouac writes in *On the Road,* movement itself is the thing:

> "Sal, we gotta go and never stop going till we get there."
> "Where we going, man?"
> "I don't know but we gotta go."

In many ways organizing time is more significant than organizing space. Hip scenes begin not with locations but with concentrations of people with free time. There can be no hangouts without time to hang, and no free time without an ethic that frees time from other demands. Hipsters can always find a new 'hood or a new hangout, but if they lose their time, sacrificing it to the job market or other soul-depleting pursuit, they can never have those hours back.

Time as we experience it, like hip, is a modern phenomenon, evolving with America's transition from a rural, Victorian society to an urban, industrial one. Industry made time a commodity, ascribing a dollar value to certain hours while considering others, namely leisure hours, as without value. The rewards of the work world lie arbitrarily in the future: having a job means literally exchanging the present for a future paycheck. Church and school, which are handmaidens to the job market, similarly train people to trade gratification in the present for a payoff down the line.

Hip flips this script, defining leisure time as productive, and working hours as time down the drain. Hip, as Whitman might have argued, is the prerogative of the loafer, the vagrant, the slacker. Instead of producing widgets or spreadsheets, hipsters produce hipness. The payoff for hip is not in the future, but in the present. (In this sense being hip differs from being an artist, which might require years of training and not be appreciated until after death.) The more useless hip is—the further from the machinations of work—the more productive, because it colonizes more time. The sociologist Harold Finestone, in a landmark study of a Chicago housing project which he published in 1957 under the title "Cats, Kicks, and Color," concluded—in delightfully mixed lingo—that "in emphasizing as he does the importance of the 'kick' [getting high] the cat is attacking the value our society places upon planning for the future and the

William Burroughs circa 1965 *(Hulton Archive/Getty Images)*

responsibility of the individual for such planning. Planning always requires some subordination and disciplining of present behavior in the interest of future rewards. . . . [T]he 'kick' appears to be a logical culmination of this emphasis."

Drugs trump other claims on time by colonizing it for their own needs. As a junked-up dealer tells his shivery customer in Burroughs's *Naked Lunch,* "I don't want your money, Honey: I want your Time." Drug time, as Burroughs said, can be pleasant or unpleasant, but it provides reliable shelter from the future—whatever happens tomorrow, it won't happen to you. Similarly, junk time makes the past irrelevant: your identity reflects not the accidents that got you here, but the substances that are on the market at any given moment. Charlie Parker once described this effect to his third wife, Doris, explaining that time was different for him. "When *you* have a bad day," he said, "there's nothing you can do about it. You have to endure it. When I have a bad day, I know where to go and what to do to make a good day out of it."

Drug trends ebb and flow with the rhythms of the economy—coke in a fast market, to keep up with time, dope in a slow one, to fill the hours.

Ecstasy served the binge economy of the 1980s and 1990s, which alter-
nated long hours of intense focus during the workweek with long hours
of focused rave. But at either speed, the promise of drugs is more time,
not less. Thomas De Quincey (1785–1859), the godfather of dope literature, addressed this promise in his classic *Confessions of an Opium Eater.*
For De Quincey, opium opened up the present, which was otherwise just
a mathematical illusion. "Of that time which we call the present," he
wrote, "hardly a hundredth part but belongs either to a past which has
fled, or to a future which is still on the wing. It has perished, or it is not
born. It was, or it is not. Yet even this approximation to the truth is infinitely false. For again subdivide that solitary drop, which only was found
to represent the present, into a lower series of similar fractions, and the
actual present which you arrest measures now but the thirty-sixth mil-
lionth of an hour." Opium allows the user to inhabit this frozen instant,
which would otherwise subdivide until it was nothing. The drug *produces*
the present tense.

Like hip, drugs spin a romance of time redeemed. Drug thinking,
which is always self-serving, treats dead time as *purposefully* dead time. Its
parameters are harsh but forgiving. "He'd wasted his entire life," says the
junkie narrator of Denis Johnson's story "Out on Bail," upon meeting an
acquaintance just out of rehab. "Such people were very dear to those of us
who'd wasted only a few years. With Kid Williams sitting across from you
it was nothing to contemplate going on like this for another month or so."
Ann Marlowe, who balanced her dope habit against the time it demanded, rationalized, "In the nod, I felt less guilty than when I simply
daydreamed, for I wrote nod time off as accounted-for leisure. . . . Time,
concretized as a powder, becomes fungible, and thus harmless. The past
is heroin that has been consumed, and the future is heroin that you have
yet to buy. There is nothing unique about the past to mourn, and nothing unique about the future to fear. For awhile."

Isolating time in the present tense might seem like a way to deny
death. If time doesn't pass, after all, how can anybody die? But the opposite is true. To live in the present, as Mailer said of Cold War hip, is to accept the terms of death. The threat of death is always in the present tense,
whereas rituals celebrating the past or future hide mortality. Planning for
the future presumes that you will be around to see it. Even apocalyptic

scenarios let you imagine the world ending rather than going on without you. Similarly, nostalgia is comforting because it revisits a past in which we know we did not die. We are invulnerable within its amber; in our pasts we are all immortal. Retro hip rests on this false assurance. Hip's continuous present tense serves as a reminder that time runs out—that we are all, as Lou says, closing in on death. In the absence of stronger religion, this acknowledgement fills the present tense with meaning.

Hip conveys this memento mori through style. The joyous fatalism of the blues, the slapstick violence of pulp, the self-invention of outlaws and confidence men, the homicidal swagger of gangsta rap, the goofball nihilism of punk—all are most compelling, and funniest, when they are rubbing elbows with death. They allow us to explore death without horror; it is out there, but not yet ours. Like the notes of a Miles Davis solo, death becomes all potential and implication, forever captured in the act of becoming. Though some people think hip is trivial, it is never far from this decidedly nontrivial acknowledgment. Squareness, on the other hand—saving for a rainy day, minding your p's and q's—is at odds with death. Remember the real estate man Flitcraft in *The Maltese Falcon* who realizes that the delusion that life can be ordered to preclude death puts one "out of step, not into step, with life." By bringing death back into the picture, hip seeks to get back in step.

The romance of drugs makes this explicit. I do not mean that people who take drugs want to die, but that drug culture provides one of our rare unblinking acknowledgements that it is coming. Martin Scorsese, who horned as many drugs as his body could withstand in the late 1970s, told the journalist Peter Biskind, "It was a matter of pushing the envelope, of being bad, seeing how much you can do. Embracing a way of life to its limit. I did a lot of drugs because I wanted to do a lot, I wanted to push all the way to the very very end, and see if I could die. That was the key thing, to see what it would be like getting close to death." This is the crux of it: a view of death without the thing itself—a present tense that does not give way to the inevitable future. Returning to the Velvets' "Heroin," death is present but at bay, a shoe ever waiting to drop. Reed thanks God that he's "good as dead," but there is no chance of his getting there, no matter how many times you listen to the song.

If drugs are hip, in the sense of enlightenment or *hipi,* it is because we use them as a surrogate for the unknowable. Mortality is beyond our understanding, but a bag of dope is a mystery that can be solved; cook it up and it will tell all of its secrets: its purity, its intent, its value. Like hip slang, which means more than it says, drugs operate as a medium of language. Their message may be warmth, joy, healing, pain and death, made democratically available to all. Which is to say, the stuff of life. In the junk self-destruction of an idol, such as Iggy or Bird, who appear both heroic and damaged, we can see the universality of their fall. There is more to enjoying these self-destructive figures, even vicariously, than egging them on. Their end awaits us all. If hip has a claim to enlightenment, it begins in this fundamental recognition.

Does this mean that self-destruction is hip?
Terry Southern believed it was worth the risk, just to numb the pain; Lou Reed got hip and out of it; Charlie Parker tried to hip colleagues away from his life. The tragic drunks and drug addicts who fill hip's rosters—Jackson Pollock, Charles Bukowski, Dorothy Parker, F. Scott Fitzgerald, Hart Crane, Billie Holiday, Hank Williams, Lenny Bruce, Jack Kerouac, Neal Cassady, John Coltrane, Chet Baker, Janis Joplin, Jimi Hendrix, Johnny Thunders, Jerry Nolan, Kurt Cobain, Darby Crash, River Phoenix and so on—all cut larger public figures because of their habits, whether they needed to or not. Their other, more extraordinary accomplishments compete for attention. Viewed through the prism of his willful self-destruction, a figure like Pollock remains forever in the present tense, spared the indignity of accruing a past or the inconsistency of outgrowing one. Such purity loves company. The streets of the East Village, Hollywood or Capitol Hill in Seattle run with angelheaded hipsters who took *Naked Lunch* or *Nevermind* too literally, now stretching their heroin highs with Klonopin.

The night Charlie Parker died, March 12, 1955, the saxophonist Frank Morgan was blowing with Dexter Gordon and Wardell Gray at the California Club in Los Angeles. Like most jazz musicians of his generation, Morgan, who was 22, had grown up idolizing Parker. The son of a guitarist, he picked up the saxophone after seeing Parker in a Detroit theater when he was seven; when he turned 17 he graduated to Parker's other habit. "I thought that one used heroin to play like Charlie Parker played," Morgan later told Gary Giddins. When the news of Parker's death reached the bandstand, the musicians called a break—and shot up. "I paid tribute to Bird by getting high," Morgan said later. "Which is what I would have done anyway. Instead of frightening me, Bird's death clouded my thinking even more. I decided it was kind of on me to carry the torch, not as a musician, but as a dope fiend." Morgan spent the next decades in and out of drug programs and the California penal system; Wardell Gray was found dead in the desert two months after Parker's death, possibly from a heroin overdose. The saxophonist Gene Ammons, who also shot up with the group that night, went on to seven years of prison time on drug charges.

One of the paradoxes of hip, as Morgan's journey underscores, is that at its most committed or single-minded, hip is not hip at all. Hip is an aesthetic of the hybrid, the mongrel. As a system of intelligence, it learns through inconsistencies, just as the larger social system learns from its tricksters and rule-breakers. Without this internal argument, hip meanders into pathology or the nerdiness of record collectors. In one direction, unleavened hip becomes hooliganism. Thrill jockeys, daredevils, litterbugs, serial dads, sideshow freaks, metal dudes, SUV owners and presidents who wear cowboy boots with suits all imagine themselves adhering to the code of the hip outsider. In the other direction, too much hip produces the peculiar species of nerd that Terry Southern served up in his story "You're Too Hip, Baby," insufferable in his boho correctness. This type is the underground version of the overachiever, poring over white-label trance singles or ironic T-shirts rather than spreadsheets or stamp collections. As Southern noted, his correctness is a drag.

In 2002, a woman named Aimee Plumley launched a blog called hipstersareannoying.com as a zoological study of this latter species. *Hipsterus reductivus,* as she saw it, had reached a critical mass in her Brooklyn neighborhood of Williamsburg, once a Polish and Italian blue-collar enclave. She rattled off a taxonomy of hipster tropes. What follows is but a fraction of her salvo:

I don't wear (I don't even own) any ridiculous trucker-style caps with mesh screen, I certainly don't fucking wear them backwards, or sideways,

I do wash my hair and like to keep it relatively trim, I don't own any big sunglasses, I don't have any of those little T-Shirts that say things about little league football teams from little nowhere American towns, or funny Jesus quips, or glittering iron-on Dukes of Hazzard decals, I don't have any tribal or comic book related tattoos, (I don't have any tattoos, if you must know) I don't hang giant pictures of paint-by-number art on the fresh sheetrock walls of the Williamsburg loft (that I don't have) that my parents (don't) rent for me. I don't go to art school, I don't come from the Midwest, I don't think Andy Warhol was brilliant, I don't think the Velvet Underground were "totally underrated," I don't own any lunch-boxes from the 1970s (or 1980s) I don't have any piercings (although during a confused stage of college I did have one briefly) I don't believe that communal living is a workable idea, I don't carry a digital camera everywhere I go shooting pictures of my other dumb hipster friends and putting them up on my dumb hipster photolog site. . . .

And so on, in the kind of prolixity only possible on the Web.

Hip's relationship to drugs, as to any single-minded obsession, requires that we know enough to know better. There's nothing hip about taking drugs to be hip. As an end in itself, drugs are no hipper than the trucker caps or *Dukes of Hazzard* T-shirts that future archaeologists will use to identify 21st-century Williamsburg. They enrich an economy without being enriched by it. The enlightenment in Frank Morgan's story speaks through the second voice in his head, which comments knowingly on the first. "In retrospect," he said, speaking of the year he picked up the needle, "I guess that's when I decided to fail. I knew enough about heroin to know that it was certain failure—that if anything would insure failure, becoming a heroin addict would be it. I had full knowledge." When he later recalibrated the lessons of Parker, he came to aim not for Bird's habit or his sax style, but the peace that Parker evinced in even the most frenetic blowing. "I don't feel I have to fail anymore," he said.

I do not mean to dismiss the drive for failure, or to denigrate it as a simple fear of success. The state of failure and forgiveness, after all, approximates man's relationship with God. It plays an important role in hip's history. This grace, which begins in error, is the beatitude for which the Beats hit the open road, or for which Monk counseled his bebop peers, "Make a mistake." But hip follows from the complexity of this relationship, not from the voice of self-destruction alone. The aesthetic of the hybrid is fulfilled only when it includes dissonance, and only when it moves toward learning and enlightenment. Drug use, like the trivia cataloged on Aimee Plumley's blog, is as likely to drive out complexity as to facilitate it.

At the start of his 1970 novel *Blue Movie,* Southern used an epigraph from T. S. Eliot that came very close to his definition of hip. "Poetry," Eliot wrote, "is not a turning loose of emotion, but an escape from emotion; it is not the expression of personality, but an escape from personality. But, of course, only those who have personality and emotions know what it means to want to escape from these things." The relationship of hip and drugs follows this paradox. Though the romance surrounds the needle and the damage, it is the uninjured self that supplies all the meaning. Drugs work as a tangible stand-in for pain, knowledge, autonomy or grace. But hip resides in the thing itself, not its stand-in. To return to the porn metaphor, even in a money shot, what matters is the unseen pleasure, not the fluid flying across the screen. The fluid, like drug habits of hipsters and wannabes, or the righteous threads of the terminally cool, is just the shimmer that gets the suckers to pay their admission, and the mess that somebody else has to clean up. Which is neither hip nor cool— nor, as we used to say in the 1980s, dope.

"it's like punk rock, but a car"

hip sells out

> Hip capitalism wasn't something on the fringes of enterprise, an occasional hippie entrepreneur selling posters or drug paraphernalia. Nor was it a purely demographic maneuver, just a different spin to sell products to a different group. What happened in the sixties is that hip became central to the way American capitalism understood itself and explained itself to the public. —THOMAS FRANK

Ray Kroc opened his first McDonald's franchise in Des Plaines, Illinois, in April 1955, the same year that Ginsberg wrote "Howl." Like the poem's audience, Kroc liked to tout his "Bohemian extraction," but in his case he meant his national origins, a synecdoche for a grinding work ethic. A beaver of American ambition, Kroc dropped out of high school at age 15 and dived into several get-rich ventures before making his first fortune with a machine that could mix five milk shakes at once. When he met Dick and Maurice (Mac) McDonald, two brothers in San Bernardino, California, who had found a way to automate the hamburger business, Kroc saw an idea he could believe in. He envisioned a postwar America *on the road,* rejecting hearth and tradition, choosing immediate gratification over domestic formality. By 1961, when he began to buy out the McDonald brothers, the company that bore their name was opening nearly a hundred new franchises a year.

The rise of Kroc's fast food empire, which took off in the 1960s, followed a convergence of activity that is pivotal to this book. Besides marking the debut of "Howl," 1955 divided the writing and publication of *On the Road*. It was the year Charlie Parker died. Miles first recorded with Coltrane that year, discovering a sound "so bad that it used to send chills through me at night," he said. Brando's brooding hipster in *The Wild One* in 1954 begat James Dean's hipster shrug in *Rebel Without a Cause* in 1955, and Elvis busted up Ed Sullivan for the first time in 1956. Mailer published "The White Negro" the next year. Comparing this hip flurry with Kroc's success a few years later, it is striking how the values of one repeated in the other. Kroc, who was Bohemian in nationality only, considered facial hair an affront and warned that you "cannot trust some people who are nonconformists," yet he was riding a change in America just as the Beats and beboppers were. The McDonald's hamburger chain sold the nation an image of itself driven by radical individualism: young, mobile, sloughing off the skin of the old—the same values for which Allen Ginsberg, then 29, hurled his human voice and body "against the harsh wall of America," sending angelheaded appetites through the negro streets at dawn looking for an angry fix, or at least a Big Mac.

Uh, bummer.

How could hip at its hippest dovetail so neatly with something as soul-depleting and antithetical as the corporate burger? The relationship between hip and commerce, which are on the surface antagonistic ideas, is a long and tangled one that neither camp tends to acknowledge, but that shapes the development of both. As the early Greenwich Village bohemian Floyd Dell noted, watching the commercialization of Village slack as early as the 1920s, "The American middle class had come to the end of its Puritan phase; it had its war-profits to spend, and it was turning to Bohemia to learn how to spend them."

Anyone whose favorite Iggy Pop song has been licensed to sell sneakers or vacation cruises knows the ambivalence that comes when the two worlds get too close together. On the one hand, there is the finky satisfaction that somebody slipped an uncut dose of Iggy—heroin addict, proto punk, freak on a leash—into the national punchbowl, using big media to bankroll a message it didn't want. For 30 seconds, the Stooges fraternity becomes a little less marginalized, no longer having to justify its perversities to the people who take cruises or wear high-performance sneaks. On the other hand, letting advertisers control the song is like making them president of the fraternity, with access to all the house activities. For a small investment, Nike or Carnival Cruise Lines gets to insert itself between you and your Iggy. So now who's the stooge?

In the matter of the great hip sellout, there have been two stock arguments. The first is that the commercial world, being empty of values itself, bogarts hip for its own venal purposes. This is a model of simple co-optation, in which hip's genuine antimaterialist, anticorporate sentiments are turned around and used to sell product. A comfort of this reading is that it has clear good guys and bad guys. The critic Herb Gold, who in 1960 derided Ginsberg-generation beatniks as "the hipster parodied and packaged as a commercial product," is a standard-bearer for this line of bohemian *essentialism*. Under this argument, co-optation transfers hip's aura to material goods like bop glasses, say, or retro cans of Pabst Blue Ribbon, treating hip as a consumer choice rather than a form of enlightenment. True hipsters dismiss the commercial variant as a bogus imitation, and keep their edge only by moving each time the commercial world catches up, a time lag that is now approaching the nanosecond.

The second, darker argument evokes the paranoia of *The Matrix:* There is no difference between commercialized hip and the real thing, because *there is no real thing.* Even at its most pure, hip is just a cog in an expansionist economy, conjured to create the radical consumers that the market needs to sell ever-newer stuff. Its fetish for novelty trains us to embrace obsolescence and constant turnover. This bohemian *"consumption ethic,"* as Malcolm Cowley called it back in the 1930s, became increasingly necessary once American industry began to produce more than people absolutely needed; it was reason to buy anyway. If core hipsters don't actually buy all the stuff, that's okay: their role is to promote *newness* itself, and maybe to appear in an occasional ad for Nike or the Gap. The broader shopping world then takes its cue from this hip vanguard.

By this reading, hip works as America's unofficial advertising medium, a triumph of style-as-substance for an economy that sells image as much as products. For what else would a wild, yea-saying overburst of American joy say but "just do it," "be your own dog" or "let UBU"? Hip's imprecation to go, man, go is exactly that of advertising; its invocation of lifestyle as a tribal value system is a brand logo made flesh. As Marshall McLuhan said, "When a thing is current, it creates currency." If this seems arch, check out the latest wave of hip-looking ads, set to alternative rock or DJ soundtracks, and try to imagine what the market is selling besides nonconformity, rebellion, jive and transracial interconnectivity.

Insurance, maybe?

These two, contradictory readings do not neatly untangle themselves; hip at various times seems to serve both functions. Neither explanation is really satisfying, and certainly neither can do justice to a complicated hip figure like Mark Twain or Andy Warhol. The relationship between hip and commerce is neither straight opposition nor simple stoogery. As Ginsberg told the writer Ronald Sukenick, discussing whether Dylan's performance at the 1965 Newport Folk Festival was a sellout, hip has other fish to fry. Selling out, Ginsberg said, was

one of those cornball ideas that people who didn't have anything to do got hung up on. I wouldn't have minded doing it if I could find what to sell out to. Geniuses don't sell out, in the sense that genius bursts the bounds of either selling out or not selling out. When somebody has real inspiration like Dylan, the move to electric is just simply the expansion of his genius into more forms, wilder forms. He's got that sense of negative capability being able to go all the way in, without necessarily losing himself. Committing himself and at the same time doing it like a poet, landing like the cat with nine lives.

By this logic, the gifted trickster can sell a riddle of himself, and use the mass media to disperse that riddle to a broad audience. In a pop culture that produced both "Subterranean Homesick Blues" and the Suburu ads that spieled, "it's like punk rock, but a car," the dichotomy of hip and commerce is too limiting.

•   •   •

he sellout question gets to the very nature of hip. Is it still hip—a
source of life, invention and meaning—once it spreads outside the
original in-group, or does it lose its hipness if it's available to anybody? In
other words, is hip essentially a loser ethic that can survive anything but
winning? Michael Harrington, a figurehead of the 1960s counterculture,
declared in 1972 that the fun was over, ruined by its own success. "Bohemia could not survive the passing of its polar opposite and precondi-
tion, middle-class morality," he wrote. "Free love and all-night drinking
and art for art's sake were consequences of a single stern imperative: thou
shalt not be bourgeois. But once the bourgeoisie itself became decadent—once businessmen started hanging nonobjective art in the board-
room—Bohemia was deprived of the stifling atmosphere without which
it could not breathe."

If hip was the special benediction of outsiders, according to this view,
then any access to the inside was a form of kryptonite. Two decades after
Harrington declared the end of the counterculture, Kurt Cobain tore
himself between indie-rock idealism and pop ambition. On the one
hand, he admired the purism of Calvin Johnson, co-owner of K Records,
an indie diehard who saw the enemy not as the people who disapproved
of punk rock but those who wanted to put it on MTV. But Cobain also
saw the Calvinists, as Johnson's circle aptly called themselves, as parochial
scolds for whom the only success was making sure no one else succeeded.
In an unsent letter written months before his suicide, Kurt renounced
them as "the fucking needy indie fascist regime."

Any study of hip's commercialization risks the cynical conclusion that
hip is a trick to make people think they're rebelling when they're just buying stuff. Though the market appears to chase hip, from another perspective it is really a step ahead. Thomas Frank, the most acute and
cranky chronicler of this hip paradox, described the vanities of would-be
rebels in a 1995 essay called "Why Johnny Can't Dissent." The minions of
corporate America, he wrote, are no longer drones in gray flannel suits.
"They're hipper than you can ever hope to be because *hip is their official
ideology,* and they're always going to be there at the poetry reading to encourage your 'rebellion' with a hearty 'right on, man!' before you even
know they're in the auditorium. You can't outrun them, or even stay
ahead of them for very long; it's their racetrack, and that's them waiting

at the finish line to congratulate you on how *outrageous* your new style is, on how you *shocked* those stuffy prudes out in the heartland."

By this logic, hip bloomed in the 1950s, as in the 1920s and 1850s, not in response to the horror of war or the cleaving of racial attitudes, but because the industrial economy needed it. Factories that were turning out new stuff needed the public to give up the old. Hip made things obsolete before they wore out. Likewise, during the urban crises of the 1960s and 1970s, when downtown neighborhoods emptied, hipster artists and punks served as the advance troops of gentrification. The more outrageous they were, the more media attention they drew, until they attracted the creative-type young professionals who drove property values up. The dot-com boom of the 1990s, which cast itself in hip's image, proved that an entire economy could soar without tangible profits, at least briefly, as long as it offered the promise of hip.

In such an omnivorous loop, even individualism has an aftermarket. Troy Pierce, the Williamsburg man who let Levi's clone his worn jeans, recognized that a life of bohemian slack itself could be understood as a commodity, stacked in shelves at local retailers. "It was weird," he said of Levis' request for his dirty trou. "They wanted to duplicate my hard work and take all these shortcuts on a year's worth of my life." But he gave up the pants. "I guess I thought it would be funny to see a stack of my jeans in a store," he said. No wonder so much of alt culture girds itself in self-conscious irony, like the cover to Nirvana's *Nevermind,* which showed a baby chasing a dollar bill in a swimming pool. That coy pose of selling-out-but-not-*really*-selling-out is a way to claim a little leverage on a system that in reality allows nothing outside it.

As usual, a little historical perspective is helpful here. In the introduction to this book, I said that hip was not a marginal fillip but a central current in American culture. It spreads in two ways: as an idea and as an influence. As an *idea,* forged in the essays of Emerson and the knot of America's racial debacle, hip gets under the skin of squares as well as hipsters, Kroc as much as Ginsberg. It is the background to much of what goes on in American culture. At odds with the values of church and state, which prefer hierarchy and delayed gratification, it is well suited to the values of the market, which has always had a place for wild yea-saying. Beginning with the economic expansion of the 19th century, as the market has usurped authority from religion and politics, the idea of hip has spread alongside.

As an *influence,* hip moves in concentric ripples—from hipsters to sympathizers to wannabes to the broader public. This is hip as foreground, the stylish acting out of the idea. It separates the hip from the square. Within the initial in-group, members develop hip gestures or codes as shorthand to speed up conversation. These gestures then spread through a series of intermediaries, some of them mass media, until cats who have never heard "Salt Peanuts" owe their walk and talk to Dizzy Gillespie. Mostly this influence travels as behavior or style rather than as an articulated principle. With each expansion of the circle, the gestures, or *form* of hip, are received more as content, overshadowing the messages they were developed to convey. When too much of the message is lost— when the gestures no longer connect to the underlying idea—hip is reduced to a commercial shell, able to flog but not to enlighten.

It is tempting to imagine a more innocent hip Eden—before MTV and cool hunters, before corporate rock, before the Fox Bros. of Chicago flogged their "leopard skin jacket as worn by Dizzy Gillespie" or *Playboy* advertised the "beat generation tieclasp!"—when hip stood apart from the marketplace. But that's like imagining those online patches will give you a bigger penis. Hip from its origins was tied to the needs of the market. The violence that brought the word *hipi* or *hepi* to the New World after 1619 was not an aesthetic or religious force but an economic one, a need for labor. White interest in black culture, and the cycle of pursuit and evasion that is the engine of hip, begin in a battle to control this economic relationship. When the African-American poet Nikki Giovanni says, "It is our willingness to forgive that both perplexes and confounds those who think they can braid their hair or drop their pants and know something about the splendor of being who we are," one reason for this perplexity is that there is no obvious market value for such understanding, whereas to understand what Snoop means when he says, "fo' shizzle my nizzle," is to follow the flow of dollars through American culture. There is commercial value in the latter. Ever since white slave owners and overseers strained to understand what the Africans were saying, getting hip paid benefits in profit and control. For the evaders, who needed ways to converse privately in their antagonists' presence, being hipper meant autonomy. If hip is a subversive intelligence cultivated by outsiders, the mainstream has always had a stake in keeping up.

During this early stage in its evolution hip was still about *process:* the invention of language and meaning, the centrality of rhythm, the pursuit of understanding and joy across racial and cultural lines. The products— the words or usages—were simply the materials at hand. They were temporary repositories for value, which circulated only among the hip. For example, slaves or slave-owners alike had access to the word *bad,* but only

290 HIP: THE HISTORY

the hip could extract the full value it carried. The word itself was not hip; next week people might stop using it or return it to its conventional definition, with no loss of meaning in the world. Hip lay in the process of attributing and shifting this meaning. It was fluid and immaterial, changing as fast as the squares could catch on. If you captured only the gestures, not the idea of invention behind them, what you caught was air.

In the 19th century, the industrial economy created a new relationship between hip and commodities. Factory work and automation, which occupied millions of Americans as early as the 1860s, disrupted the natural connection between people and the objects they lived with. Marx called the condition commodity fetishism. Instead of sitting in furniture they made themselves, workers who moved widgets along a belt had no connection with the final product or its use. As the historian Jackson Lears has written, "things were isolated from their origins and seemed to move mysteriously on their own: a different sort of fetishism emerged . . . requiring people to jettison their cultural baggage if they were to stay on the train of progress." Part of that baggage, he added, "consisted of goods rendered outmoded by stylistic change and planned obsolescence." Commodity fetishism valued the acquisition of things while devaluing the things themselves.

Like hipster slang, which endowed words with new meanings, this process changed the value of objects. It endowed them with an aura based on qualities like newness, status or sex appeal, rather than such mundane factors as how well they worked. You could become attached to this aura, independent of the things themselves. Since the aura was free-floating, it could then be shifted to the next line of products. As a kind of coded information that not everyone could see, this aura looked a lot like hip.

The evolution of hip from process to product mirrored the rise of advertising. The first four hip convergences all coincided with watershed moments in the ad trade. Ads also traffic in the insubstantial aura around things, rather than the things themselves. Like hip, advertising shifts value among temporary repositories, abandoning the old ones simply because they are not new.

The American Renaissance of the 1850s, the first hip convergence, followed close on the opening of the first advertising agency in 1841, and the rise of P. T. Barnum, huckster and trickster, who raised hype to an art form. Like the primitive ads, which were largely for patent medicines, the major writers sought to endow objects with ineffable qualities that only some could see. As Emerson asked in "The American Scholar," in the study of objects, "what is classification but the perceiving that these objects are not chaotic, and are not foreign, but have a law which is also a law of the human mind?" For the writers, the key to unlocking this law—this connection between person and object—was contemplation; for the ads, it was the act of buying. The writers' calls for nonconformity, individualism and celebration of the self all became staples of the ad business, even if the austerity of Walden or Concord did not.

The second hip convergence, which included the Greenwich Village moderns, the Lost Generation and the Harlem Renaissance, coincided with the first golden age of advertising, when revenues soared from $682 million in 1914 to almost $3 billion in 1929. Hart Crane, Sherwood Anderson and F. Scott Fitzgerald, signature voices of hip, all turned a dollar writing ad copy, prefiguring the crossovers of Ginsberg and Warhol in the next hip groundswell. Dorothy Parker penned the immortal ad caption, "Brevity is the soul of lingerie." Consolidated for the first time in New York, the ad business wormed its jazzy pleasures and late-Victorian scolds into every corner of America. It was not quite entertainment or pedagogy, but had trappings of each—a blurrer of boundaries, obscuring its own motives in the process. It pushed the culture toward the hybrid. "Only in America was advertising the main or sole backer of all the mass media save film," Ann Douglas writes; "only in America was advertising itself a medium of entertainment high and low. Only there was it promoted and vivified by some of the country's most talented performers, writers, and stars."

Hip was aligned with modernism, and advertising was modernism's mass medium. "Modernism," the ad executive Ernest Elmo Calkins wrote, "offered the opportunity of expressing the inexpressible, of suggesting not so much a motor car as speed, not so much a gown as style, not so much a compact as beauty." For the boys at the agencies, this was gravy. By capturing intermediary qualities like speed or style, modernism put itself in the gap between people and objects, in the same way that slang gets between people and words, or jazz improvisation comes between musicians and the written note. All sell the experience, not the underlying thing. Modernism gave advertising a voice that could promise more than material goods. What it promised, in fact, was advertising itself. As Burt Manning, the CEO of the J. Walter Thompson agency, said about a beer campaign in 1985, "People don't always drink the beer; they drink the advertising." A paradox of advertising is that like hip, it has little interest in the materials to which it is provisionally attached.

Through the new practice of public opinion polling, advertising in this period geared itself to knowledge of the microrebellions that made up modern America. Polling was interested in the ways in which real citizens diverged from the official portrait of themselves. These divergences, or rebellions, revealed where products were needed and at what prices. Captured by market researchers, they were the engines of the new. Ads, in turn, exploited the anxieties the research uncovered, posing them as problems that only the advertised products could solve.

Before leaving behind the 1920s, let me recap some of the ways the commercial realm had entwined itself with hip, and which remain part of hip today. Both rallied individuals against the constraints of church and state. Both set the values of leisure above those of the workplace: the real you was defined by your rebellions and desires, not your industry, obedience and sacrifice. Both attached their aura to the objects from which people had been disconnected through commodity fetishism. And both spread opportunistically through new technologies and media, blurring distinctions between high culture and low. Though the Lost Generation novelist Winifred Bryher might have spoken for her hip circle when she said, "If a manuscript was sold to an established publisher, its author was regarded as a black sheep," the hip and commercial worlds sustained each other more than the rhetoric let on.

In the third hip convergence—the Cold War boogie of bebop and the Beats—the growth of consumer brands and the advent of television corralled both the form and content of hip into the business of selling. Though brands and logos had been around for decades, mainly to assure uniform quality, the economic boom after World War II changed their function. Naomi Klein described this change in her 2000 book *No Logo*, about the insidious expansion of brands and logos. "By the end of the

1940s there was a burgeoning awareness that a brand wasn't just a mascot or a catchphrase or a picture printed on the label of a company's product; the company as a whole could have a brand identity or a 'corporate consciousness,' as this ephemeral quality was termed at the time." Brand identity invested its powers in the logo, which was pure information. It branded the consumers who bought its products as much as the products themselves.

Where conventional advertising touts a product's quality or price, brands and logos operate like creeds, creating tribes in the same way that hip does. By definition they are bigger than the stuff gathered under them. The products become offshoots of the brand, rather than the other way around. A good brand identity—say, Harley-Davidson—can apply as easily to T-shirts or fajitas as motorcycles. "What is a brand?" the ad creator Lance Jensen asked me, on a winter morning in his Boston loft office. In a famous 1999 ad for Volkswagen, Jensen had used Nick Drake's song "Pink Moon," sparking a Drake revival long after Drake had killed himself with an overdose of antidepressants. Jensen had a snowboard in one corner of his office and was playing a stream of alternative rock. "Is a brand products?" he asked. "I think it's a set of ideals, an aesthetic sensibility. Branding advertising is not about, 'Come on down, on sale now.' "

Since these ideals do not spring from the products, they have to come from someplace, and they have to make people want to participate in their community. One place they come from is hip. As information behaved more like a commodity, bought and sold in the shape of brand logos, the market began less to co-opt hip than to become it.

Television, introduced in 1948, spread hip's gestures in ways that would have been unimaginable just a few years before. The tube caught on faster than any medium before it. At the end of that first year, 0.4 percent of American homes had TV's. By 1954, 56 percent had sets, and by 1958, a decade after its introduction, 83 percent had them. The box created new relationships between people and culture outside their immediate circles. The historian Michael Kammen defines this change as one from popular culture to mass culture. Popular culture, which Kammen dates from the circuses that roamed America in the 1790s to the middle of the 20th century, transmitted values and entertainment through books, magazines, state fairs, bowling leagues, museums, etc. These drew together people of a town, region or educational level, required active participation and set their brow for a limited slice of the population. The very poor or very rich were seldom part of the fray.

Mass culture hits everyone at the same time. It requires only passive involvement, for which it delivers novelty and celebrity as ends in themselves. Because it broadcasts its message everywhere at once, rather than dragging it from town to town like a circus or road show, mass culture allows no lag between the time someone introduces a new style or idea and the time everybody knows about it; it cut the half-life of newness to nothing.

Cold War hip, one source of newness, caught the first updraft of mass culture; it was both magnified and diminished by the process. Within a few months of *On The Road*'s publication, thousands had read its portrait of two friends in a vagabond search for meaning. But millions could tell you what a Beat was, thanks to *Life* magazine and other mass-circulation periodicals and television. As simplified for mass consumption, Beat was now a scruffy curiosity, and Kerouac was no longer a difficult, sometimes depressive artist but a handsome rebel romantic figure. This is the difference between the popular culture of book publishing and the mass culture of celebrity. Popular culture can express a particular point of view and belongs to the class from which it originates; mass culture belongs to everybody. Mass culture is both the event and its context.

Cold War hip might seem antithetical to this commercial grab. The bebop pioneers at Minton's shunned the mass appeal of swing and the dance hall. The Beats renounced the material ambitions that made the marketplace run. As Gary Snyder wrote, "Better to live simply, be poor, and have the time to wander and write and *dig* (meaning to penetrate and absorb and enjoy what was going on in the world). . . . It is one of those few times in American history that a section of the population has freely chosen to disaffiliate itself from 'the American standard of living' and all that goes with it—in the name of freedom." This was the era when business bestsellers like William H. Whyte's *The Organization Man* and Sloan Wilson's *The Man in the Gray Flannel Suit* described a towering corporate hierarchy. Hipsters wanted no part of its oppressive conformity.

As it turns out, though, neither did the business world. *The Organization Man* and *The Man in the Gray Flannel Suit*, as Thomas Frank has pointed out, were both diatribes against conformity, which even managers could see impeded company creativity. Though the Eisenhower years are often portrayed as a battle between the forces of rock and roll and the wet blanket of the military-industrial complex, really the two sides shared many values. Even as collegiate bohemians turned on to *Naked Lunch* or *On the Road,* the corporate culture saw itself as trying to break out of the same box. Only instead of creating poetry or jazz, it imagined new ads or products or models of corporate individualism.

As Frank argues, smart executives in the 1950s and 1960s saw hip not as a threat to capitalism, but a way to purify it, overriding the inhibitions that held capitalism back. "Madison Avenue," he writes, "found in the ideas of people like Jerry Rubin a continuing—even a heightened—commitment to the values and mores of the consumer society." The virtues of the straight world, such as tradition, caution and prudence, would not sell all the new gizmos and goods that American factories were now producing. An expanding economy needs its troublemakers and tricksters, people who invent new desires that can be satisfied by new products. Though hip professed disdain for material goods, the market wasn't selling material goods: it was selling the thrill of buying them and discarding them. In other words, it was selling change. Hip's call to drop your old life and seek a more satisfying one sounded like *ka-ching* in the market. Though some of these new seekers might find time to wander and write and *dig,* for others the new life would also require a new refrigerator, coffee mugs and dish towels *at a minimum.*

Hip capitalism in this period exploited what was by then an unspoken truth: the values of hip and those of corporate America complemented each other neatly. Rebellion resonated as enticingly inside the office tower as on the street. When Kerouac wrote his often quoted passage, "The only people for me are the mad ones, the ones who are mad to live, mad to talk, mad to be saved, desirous of everything at the same time, the ones who never yawn or say a commonplace thing, but burn, burn, burn like fabulous yellow roman candles exploding like spiders across the stars and in the middle you see the blue centerlight pop and everybody goes 'Awww!' "—well, you can only imagine the marketing director who wished he'd thought of the line first, fingering his beat generation tieclasp as he rode the commuter train home with the words "desirous of everything at the same time" underlined in his dog-eared copy of *On the Road.*

To return to Kammen's terms, this hip capitalism was a form of mass culture playing with the toys of popular culture. A soloist at Minton's or a poet at the Six Gallery could inspire and influence a roomful of people; a Blue Note recording or City Lights book could reach thousands. Either was a form of popular culture. It required attention, effort and an open mind. You could argue with it. It lent itself to hours of discussion, by which it reached larger circles of coconspirators. Mass culture, by contrast, could distribute the same values or gestures to millions instantaneously, with no demand for participation or further inquiry. You didn't argue with it, you just changed the channel. It called only for approval or disapproval, and provided rewards for each.

Hip resistance to this bigfooting seemed quaint in comparison. By definition, a turn away from mass culture meant a refusal to communicate, at least to the full extent now available. By mass culture's terms it was to embrace one's own irrelevance, to willingly become Ellison's invisible man. After *Life* magazine ran a cartoonish feature story on the Beat writers in 1957, accompanied by photographs of a "beat chick" in a "typical Beatnik pad," the underground photographer Fred McDarrah lampooned this co-optation, offering to rent Beat poets for all occasions. His ads promised: "Rent a Genuine Beatnik. Fully Equipped. Eye-Shades, Beard, Dirty Shirt. With or Without Sandals. Special Discounts for No Beard or No Bath." Joke or not, the business provided some needed money to Ted Joans and other serious poets, who relished the opportunity to "get to the so-called squares," as Joans put it.

Yet the mass culture absorbed such satire without a bump. Within two years, instead of renting a Beatnik, Americans could bring one into the living room for free just by turning on Maynard G. Krebs and *The Many Loves of Dobie Gillis.* By 1968, corporations could pose as hip themselves, as Columbia Records did in a notorious ad that declared, "The Man Can't Bust Our Music," with a picture of seven men in a jail cell—as if the prospect of arrest, especially in a year of demonstrations for peace and civil rights, were simply the makings of a marketing category. (The ad, remarkably, was for Columbia's classical recordings, including the time piece *Switched On Bach.*) Opposition to the state was hip, and the market, which has always sought leverage over government, was happy to play along.

• • •

In the fourth hip convergence, from the mid-1970s to the early 1980s, youth culture turned not against the establishment but against itself. I have dealt cursorily in this book with the counterculture of the 1960s, on the grounds that its hippest elements built on the stirrings of the Beats and beboppers. The hip subcultures that emerged in the 1970s, on the other hand, built on razed ground. This was the bloom of the do-it-yourself, or DIY, underground: hip hop and punk, fanzines and independent film, the golden age of graffiti. In Kammen's terminology, all were attempts to etch pockets of popular culture within the context of mass culture. The enemy was not your dad, but Peter Frampton and the corporation supporting him. The idioms were adversarial or provocative, which kept the mainstream out and forced the audience to be active participants rather than passive spectators.

For the 1960s counterculture, one of the symbolic turning points had been the assassination of John F. Kennedy in 1963, which was a death of the prodigal son. Youth had been sacrificed, replaced by the venal father figure of Lyndon Johnson; youth culture rebelled. For the DIY convergence, the symbolic equivalent was the resignation of Richard Nixon in 1974. The father was gone—not just in American households, where mothers increasingly were on their own, but in the economy, where corporations were in recession, and now in the political sphere, which was supposed to hold the nation together. The ripple effects were far-reaching. In the absence of a father, youth cultures organized around peer approval and support. Break-dancers, graffiti writers, rappers, squatters and anarchists formed DIY families. Established churches and synagogues lost members to DIY new age sects, which did not need an ordained father. Punks created their own music business; zinesters, their own press.

"None of the kids I grew up with had fathers in the home," said Kris Parker, better known as KRS-One, who ran away from a single-parent home and started his rap career while living in a men's shelter in the Bronx.

Someone who doesn't come from a family feels no way about embarrassing himself culturally. If everybody's doing the uprock [dance style], and that's the tradition, those who are in a family are locked to a tradi-

tion, because their power is locked to the family, and if you break the tradition you break your bond with the family. Those that don't come from
a family, it's easier to break the tradition and do new things. The name
you choose would be a freestyle name, a name that was not ever used before, because it's not linked to anything. Your name is what links you to
your family tree. This person would call himself KRS-One: not linked to
anything. This person calls himself Flava Flav. He's searching for identity,
searching for a home, searching for family. You start doing graffiti: I exist,
and not only do I exist, I have expression, I have thought.

In the poor neighborhoods of Harlem, the South Bronx and the
Lower East Side, where paternal neglect was particularly acute, new tribes
formed around longstanding hip principles. Without the father, they
preached reinvention and clique loyalty, and girded themselves in new
language. As in previous hip convergences, inner circles formed within
dead zones in the real estate market, where they pushed each other to extreme behaviors. They policed their perimeters by scaring off outsiders,
then disseminated the results to the next ring of sympathizers.

The parallels were uncanny. Uptown, a Jamaican man named Clive
Campbell called himself Kool DJ Herc and pulled apart records nobody
wanted, isolating the "break beats," or strong percussive sections, and repeating them on two turntables. Downtown, pseudonymous musicians
like Dee Dee Ramone or Stiv Bators pulled apart old pop forms that had
lost their savor, hammering them to their own equivalent of the break
beat. Graffiti writers and break-dancers (originally known as b-boys and
b-girls) twisted letters or bodies into warlike pantomimes. Without the
father, the subcultures needed to support themselves by turning their play
into work. Hip in the age of DIY came with a strain of guerilla capitalism.

The barriers to entry were low. You didn't need formal training or the
support of a major corporation, and the materials were minimal: boosted
Krylon, two turntables, pawn-shop guitars, access to a photocopier. Because anybody could do it, DIY collapsed the distinction between the
people producing the work and those consuming it, eliminating the need
for entertainment conglomerates to fill the gap. Anyone could kick it like
Dee Dee Ramone or the Bronx breakdance team the Nigger Twins,
though the latter would take work. The ethos was local: graffiti legends

Andy Warhol

like TAKI 183 or JULIO 204 represented their street numbers every time they tagged; rap nurtured rivalries between boroughs and eventually coasts; punk clustered in pockets or "scenes"; zines circulated on shelves at record stores or outside dive clubs.

For a spiritual godfather, both economically and creatively, the players built on the work of Andy Warhol (ca. 1927–1987). Since the early 1960s Warhol had used mass culture's symbols, like a Brillo box or an image of Elvis, to comment on itself. In some cases the connection with Warhol was literal. Punks at CBGB worshipped the Velvet Underground, who had played their first shows under his imprimatur; in the back room at Max's Kansas City, where Warhol held nightly court, his Superstars mingled with punk's new cast of self-invented legends, including Patti Smith, Deborah Harry and various Ramones. Fred Brathwaite, a member of the Fabulous Five graffiti crew who called himself Fab 5 Freddy, in 1980 connected the dots between his work and Warhol's by painting an entire subway car with Campbell's soup cans. The following year he forged another connection, curating a graffiti show called *Beyond Words* at the downtown Mudd Club that brought together the worlds of punk, graf and rap.

Like Warhol, DIY manipulated the folk imagery of mass culture, removing it from its normal context and holding it up for inspection or ridicule. Hip hop DJs made new sounds from old beats; punk bands like the Ramones and Blondie played with the conventions of 1960s bubblegum pop; graffiti tags worked like colorful ad logos for the writers. Many writers had more than one tag, as if launching multiple lines of merchandise. The performers presented themselves as products, with names like Cheetah Chrome or Grandmaster Caz. Though the rhetoric was often rebellious, most of the work did not so much oppose mass culture as commandeer its resources—brand logos, celebrity faces, publicity and mass media—to build alternative networks. This was a way to turn away from mass culture without becoming irrelevant or invisible.

The alternative scenes also offered an answer to the mainstreaming of hip, which Michael Harrington and other old-timers had taken to be its death knell. If mass entertainment had co-opted bohemian rebellion, leaving it nothing to rebel against, the DIY underground simply internalized the opposition, acting like an immune system at war with its own body. Hip-hop, punk, graffiti and indie film all doled out abuse along with membership. There was a puritan streak to the idioms; as in the pogo dance, precursor to the mosh pit, there were few pleasures without self-inflicted pains. If the mainstream world of the 1970s had become too cozy with rebellion, hip had to reject parts of itself.

Like past hip movements, the DIY ethic reflected changes in the economy. The hip convergences of the 1920s and 1950s responded to boom years. Production was up, and hip stimulated consumption. The economy of the mid 1970s, on the other hand, was a bust. Behemoth corporations like IBM and General Motors lost ground to more nimble competitors. Hip answered with a kind of bootstrap entrepreneurialism, promulgated through indie seven-inch singles, outlaw block parties, fly-by-night screenings and Krylon ubiquity. Without a father, the tribes claimed their own space and resources. Again, the parallels are striking: hip-hoppers commandeered electricity from public streetlamps; Tom Verlaine and Richard Lloyd lied their way into CBGB, telling owner Hilly Kristal they played Country, Bluegrass and Blues. Graffiti writers spread the word—the *logos,* the logo—on every inch of visible surface, reclaiming public space just as the boom box turned municipal sidewalks into private sonic domains. The new underground did not invalidate hip capitalism so much as break it into smaller rebel cells.

Punk, hip-hop, zines and indie film all glamorized the hipster as boho entrepreneur, using guerilla media to consolidate small bands of likeminded souls. "We was young entrepreneurs, when we didn't know we was entrepreneurs," said Afrika Bambaataa, who in the early 1970s graduated from the Black Spades gang to graffiti (all the gangs had graffiti writers to mark out their turf) to throwing parties at the Bronx River Community Center, part of a public housing project in the Soundview section of the South Bronx. As Bambaataa put it, hustle was everything. "[T]he thing was getting out there and doing promotions, hitting all the high schools or the junior high schools, hitting all the different communities, walking up and down the street doing hand-to-hand contact, leaving flyers in record stores, and if you got on the bus, sticking it up on the bus signs—you'd cover over the advertising signs. It was a lot of work."

If corporate brands produced marketing that acted like culture, the new underground produced culture that acted like marketing. Dispensing with costly infrastructure or inventory (namely, formal training or expensive gear), DIY culture spread through bold gestures, like punk's spiked hair or hip hop's break beats, for a community defined by the ideas behind the gestures. As Lance Jensen said about brand advertising, the essence of punk or hip-hop was not the products but the ideals and aesthetic sensibilities. The products were secondary. If you wanted to know what punk or hip hop was, you were better off looking at the fans than listening to the records. Punk could have survived without the records, but the records would not have made sense without punk.

If this seems contrary to the way big business does business, it was exactly how brand-based companies like Calvin Klein or Nike were starting to move. As Naomi Klein writes,

> These pioneers made the bold claim that producing goods was only an incidental part of their operations, and that thanks to recent victories in trade liberalization and labor-law reform, they were able to have their products made for them by contractors, many of them overseas. What these companies produced primarily were not things, they said, but *images* of their brands. Their real work lay not in manufacturing but in

marketing. This formula, needless to say, has proved enormously profitable, and its success has companies competing in a race toward weightlessness: whoever owns the least, has the fewest employees on the payroll and produces the most powerful images, as opposed to products, wins the race.

In other words, they did what Warhol was doing: letting others produce the raw materials (in Warhol's case, the Brillo logos or dance-step diagrams), while adding a layer of meaning or value on top. As with Warhol's soup cans or Marilyn Monroe silk-screens, the images produced by Calvin Klein, Nike and others were both sexy and impersonal. These images spoke naturally in the language of hip because they came from the same place and served the same function. Like hip, they were a form of antimaterialism that was not above turning a profit.

On August 1, 1981, a new cable television network introduced a concept that fused DIY culture and corporate branding: a wholly-branded network whose programming and advertising were the same stuff. The new network, MTV, played nothing but promotional videos that were produced and paid for by record companies or performers in order to sell records. Like Calvin Klein, the channel didn't have to manufacture anything; all it had to do was to apply its stamp. Everything on MTV was selling something, and all of it in turn was selling MTV. In the parlance of ad agencies, everything heroed the network. It was a seamless commercial universe, with no disjunction when the programming broke for a sales pitch because the programming *was* a sales pitch. Instead of sitcoms or game shows that might have required internal consistency, there was just a brand identity and a brand style. The brand style was the visual quick-cut or non sequitur, borrowed from avant-garde film. The brand identity was the universe of selling as rendered through the visual vocabulary of hip.

The performers did not just lend their hip quotient to the network; to a great extent, they gave it away. They became salesmen and actors, pretending not to be the very thing the audience admired, rock stars. The channel diminished the products—the performers—in favor of the brand. Though MTV's ratings have never quite matched its public profile, it was mass culture that fed on the idiosyncrasies of popular culture. When Henry Rollins flashed his tattoos or Public Enemy strapped on giant clocks, these gestures, which were essentially fringe, could reach every adolescent community in the United States at the same time, regardless of how the locals felt. Because the tattoos or clocks first arrived through MTV—that is, as part of the MTV brand—there was no gap between the original thing and the inevitable fan imitations. Whether you were Flava Flav or a kid in Kenosha, your clock referred to the network. If anything, the knockoffs were more authentic because their bearers weren't trying to sell anything. Like the performers, they were just participating in the brand identity of MTV.

The network saw few limits to what it could fit into that universe. Frank Biondi, the president of MTV's parent company, Viacom, told the journalist John Seabrook in 1994, "You see Disney going into the cruise business. Maybe there will be MTV cruises and MTV special events. MTV's mission is connecting to the audience, to the MTV Generation, which we didn't even name—your side did—but which has become like Kleenex or Xerox. We want to provide a point of view for the MTV Generation." In this universe, even the audience becomes a brand extension, for which the mothership provides a point of view. In the Public Enemy example above, it is MTV that provides a branded meaning—rebellion, currency, solidarity—for the clock. The cruises have yet to materialize, but as the network has replaced music videos with reality shows like *Road Rules* or *Punk'd*, the audience is now watching a branded version of itself.

This resolved one of the differences between advertising and hip. In the pre-MTV era, advertising wanted its audience always to keep up, to value the same things it did, whereas hip moved ahead of the crowd. MTV changed that. The essence of the MTV brand was that it was always ahead; yet you never got left behind because you had already bought into the MTV universe. Even if you weren't an alpha trendsetter, you became an alpha by association. In the last two decades advertising has mimicked this logic as well. This can be seen in the marketing campaigns of cool hunters, who scout malls and urban hangouts for the barely perceptible twitches of hip tastemakers, and of "viral" marketers, who attempt to spread these twitches to the broader public without being seen as intermediary. Instead of broadcasting to the potential sales market like conventional ads, cool hunters and viral marketers try to reach small subsets of the market—identified as "innovators" and "early adopters," the market version of hipsters—in expectation that the more mainstream "early majority" and "late majority" will follow suit. A viral marketer, for example, might hire hip-looking people to order Hennessey martinis in a bar in order to *infect* the behavior of the bar's wannabes. These schemes view hip as not opposed to mainstream values but simply a market cycle ahead of them.

W hich returns us to the question: can mass hip ever be hip?
The cynical conclusion to draw from all this complicity between hip and commerce is that you can't win. It makes little difference whether the mainstream co-opts hip and remakes it as a bogus imitation, or whether hip was an engine of commerce all along, led by a vanguard of what might be called black-collar workers. The effect is the same. As Naomi Klien notes,

> The indie skateboarders and snowboarders all have Vans sneaker contracts, road hockey is fodder for beer commercials, inner-city redevelopment projects are sponsored by Wells Fargo, and the free festivals have all been banned, replaced with the annual Tribal Gathering, an electronic music festival that bills itself as a "strike back against the establishment and clubland's evil empire of mediocrity, commercialism, and the creeping corporate capitalism of our cosmic counter-culture" and where the organizers regularly confiscate bottled water that has not been purchased on the premises, despite the fact that the number-one cause of death at raves is dehydration.

Because mass culture eliminated the time lag between innovation and passive consumption—between process and product—there is no resistance it has not already colonized. No amount of wild yea-saying will put you outside the needs of the market, because wild yea-sayers are precisely what the market needs.

MTV and the rise of cool hunters proved that the counterculture of

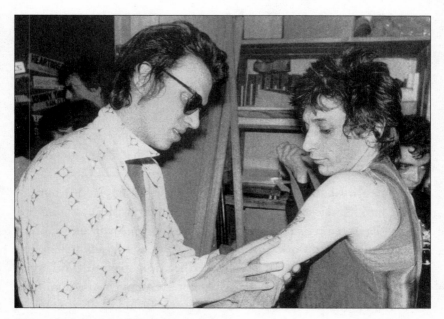

Richard Hell and Johnny Thunders

the 1960s had it wrong: that the personal was *not* the political, and that a stylistic license to ill—to fly your freak flag, your gangsta pathology, your anarchy A, your s/m gear—did not translate into political or economic change. All it translated into was iller styling. Sex, drugs and rock and roll were not the revolution; they were the fun the revolution promised. The era that produced punk and hip-hop and MTV also produced Reagan youth. Freed from the stifling behavioral conservatism of the 1950s, they replicated the era's political conservatism. Hip's sway became both more far-reaching and less pointed, unable to offend anyone but the knee-jerk right, whose reactions seemed coordinated to sell Madonna albums. If these guys didn't fulminate, she'd have had to pay someone to do the job.

But it is also possible to see a less sinister relationship between hip and commerce, more subtle than the simple dialectic of good guys and bad guys. If hip were just a salvo against the mainstream, we would have to look at it as a flop. The mainstream will always be there. To see hip simply as rebellion, as Ginsberg wrote his father, "misses the huge awful point." Even without corporate co-optation, rebellion is mainly an illusion of freedom, because ultimately rebels are chained to whatever they're rebelling against. This is one reason full-time rebels can be a bore, especially once they get tenure. By the same token, if hip meant pious withdrawal from the forces that make the nation run, it would be a marginal diversion, like the righteous asceticism of the indie-rock Calvinists. At most it would be a form of martyrdom. More likely it would have fizzled into disuse years ago.

Hip has survived as a shaping force of American life because it is constitutionally impure. After Ronald Sukenick published *Down and In: Life in the Underground,* a romantic portrait of the Village in the Cold War years, the artist and downtown character Larry Rivers chided him for buying into the slacker mythos. For all the drunk-in-the-afternoon theatrics, Rivers reminded Sukenick, "[h]ardly anyone without a pretty strong ambition and work ethic has left us anything to think well of outside its behind-the-scenes melodrama." To chide Cobain or Ginsberg or Miles for their ambition—or worse, to not even notice—is to miss the ways that ambition informed their best work, including their carefully crafted public selves. Hip becomes relevant precisely when it is impure, jumping in the pit with the beast of capitalism—feeding it, resisting it, exploiting it, shaping it. Co-opting *it,* even as it is co-opted in return. As students of the civil rights movement have learned, the choice between autonomy and access—between Malcolm X and Martin Luther King—is a false dichotomy; the only appropriate choice is both. If hip is a measure of enlightenment, it is only reasonable to expect its truths to play out in the marketplace as well—to open avenues of access even as they provide the buffer of autonomy.

If we lay aside the question of authenticity, which is dubious anyway, hip continues to be relevant not despite its contact with commerce but in proportion to it. Commercial hip is less a betrayal of the legacy than part of its natural evolution. With its traffic in enlightenment, its coded language, its viral distribution networks and its framing of the immaterial, hip anticipated and helped shape the information economy that we now live in. Power and resources in America now move mainly through the realm of information and images, and for individuals hip is a foothold in this realm. In other words, hip was in the market before the market was. It does not wither in the mainstream because it was there first. If it becomes more diffuse through mass culture, it also has some effects that are below the radar. For instance, mass hip is one of America's protections against religious or political fundamentalism. It needs the market to do this job.

Hip also uses the market against itself. When you see those hip-driven ads with the righteous soundtracks, it is worth remembering the basic transaction of advertising: you get paid in entertainment value for your attention to a message selling the product. Since the 1960s, as ads became more hip, advertisers have had to pay you increasingly more for less of your attention. Advertising is one of the few businesses in America that rush to spend more money to establish progressively less effective media. It is often better at communicating hip's values than the names of its products. Tim Barnes, a New York downtown musician and ad editor who has convinced agencies to use such noncommercial acts as the Sea and Cake, Faust and the experimental jazz drummer Milford Graves, argues that a good sell-out pimps the commercial world while being pimped by it. "We're putting money back into that fringe of popular culture," Barnes said. "We're able subversively to put some of these groups into the living rooms of America. Certain fans may get upset. But I don't really know how to answer that." The Nick Drake VW ad probably sold more CDs than cars, and did more to promote indie culture than car culture. Hip did that, claiming access and autonomy, and a sponsor to foot the bill.

Some fruits of hip's dance with commerce are obvious: for instance, these days rhythm is everywhere. The roots of the blues may lie in African Americans' alienation from the marketplace, but the music came into its own through the processes of the market. Other effects are more subterranean. If radical individualism created the modern consumer, it is also likely that the respect granted the radical consumer has facilitated other liberties, like gay acceptance and the multiracial embrace of hip-hop culture. In most cities in America, there are places where a pierced, tattooed couple of different races and the same sex can walk into a room without drawing a second glance. To dismiss this as merely a stylization of rebellion, just because the couple isn't really rebelling against anything, is to believe that the essence of liberty lies in the battle, not in the enjoyment of it. The fact that commerce and mass media made it possible does not make it less hip.

A half century after Ginsberg described the mass media as "exactly the places where the deepest and most personal sensitivities and confessions of reality are most prohibited, mocked, suppressed," these same sensitivities now generate record contracts, ratings, development deals, brands, political campaigns and lifestyle magazines. Mass culture's identification with hip has demanded a hipper look at the formulas of race, class, gender and so on. As Leon E. Wynter argues in *American Skin: Pop Culture, Big Business and the End of White America,* the confluence of hip and advertising has produced a realm where race is a quantity to be played with and polished, and whiteness by itself is a drag. This "transracial vision" has thrived in the mainstream "not because it's politically correct but because it's how America wants to see itself: as a unified multiracial society." Hip did that, too.

This does not mean that mass hip is not ultimately self-limiting. If it relies on the approval of mass culture for currency, how hip can it really be? By taking hip out of the hands of hipsters, and by collapsing the lag time for phenomena to develop, mass culture devalues hip in the same way that branding devalues commodities. All that matters is the next acquisition or the next hip trend. The DIY movements of the late 1970s and 1980s showed the possibilities of carving popular culture out of mass culture, using mass media to reach small communities through pointed, personal communiqués. What they found was that there were pockets of hip everywhere: b-boys in South Dakota as well as the South Bronx, graf writers in the Netherlands who were influenced by their Brooklyn counterparts, and vice versa. These pockets acted like the individuals in a hip inner circle, pushing each other to more intricately hip expressions rather than toward a generic middle ground.

The next hip convergence, which will be the focus of the following chapter, built on this model of radical entrepreneurship and decentralized networks, piggybacking on yet another revolution in new media. The Internet connected communities around ideas without assigning value to one idea over another. It was active, not passive; democratic, not hierarchical; maddeningly specific, not bound to the least common denominator. Moreover, it offered something hip had not seen before, a vision of technology creating a future that was freer—and hipper—than the past. As early as the 1840s, Alexis de Tocqueville had warned that Emersonian individualism left Americans vulnerable to an "immense, protective power which is alone responsible for securing their enjoyment [and which] gladly works for their happiness but wants to be sole agent and judge of it." A century and a half later, the Internet freed Emerson's heirs from this threat. The more powerful the Net became, the less possible it was for any power to be sole agent and judge. Its traffic was pure enlightenment, at least in theory. Yet even as the new media sidestepped the tyranny of mass culture, they posed their own threat to hip.

do geeks dream of html sheep?

a digressive journey through digital hip

Today, coolness isn't outright rebellion. It's rebellion from within. It's the ability to say, "I work here and I'm cool."...Cool speaks to those of us who rebel against the corporate culture, but who are content to stay within the corporation. Cool companies are those that have found a way to make the corporate culture mean something to people who's [sic] life is dominated by work.

—ALAN LIU,
professor of English,
University of California, Santa Barbara

A lot of this stuff was started by a bunch of people on drugs who had a tendency to play with computers. The people on the, let's say, opposite side of the counterculture, they started showering money on you. It was like, "You guys are a bunch of freaks who are completely different from us, so obviously you must know what you're doing. Here, have a bunch of money." That changed everything.

—PATRICK KROUPA, aka Lord Digital

Some years ago I went looking for a used drum set through ads in the *Village Voice.* At the risk of dating myself, I will tell you that these were new wave times and called for new wave measures. You might expect that the people you'd meet selling their drums would be like the people who sell their motorcycles: either aging guys who lose their taste for the big noise, or gearheads who want more power and accessories, possibly involving a gong. But this was not my experience. Instead I found single women with very young babies, low regard for drums and even lower regard for drummers. The set I bought had not been played in months, or more than enough time for the previous owner to have sent a postcard relating his whereabouts, if he'd had the decency to mail one.

There are lessons to be drawn from these encounters, not least regarding the wisdom of opening your womb to a man who spreads his legs on the job. (Can it be a coincidence that traveling salesmen, the Johnny Appleseeds of American sexual humor, are also called drummers?) Hip's history is strewn with the kind of blind trust these women offered and the fast feet the drummers showed in return. But amatory advice, sadly, is not our business here. Instead my questions concern the different strains of individualism that slice several ways through these lives. First, there are the I'm-going-out-for-cigarettes disappearances of the drummers, who marched to their own beat because that's what drummers do. Hip has long been invoked to rationalize this unfortunate flight. Modern critics like Quentin Anderson trace such behavior back to the legacy of Emerson, on the grounds that his counsel to "Trust thyself: every heart vibrates to that iron string," was just a fancy way of saying, *Slip out the back, Jack,* or *Dust my broom.* Emerson's focus on self-reliance, the argument goes, ignores our responsibility to people around us, especially when that responsibility gets sticky.

Yet there is another, nimbler ideal of individualism in the drums themselves. In my shopping ventures, most of the sets had belonged to jazzmen; rock drummers invest too much of their adolescence in their drums to leave them behind during such an adolescent act. So the drums came with a jazz relationship to the world around them. Ralph Ellison, whose parents named him after the mighty individualist of Concord, observed that the individual in jazz is locked in a battle between subordination to the group and devotion to his own badass strut. "True jazz," Ellison believed, "is an art of individual assertion within and against the group. Each true jazz moment (as distinct from the uninspired commercial performance) springs from a contest in which each artist challenges all the rest; each solo flight, or improvisation, represents (like the successive canvases of a painter) a definition of his identity: as individual, as member of the collectivity and as a link in the chain of tradition." Without both group cohesiveness and individual flights away from the center, a combo will not fly.

This might seem like a digression from my new wave improprieties, and especially from our broader topic of Internet hip—precisely the kind of evasion you'd expect from a drummer. But it is not so easy to get there from here. By the peculiarities of hip time, nothing is further from hip than what was hip yesterday, and the days of Internet hip, when otherwise admirable people used prefixes like *digi* and *cyber* as markers of cool, now seem more remote than Concord or even skinny ties. How inaccessible now are the days when the futurist Paul Saffo proclaimed, in the fourth issue of *Wired* magazine, that "just as the beatniks anticipated the hippies, cyberpunks are setting the stage for a coming digital counterculture that will turn the '90s zeitgeist utterly on its head." If you wrote that today, concerned friends would call a nurse. Come the revolution, someone will remember that Louis Rossetto, who founded *Wired* with his partner, Jane Metcalfe, originally wanted to call it *DigIt,* a pun on "digit" and "dig it," but for now this seems like a relic from the land before time, as far away as 1,200-baud modems and Billy Idol's 1993 album *Cyberpunk.*

Yet this era truly did transform the boundaries of hip. From about 1984, when William Gibson's novel *Neuromancer* introduced the term *cyberspace,* to roughly 1996, when AOL brought suburban domesticity to the Web, the social circle that identified itself with new technology was almost Darwinian in its intelligence, curiosity, daring and style. This was the new bohemia, existing in electronic neighborhoods others didn't even know existed. Networks of silicon microchips, built to withstand military attack, transferred tremendous resources of information from big corporations and government to the desktops of geeks, creating a new outsider in-crowd, with its own language, values and dress. The promise of personal computers was that they would make all existing authority obsolete: not just government, but school, blue chip corporations, church—even parents, who inevitably did not understand the new box as well as their kids. They made real an individualism Emerson only threw words at. And in contrast to the industrial era, in which machines were seen as dehumanizing, or the nuclear era, in which technology was seen as deadly, the age of the Internet promised to make life more interesting, free and clean.

Since the invention of the cylinder press in 1847, hip has risen symbiotically with new technologies and media. It grows with them and sells their wares. The wired revolution provided a complete universe to hang out in, where the hierarchies of real life, or rl, did not apply. To belong, all you needed was to have knowledge, or as the Wolofs said, to be a *hipikat*. Nerd power, which is usually a gambit of the future, in the way that pocket protectors sacrifice a little dignity today for an unstained shirt tomorrow, now translated excitingly to the present tense. Patrick Kroupa, who in the 1980s made a name as the teenage hacker Lord Digital, remembered a sudden reversal of authority, like the opening of a new frontier. "You could use the computer as a fulcrum to get actual power," he said. "It was very neat, because when you're a kid you don't really have any power. You don't have the opportunity to change reality. But with this box you could do that. It was like being superheroes and supervillains. When you're in high school, it's like, 'Hey, I'm being arrested by the Secret Service.' 'You are? Wow, that's awesome.' "

More important for our story, computers were transforming the relationship between hip and work. Employment, and the cycle of working to consume, had long been the enemies of hip. But as the commercial marketplace increasingly stamped its brands over leisure time and space, it was the workplace that was becoming more individualistic, cooler, closer to Ellison's vision of the jazz ensemble, with its assertion of the individual within and against the group. At Apple, glassy-eyed geeks wore T-shirts that said, "Working 90 Hours a Week And Loving It." Netscape, one of the most dynamic new companies, replaced the traditional personnel director with a Director of Bringing in the Cool People. Her name was Margie Mader, and it was her job to make sure the revolution would be webcast—to refine the office to accommodate coolness, but also to refine cool so it did not interfere with the maniacal work ethic. Cool, she said "is being redefined from how you look to how you think. Cool is about intelligence and innovation. It's about the ability to change, impact, innovate and collaborate. It's about throwing away the traditional ways of doing business and finding a new way. It's about getting out of your comfort zone."

Such rhetoric now seems like kitsch, but it also signified a shift in the relationship of work to play. Computers blurred the line between the two worlds: hacking code for an Internet start-up used the same muscles as playing Doom or downloading porn on line. The job, once the nemesis of hip, now meant membership in an elite tribe and access to the best machines. If work offered coolly modernist digs, alt music, high bandwidth, strong coffee and twisted peers, why would you want to go home to a medium-tech crib? Why shred on the electric guitar when you could make more noise with more freedom as a web developer, and use the money to remake your home in the DayGlo image of your workspace?

The speed of technology undercut one of the restraining forces of the square world: the hierarchy of seniority. Now you really couldn't trust most people over 30. Where work was once old people's revenge on the young, tech turned youth loose on playgrounds of money and gear that were even younger, more mobile than they were—a prosthesis belonging only to the swiftest. Offices added swimming pools, slides, masseuses or, like a high-tech compound in Reston, Virginia, a jukebox inside a '57 Chevy. Four decades after Sloan Wilson's *The Man in the Gray Flannel Suit,* executive trade journals advised even nontech companies to model themselves on cool, computers and koosh balls. "Any company in any industry in any location can and should strive for coolness," read an article for human resources execs. "Why? Because it's great for the bottom line."

Howard Rheingold, a veteran of the San Francisco counterculture who became an Internet guru, saw the freak flag of Haight-Ashbury—the exchange of radical ideas, ecstatic music and old-fangled groping—as reborn in the instant offices springing up in San Francisco's Multimedia Gulch, a former no-man's land south of Market Street. Instead of dropping out, the players were dropping in. "For most of those young dotcomers, hanging around the office was their social life," Rheingold said. "That was where they met people. They were not really *working* 100 hours a week, they were *at the office* 100 hours a week. I know because I employed them. They were playing naked Twister at two in the morning."

Wired, which launched in 1993, became the mouthpiece of the new Internet hip. It trumpeted an electronic utopia, exalting "the information rich . . . the most powerful people on the planet today. You and the information technology you wield are completely transforming our lives, our families, our neighborhoods, our educations, our jobs, our governments,

Ad spread from the inaugural issue of *Wired* magazine

our world." The first issue opened with an ad spread of a Native American man with a dyed Mohawk facing a punk teenager with the same Technicolor 'do. Beneath the first picture, block letters spelled out CHIEF; beneath the kid, OUTCAST. The message was clear: the strange new magazine was a manifesto for these newly powerful outcasts, with ecstatic colors and corporate sponsorship to boot.

The rhetoric was so hip-driven that by the third issue, it declared even its own m.o. over: "The Net used to have a somewhat Bohemian air," began an item on the magazine's "Hype List" for July/August 1993.

> But within the last year or so the Net has become the Establishment. In short, cyberspace is undergoing rapid gentrification now that every random salary-man has access to the Net. But just as the Village in New York still keeps a few artists amidst the stockbrokers for "atmosphere," so the Net now puts up with, even canonizes, a few properly behaved aging and toothless hackers. It seems no matter where you turn there is some hacker-cum-Net.pioneer expounding on The Good Old Days while an audience of accountants listens politely. The settlers have taken over cyberspace, and now the natives dance for trinkets.

That *Wired* was leading the dance was never mentioned.

As hollow as much of the hype proved, even in its collapse the Internet bubble has left the worlds of work, play, money and hip substantially changed. But before we play these changes, let us take another detour—an excursion on the version. If you'll bear with me, we are circling our way toward these changes through a network of links.

The first link is the drums. If the story of hip in the 20th century was the growth of the rhythm nation, with all the enlightenment and empathy that entailed, the jazz group carried the load the first half of the way. From the turn of the last century to the dawn of rock and roll, the jazz ensemble was the principal vehicle for spreading rhythm across America. With its Emersonian balance of individualism and unity, jazz gave America an image of itself as synthesizing from all over—from Africa and Europe, high society and low, from the wellsprings of comedy and tragedy—all in magical, cacophonous, *progressive* conspiracy. In the looking glass of jazz, Americans could imagine themselves across the boundaries that constricted them in daily life. Like the jazz ensemble, they were united in their difference.

Think of the collective improvisation on Louis Armstrong's 1928 recording of King Oliver's "West End Blues," made with the Hot Five. After Louis's opening break, each musician juggles a piece of the melody yet seems wholly independent of the others. The tune materializes as if by its own accord, without any of the players seeming to worry about where he fits in. Armstrong once wrote that if each musician "had his own way and could play as he wanted, all you would get would be a lot of jumbled-up, crazy noise." Yet the effect of "West End Blues" is just the opposite: that of every man having his own way, producing a coherence that is greater than the sum of its parts. By the time of Ornette Coleman's atomized *The Shape of Jazz to Come* (1959) or *Free Jazz* (1960), the jazz ensemble could hold together without even the suggestion of a consensus; independence was its own organizing principle.

This gives us another pass at Emerson, more felicitous than that provided by our wayward drummers. In an 1844 lecture on "New England Reformers," Emerson outlined a model of the state that worked a lot like Armstrong's Hot Five or Ornette's Double Quartet. "The union is only perfect," he said, "when all the uniters are isolated." In contrast to a classical ensemble, where everybody has to follow the composer's score, Emerson saw government functioning most productively like the Hot Five: the central plan would be there but not there, with none of the players shackled to its authority or each other. "Each man, if he attempts to join himself to others, is on all sides cramped and diminished of his proportion," Emerson wrote, "and the stricter the union the smaller and the more pitiful he is. But leave him alone to recognize in every hour and place the secret soul, he will go up and down doing the works of a true member, and, to the astonishment of all the work will be done with concert, though no man spoke. Government will be adamantine without any governor. The union must be ideal in actual individualism."

This collective freestyle, as envisioned by Emerson or Armstrong, constitutes an intelligent system, with built-in room for tricksters and contradiction. It absorbs the intelligence of its members, rather than bending them to a single ideal. At all moments its order is disintegrating into a new one—which, in turn, is on the way to becoming something else. Like the definitions of cool that Robert Farris Thompson found across the linguistic spectrum of Africa, this arrangement combines composure in individuals with stability in the group—while allowing maximum license to both. As a hybrid of African America, jazz also carries the burden of collective memory. For a population historically denied its ancestry, jazz's freedom amid order links modern America to a past that might otherwise have been lost. The music is a reminder, always invented anew, of where American culture comes from. Even when it seems to speak in trifles like cool poses or junkie shuffle, its rhythms are also telling stories.

The music also performed a *prospective* cultural function. Our experiences of culture, as Brian Eno says, "prepare us for acts of improvisation by getting us used to the idea of enjoying uncertainty." A jazz piece like "West End Blues" promises to be different each time it is performed, in ways over which the audience has no control. Listeners, then, learn to embrace change even if the ends are not clear. We want our music to take us someplace new each time, even if we're just playing the same CD over and over. To paraphrase the Greek philosopher Heraclitus, you can't step into the same "West End Blues" twice.

The medium for these messages has been personal technology. Jazz begins with the advent of machines that allowed listeners to consume music as individuals, not just as part of a concert audience. Though the music came into being before its encounters with technology, it matured with them. Piano rolls spread ragtime into private living rooms. Records and radio moved it quickly into millions of homes. Jazz spurred the spread of the machines, and the machines spread the footprint of jazz. Through these new media, which had their own agenda regarding the individual and the collective, jazz offered complex, Emersonian models of how people might get on in the world.

Of course, jazz no longer serves this function. The job of spreading rhythm as the cutting edge of invention, which passed to rock and R&B musicians in the 1960s, is now handled most deftly by DJs. Audiences at the Village Vanguard who catch the right set on the right night can still witness brilliant flights of invention; but culturally, the uncertainties for which it prepares listeners will be narrowly circumscribed, the stakes low. What happens in the club has long ceased to move with what happens outside. The preservationist movement begun by Wynton Marsalis in the 1980s emphasizes jazz's current role of extending ties with the past, not breaking ties with the present. The musicians may have kept up their vitality, but the metaphors have not, and the overall effects are largely the same: for an increasingly refined audience, jazz can affirm and confirm, but it can rarely undermine.

For the first half of the 20th century, the jazz ensemble reflected American industry. Its products were always new and improved, efficiently produced through rhythmic repetition. Jazz was a union business in a union economy. Until production changed there was no real reason for music to. But production did change, in ways that the music didn't follow. The management theorist Peter Drucker, who coined the term *knowledge worker* to describe the folks who replaced jazz's blue-collar analogs, outlined this transformation in 1993. "No class in history has ever risen as fast as the blue-collar worker and no class has ever fallen as fast," he said, as if he were talking about jazz. "All within less than a century. In 1900 the blue-collar worker was still a proletarian. Trade unions were still either totally illegal or barely tolerated. There was no job security. There was no eight-hour day. There was no health insurance (except in Germany). Fifty years later, the blue-collar worker seemed to dominate every single developed society. Now we have a Secretary of Labor [Robert Reich] who openly declared, in *The Work of Nations,* that the blue-collar worker doesn't matter. And the unions accepted him."

Jazz rode the first half of this history as the sound of American popular music; in the second it became a music without a country, seeking shelter in institutions or overseas. Though jazz fans blame the commercial bigfooting of rock and roll or the overzealous flight into the avant garde, jazz lost its hold on the American consciousness precisely when the patterns of American society to which it gave meaning—the way we worked, produced, manufactured—went into decline, outshined by the more abstract economy of the brand. Jazz was about the means of production as the country began to see production as a drag. As Drucker said, "The traditional factors of production—land, labor and capital—are becoming restraints rather than driving forces. Knowledge is becoming the one critical factor of production."

DJ culture, which is about the manipulation of information, reflects the economy at the start of the new century. DJs, whether in hip-hop or the various niche republics of dance music, do basically what global brands do: they repackage materials made elsewhere, overlaying them with moods or images, transmitting the goods electronically across boundaries of race and nationality. A DJ like Paul Oakenfold or John Digweed is the brand, no matter who makes the music he spins, in the same way that Calvin Klein is the brand, no matter who makes the jeans. DJs themselves are as mobile and stateless as their grooves.

Paul Miller, a Bowdoin graduate who calls himself DJ Spooky That Subliminal Kid, after a character in William S. Burroughs's *Nova Express,* described the mix as a flow of disembodied information across borders. "It somehow goes with the paradigm of the time—migrational, nomadic, completely decentered and just floating," he said. "You can go to Goa, for example, and you'll see Israeli DJ's playing trance, and you go to an island nearby and there's some Indian guy spinning South Asian dub and this is all so weirdly current. It's the first time people have been able to compare notes on things so quickly, and with the ease of the Internet, mixes go around the world."

The cult DJ products of the 2000s, known as "mash-ups," thrive on perverse ecumenicalism, throwing a vocal by Destiny's Child on top of a sampled Nirvana track, or a Jay-Z rap over the Beatles, daring the fans of either to dis the other. The original products, like the sweatshop that makes jeans, are interchangeable, of little value. As a DJ, said Spooky, "You're sort of destroying this received object from the corporate culture and then putting your own spin on it. Instead of receiving as a passive consumer, you begin to transmit. . . . I put my own imprints on all these songs, and then change them. In a certain sense it's beyond computer hacking. It's reality hacking." This describes the economy at the start of the new century, in the same way that "West End Blues" defined America on the eve of the Depression. The country can see its refractions more clearly in a digital sampling device than in a quintet on a bandstand.

It is a commonplace that DJ culture (like video games or the Internet) is the new rock and roll or the new jazz, but it is unclear what this might mean—except perhaps that DJs get laid a lot, and that kids shopping for used turntables should prepare to hear tales of fecklessness and woe. We seldom stop to ask what it meant to be the old jazz in the first place. In a puckish 1956 essay titled "What's 'American' About America," John Atlee Kouwenhoven named twelve things that he felt defined the country:

1. The Manhattan skyline
2. The gridiron town plan
3. The skyscraper
4. The Model-T Ford
5. Jazz
6. The Constitution
7. Mark Twain's writing
8. Whitman's Leaves of Grass
9. Comic strips
10. Soap operas
11. Assembly-line production
12. Chewing gum

What they share, he said—what's *American* about them—is that they are organized episodically, through repetition, without meaningful beginnings or ends. (I'm oversimplifying, but only to get us to the Internet more quickly, promise.) A glass-box skyscraper does not come to a crescendo at the top; it simply runs out of stories. Chewing gum and the last part of *Huck Finn* irritate formalists because they keep rolling without denouement, like the river itself. Similarly, a jazz performance does not move toward a goal or tell a linear story in the manner of a classical composition. A soloist could flow for 24 bars or, like Coltrane, for 24 minutes. Instead of developing themes, jazz musicians pull them apart; by the time Parker is through with the changes to "I Got Rhythm," there is nothing left but bird feathers. Like Parker at the Argyle Show Bar in Chicago, when he nodded in and out on the bandstand, you can wake up in any part of a jazz piece without needing to know what came before; what matters is the flow of the present moment.

This, Kouwenhoven said (again, I'm oversimplifying), is a framework for understanding America, and a quality shared by each of his distinguishing dozen. To which I would add two more that were not available in 1956, and that may not seem American at all: electronic dance music and the Internet.

Like dance music and the Internet, the items on Kouwenhoven's list are best understood as matters of process rather than product. A Model-T Ford is a boxy, cumbersome thing, but the process that turned it out is a thing of wonder. Ditto the Big Mac, which gave people a place to go in their later Fords. The essence of each, as Twain said of the humorous story, lies in the telling, not the end results. Returning us to Concord, Kouwenhoven cites Emerson's fascination with the way "becoming somewhat else is the perpetual game of nature," and his belief that man is great "not in his goals but in his transitions." This contradicts the theology Emerson learned at Harvard Divinity School, but is not so far from the orientation with which Jack Kerouac followed Whitman out onto the open road. In the 1970s, it described the ethos with which Afrika Bambaataa built his following at the Bronx River Community Center, in the days before rappers eclipsed the DJs behind them.

What Bambaataa did, like Kool Herc before him, was to piece together bits of music, or breaks, that were on their way to somewhere else: the intro to "Apache" by the Incredible Bongo Band, or the breakdown to James Brown's "Funky Drummer." Defining his ethos, Bam wrote: "Break music is that certain part of the record that you just be waiting for to come up and when that certain part comes, that percussion part with all those drums, congas, it makes you dance real wild. You just let all your feelings go, but that break is so short in the record, you get mad, because the break was not long enough for you to really get down to do your thing. As soon as the break part comes, boom, the singing or music part comes right back and the break part is gone."

Joseph Sadler, a Bronx electronics student who called himself Grandmaster Flash, invented a device called a crossfader that allowed him to hear one turntable while playing another, and so extend a break seamlessly. By "backspinning," or rotating one turntable backward until the needle reached the beginning of a break, he could freeze the music in this moment of transition, never to arrive at its destination. It became perpetually *on the road,* as opposed to, say, taking up residence in a garden apartment complex outside Chicago.

Hip has both encouraged this focus on process and arisen from it, like the riddle of the chicken and the egg. The focus shapes hip's present tense, and hip shapes the focus. If you are wondering why this is American— why the soap opera did not originate in Mexico, say, where the *telenovela* now reigns supreme—it is perhaps because the metaphors that connect Bronx River to the mad Ahab driving of Neal Cassady also reach farther into American history and geography. For most of its colonial history, the topography of North America had no endings, only successive frontiers. It was a process, like a stick of gum or a repeated break beat.

Similarly, the African-American trickster tales, or the contemplative loafing of Whitman and Thoreau, were whole in the moment, but are revealed as ongoing processes in the long view. The wisdom of a trickster tale or a leaf of grass accumulates through repetition and mutation. The Signifying Monkey tales, for example, should be viewed as a single ongoing story, with a different ending each time. You chew it like a stick of gum. Sometimes the Monkey wins, sometimes the Lion gets the last bite, but the tale keeps going either way. We don't get rid of the old version each time a new one comes along; we just add both to the pile, contradictions and all.

If this is getting too abstract, think about the difference between St. Patrick's Cathedral in midtown Manhattan, which is very Old World, and the skyscraper grid of Rockefeller Center across the street, which is New. Any point in the facade of St. Patrick's bears a specific relationship with the other points and with God; its meaning lies in the sum of these relationships. If you added another clerestory it would throw everything out of whack. By contrast, on the rectangular grid of Rockefeller Center, any piece of the grid tells you the same information about the design of the whole; the meaning of the building lies in the *process* of adding window upon window, not in the sum. If you added another row or column of windows, the result would not be different, just more.

What I'm getting at is this: the Internet and DJ culture are organized like the Signifying Monkey canon or the windows in Rockefeller Center, not like St. Patrick's Cathedral or Bach's Mass in B Minor or *War and Peace*. In 1984, William Gibson III, a Virginia native writing in Vancouver, gave this arrangement a name and a blueprint, conceived after watching a bunch of teenagers playing video games at a Vancouver arcade. The name was cyberspace. He defined it as:

> A consensual hallucination experienced daily by billions of legitimate operators, in every nation, by children being taught mathematical concepts . . . A graphic representation of data abstracted from the banks of every computer in the human system. Unthinkable complexity. Lines of light ranged in the nonspace of the mind, clusters and constellations of data. Like city lights, receding. . . .

Cyberspace, which appeared in Gibson's debut novel, *Neuromancer*, was the metaphorical place where telephone conversations took place or where computer "modulator-demodulators," or modems, exchanged handshakes. It was the *Matrix* before the sequels.

What was hip about this matrix, as Gibson drew it, was the anarchy of information and identity. Like the Signifying Monkey canon or the grid of Rockefeller Center, cyberspace was pure process, without hierarchy or organizing conceit. Every path was equal, every kink accounted for. The domain extended modularly; no idea stepped on any other. Gibson's protagonist, a hacker named Case, worked this interzone like a cowboy, or like the kids at the Vancouver arcade, whose furtive play made it into the book as "a kind of ghostly teenage DNA at work in the Sprawl, something that carried the coded precepts of various short-lived subcults and replicated them at odd intervals." Jacking in through a prosthetic port, Case found his real identity in its digital expanses. Cyberspace was not a wiring scheme but a culture, extending the boundaries of the self:

> This was it. This was what he was, who he was, his being. He forgot to eat. Molly left cartons of rice and foam trays of sushi on the corner of the long table. Sometimes he resented having to leave the deck to use the chemical toilet they'd set up in a corner of the loft. Ice patterns [an acronym for intrusion countermeasures electronics] formed and re-formed on the screen as he probed for gaps, skirted the most obvious traps, and mapped the route he'd take through Sense/Net's ice. It was good ice. Wonderful ice. Its patterns burned there while he lay with his arm under Molly's shoulders, watching the red dawn through the steel grid of the skylight. Its rainbow pixel maze was the first thing he saw when he woke. He'd go straight to the deck, not bothering to dress, and jack in. He was cutting it. He was working. He lost track of days.

It is an old saw that science fiction is about the present, not the future, and *Neuromancer*—along with Vernor Vinge's novel *True Names* (1981), David Cronenberg's 1983 movie *Videodrome* and Ridley Scott's 1982 *Blade Runner,* based on the Philip K. Dick novel *Do Androids Dream of Electric Sheep?*—described an anarchic intelligence that was already loose in the circuitry of the late 20th century. As the critic Istvan Csicsery-Ronay Jr. has observed, sci-fi in this period was no longer about rockets shooting into outer space, but about a breakdown of urban inner space under unchecked technology and media. The personal computer, introduced in 1974, was beginning to level the playing field for information, putting enormous processing power literally at the fingertips of individuals. At the same time, corporations were seeking to brand the private worlds of fantasy and image. The lines between data and self were blurring. As the character Brian O'Blivion (Jack Creley) says in *Videodrome,* "Whatever appears on the television screen emerges as raw experience for those who watch it. Therefore, television is reality, and reality is less than television. . . . Your reality is already half video hallucination."

Gibson filled this consensual hallucination with new slang, drugs, crime, dub and corporate superpowers. The sprawl was beautiful and

Videodrome

lawless, cyber and punk. Pleasure, toward which Americans have often expressed ambivalence, was both enhanced and suspect. It was unreal. From the novel's first line the presence of media was oppressive: "The sky above the port was the color of television, turned to a dead channel."

Gibson himself was barely a dabbler in the tech world, writing not on a computer but a 1927 Hermes typewriter. His vision in *Neuromancer* and "Johnny Mnemonic," the 1980 short story that laid out many of the novel's themes, drew loosely from William Burroughs, who was experimenting with a form of science fiction around this time. For Burroughs, whose worldview was shaped in part by addiction, control was a virus that replicated itself through language and technology. Like many people his age, Gibson, who was born in 1948, discovered Burroughs as a teenager, through an excerpt from *Naked Lunch* in a 35-cent Beat anthology, and was knocked out. "That was one of the most hallucinatory pieces of prose in the English language," he said. "Reading that was like being impregnated with a virus." Like Burroughs, Gibson treated drugs and even sex as synthetic experiences, enhanced by technology but also prone to its capacities for manipulation. As the British critic Dani Cavallaro points out, "in a culture saturated with artificial substances (be they legal or illegal), the notion of what is 'good' for you is bound to become increasingly hazy." Best of all, faster than you could say teledildonics, Gibson's geeks parlayed their computer skills into all the sex they could handle.

For the kids who were already experiencing their identities through video games or computers, *Neuromancer* presented a world in which their critics were irrelevant. Inspired by *Naked Lunch,* the book hit like *On the Road,* less a literary event than a rock one. "All I did was free up the fashion options of computer kids," Gibson said a decade later. "So that they could dress like early Bruce Springsteen and still be computer guys. I had never run into any serious computer types who had leather jackets, they had sort of lumpy shirts." *Neuromancer* gave them their inner hipster.

Patrick Kroupa was one of those kids. At the time *Neuromancer* came out, he was an overly bright teenager living in Spanish Harlem, bouncing from school to school, finding his peer group and obsession in the labyrinthine world of telephone computer systems and online bulletin boards. Here he could transform himself from adolescent into Lord Digital. "Gibson basically created a whole mythology of technology and computers and let people assume these different archetypes," he said. After *Neuromancer,* he and his peers "weren't just a bunch of geeks; it was suddenly like, wow, this is cool." He joined the ranks of the hacker underground: Inner Circle, then Knights of Shadow, then the notorious Legion of Doom, who in 1990 inspired one of the biggest federal crackdowns ever on a bunch of adolescents and postadolescents. In a common overlap of countercultures, Kroupa also got involved with a Yippie offshoot called Technological Assistance Program (TAP/YIPL), which published telephone and credit card scams and other underground information, including the private phone numbers of the White House and Buckingham Palace.

Like geeks immemorial, these hackers were isolated in their high schools but connected through their electronic subculture. Its pulse came "rushing through the phone line like heroin through an addict's veins," wrote a hacker named the Mentor in the St. Louis zine *Phrack.* The Mentor echoed the hero of *Neuromancer,* announcing, " 'This is it . . . this is where I belong,' " before declaring, "This is our world now." Within this world they held enormous power, limited only by their intelligence and curiosity, not their place in the high school food chain. *Neuromancer* gave them direction and romance. "What Gibson wrote about didn't exist then," Kroupa said. "But a lot of people thought, 'This is a pretty neat fantasy,' and they went about trying to make it a reality." (Kroupa is now a lawful geek in Florida and proselyte for Ibogaine, a treatment for heroin addiction that is banned in the United States but available elsewhere.)

In truth, much of Gibson's world was already a reality. Even without computers, Bambaataa's Zulu Nation, a loose organization that gave parties and promoted peace and survival, posed a model of a future society that was stateless, borderless, trafficking information through the codes of b-boying (break dancing) and Bam's recombinant break beats. Without leaving the borough they moved packets of information and identity around the world. Jazzy Jay, who did much of the hands-on spinning, said he often didn't know what records Bam had handed him until he dropped the needle. Balinese Monkey Chants mixed with Trinidadian soca and the theme from *The Andy Griffith Show*. Then, like 'Trane, Jazzy could juggle a beat for 24 bars or 24 minutes.

Technology and Gibson's cyberspace simply extended this metaphor. With a cheap computer and software, music could flow independent of instruments—that is, without origin, existing in the electronic sphere of the consensual hallucination. Bambaataa and his crew Soulsonic Force turned the European electro-cool of "Trans-Europe Express," by the German group Kraftwerk, into the global sound of the South Bronx on their epochal "Planet Rock" (1982). The maxim that "information wants to be free," a staple of Internet hip, shook the walls of Bronx River long before it hit *Wired* magazine.

The structure of DJ music—of music without musicians or musical instruments—jumbled the categories into which music is often divided: distinctions of time period, region, style, even performer. Everything was available to everyone. Think of the packets that make up digital music as the windows on the Rockefeller Center grid. Regardless of where they are or what goes on behind them, all have the same value and can be shuffled in any combination. A kid in a bedroom in Kansas City or Copenhagen can kick it *exactly* like Clyde Stubblefield, the funky drummer behind "Funky Drummer," or throw a didgeridoo over a bassline from Studio One in Jamaica and a beat from a vintage Roland-808 sequencer, all without leaving home. In a home studio in Lower Manhattan, Moby could channel the 1940s gospel singer Vera Hall swooning "Oh, Lawdy, troubles so hard / Don't nobody know my troubles but God," a sequence of ones and zeros no different from the thumping beat or the credits on the CD booklet. Bits are bits. Digital sampling devices collapsed the history of popular music, or the hierarchy of taste, into the same present tense. Freed of chronology or geography, the sounds were connected like the links on the Web: change the sequence and you got a whole new mix.

There is an element of the nonrational in this. How can you have "Funky Drummer" without a funky drummer? In modern secular society, a presence of information without a material dimension is pretty close to a definition of God. The consensual hallucination of cyberspace—that is, the *nonrational* awareness—is big enough to resemble eternity, the place you go when you leave time and space. Long after commodity fetishism divided society from the objects around it, the logic of the Internet or DJ culture carries this dualism to its natural conclusion: the physical objects that hold samples or computer codes are practically irrelevant. The information doesn't exist to give the objects meaning; it is whole in itself.

This relationship is fundamentally metaphysical, exalting something that cannot be seen or touched. It is no coincidence that the Internet became a pipeline for the spiritual, from neo-paganism to www.kabbalah.com, or that much of the traffic moved outside the hierarchies of church, synagogue or mosque. If cyberspace is eternity, eternity is flat. It looks less like the oppressive authority of the Puritans and more like Ishmael Reed's voodoo aesthetic, the slack Buddhism of the Beats, or what DuBois called the communism of the African forests. It is enlightenment without proscription, making pathways for unlimited dissent or difference: a model of spiritual hip.

The dance floor, similarly, runs on ritual transcendence, with or without chemical sacrament. Rave culture extends plateaus of ecstasy for as long as the microchips hold out. The anonymity of the beats is part of the experience; they are bodiless, pure information or spirit. In the book *Last Night A DJ Saved My Life: The History of the Disc Jockey* (2000), the British writers Bill Brewster and Frank Broughton argue that DJs, in digging up and dispensing arcane bits of musical information, are like shamans.

(This is a bit of a tautology, because most of us know shamans only as the front half of such metaphors, but let's not get hung up.) "It is the DJ who presides at our festivals of transcendence. Like the witchdoctor, we know he's just a normal guy really—I mean look at him—but when he wipes away our everyday lives with holy drums and sanctified basslines, we are quite prepared to think of him as a god, or at the very least a sacred intermediary, the man who can get the great one to return our calls."

This, of course, is the role of the trickster, of Hermes or Esu-Elegbara, who mediated between mortals and the gods. And it was the fundamental promise of hip in the early age of the Internet: the farther you went into the machine, or the more deftly you traversed the consensual hallucination, the closer you came to pure enlightenment. Anybody could get there with the right skills. And maybe get rich to boot.

One of the first myths of cyberspace is that its founding members were all hacker kids and hippies, and that its politics were *Star Trek* liberal. It's easy to see where this myth came from, and how it fed the image of Internet hip. After all, people dressed funky, listened to weird music and as a group were not averse to alt.sex or chemical enlightenment. At times cyberspace seemed an extension of the drug culture—a consensual hallucination *indeed*. But the digital world has other roots as well, and other claims to the legacy of Emerson. Even in the nonhierarchical sprawl of digital culture, where any Amazon temp can send interoffice email to Jeff Bezos, it is worth asking, cui bono: who benefits, and whose name is on the door? In the inventory of cyberspace subcultures, the one that created it often gets overlooked.

In 1974, an inventor named Theodor Holm Nelson, son of the actress Celeste Holm and the director Ralph Nelson (*Lilies of the Field*), published a manifesto called *Computer Lib,* which became a cult classic in tech circles. Ted Nelson, who coined the term *hypertext* in the 1960s, is no ordinary crank, though this does not mean he isn't a crank. He was almost expelled from Swarthmore College in the 1950's for his immoderate defense of sexual liberation, and later liked to take potshots at cyberspace's more practical visionaries while anointing himself "the Orson Welles of software." *Computer Lib,* published just months before the release of the first commercially available personal computer, described the possibilities of a world in which information had no borders. "Computer Power to the People" was one of his slogans. In the book he cited a survey that revealed a subcultural proclivity of the early digerati. Fifty percent of the registered members of New York's Libertarian Party, the Emersonian fringe of the right wing, were computer professionals.

One of these libertarians, registered or not, was Louis Rossetto Jr., the future founder of *Wired*. Raised in the stuffy suburb of Great Neck, Long Island, the son of a Mergenthaler Linotype executive, Rossetto arrived at Columbia College in 1967 as radicals from Students for a Democratic Society were battling the administration for control of the campus. Rossetto had long hair, a profound antipathy to the war, and no interest in the student left. He hung out with anarchists and became president of the Columbia Young Republicans, but his passions lay with a more aggressive conservative movement. With a fellow Columbia student named Stan Lehr, he wrote a 1971 cover story for the *New York Times Magazine* heralding "The New Right Credo—Libertarianism." This credo was essentially a free-market version of anarchism, or, as Karl Hess, a libertarian figurehead and former Goldwater speechwriter, called it, "anarchocapitalism." Rossetto and Lehr, who appeared on the magazine's cover, argued against taxation, the draft, the federal highway system, drug laws and any government intervention in citizens' lives, except to keep them from capping each other.

Years before the Reagan right declared government an evil parasite, Rossetto and Lehr argued for shrinking it to the bare minimum. (In reality, of course, Reagan expanded government by running up the biggest deficits in American history.) Echoing Emerson's belief that "to be great is to be misunderstood," the authors contended that full-tilt individualism made the country dynamic; collective effort and group-think brought only mediocrity and Soviet bureaucracy. The article listed the architects of libertarianism, including Hess, Ayn Rand, the science fiction writer Robert Heinlein, the 17th-century philosopher Baruch Spinoza, the economist Ludwig von Mises and the writer Freidrich A. Hayek, whose 1944 *The Road to Serfdom* warned of the wages of state control. In decades to come, these would become guiding spirits of Silicon Valley.

For the misfits of high tech, libertarianism was both mission and social contract. It separated what was most anti-hip about the right—like its intrusive moralism, corporate hierarchy or all that "thou shalt not" stuff—from what was potentially liberating, like access to the free market. Hip was always more friendly toward the market than toward its restraining institutions, the church and state. Libertarianism opened access to pocket money, even if you weren't a suit or a middle management drone. It accommodated all contrary pleasures, ideas and enlightenment. It was like Kerouac's mad ones, who were "desirous of everything at the same time." All values were as viable as the market said they were. If, as Albert Goldman believed, the roots of the counterculture were in the criminal underworld, libertarians were philosophically even closer to the source; they rejected laws the hippies didn't bother with. In the *Times* magazine piece, Rossetto and Lehr approvingly quoted an unnamed classmate to the effect that, "As the New Left drifts further into rigid Marxism, it is getting straighter and straighter, while we [libertarians] are getting progressively looser and freakier."

This was a perfect belief system for the Internet, which by its structure resisted taxation or policing. By the time Rossetto and Jane Metcalfe launched *Wired* in 1993 (after Rossetto ghostwrote a juicy tell-all called *Ultimate Porno*, for an assistant director on the smut epic *Caligula*), Internet mythology brought together hackers' grunge romance with the right-wing turbocapitalism of its new mogul class, sometimes cloaking one in the other. The tech barons were as feral and smart and Gibsonian as the hackers; they just had bigger investors. "Capitalism used to be seen as those guys off at GE or Bank of America," said Howard Rheingold. "Suddenly you could be two Stanford students [David Filo and Jerry Yang, founders of Yahoo!], and you could go buy GE a couple years later. Old money that had taken most of the century to amass was suddenly eclipsed, not just by new money, but new money that was based on technical knowledge. That was enormously, intoxicatingly empowering. It was capitalism, but it was the American Dream."

In the previous chapter I observed that during periods of increased industrial production, hip has served as an ethos of *ka-ching* consumerism. But the new economics of the Internet, like the DJ culture, were not about production and consumption. They were about the distribution of belief. You didn't sell widgets, you sold belief in a story about widgets. Until the belief system crashed, in a cataclysm of suddenly worthless paper, it was amazing what investors would cough up. One underlying belief was that information should be free. The key was to remove all bottlenecks. As *Wired*'s Kevin Kelly liked to say, attributing the remark to Gibson, "The future is already here—it's just unevenly distributed." On the Internet, data flowed around whatever tried to restrain it. Authorities like doctors, lawyers or stockbrokers, who had long been sole gatekeepers to information, were suddenly competing with real-time stock quotes or usenet groups dispensing legal or medical advice. Entertainment corporations, which had been gatekeepers to copyrighted movies or music, suddenly found that anyone could download the new Metallica album without them.

To work for the new media companies that were opening this frontier was to be part of the undermining of old authority. That was pretty hip. The old dilemma of selling out did not apply. No matter how hard you worked, it was in the interest of increasing personal access to information, not restricting it. In other words, what you were working at was hip.

If money was information—both in the sense of moving as ones and zeros and that of financing the gear to harvest more info—then money itself could be hip. It came in new denominations (stock options), enriched new people (geeks) and rose to new highs. This was a fulfillment of the information economy: even money was perceived in terms of image. The titans of the World Wide Web, the navigational system that began mapping the Net in 1992, were rock stars; *Wired* was their *Rolling Stone,* as its editors never tired of braying. For old school hipsters, this could be disorienting. Jim Marshall, a writer and radio disc jockey who also calls himself the Hound, runs a bar called the Lakeside Lounge on Avenue B in the East Village, where there's Iggy on the jukebox and the ghost of Charlie Parker is never far away. In an era of vanishing dives, the Lakeside is what anyone would call a fine place. Marshall has been dismayed to hear the new language infiltrating its smoke-free air. He moved to the neighborhood in the late 1970s for the connection to William Burroughs and the Velvet Underground, and because the drug traffic kept the rents down. The new dot-com crowd, he said, were the people he moved there to escape. "I heard two kids in here, maybe 25, talking about their retirement plans," he said. "My whole world is gone." But the corporate world these customers inhabited was not the one he rejected. In the new workplace, work was like play; if you played hard and smart, why shouldn't you make buckets of ducats?

The hip answer to this question in the past was easy: just look at the snots who had money. Did you want to roll with them, or with Whitman and Sun Ra? Money was old money; it was slow and clogged up the hip circulation of culture. Because old money wants to stay where it is (i.e., in the pockets of the rich), it reinforces the divisions in society—the ones hip exists to cross. Yet other money, hip money, has always moved outside of this framework: in the economy of the outlaw, the drug dealer, the hard-boiled dick, the high roller, the decadent rock star or hip-hop baller. Ma Rainey, an early progenitor of bling, wore diamonds, a tiara, gold teeth and a chain made of $20 gold pieces. All of these alternatives moved wealth from the bottom up, breaking lines rather than reinforcing them. When Snoop Dogg appears on awards ceremonies flaunting a white gold chalice, it is not just an homage to status materialism but also a refutation of it, like burning bills or tossing them into the stock exchange—a grand FU. If money could be agile, moving at the speed of DJ Spooky's subliminal circuitry, it could be as neutral as the samples themselves. What mattered would be how you mixed them.

One peculiarity of technology is that it scorns money for the same reason hip does: because money holds it back. Technology bites the people who pay the most for it. The first version of any new technology, like automobiles or computer modems, is tremendously expensive, and so it sucks up to the rich. But it cannot live in this insular ecosystem. Unless it is a monopoly, as the phone system became, competition and technical advances will drive the price down and the market outward. The rich pay fortunes for primitive machines so the poor can get the next generation. The better the tech, the faster it lowballs itself. Value is a dead weight.

To illustrate what I mean, the other day I was looking for the 1890s address of the Sulzberger family, owners of the *New York Times,* and through a company archivist I eventually found it—on West 120th Street in Harlem—in an old telephone directory. This tells you something about the relationship between wealth and technology. In its early years, the phone was a marker of class, and the directory was like a private club. Anyone who could afford this new status object would be proud to publish his (rarely her) number in a directory. They wouldn't worry about getting calls from the rabble because the rabble did not have telephones. Now, when peasants in the fields of Vietnam have cell phones powerful enough to steer battleships, if you wanted to find the Sulzberger address you would no more look in the telephone book than you would pound the pavement on 120th Street. The phone directory belongs to the rabble, and the phone grid puts paupers on the same level as princes.

In this way technology is different from diamonds or real estate, which conserve privilege rather than distributing it. Tech resists the bottlenecks of class. A society organized around material wealth tries to gather it in stacks; one organized around technology, like the phone system, wants to scatter it horizontally. If 10 percent of the population owned 70 percent of the phones or monopolized 70 percent of the good TV shows, the system would revolt. The printing press, radio, television, CDs, cell phones and the Internet all moved in the way of the telephone. Created in the image of the elite, they all gave the masses a medium for speaking back. (Sometimes rudely: If you thought cable television would mean the BBC, say hello to pro wrestling; the Internet may have been created for research scientists and the military, but its early killer app was porn.)

Not coincidentally, all these media became vehicles for spreading rhythm and Emersonian individualism, sometimes contrary to the intentions of their inventors and first patrons. A decade after Time Warner, one of the richest media conglomerates in the world, aligned its fortunes with AOL, millions of AOL subscribers were using the service to rip free MP3's of Warner songs, threatening the entire music industry. When George W. S. Trow writes about the death of the Eisenhower empire, back when it really was the empire—"the control system that produced our money, our dominance, our unique position in the world"—he is talking in part about the way the economy of technology, which seeks ever poorer customers, has superceded the economy of diamonds and real estate.

This upheaval has at every step extended hip's gospel. Its pace is now such that it is at the point of eating itself. In recent years giant media conglomerates like AOL Time Warner, or telcoms like Global Crossing and WorldCom, hemorrhaged fortunes even while they added customers, because they were in a race to make their product less valuable, turning a privilege into a commonplace. (Executive corruption or incompetence helped as well.) As annoying as cell phones are, they are subversive in a way that leather jackets cannot not be, because they bite the hand that markets them. The wealth of technology, in the end, is closer to the poverty of Jack Kerouac: everything belongs to me because I am poor.

In Don DeLillo's 1997 novel *Underworld,* an artist named Klara Sax, who paints disused B-52 fuselages in the desert, describes a sense of imbalance left by the end of the Cold War. The Berlin Wall fell in 1989; the Soviet Union collapsed two years later. Without the symmetry created by two opposing superpowers, she says, the old points of reference disappeared. The Cold War had created monumental hierarchies, against which everything took its measure, in the same way the details on the facade of St. Patrick's Cathedral all take their meaning from their unique relationship with God. Without it, she says, "Many things that were anchored to the balance of power and the balance of terror seem to be undone, unstuck. Things have no limits now. Money has no limits. I don't understand money anymore. Money is undone. Violence is undone, violence is easier now, it's uprooted, out of control, it has no measure anymore, it has no level of values."

Afrika Bambaataa

So much of hip's history is based on a relationship of polarities: black and white, high culture and low, mainstream and underground, insider and outsider. Hip worked the ground between the poles, shuttling intelligence across the gap or conspiring with one side to elude the other. Black English, for example, both eludes curious whites *and* enriches their vocabularies. Mass culture, which in the Cold War era built up a titanic mainstream, invited a counteroffensive of hip dissent and satire. You could tell what side anything was on because there were only two sides. Something was on the bus or off the bus. As Mailer wrote in "The White Negro," "One is Hip or one is Square (the alternative which each new generation coming into American life is beginning to feel), one is a rebel or one conforms, one is a frontiersman in the Wild West of American night life, or else a Square cell, trapped in the totalitarian tissues of American society, doomed willy-nilly to conform if one is to succeed." When DeLillo's character pines for the fixed ground rules of the Cold War, part of what she misses are the clear boundaries of mass culture.

By contrast, digital culture has no inside and outside. To the extent that Mailer's binary system ever held up—and someone as iconoclastic *and* conventionally ambitious as Mailer should question his own premise—it no longer passes even as an illusion. There is no center to be alternative to. In place of the old hierarchies is the digital grid of the Internet or the DJ decks, where everybody occupies an equivalent of one of the windows in Rockefeller Center. All are zeroes and ones. Once-marginalized figures like white supremacists or enema enthusiasts can now travel in communities of kindred spirits, oblivious to any outside opinion, the same as jocks or young Republicans. Destiny's Child really is no different from Nirvana; old field recordings gathered by Alan Lomax are as current as new beats by Moby. One-man blogs like Gawker.com, started by a former equity analyst, or a Web site showing an animated character taking a dump, created by a struggling freelance animator named Tom Winkler, transmit information in the same way as large media conglomerates. In early 2000, Winkler's www.doodie.com was getting 9.5 million visitors a month, comparable to some of AOL Time Warner's sites.

Though digital culture seeks ever smaller, more specific domains, it is not a return to popular culture, in the sense that Michael Kammen uses the term, but a post-mass culture. The model for popular culture was a broad cross section of a local population rubbing elbows at the same county fair; by contrast, the Net unites funnel-cake fanatics worldwide. This poses some challenges to hip. By its nature, hip is an operating system of alpha hipsters: we gravitate toward Miles or Twain or the guy down the block because of something in them that is familiar, then follow them into realms that are not. Hip needs this interplay of alphas and admirers (who may become the next alphas). A truly disconnected individualist may have a blues to sing, but it is not a hip blues. Hip is a reason to cross the street or cross the tracks, to leave behind the familiar and consensual. At Minton's Playhouse or on Twain's river, as Eno says, the improvisations get us used to the idea of enjoying uncertainty. The contact is enlightening. To get from the square exurbs to the hip inside you have to brush against people in each circle along the way. The boundary-crossing, in turn, speeds the pace at which the people involved learn to enjoy uncertainty.

There is something at stake any time we cross from one circle to another, a simultaneous relinquishing and hardening of the self. The alternative is solipsism. For this to happen—for people to agree to be changed by something unlike themselves—there must be a cohesiveness to the individualism, like that emerging from "West End Blues." People who do not walk a certain way must agree that the people who do are hip. There must be a consensus that Monk's porkpie hat is hip, but that Weezer's sweaters are lame. When hipsters challenge the taste hierarchies of the mainstream, it is not to argue that there should be no taste hierarchies, just that Charles Bukowski or Richard Pryor belong above Barbra Streisand or Philip Roth—if not on objective aesthetic grounds, then on the highly subjective grounds of hip.

The Net, by contrast, is an operating system that does not need alphas. It defeats authority. Its consensuses are micro—*within* subgroups rather than *between* them. We visit Web sites to learn about things we are already interested in, not to see what the people there are into. If the experience on any site does not confirm what you already believe, you are probably out of there. There's always another site waiting to provide this confirmation; there's a streaming audio source that plays only your brand of Mexican ska or Danish hip-hop. Even peer-to-peer networks, like those that share music files, are united mainly by their resistance to hierarchy, including that of intellectual property rights. Cher fans download Cher; fans of Super Furry Animals download their favorites. There's no need for either to encounter the other or justify their tastes.

This is a new condition of hip. Without a mainstream, the society formed around the Internet has no need for an alternative. Everyone is alternative now. Even athletes, once the most aggressively square people on the planet, now swagger like rap thugs. They are all misfits. There is no dominant square ideology, just niche cults that chug along independent of anything but themselves. The patrons at Jim Marshall's Lakeside Lounge, listening to a swamp jukebox and talking about their retirement plans, are not the hipsters the neighborhood once had, but it would be parochial to assume that they cannot be hip. From its beginnings hip has shaped itself to the economy and technology of its time. These have changed, and so has hip. (Though let's not rule out the possibility that Marshall's customers are just a couple of assholes talking about their retirement plans.) In this universe, the last thing you'd cop to is being a hipster.

In the concluding chapter, I'll talk about where hip goes now that its ideology has become the mainstream's. In the meantime, while it is natural to sympathize with Klara Sax or Jim Marshall, there is nothing to be gained by laments for a lost unspoiled age. Hip resists such resistance to change; that's part of what makes it hip. While its collective memory preserves the past, it also destroys it to begin anew. Its loftiest tradition is this self-destruction. The battles of hip's past are over and hip has won. In the post-hip era, the new battles begin.

everybody's hip

superficial reflections on the white caucasian

> [T]his whole hipster thing is the most interesting cultural phenomena our generation has put forth, like it or not...maybe the whole hipsterization of downtown was happening well before 2001, but i don't think it became prevalent until post-9/11.
>
> —"C,"www.hipstersareannoying.com

On the question of what is post-hip, Tower of Power has kept a discreet silence.

We are left on our own, then, to account for what happens when nearly everybody is hip. After 300-odd years of *hipi* and *hepi*, of Emerson and Ellison, the old binaries of black and white, alternative and mainstream, no longer go very far. "You know it's gone to hell," as Charles Barkley said in 2000, "when the best rapper out there is a white guy and the best golfer is a black guy." The squarest of American institutions, from gardening manuals to Army recruitment ads, now market themselves in two strengths: hip and hipper. Stockbrokers download alternative trance music, and Jim Crow memorabilia sells as kitsch on eBay. Hip has reached another new beginning, this one dressed in an ironic Little League T-shirt and gothic-script tattoo. It has passed from hip to "hip." The inverted commas say, "We're both too hip to care about this hip stuff, but, you know, isn't that pretty hip?" They are the raised eyebrow of post-hip.

We noted earlier that few things are as unhip as what was hip five minutes ago. In this way hip is like Menudo. Old members don't mature, they just lie low until it is safe for them to resurface as Ricky Martin—or in the case of hip, as retro styles, like the graphics on old Blue Note album covers. The corollary to this is that for hipsters of any vintage, whatever comes along five minutes after them seems lightweight and contrived. One's own sliver of hipness entails rigor and substance, it seems, but anything slightly older or newer feels corny or unschooled.

This prejudice is nearly as old as hip itself. To the Greenwich Village bohemians of the 1910s, the newcomers who moved in after the Great War seemed without weight. Similarly, Kerouac's crowd saw the beatnik swarm after *On the Road* as wannabes, cloned through ads in the back of *Esquire*. Beatnik purists, in turn, often judged the 1960s hippies as spoiled college kids in goofy colors. And Woodstock diehards could only watch in despair when their legacy metastasized into new age and the Eagles a decade later. (A small matter, you might say, but try reading this book while humming "Desperado.") And so it goes. These schisms help explain the longevity of the hip process: for all its forward thrust it never actually gets anywhere, because it always starts anew from the same place.

With this bias in mind, we come to the mash-up mix of the 00s: trucker hats, Pabst Blue Ribbon, Jenna Jameson, coke (again), "blackting," bhangra beats, homo thugs, retro afros, redneck rock, Friendster, bling, bikram yoga, new wave (again!), nerdistans, faux-hawks, pole dancing and the strangely common belief that being from the Midwest or Canada constitutes a story. Urban anthropologists can spot post-hip by its prefixes and quotation marks, a politically incorrect mix of neo-shitkicker, nuevo-blaxploitation, and kimchi kitsch. To the above inventory, add metrosexuality, *McSweeney's*, Vicodin, flash mobs, smart mobs, thumb tribes, "extreme" everything, free folk and the return of no wave. If any or all of these have passed to the trend boneyard (or Urban Outfitters) by the time you read this, please substitute whatever arose in their stead.

Strictly speaking, these trends are not the meat of our story here.

They are just the points where hip meets the marketplace. The media may hawk each as an event, but hip's essence lies in the processes below the surface, which tie the trends to a longer history. Like the word *bad*, which I've used as an example throughout this book, the various T-shirts or bhangra moves become temporary repositories for meaning, which might at other times be shuttled elsewhere. Just as there is nothing inherent to *bad* that allows it to play this role, you should not sweat the inherent hipness of whatever indie band sounds most like Lynyrd Skynyrd this week. What's hip is the meaning, if any, that this post-camp aesthetic has momentarily been called upon to harbor. To explore this, let us look at how meaning comes to hip.

As a starting point, take the romance of the open road. From *Moby-Dick* to the peregrinations of modern DJs, the ubiquity of travel or rootlessness in hip is uncanny. It is hip's archetypal story. As told by Mark Twain or Muddy Waters, or in the slave sermons about exodus, this tale is episodic or open-ended, more concerned with motion and process than arrival. Its protagonist leaves behind a past life and the people who knew him by it, and is transformed by the journey. The itinerant bluesman, Beat hitchhiker, hobo, outlaw or free-clicking Web-head all fall into this drift. Jazz improvisations or DJ mixes repeat the journey in music, transforming a tune rather than composing it. The hip hero gathers no moss. We think of Huck or Sal, or Jesse James or Lord Digital, as traveling without baggage, reinventing themselves through the motion of the road.

What is missing from the story is what the travelers bring to us when they arrive. This begs a second look. Along with their own epiphanies, the road warriors also transport ideas and knowledge from one place to another. Their adventures, in turn, seduce other travelers into motion. A broader portrait of hip and the road is one of wholesale redistribution, funneling certain outsiders and skills to places where they reach critical mass. It moved eastern European Jews and black southern sharecroppers to northern cities in the early part of the 20th century, and poets and jazzmen to the coasts in the middle. Where its lines come together hip flourishes. A way to look at hip is as a map of people in motion.

In trying to account for hip's existence over the course of this book,

I've resisted explanations that run counter to market Darwinism. Though hip is a romantic ideal, romance without finance is unpersuasive. Movements in America that don't turn a profit tend to have short lives (even religion, because it preaches obedience and delayed gratification, creates a productive workforce). Though hip seems to encourage sloth and underachievement, as we've noted in earlier chapters, it has spiked when the economy needed something to promote consumption. The hip convergences of the 1850s, 1910s, 1950s and 1990s all coincided with manufacturing booms for which the bohemian rallying cry—*out with the old, in with the new*—spoke to the radicalized consumer. When America's stores flogged revolutionary new products, hip called for lifestyle revolution and immediate kicks. Where religion creates workers, hip creates consumers.

Yet there is another way to line up these dates. Each coincided with a boom in migration or immigration, or an influx of ideas from abroad. For example, the first decades of the 20th century, which produced the prototypes of modern hip—the Village bohemians and early Harlem Renaissance—saw more immigration than any previous period in American history. Immigrants to the Lower East Side met up with blacks making the Great Migration from the South, combining in the hip hybrids of the Jazz Age. The next time immigration reached this level was at the end of the century, when polyglot enclaves in New York and San Francisco generated the style rebellions of Internet hip and post-hip. Even in the periods after the two world wars, when the government restricted immigration, ideas from abroad served as catalysts for hip, entering the country with returning servicemen and expats. In these two periods the Lost Generation synthesized ideas from Europe, the Beats from Asia and the bop musicians from Africa and Cuba. When knowledge moves and clusters, hip blooms.

This flow suggests another meaning to hip's romance of the road. Immigration pulls self-selected individuals from the rest of the world to the United States, concentrating them in low-rent districts of major cities. At the same time, young nomads from all over America, also self-selected, converge on many of the same spots. In different periods immigration has brought many of the world's great artists, intellectuals, dissidents, iconoclasts, pariahs, heretics, students and freaks to America.

The nation's greatest strength, the economist Richard Florida has suggested, may not be its native gumption but its access to other countries' brainpower and initiative. Hip—the combination of freedom and intelligence—is part of the draw. It brings self-starters, self-inventors and a predisposition to youth culture: in immigrant homes, it is common for the youngest members to be most fluent in the new language and customs, and to lead their parents toward their romance of America. Hip permeates this romance.

Hip does not happen just anywhere. It clusters in some areas and depletes others. It is an epidemiology of enlightenment. Viewed from above, it looks like a jumble of bicycle spokes coming together in a few distinct hubs, then radiating back out. Take bebop as an example. Though Charlie Parker learned his skills in Kansas City and Dizzy Gillespie in South Carolina, and though both men worked these skills on the road, hip needed Harlem and Minton's for bop to gel as a full-service lifestyle, with its own language, fashion, drugs, politics and philosophy. Even before Henry Minton set up shop, bop needed the Great Migration and the Harlem Renaissance of the 1920s to move artists, intellectuals, writers, radicals, revelers, Negrotarians, dancers, dealers and dollars to Harlem, and it needed the European avant-garde that relocated to New York in the 1930s to escape Hitler. It needed Juilliard and the Mighty Mezz, the man with the righteous bush. Perhaps it needed Sicilian heroin syndicates and Parker's Ukrainian drinking buddies on the Lower East Side.

None of these elements was indigenous to New York. When enough of them add up, the density of skills, information and noise scares some people but liberates others. Squares wring their hands; hipsters push each other to wilder styles—now that there are battle lines, folks can battle. It is no coincidence that bop or Beat did not happen in a more segregated city like Chicago or Memphis, or a more stratified one like Charleston or Kennebunkport, or a less Euro-accessible one like Los Angeles or Detroit, or in the wide-open spaces of Wyoming or New Mexico. Smaller hip towns did not have enough gravitational pull or good drummers to bring the scenes together; they got them on the bounce. The phenomena may not have needed New Yorkers (apologies to Monk and Bud), but they needed New York—they needed the mix. Pulp needed Raymond Chandler's Los Angeles, and cartoons needed the Fleischer brothers' multiethnic Brooklyn.

And to get people there, all of them needed hip and the romance of the road.

The first migration in this book, of course, is the passage to America. This journey is asymmetric, beginning very differently in Europe and Africa. Hip's history starts with this asymmetry in the new land. In the same way that bop needs Minton's as a creation myth, hip needs this journey and first encounter. Its first artifact is the word *hip* itself, which bears its own record of travel. The transit of *hipi* to hip, which passed unremarked in most textbooks, opens an alternative history of race in America. This book has been about that history. From this first synthesis, hip's broader story unfolds in macrocosm.

The macro story of hip and the road, like the micro narratives of individual journeys, shapes each of the six hip convergences. The rise of minstrelsy, the blues and the American Renaissance of the 1850s, hip's first vehicles, all reflected the strangeness of this original migration and encounter in the new land. As America's first popular culture, minstrelsy recorded white immigrants' experience of blacks; the blues, the first art form created by African Americans *as Americans,* recorded black immigrants' experience among whites. Both forms were new and strange; they were transitory chronicles of a world that was inventing itself as rapidly as its chroniclers were.

Emerson, Thoreau, Whitman and Melville added an interest in Eastern philosophy and spiritual tradition. But they captured this transition incompletely, because they concerned themselves only with how the nation invented new identities, not with the bits of Africa and Europe the two groups brought. This is one tendency of the hip road narrative: it sheds the past to allow reinvention in the present. This process jibes with Emerson's ideal of individualism, since the past ties are mainly collective, defined by class, ethnicity, nationality or tribe, while the self we invent is individual. (Conveniently glossed are the country's indigenous cultures, whose identities predate these reinventions).

The portraits of migration from the 1850s were also incomplete because slavery artifically limited African Americans' movements. After emancipation, blacks could move where circumstances favored them. In the subsequent hip convergences, black migrants and their descendants met waves of white travelers and foreign immigrants, first from Europe, then much later, during the tech boom of the 1980s and 1990s, from Asia, the Pacific Islands and Latin America. Where these diverse tribes went, and whence they packed up, determined the geography of hip.

As I said above, hip does not happen just anywhere. It requires population density, so that people rub against each other, and so that the misfits, dissidents and outcasts can find each other. In close quarters they trade bits of style, skill and language, mangling each other's gifts to produce something hybrid and new. Within this dense population, hip also requires diversity, for the same reason that evolution requires diversity in the DNA. It is not hip if it is monocultural or unchanging. And it requires new apostates to unseat the old. These newcomers, whether from Kansas City or Bangalore, start bands or zines or hole-in-the-wall design studios, or fill bars and cafés to escape their apartments. Some hit the streets to get away from their parents or make noise. They outshine

Williamsburg, Brooklyn, 2003

the previous wave of arrivals and attract the next—who, in turn, will outshine them. Their influx makes streets lively after dark, attracts more newcomers and moves money and information among hip's concentric circles. There is nothing as dead as a place that relies on its licit thrills or moldy traditions.

Though many Americans say they pine for old-school ethnic communities where neighbors look out for one another, hip seeks the anonymity of the big city. In neighborhoods where people greet each other with a generic "Wha'sup, player," hip moves freely; neighborhoods where they say, "Tony, your mother needs you home right now," tend to repel outsiders and stifle diversity. Hip communities replicate the flux of the road. Hipsters often think of themselves as flowing toward cheap rents, but this is only half of the story. Drawn to meccas like New York, San Francisco, Seattle or Portland, they come first despite the high rents, then find liminal neighborhoods like Williamsburg or the Mission where the dress codes and real estate values are slack. When they reach critical mass there they comprise a hip scene—which jacks the rents, pushing the next arrivals to the next benighted 'hood. If they really just wanted cheap rents they could stay home in bumfuck.

Like the retail theory of hip, which holds that hip exists to stimulate consumption, all this migration and immigration align hip with a flow of money. Hip may look like poverty and slackness, but it runs with or attracts wealth. Richard Florida and Gary Gates, an economist at the Urban Institute, have shown that the cities that cultivate these hipster tribes—musicians, artists, immigrants, bohemians, writers, designers, Web developers, gays and lesbians—are the cities that get rich.

Immigrants and other outsiders do not just materialize in a place. Something has to get them there. Ellis Island gave New York the edge in the early 20th century. The city provided more cultural experiences and more ways to fit in than anywhere else. Drugs, bagels, jazz, hookers, import punk singles and underground zines followed. In the 1970s and 1980s, the libertarian politics of Silicon Valley made it a welcoming place for immigrants with certain skills or ambitions. It was okay to be different there. These immigrants, in turn, converged with the old freak culture of Haight-Ashbury, the gay culture of the Castro and the residual Beat legacy of North Beach, which also had been allowed to linger or grow. Some newcomers clustered in nerdistans, or geek ghettos.

The money they attracted, which fueled the dot-com boom, left behind Eastern Establishment families and banks and the dinosaurs of the Rust Belt. It moved not just from square to hip, but from rooted populations to migratory ones. Immigrants started about 25 percent of new companies in Silicon Valley after 1980. This is a model of how hip and wealth run together, even though alpha hipsters—the ones who pore over Foucault and Fugazi and cheap drugs—don't necessarily get rich. They just set the stage for creative diversity and enterprise. "The great cultural legacy of the sixties," Richard Florida writes, "was not Woodstock after all, but something that had evolved at the other end of the continent. It was Silicon Valley."

The hip tribes of Seattle, Portland, Toronto, Austin, Providence, San Diego or Chapel Hill (source of the great 1990 loafing anthem, "Slack Motherfucker," by Superchunk) arrived via similar migrations and encountered similar boom times. The places that had young, mobile populations had dive bars, DJs, coffee shops, rock clubs, tattoo parlors and alt music shops—and the places that had these things got venture capital money. Entrepreneurs, whether drug dealers, indie label guys or the founders of future Fortune 500 companies, share a lot of the same instincts and seek many of the same pleasures. All create wealth: for most of the 20th century, the best predictor of economic growth for cities was the density of skills in the population, not the companies or government infrastructure. Hip comes with a diversity of ideas and skills. Money seeks the same combination.

Economists disagree about just how hip and economic growth are related. Edward Glaeser of Harvard believes that cities now provide mainly consumer experiences, and that skilled workers and companies follow bohemians because they're fun to watch. These followers might include, perhaps, the guys discussing retirement options in Jim Marshall's Lakeside Lounge. Florida and Gates believe that the same ecosystems that favor bohemians also favor entrepreneurs, for reasons that are not yet clear. Either way, hip plays both cause and effect in this equation. It attracts diverse people to a place, then accrues from their density, diversity and tolerance. If you wanted to find this population and get rich, you could look at where hip is. And if you were among the hip, you would be there already.

In immigrant communities, hip serves another function as well. Because foreign-born parents often engage their new country through their children, hip becomes the path of acculturation. Many kids absorb hip's values and accessories even before they arrive. The sociologist Ruben Rumbaut calls this the consciousness of generation 1.5, who arrive as foreign children and grow up to be American teens. Hip allows them to be both American and unassimilated. It's a way in, in the same way that Baraka's field hand, who looks up from his toil and says, "Oh, Ahm tired a dis mess, / Oh, yes, Ahm so tired a dis mess," expresses a consciousness that understands both hip and America. Hip welcomes difference; it is attractive. After all, who wouldn't rather enter the America of Ralph Ellison and Fischerspooner than the cold one of Robert McNamara and Donald Rumsfeld? Since skilled immigrants create wealth, hip serves the economy in three ways: it beckons them to America, puts them where they can use their skills and brands them as Americans. For a nation without roots, hip translates motion as order—in other words, as home.

The other outsiders who add meaning to hip's romance of the road are gays and lesbians. Gays have been at or near the center of every hip convergence. Their story, too, begins with movement. In a mobile society, people do not remain where they are not wanted, or where they cannot meet romantic partners. Born everywhere, gays and lesbians tend to seek the cover of dense communities, where they are not the only gay person they know. In close proximity, they cultivate codes of language, aesthetics and humor; camp could only have come from concentrated gay ghettos. These ghettos pop up where people, gay as well as straight, feel free to act out. Even in the age of *Queer Eye for the Straight Guy*, when gay is everywhere, wherever you find a gay bar, chances are you'll also find a bohemian enclave. And where you don't, you won't. Hip attracts more hip.

Using 2000 census figures, which count gay couples, Florida and Gates found that cities with large gay communities also had expanding economies. Cities like Cincinnati, whose charter at the time of writing prohibited it from passing gay rights legislation, fall behind economically, because they cannot attract skilled workers. Even open-minded straight people don't want to move there. Gays, artists and bohemians remain hip's residential front line, remaking neighborhoods like

Williamsburg, Silver Lake, Newark, Southwest Baltimore, Deep Ellum, Chicago's Lakeview and Wicker Park, the Castro and their equivalents in other cities. Hip moves where they do, and economic growth follows.

A t this point you may be wondering, What does this have to do with the meaning of a trucker hat?

For the uninitiated, the trucker hat, or mesh hat, is a baseball cap with a foam-padded front panel and a one-size-fits-all plastic snap in back. It is an ugly piece of work. Classic models feature logos for Von Dutch car "kustomizers," Stroh's beer, or other emblem of their blue-collar roots, and may be worn facing front or to the side. Spotted in the early 2000s on Pharrell Williams of the Neptunes and Johnny Knoxville of *Jackass,* by late 2002 they reached the saturation point in hipster enclaves, and by mid-2003 they were in Barney's, the upscale clothing store. Rewriting the rules of chronology, they went from being *so* last week to *so* three months ago in about a week and a half. Their swift arc, born on a wave of white trash chic, seems counter to hip's romance of the road: they're from nowheresville and proud of it.

The life of a hat is rarely an unencumbered one. Hat color distinguishes heroes from villains, and your hat is what you keep secrets under. Nothing says "I'm enjoying the show" like a 10-gallon hat in your lap. The Cat in the Hat and the Man in the Big Yellow Hat show American children that their guardians will both fail them and dress to embarrass them—a key lesson for larval hipsters. In some jazz circles of the 1940s and 1950s your hat was your honey, but in the hip hop 1990s you didn't want your cap peeled. Berets, porkpies, fedoras, yarmulkes, Kangols, skullies, hoodies, jimmy hats, John Waters's boater and those regrettable straw cowboy hats of 2001 fill hip's history. They keep its lid on. Without hats, hipsters would have to develop "hat head" by artificial means.

The semiotics of the trucker hat follows a noble precedent. In his 1981 essay "Within the Context of No Context," George W. S. Trow wrote about growing up believing that he would someday wear a fedora like his father's, and that this hat would signal his place in society. But by the 1960s, when he reached adulthood, society had changed, and so had the fedora's meaning. "I have, in fact, worn a fedora hat," he wrote, but only as an ironic gesture.

> Irony has seeped into the felt of any fedora hat I have ever owned—not out of any wish of mine but out of necessity. A fedora hat worn by me without the necessary protective irony would eat through my head and kill me. I was born into the upper middle class in 1943, and one of the strange turns my life has taken is this: I was taught by my parents to believe that the traditional manners of the high bourgeoisie, properly acquired, would give me a certain dignity, which would protect me from embarrassment. It has turned out that I am able to do almost anything but act according to those modes—this because I deeply believe that those modes are suffused with an embarrassment so powerful that it can kill. It turns out that while I am at home in many strange places, I am not free even to visit the territory I was expected to inhabit effortlessly. To wear a fedora, I must first torture it out of shape so that it can be cleaned of the embarrassment in it.

Irony and embarrassment, of course, are perspectives of context. They judge something from one context according to the values of another. In Trow's case, irony measures the distance between his father's fedora and his own. It is a form of signifying. A fedora worn in irony says, "the old commuter world is passé, but we also miss its comforts." For the class that lost the old privilege, this second meaning is a replacement privilege.

The obvious contexts for the ironic trucker hat are September 11 and the collapse of the dot-com bubble. Against this backdrop, post-hip flaunts downward mobility and small town security as fashion accessories. Also, after the hollow symbolic wealth of the previous decade, the new era explores symbolic *authenticity,* fabricating roots rather than aspirations. And as American political power moves toward Christian evangelicals, who take a very orthodox view of enlightenment, post-hip mocks the boundaries of orthodoxy itself. Its first targets, appropriately, are the orthodoxies that call themselves hip. When hipsters start dancing to old Journey records, it is on the graves of hip pieties past.

But there's a broader, more interesting context for the emergence of

Caucasian kitsch. Viewed through the prism of migration and immigration, the trucker hat tells a story about hip's changing demographics. Like Trow's fedora, it riffs ironically on its demo. Pulled out of its white, working-class, all-American context, it identifies the most diverse, multicultural, middle-class and ethnic-marketed generation in American history. Between 1970 and 2000, the immigrant population in the United States tripled, from 9.6 million to 28.4 million. After the tight borders of the 1960s and 1970s, when the parents of today's hipsters came of age, America now accepts more immigrants than the rest of the world combined. One in five Americans is now either an immigrant or has a foreign-born parent. In New York, 40 percent of the population at the turn of the century was foreign-born. Latinos passed African Americans as the nation's largest minority group. These changes were most pronounced among younger people. In Los Angeles's public school system, for example, Latinos in 2001 made up 71 percent of the students. The generation gap now is less a matter of sex, drugs and rock and roll than demographics.

Williamsburg, Brooklyn, 2003

For the post-hip generation, the black and white poles that for so long defined race have given way to a kaleidoscope of color, race and ethnicity, made even more complicated by crosscurrents of class and sexual orientation. This generation's world is not that of their boomer parents, however hip those parents think they are. Born around the time of the first rap single, the Sugarhill Gang's "Rapper's Delight," in 1979, and raised with anime, *Sabado Gigante,* gender studies and fusion cuisine, post-hipsters never knew a time when hip-hop was not the dominant cultural force or when you couldn't change your ethnic surround by clicking a remote control. In this churn, many middle-class blacks, whose numbers doubled in the last 20 years, get their ghetto fix through rap videos, and Asian Americans debate the "realness" of the banana or Twinkie, the Eastern equivalents of the Oreo. Cholos trade poses with gangstas. Race is something they arrive at as well as come with. More than any past generation they have grown up omniracial, at least in their recreations. Many can't remember back when ketchup outsold salsa or queer was an insult.

To a great extent this blurring of lines finally exposes what has been a fallacy all along. The dichotomy of black and white rests on the fiction of the one-drop rule, which hides the complexities of our racial history. In 1958, the anthropologist Robert P. Stuckert of Ohio State proposed, in a peer-reviewed article, that more Americans with African ancestors were living as white than black. Though Stuckert relied on some fuzzy math, his broader point is provocative. It suggests that America's population is like its pop culture: elusive of origin, hybrid, casually labeled black or white when it might really be anything in between. Like the romance of the road, this mix reveals itself more in its processes than in the racial poles that have been contrived to describe it. The labels "black" and "white" are nowhere near as interesting as the road stories they hide. As scientific terms they are meaningless, and as historical terms they erase whole histories of intermingling and crossover—many unhappy, some atrocious, but by no means all. If the one-drop rule were reversed, so that anyone with a drop of European blood was considered white, enormous swaths of culture would arbitrarily change sides overnight.

In this spirit, the trucker hat and other post-hip accessories play with the meaning of whiteness in a multicultural world. They make white visible. Without the black/white dichotomy to anchor it, and without numerical dominance to give it weight, whiteness is up for grabs. Especially in cities that are now "majority-minority," or less than half non-Hispanic white, whiteness is no longer the baseline, something taken for granted; it's something to be explored, turned sideways, debated for its currency. It's a mask, like burnt cork or "blackting," the slang word for acting black. Caucasian kitsch—which includes redneck rock, wife-beater tank tops, homey Little League T-shirts, corn dogs, drag racing, demolition derby and *Vice* magazine—packages whiteness as a fashion commodity that can be donned or doffed according to one's dating needs. Post-hip treats whiteness the way fashion and entertainment have historically treated blackness. It swaths white identity not in race pride but in quotation marks. Whiteness doesn't define you, you define it—and you don't have to be white to wear it.

After generations of white negro hipsters, the trucker hat introduces the hipster as White White Boy. He is a *white*face minstrel. The white white boy may be any shade, from the pale tones of County Cork to the darker hues of San Salvador, Kenya or Seoul. The history of the white negro has not come to the end, but without the binary opposition of black and white, it has come to *an* end. It is now just one mask among many. Hip moves on, as it always does.

Before it leaves him, though, a proper send-off is in order. The white negro, or wigger, or wigga, or white boy who stole the blues, has been a central player in this history from the outset. His family tree runs from Daddy Rice to Twain to Elvis to Eminem, a succession that has held America's imagination for the better part of two centuries. The nation would not be what it is without him. If white supremacy is America's original sin, the white negro is a character born after the fall, conjured to imagine a return to grace without sacrifice. As Greg Tate put it in the title of a 2003 essay collection, the wigga as cultural emissary takes everything but the burden.

Like many characters in this book, the white boy who stole the blues is a trickster of sorts: self-serving, indeterminate, navigating between two worlds. He trespasses where he is not wanted. Like Esu-Elegbara, the Yoruban trickster who brought humans the gift of divination, he reveals inaccessible knowledge, but never directly, only through his own second-hand translations. His thefts are the beginning of meaning. As Lewis Hyde notes, things don't need meaning until they can be moved from one context to another; before that they just need names. As with other tricksters, the white boy's motives are not always well understood.

The misconception about the white negro is that he wants to be black. This construes race like the traditional notion of travel: you cross the road to get to the other side. But it misses the hip version, which seeks motion for its own sake. The hip traveler, like Kerouac or Robert Johnson, does not step into the road to get to the other side. He's in it for the ride, most himself when he is in the middle. Perhaps there are some white negroes who want to cross over; Mezz Mezzrow and Johnny Otis spring to mind. But as an end, that's self-defeating, like any other form of cultural assimilation. It means giving up the one thing you know is yours. It becomes a process of losing without gaining, a form of erasure. As Eminem raps, mocking this orthodoxy, "How the fuck can I be white—I don't even exist?" As an attraction such a figure would be a bust. America loves profit, not loss.

But let us think again about theft. A thief does not steal a television set in order to have a TV. He steals it to have two: the one he had before, plus the new one. What the white negro wants is not to be black but to be both: to be free of the fallacy, derived from the one-drop rule, that he need be one thing or the other. Hip is what Robert Wright calls a non-zero sum game, moving from simple states toward complex ones, adding new layers without giving up the old. This is another reason hip endures: it is a system of increase. It moves in the opposite direction of the one-drop rule, which reduces complexity to a self-justifying myth. The one-drop rule erases knowledge of the ways we are intertwined. Hip seeks fullness and paradox among the erasures.

The white negro is just one model of hip complexity. He claims what DuBois, in *The Souls of Black Folk,* called African Americans' innate *twoness:* "two souls, two thoughts, two unreconciled strivings." Hip identity is like black English or the ironic trucker hat, infused with multiple, competing meanings—not one thing or the other, but both. It connects the license of Whitman, who boasted, "Of every hue and cast am I," with the nuances of Chuck D's laconic native sons: "if you go up to somebody and he says, 'nigga bugging,' he's saying a lot of things besides nigga bugging."

Hip enlightenment begins in this double consciousness, often racial but not necessarily so. It communicates in language that means more than one thing, or through the layered contexts of irony. It signifies. In the manner of Mailer's wise primitive or the irrational intelligence of cartoons, it adds knowledge through contradiction.

This is an imperfect model of intelligence. There is a reason our rule-makers try to resolve contradictions. Carl Jung thought tricksters were "stupider than the animals" because even the dumbest animals know their natures, whereas tricksters often get into trouble by thinking they are something else. Because the hipster is both inside himself and outside, he can be seduced by failure and self-destruction, treating the self as a third party. To destroy yourself is to become subject and object—the more dispassionately, the greater the distance between the two. This, you'll remember, is Terry Southern's grim definition of hip, to be permanently on the nod. But even this path contributes to an underlying intelligence: the trickster is always learning and teaching.

In the ethnic sprawl of the 21st century, the two poles of race no longer organize American life as they once did, for white people or black. And so they no longer organize hip. The playing field is much broader. The white boy who steals only the blues is not a hipster but an underachiever. There's too much else to grab. Yet race was never hip's only dichotomy, just the one that called most urgently for correction. Bob Holman, in a tribute to Gregory Corso, captured this impulse against dualism in a poem called "The Poet's Choice," which was three words long: "I'll take both." Nor is the movement toward more complex states limited to twoness. Throughout this history hip has adapted to the metaphors of new technology, and the metaphors of the Internet and video games allow you to be many more than two. Hipness is still what it always was, an access to ways of thought that don't go together, to rule and misrule. It just has more balls to juggle.

For hipsters of any bearing, the goal remains the same: to be not one thing but two, or three, or four. The episodic nature of the road—or Twain's winding river, the grid of Rockefeller Center, or DJ Spooky's digital beats—makes it possible simply to expand the metaphor, to straddle as many lines as you can find. Hip pulls ever toward this model, always failing to get there, and always starting anew. This is another reason hip keeps going, and will continue after you and I and Eminem and Netscape are gone: it is always wrong on the way to being right. To be hip is to believe in the possibility of reinvention—to understand oneself as between states, neither one nor the other, without original sin, forever on the road. Or as they said in Wolof: to see, to open one's eyes.

notes

Preface

1 "I know your type": Scott Isler, "Transactional Analysis with Lou Reed," *Trouser Press*, no. 36, February 1979.

Introduction

4 "[T]he Negro looks at the white man": Ralph Ellison, "Change the Joke and Slip the Yoke," in *The Collected Essays of Ralph Ellison* (New York: Modern Library, 1995), 109.

6 "implement change after the fact": William S. Burroughs, quoted in Ann Charters, ed., *The Portable Beat Reader* (New York: Penguin, 1992), xxxi.

7 "There is a difference between being off-white": Al Sharpton, in John D. Thomas, "The Playboy.Comversation," available at http://www.playboy.com/features/ dotcomversation/sharpton/index.html, October 2003.

7 "Nowadays it's hip not to be married": John Lennon, quoted in "Playboy Interview," *Playboy*, September 1980.

9 "There's only one thing to do": Tom Wolfe, *The Electric Kool-Aid Acid Test* (New York: Bantam, 1999), 224.

11 Andy Warhol formally became the patron: Lewis MacAdams, *Birth of the Cool: Beat, Bebop, and the American Avant-Garde* (New York: Free Press, 2001), 242.

11 a world that was doubly foreign: LeRoi Jones [Amiri Baraka], *Blues People: The Negro Experience in White America and the Music That Developed from It* (New York: William Morrow, 1963), 1.

11 "the lawless germinal element": David S. Reynolds, *Walt Whitman's America: A Cultural Biography* (New York: Vintage, 1996), 319.

11 "real genius underneath": Ibid., 320.

12 "having one's hip boots on": Quoted in Gene Sculatti, ed., *Too Cool* (New York: St. Martin's Press, 1993), 16.

12 "Hip . . . is the sophistication of the wise primitive": Norman Mailer, "The White Negro: Superficial Reflections on the Hipster," in *Advertisements for Myself* (Cambridge, Mass.: Harvard University Press, 1992), 343.

12 "[I]f the fate of twentieth-century man":   Ibid., 339.

14 Levi's borrows the pants: Austin Bunn, "Not Fade Away," *New York Times Magazine*, December 1, 2002, sec. 6, 60.

1 | In the Beginning There Was Rhythm

17 "Do you know what a nerd is?":   Interview by Kevin Kelly, "Gossip Is Philosophy," *Wired*, May 1995, 149.

17 "About the last of August":   Hugh Thomas, *The Slave Trade: The Story of the Atlantic Slave Trade, 1440–1870* (New York: Simon & Schuster, 1997), 174.

17 not the first African slaves: Ibid., 174.

18 a 1624 census of Virginia: Ibid.

18 around 600,000 to 650,000 Africans: Peter Kolchin, *American Slavery, 1619–1877* (New York: Hill & Wang, 1993), 22.

20 "slave owners usually hired white workers":   Thomas Sowell, *Ethnic America: A History* (New York: Basic Books, 1981), 187.

20 Slave narratives: Henry Louis Gates Jr., ed., *The Classic Slave Narratives* (New York: Signet Classic, 2002), 1.

20 "They used to tie me down":   Tom Wilson, quoted in John W. Blassingame, *Slave Testimony: Two Centuries of Letters, Speeches, Interviews, and Autobiographies* (Baton Rouge: Louisiana State University Press, 1977), 339.

21 most slaves in North America: Ira Berlin, *Many Thousands Gone: The First Two Centuries of Slavery in North America* (Cambridge, Mass.: Belknap Press of Harvard University Press, 1998), 17.

21 "My Mistus use'ta look at my dress":   Sarah Fitzpatrick, in Blassingame, 643.

22 black slaves born in America outnumbered those born in Africa: Kolchin, 38.

22 "Negro women are carrying black and white babies":   Fredrick Law Olmsted, *The Cotton Kingdom: A Traveller's Observations on Cotton and Slavery in the American Slave States*, quoted in Kolchin, 117.

22 "both blacks and whites held a mix of quasi-English":   Mechal Sobel, *The World They Made Together*, quoted in Kolchin, 60.

23 "In language, the African tradition aims at circumlocution":   Ernest Borneman, "The Roots of Jazz," in Nat Hentoff and Albert J. McCarthy, eds., *Jazz* (New York: Rinehart, 1959), 17.

23 "hints of a future theory":   Walt Whitman, quoted in Reynolds, *Walt Whitman's America*, 320.

23 a record of "brutal necessity":   James Baldwin, "If Black English Isn't a Language, Then Tell Me, What Is?" in *Collected Essays* (New York: Library of America, 1998), 781, 782.

24 "The slaves, in effect, learned to communicate":   Eugene D. Genovese, *Roll, Jordan, Roll: The World the Slaves Made* (New York: Random House, 1974), 437.

25 evangelical revivals: Kolchin, 55.

26 "the only institution of the Negroes": W. E. B. DuBois, "Some Efforts of Negro Americans for Their Own Social Betterment, Report of an Investigation under the Direction of Atlanta University, 1898," (Atlanta: Atlanta University Press, 1898), 4, 43, repr. in Sterling Stuckey, *Slave Culture: Nationalist Theory and the Foundations of Black America* (New York: Oxford University Press, 1987), 257.

26 more children of mixed unions were born: Genovese, 415.

26 "Do not many of our pretty white girls":   J. J. Flournoy, in ibid., 422.

27 "Like the patriarchs of old":   Mary Boykin Chesnut, quoted in ibid., 426.

27 "Notably absent from Southern slave folklore":   Kolchin, 154.

27 Their prominence in slave tales: For analysis of Michael Flusche's argument, see ibid.

28 Dickens called William Henry Lane: For Dickens on Master Juba, see James O. Horton and Lois E. Horton, *In Hope of Liberty: Culture, Community and Protest Among Northern Free Blacks, 1700–1860* (New York: Oxford University Press, 1997), 159.

28 "the Only Simon Pure Negro Troupe": Kwame Anthony Appiah and Henry Louis Gates Jr., eds., *Africana: The Encyclopedia of the African and African American Experience* (New York: Basic Civitas Books, 1999), 1319.

28 Rice, born May 20, 1808: The life of Daddy Rice is discussed in W. T. Lhamon Jr., *Raising Cain: Blackface Performance from Jim Crow to Hip Hop* (Cambridge, Mass.: Harvard University Press, 2000), 156.

28 Dressed in a ragged blue coat: For a discussion of Jim Crow, Zip Coon and the form of minstrel show, see Nick Tosches, *Where Dead Voices Gather* (Boston: Little, Brown, 2001), 10.

28 The first minstrel characters performed: See Lhamon, p. 59.

29 the standard minstrel show consisted: Eric Lott, *Love and Theft: Blackface Minstrelsy and the American Working Class* (New York: Oxford University Press, 1995), 5.

29 Some southern cities: Ibid., 38.

29 "the best Ethiopian song-writer": Tosches, 17.

29 or even south of Cincinnati: Ibid., 16.

29 wrote and performed minstrel tunes: Berlin's years at Nigger Mike's are discussed in Ann Douglas, *Terrible Honesty: Mongrel Manhattan in the 1920s* (New York: Farrar, Straus & Giroux, 1994), 357.

29 consider the anthem "Dixie": Dan Emmett and the Snowdens are detailed in Drew Gilpin Faust, "What They Say About 'Dixie,' " *New York Times*, January 9, 1994, sec. 7, 20.

29 all worked in or beside blackface: The ubiquity of performers who worked in blackface or with blackface minstrels is discussed in Bart Bull, "Does This Road Go to Little Rock?" (Unpublished manuscript, Los Angeles), Appiah and Gates, and Tosches.

29 Dizzy Gillespie gave his first public performance: Appiah and Gates, 1319.

29 "all modern American literature": Ernest Hemingway, quoted in Bruce Cook, *The Beat Generation* (Westport, Conn.: Greenwood, 1983), 36.

29 Blackface played a key role: For the importance of minstrelsy in film, see Lott, 5.

29 *Amos 'n' Andy*: For more on this once-popular program, see Mel Watkins, *On the Real Side: Laughing, Lying and Signifying* (New York: Touchstone, 1995), 275–285.

30 "the commodification of nigga culture": Bill Stephney, quoted in Rick Marin, Susan Miller et al., "Coming Up Roses," *Newsweek*, July 15, 1996, 45.

30 "the filthy scum of white society": Frederick Douglass, quoted in Tosches, 16.

30 "is something gained, when the colored man": Frederick Douglass, quoted in Lott, 37.

30 "the only completely original contribution": James Weldon Johnson, *Black Manhattan*, quoted in Douglas, *Terrible Honesty*, 76.

30 "A lot of black people": Ishmael Reed, in "Hiphoprisy: A Conversation with Michael Franti and Ishmael Reed," moderated by Bill Adler, *Transition*, Summer 1992, 8.

30 "The white imagination": Josephine Baker, quoted in Ben Ratliff, "Fixing, for Now, the Image of Jazz," *New York Times*, January 7, 2001, sec. 2, 1.

31 "Born theoretically white": Leslie Fiedler, quoted in Lott, 53.

31 "Blacks imitating and fooling whites": Douglas, *Terrible Honesty*, 76.

32 "When America became important enough to the African": Baraka, xii.

32 "one of the most beautiful spots on earth": Francis Davis, *The History of the Blues: The Roots, the Music, the People—from Charley Patton to Robert Cray* (New York: Hyperion, 1995), 18.

33 three distinct musical traditions: See the discussion of different schools of African music in America in Robert Palmer, *Deep Blues* (New York: Penguin, 1992), 27–28.

34 the firms of C. F. Martin and Orville Gibson: Influence of the guitar is discussed in Paul Oliver, *The Story of the Blues* (Boston: Northeastern University Press, 1969), 28.

35 flattened notes for emphasis of feeling: For a discussion of pitch-tone aesthetics and other surviving African influences, see Palmer, 29.

35 the emerging individualized music: Ibid., 42.

35 "A big black man will walk up there":   For this and a discussion of both Johnson and the crossroads myth, see ibid., 60.

36 "Mighty seldom I played for colored":   Sam Chatmon, quoted in Davis, 23.

2 | The O.G.'s

39 "Whitman is a rowdy":   James Russell Lowell, quoted in Edwin G. Burrows and Mike Wallace, *Gotham: A History of New York City to 1898* (New York: Oxford University Press, 1999), 710.

39 "a stage for transformation":   Bharati Mukherjee, quoted in Diana L. Eck, *A New Religious America* (San Francisco: HarperSanFrancisco, 2001), 339.

41 "This is what you shall do: Love the earth":   Walt Whitman, quoted in John Tytell, *Naked Angels: The Classic Account of Three Who Changed America's Literature* (New York: Grove, 1976), 224.

42 "Our admiration of the Antique":   Ralph Waldo Emerson, "History," quoted in F. O. Matthiessen, *American Renaissance: Art and Expression in the Age of Emerson and Whitman* (New York: Oxford University Press, 1941), 646.

42 "has no use for history":   Mary McCarthy, "Burroughs' *Naked Lunch*," in Ann Charters, ed., *Beat Down to Your Soul: What Was the Beat Generation? Memoirs, Notes, Protests, Attacks, and Apologies—from the Beat Explosion That Rocked the World* (New York: Penguin, 2001), 358.

42 "shall have free Liberty to keepe away from us":   Nathaniel Ward, quoted in Daniel J. Boorstin, "How Orthodoxy Made the Puritans Practical," in *The Daniel J. Boorstin Reader* (New York: Modern Library, 1995), 12.

43 the death penalty for Quakers: This and other tales of religious intolerance can be found in Daniel J. Boorstin, "The Quest for Martyrdom," in ibid., 23.

43 African-American preachers: The styles and influence of black clergymen are discussed in David S. Reynolds, *Beneath the American Renaissance: The Subversive Imagination in the Age of Emerson and Melville* (Cambridge, Mass.: Harvard University Press, 1988), 17.

43 "black and white, poet and grocer":   Matthiessen, 127.

43 Taylor's relationship with Melville and Emerson: in Reynolds, *Beneath*, 20–21.

44 "I embrace the common":   Ralph Waldo Emerson, quoted in Matthiessen, 34.

44 "in conspiracy against the manhood":   Ralph Waldo Emerson, *The Portable Emerson* (New York: Viking, 1946), 17.

44 "A boy is in the parlor":   Ibid., 16.

44 "the only true America":   Henry David Thoreau, *Walden and Other Writings* (New York: MetroBooks, 2001), 171.

44 "[e]verything belongs to me because I am poor":   Jack Kerouac, *Visions of Cody* (New York: Penguin, 1972), 33.

45 "the myths Asiatic":   Walt Whitman, quoted in Reynolds, *Beneath*, 41.

45 "a vast unorganized array":   Eugene Taylor, *Shadow Culture: Psychology and Spirituality in America* (Washington, D.C.: Counterpoint, 1999), 9.

45 "holds exactly the opposite prejudices":   Ibid., 12–13.

45 "I look upon the size of certain American cities":   Alexis de Tocqueville, quoted

in Paul Boyer, *Urban Masses and Moral Order in America, 1820–1920* (Cambridge, Mass.: Harvard University Press, 1978), 3.

45 the urban population grew: See ibid., 67.

46 Five million immigrants came to the north: James Playsted Wood, *The Story of Advertising* (New York: Roland Press, 1958), 105. For discussion of changing composition of immigrant groups, see Samuel Eliot Morison, *The Oxford History of the American People, Vol. 3: 1869 Through the Death of John F. Kennedy, 1963* (New York: Penguin, 1975), 80.

46 60 percent of free blacks: Kolchin, 82.

46 more than 200 major gang wars: Boyer, 69.

46 a hotbed of single working women: See Burrows and Wallace, 801.

46 "startling color combinations": Ibid., 813.

47 2 million Americans: Morison, 72.

47 "You two green-horns!": Herman Melville, *The Confidence-Man* (New York: Penguin, 1990), 42.

48 Born in 1819 in West Hills, Long Island: For a discussion of Whitman's childhood, see Gay Allen Wilson, introduction to Walt Whitman, *Leaves of Grass* (New York: Signet Classic, 1954) v–xx.

48 "one of the roughs": Burrows and Wallace, 708–709.

48 "this great, dirty, blustering, glorious, ill-lighted": Walt Whitman, quoted in ibid., 706.

48 opened a basement beer hall: See the description of Pfaff's in *Greenwich Village Gazette*, available at www.gvny.com.

49 Clapp's circle: See Burrows and Wallace, 711.

49 "eccentric garb of rough blue and gray fabric": William Winter, quoted in Luc Sante, *Low Life: Lures and Snares of Old New York* (New York: Farrar, Straus & Giroux, 1991), 325.

49 "[m]any of slang words among fighting men": Walt Whitman, quoted in Reynolds, *Walt Whitman's America*, 320.

49 "Behavior lawless as snowflakes": Walt Whitman, "Song of Myself," in *Leaves*, 84.

49 loafing was an established franchise: Whitman's admirable loafing gets its due in Reynolds, *Walt Whitman's America*, 64–65.

49 "I loafe and invite my soul": Whitman, "Song of Myself," 49.

50 "Walt Whitman, a kosmos": Ibid., 43.

50 he denied that he was homosexual: The question of Whitman's sexuality has never been settled beyond reasonable doubt. Likely his life was more complicated than any modern label. The story of the Sodom School and Whitman's denials of homosexuality are in Reynolds, *Walt Whitman's America*, 70–71.

50 "I mind how once we lay": Whitman, "Song of Myself," 52.

51 Astor Place Riot: good description of conditions leading up to Astor Place Riot, see Reynolds, *Walt Whitman's America*, 164.

52 Already there had been riots: Ibid., 163.

52 On Macready's opening night: Ibid., 164.

52 For the next performance: On the city's preparations to prevent riots, and careful overview of the events, see Burrows and Wallace, 763.

52 crowd of 10,000 to 15,000 people: For body counts and an overview of the riot, see Barbara Lewis, Museum of the City of New York, www.mcny.org, and Burrows and Wallace, 764.

52 Thoreau had advised American writers to reject "imported symbols": Matthiessen, 83.

52 "the barbarism and materialism of the times": Ralph Waldo Emerson, quoted in ibid., 29.

52 "peculiarly American combination": Reynolds, *Beneath*, 91.

53 "the enemy, this word culture": Walt Whitman, quoted in Michael Kammen, *American Culture, American Tastes: Social Change and the 20th Century* (New York: Alfred A. Knopf, 1999), 29.

53 "a book for the criminal classes": Walt Whitman, quoted in Reynolds, *Beneath*, 312.

53 "I went to the woods because I wished to live deliberately": Thoreau, 75.

53 "civilized in externals but a savage at heart": Herman Melville, quoted in Reynolds, *Beneath*, 181.

53 "to find the significance of life in subjective experience": Alan Watts, "Beat Zen, Square Zen, and Zen," in Ann Charters, ed., *The Portable Beat Reader* (New York: Penguin, 1992), 611.

54 "I have now a library": Henry David Thoreau, quoted in Matthiessen, x.

54 "though I have wrote the Gospels in this century": Herman Melville, quoted in Reynolds, *Beneath*, 291.

54 "full of riffs, man": Ralph Ellison, in Albert Murray and John F. Callahan, eds., *Trading Twelves: The Selected Letters of Ralph Ellison and Albert Murray* (New York: Modern Library, 2000), 170.

54 "Death of a Once Popular Author": Stephen Matterson, introduction to Melville, *Confidence-Man*, ix.

54 "Henry Melville": Douglas, *Terrible Honesty*, 344–345.

54 another new voice, the squeal of advertising: For more on Volney Palmer and the early years of the advertising game, see Wood, 137.

54 "the day will come": Volney Palmer, quoted in Burrows and Wallace, 679.

55 Palmer's old age: For more on Greeley's relationship with the difficult Volney Palmer, see Wood, 137.

55 Palmer's revolution was in effect: For a discussion of the expansion in ad business, see Frank Spencer Presbrey, *The History and Development of Advertising* (Westport, Conn.: Greenwood Press, 1968), 210.

55 "People keep seeing destruction or rebellion": Allen and Louis Ginsberg, *Family Business: Selected Letters Between a Father and a Son* (New York: Bloomsbury, 2001) 80–83, quoted in Charters, *Beat Down*, 1.

56 "If any one imagines that this law is lax": Ralph Waldo Emerson, "The American Scholar," in *Portable Emerson*, 26.

56 "[Who] need be afraid of the merge?": Walt Whitman, quoted in Tytell, 226.

3 | My Black/White Roots

57 "It is the glory of the present age": Randolph Bourne, "Youth," in *The Radical Will: Randolph Bourne Selected Writings 1911–1918* (New York: Urizen Books, 1977), 104.

58 "In the African sense": Robert Farris Thompson, interview with author, 2003.

60 "[t]he reason the New York boys became such high-class musicians": Tom Davin, "Conversations with James P. Johnson," *Jazz Review*, June 1960, p. 16.

60 Ethel Barrymore, doyenne: Langston Hughes, *The Big Sea* (New York: Hill & Wang, 1963), 228.

62 "the world has changed less since the time of Jesus Christ": Charles Péguy, quoted in Robert Hughes, *The Shock of the New*, rev. ed. (New York: Alfred A. Knopf, 1991), 9.

62 New technologies moved people and information: For a discussion of the impact of powered flight and the Model T, see Morison, 225.

62 revenues rose to $3 billion: Douglas, *Terrible Honesty*, 64.

62 town crier yielded: For a discussion of the rise of media, including film receipts, see ibid., 61.

62 population that consumed this culture: Boyer, 189.

62 one-third of all Americans: Immigration figures from U.S. Census report, "Pro-

file of the Foreign-Born Population in the United States: 2000," December 2001, 23–206.

63 "Culture," he wrote, "follows money":   F. Scott Fitzgerald, quoted in Douglas, *Terrible Honesty*, 4.

63 born Ferdinand Joseph Lamothe: Morton's New Orleans years and milieu described in Ted Gioia, *The History of Jazz* (New York: Oxford University Press, 1997), 31.

64 according to one legend: This is likely an apocryphal story, but it is typical of the myths Morton wove around himself. See Gioia, 41.

64 "If you can't manage to put tinges of Spanish in your tunes":   Jelly Roll Morton, quoted in Gary Giddins, *Visions of Jazz: The First Century* (New York: Oxford University Press, 1998), 70.

64 Any tune could be fit to any idiom: For the transit of tunes between idioms, see Davin.

65 changed the way Americans danced: James Lincoln Collier, *The Making of Jazz: A Comprehensive History* (Boston: Houghton Mifflin, 1978), 76.

65 the Charleston is little more than a recasting: Baraka, 17.

65 were up to 100 million: Collier, 78.

66 Original Dixieland Jazz Band: Collier, 72–73.

66 brought the blues out of the Harlem cabarets: Mamie Smith's recording was both a landmark and a new turn in the history of exploitation, by which African Americans were judged by their stage characters. The recording is discussed in Douglas, *Terrible Honesty*, 391.

66 "[W]hen you came into a place you had a three-way play": James P. Johnson, in Davin, 14.

67 more than 300 gospel and blues: Gioia, 17.

67 "Perhaps one reason many American Negroes sing a sad song happy":   Thompson wrote two versions of this essay; this is from the first. Robert Farris Thompson, "Toward an Aesthetic of the Cool," *African Forum*, 1966, 85–86.

68 "so many radical young people":   Randolph Bourne, "Youth," 104–105.

68 "proletariat of the arts":   Malcolm Cowley was the most arch and incisive chronicler of the Lost Generation, but had little empathy with prior Village bohemians. See *Exile's Return* (New York: Penguin, 1976), 48.

69 "a Murger complex":   For good evocations of the Village scene, see Allen Churchill, *The Improper Bohemians: A Re-Creation of Greenwich Village in Its Heyday* (New York: Dutton, 1959), 238.

70 Rebellion in the Village: The plights of Sanger, Goldman, Berkman and the moderns are inventoried well in Christine Stansell, *American Moderns: Bohemian New York and the Creation of a New Century* (New York: Henry Holt, 2000), 37.

70 Hammerstein offered her a thousand dollars: Ibid., 85.

71 the Justice Department cracked down: Ibid., 315.

71 ordered the arrest: More on the Palmer Raids can be found in Morison, 217.

71 barred from the mails: The crackdown on the mails smothered communication between the moderns and the outside world, and between themselves. Stansell, 316.

71 Mabel Dodge moved her salon: Ibid., 317–318.

71 "As We Are Reported":   The article is cited in Churchill, 251.

71 "I had rapidly become a mythological figure":   Mabel Dodge, quoted in Stansell, 103.

71 "neither wit nor beauty":   Max Eastman, quoted in Churchill, 16.

71 "The faculty I had for not saying much":   Mabel Dodge, quoted in Stansell, 103.

72 "grown up to find all Gods dead":   F. Scott Fitzgerald, *This Side of Paradise* (New York: Modern Library, 1996), 322.

72 "It was characteristic of the Jazz Age":   F. Scott Fitzgerald, *The Jazz Age* (New York: New Directions Bibelot, 1996), 3.

72 the French ambulance corps: The corps and the damage seen are described in Cowley, 38.

72 "The Village in 1919 was like a conquered country": Ibid., 71.

72 Reared in Baltimore: Stein's education and the weight of her breasts are courtesy of James R. Mellow, *Hemingway: A Life without Consequences* (Boston: Houghton Mifflin, 1992), 148.

73 "It became the period of being twenty-six": Gertrude Stein, *The Autobiography of Alice B. Toklas* (New York: Modern Library, 1993), 212.

73 were not so much expatriates: The generation's rootlessness and loss of *patria* are discussed in Noel Riley Fitch, *Sylvia Beach and the Lost Generation* (New York: Norton, 1983), 162.

73 "Dinners, soirees, poets": Hart Crane, quoted in Mellow, 173.

74 "deracination" of industrial society: This concept is discussed in Cowley, 28.

74 "People have done me the honor of believing I'm an animal": Josephine Baker, quoted in Douglas, *Terrible Honesty,* 52.

74 "an idiom for the proper transposition of jazz into words": Crane, quoted in Paul L. Mariani, *The Broken Tower: A Life of Hart Crane* (New York: W.W. Norton, 1999), 91.

74 announced she had launched: For Melanctha as the source of 20th-century literature, see the demure account by Stein, 54.

74 "the scum of Greenwich Village": Ernest Hemingway, quoted in Mellow, 164.

74 "He usually wore workman's clothes": Eugène Jolas, quoted in Robert Kiely, "Lost Man of the Lost Generation," *New York Times,* January 3, 1999, sec. 7, 20.

75 "Hemingway poses as a non-literary sportsman": Ellison, "Change the Joke and Slip the Yoke," in *Collected Essays,* 109.

75 "It was like a course in bull-fighting": Ernest Hemingway, *The Sun Also Rises* (New York: Scribner's, 1926), 219–220.

75 "his great studies into fear": Fitzgerald's quote, along with other assessments of his peer and rival, are in Mellow, 307.

75 At the turn of the century: Good overview of the Harlem Renaissance motives and movements in Richard B. Sherman, *The Negro and the City* (Englewood Cliffs, NJ: Prentice-Hall, 1970), 5.

76 African Americans' future: Booker T. Washington's agrarian plan is in Ibid., 1.

76 half a million blacks left the debt cycle: A good overview of roots and patterns of the Great Migration can be found in Nicholas Lemann, *The Promised Land: The Great Black Migration and How It Changed America* (New York, Vintage, 1992), 16.

76 the price of cotton in the Mississippi Delta plunged: Ibid., 15.

76 African Americans in the North tripled: For the changing northern demographics, see Douglas, *Terrible Honesty,* 73.

77 "[i]n ten years Negroes have been actually transported": Charles S. Johnson, quoted in ibid., 74.

77 "the migrant masses, shifting from countryside to city,": Alain Locke, "Enter the New Negro," in Sherman, 91.

77 "[j]azz, the blues, Negro spirituals, all stimulate me enormously": Carl Van Vechten, caught in an unflatteringly—and uncharacteristically—flip phrase, quoted in David Levering Lewis, *When Harlem Was in Vogue* (New York: Penguin, 1997), 98.

78 Langston Hughes (1902–1967): John Henrik Clarke, ed., *Harlem: A Community in Transition* (New York: Citadel, 1964), 62.

78 "It was a period when almost any Harlem Negro": Langston Hughes, *Big Sea,* 228–229.

78 Harlem hostess A'Lelia Walker: For good descriptions of Walker's parties and other splendid indulgences, see Lewis, 166.

78 "You go sort of primitive up there": Jimmy Durante, quoted in Steven Watson,

The Harlem Renaissance: Hub of African-American Culture, 1920–1930 (New York: Pantheon, 1996), 5.

79 "The Old Negro goes":   Quoted in Lewis, 24.

79 The Civic Club, known for its liberal politics: As usual, Lewis has the best descriptions of the meeting and its social surround. See Lewis, 90–94.

79 "midwives of the Harlem Renaissance":   Ibid., 121.

79 "The world does not know that a people is great":   James Weldon Johnson, quoted in ibid., 149.

79 "We claim no part of racial dearth":   Gwendolyn Bennett, quoted in ibid., 94.

80 "What American literature decidedly needs at this moment":   Carl Van Doren, quoted in ibid., 93–94.

80 " '[T]hat good-for-nothing, trashy Negro' ":   Zora Neale Hurston, *Dust Tracks on a Road* (New York: HarperPerennial, 1996), 178.

80 "more to gain from the rich background of English and American poetry":   Countee Cullen, quoted in Douglas, *Terrible Honesty,* 340.

81 "And as for the cultured Negroes":   Langston Hughes, *The Ways of White Folks* (New York: Vintage, 1990), 110.

81 "We sensed that the black cultural as well as moral leaders":   Benny Carter, quoted in Gioia, 95.

82 "Among those who disliked this form of entertainment":   Willie "the Lion" Smith, quoted in ibid., 95.

82 "thinking the Negroes loved to have them there":   Hughes, *Big Sea,* 225.

82 "White readers just don't expect Negroes to be like this":   White editor to Jessie Fauset, quoted in Lewis, 124.

82 "finished running their inheritance":   Charlotte Mason, quoted in ibid., 155.

82 "These people who was coming to make records":   Sidney Bechet, quoted in ibid., 172.

83 no figure was as freighted: A good thumbnail biography of Van Vechten's preHarlem years can be found in Nathan Irvin Huggins, *Harlem Renaissance* (New York: Oxford University Press, 1971), 93–95.

83 "almost an addiction":   Carl Van Vechten, in Douglas, *Terrible Honesty,* 288.

84 "Don't let *nobody* tell you you can't sing":   Bessie Smith, quoted in Lewis, 183. On the same occasion, she slugged Fania Marinoff, Van Vechten's wife, after Marinoff tried to kiss her.

84 forfeited much of his goodwill: For the negative reaction to Van Vechten after *Nigger Heaven,* see Lewis, 181.

84 "If you young Negro intellectuals don't get busy":   Carl Van Vechten, *Nigger Heaven,* quoted in Lewis, 187.

85 "the picture within a picture within a picture":   Baraka, 110.

86 "Be yourselves!":   Eugene O'Neill, quoted in Lewis, 115.

4 | Would a Hipster Hit a Lady?

87 "From thirty feet away she looked like a lot of class":   Raymond Chandler, *The High Window* (New York: Vintage, 1988), chap. 5.

87 uncomfortable with its own manhood: Jung's travels in America are recounted in "America Facing Its Most Tragic Moment," *New York Times Magazine,* September 29, 1912.

88 "unfurling and flying and hissing at incredible speeds":   Jack Kerouac, *On the Road* (New York: Penguin, 2003), 237.

89 "yield up his liberty, his property and his soul":   H. L. Mencken, "In Defense of Women," quoted in Barbara Ehrenreich, *The Hearts of Men: American Dreams and the Flight from Commitment* (New York: Anchor, 1987), 6.

89 "profound national impulse [that] drives the hundred millions":   Carl Van

Doren, "The Negro Renaissance," *Century Magazine,* quoted in Gilbert Osofsky, *Harlem: The Making of a Ghetto* (Chicago: Ivan R. Dee, 1966), 180.

90 "He felt like somebody had taken the lid off life": Dashiell Hammett, *The Maltese Falcon,* in *The Complete Novels* (New York: Literary Classics of the United States, 1999), 444.

90 "out of step, and not into step, with life": Ibid.

91 "I giggled and socked him": Raymond Chandler, *Farewell My Lovely,* in *The Big Sleep and Farewell My Lovely* (New York: Modern Library, 1995), 405.

92 "And Darkness and Decay and Death": Edgar Allan Poe, "The Masque of the Red Death," quoted in Reynolds, *Beneath,* 238.

93 "No one in this world, so far as I know": H. L. Mencken, *Chicago Tribune,* September 19, 1926.

93 "[R]ight and wrong are not written on the statues for me": Carroll John Daly, quoted in William Marling, "Hard-Boiled Fiction," Case Western Reserve University, available at http://www.cwru.edu/artsci/engl/marling/hardboiled.

95 "Hammett gave murder back to the kind of people that commit it": Raymond Chandler, "The Simple Art of Murder," quoted in Daniel Stashower, "A Thin Man Who Made Memorable Use Of His Spade," *Smithsonian,* May 1, 1994, 114.

95 "Everybody," as Spade says, "has something to hide": Hammett, *Maltese Falcon,* 517.

95 "We didn't exactly believe your story": Ibid., 416.

96 "not as sick as I would feel if I had a salaried job": Raymond Chandler, *Farewell, My Lovely* (New York: Vintage Books, 1976), 191.

96 "I first heard Personville called Poisonville": Hammett, *Red Harvest,* in *The Complete Novels,* 5.

97 "Once you have had to lead a platoon": Raymond Chandler, quoted in Frank MacShane, *The Life of Raymond Chandler* (New York: Dutton, 1976), 29.

97 English public schools: Chandler's upbringing and disastrous oil career are discussed in ibid., 20–40.

97 MGM screen test: McCoy's travails in Marling, available at http://www.cwru.edu/artsci/engl/marling/hardboiled/McCoy.html.

98 "loitered on the corners": Nathanael West, *Miss Lonelyhearts and The Day of the Locust* (New York: New Directions, 1969), 60.

98 "I used to like this town": Raymond Chandler, *The Little Sister,* quoted in Philip Durham, "Raymond Chandler's Los Angeles," in John Caughee and LaRee Caughey, eds., *Los Angeles: Biography of a City* (Los Angeles: University of California Press, 1977), 333–334.

99 Los Angeles was built for pulp disillusionment: Chandler's perception of Los Angeles as myth is discussed in MacShane, 64.

99 "The ignorant, hopelessly un-American type of foreigner": Charles Fletcher Lummis, quoted in Kevin Starr, *Inventing the Dream: California through the Progressive Era* (New York: Oxford University Press, 1985), 89. See Starr for accounts of the city's founding and abuse of political influence.

99 "I smelled Los Angeles before I got to it": Raymond Chandler, *The Little Sister* (New York: Vintage Books, 1988), chapter 13. This is Chandler at his most bitter.

100 "an utter swine": Raymond Chandler, quoted in MacShane, 4.

100 "An hour crawled by like a sick cockroach": Raymond Chandler, *The Long Goodbye* (New York: Vintage, 1992), 137. This novel was Chandler's attempt to transcend pulp, and richer than his previous books.

100 "All I wanted when I began": Raymond Chandler, from a letter dated January 7, 1945, quoted in Joyce Carol Oates, "The Simple Art of Murder," *New York Review of Books,* December 21, 1995, 40.

100 "parvenu insecurity": Raymond Chandler, quoted in MacShane, 10.

100 hero's "moral and intellectual force": Raymond Chandler, "The Simple Art of Murder," quoted in MacShane, 70.

100 "To hell with the rich": Raymond Chandler, *The Big Sleep* (New York: Vintage/Black Lizard, 1992), 64.

101 "I watched the band of white": Chandler, *Long Goodbye*, 87.

101 "desire is all there is": Geoffrey O'Brien, *Hardboiled America: Lurid Paperbacks and the Masters of Noir* (New York: Da Capo, 1997), 70. O'Brien provides an excellent overview of the pulp pantheon.

103 "the corpse on reprieve within each of us": Andre Bazin, quoted in James Naremore, "American Film Noir: The History of an Idea," *Film Quarterly*, December 1, 1995.

103 "every kind of writer I detest": Raymond Chandler, in a pissy, competitive mode, quoted in MacShane, 101.

104 "Striking at people that way": Jim Thompson, *The Killer Inside Me* (New York: Vintage, 1991), 5.

104 "You can do that, split yourself in two parts": Jim Thompson, *Savage Night* (Berkeley: Black Lizard, 1985), 95.

104 "Hollywood basically killed him off": His sister's remarks, and excellent overview of Thompson's life and work, are in Robert Polito, *Savage Art: A Biography of Jim Thompson* (New York: Vintage, 1996), 392–402.

104 "nothing but desert, parched": Jim Thompson, quoted in Polito, 366.

105 "biggest, baddest, sickest, ugliest": Ellroy's sentiments, along with biographical details, can be found in Jim Shelley, "Portrait: A Genre's Demon Dog," *Guardian*, January 7, 1995.

105 "Try and pick up every waitress": The quote and biographical details are from Steve Boisson, "James Ellroy, Crossing the Dividing Line," *Writer's Digest*, July 1, 1996, 26.

105 "If there's one rule I'd like to break": James Ellroy, interviewed in ibid.

105 "your shakedown artist, your rogue cop": Ibid.

105 cut the manuscript: Ellroy describes the honing of his style in ibid.

105 "telegraphic shorthand style": Ibid.

106 "Hip hop lives in the world": Greg Tate, *Flyboy in the Buttermilk: Essays on Contemporary America* (New York: Simon & Schuster, 1992), 129. For two decades, Tate has been the most incisive commentator on the play of art and politics in hip-hop.

106 Bambaataa, born Kevin Donovan: Bambaataa's background and the origins of his name are in David Toop, *Rap Attack 2: African Rap to Global Hip Hop* (New York: Serpent's Tail, 1991), 56.

107 "They had graffiti artists, breakdancers": Ice-T, in Brian Cross, *It's Not about a Salary: Rap, Race and Resistance in Los Angeles* (New York: Verso, 1993), 183–184.

108 "I am a nightmare walking": Ice-T, "Colors," *Colors*, CD, Warner, 1998.

108 "The boy JB," Eazy-E, "Boyz-N-the Hood": *Eazy-Duz-It*, CD, Ruthless/Priority, 1988.

109 "But why be a thug?": Kevin Powell, "This Thug's Life," in Alan Light and *Vibe* magazine, eds., *Tupac Shakur* (New York: Crown, 1997) p. 29.

109 "where cowards die": Tupac Shakur, "California Love," *All Eyez on Me*, CD, Death Row, 1996.

109 "a fool not to be born a Frenchman": This and the other European reactions to noir and pulp in Naremore.

109 "They didn't get it": Dream Hampton, interview with author, 2002.

110 "I'm expressing with my full capabilities": N.W.A., "Express Yourself," *Straight Outta Compton*, CD, Ruthless/Priority, 1988.

110 "What did it matter where you lay once you were dead?": Chandler, *Big Sleep*, 228.

5 | The Golden Age of Hip, Part 1

111 "The goatee, beret, and window-pane glasses were no accidents": Baraka, 201.

111 Parker arrived at the club: The account of the Argyle Show Bar incident is drawn from Miles Davis with Quincy Troupe, *Miles: The Autobiography* (New York: Simon & Schuster, 1989), 107–108, and Al Aronowitz, "Retropop Scene: Bird's Christmas," Blacklisted Journalist, col. 4, December 1, 1995, available at http://www.bigmagic.com/pages/blackj/column4.html.

112 "[Y]ou'd see hundreds of heads nodding": Jack Kerouac, "Lamb, No Lion" in Ann Charters, ed., *The Portable Jack Kerouac* (New York: Viking, 1995), 564.

113 "Be-bop cut us off completely": Gilbert Sorrentino, "Remembrances of Bop in New York, 1945–1950," in *Kulchur,* Summer 1963.

113 "We were the first generation to rebel": Don Asher and Hampton Hawes, *Raise Up off Me: A Portrait of Hampton Hawes* (New York: Thunder's Mouth Press, 2001), 8.

113 The son of an itinerant entertainer: Parker's childhood is described in Ira Gitler, *The Masters of Bebop,* exp. ed. (New York: Da Capo, 2001), 17.

113 One day in December 1939: Details of Parker's discovery of bop changes are related in Michael Levin and John S. Wilson, "No Bop Roots in Jazz: Parker," from *Down Beat,* September 9, 1949, in Carl Woideck, ed., *The Charlie Parker Companion: Six Decades of Commentary* (New York: Schirmer, 1999), 71.

114 "[T]he moment I heard Charlie Parker": Dizzie Gillespie with Al Fraser, *To BE or Not . . . to BOP* (Garden City, N.Y.: Doubleday, 1979), 116–117.

114 the other half of his heartbeat: Parker and Dizzy's relationship and closeness are discussed in Giddins, *Visions of Jazz,* 265. Here and elsewhere, Giddins provides the most sensitive, thoughtful analysis of the musical changes wrought by bop.

114 his playing pitted the past against the future: For a good analysis of Monk's piano style, see Laurent de Wilde, *Monk* (New York: Marlowe, 1997), 2–20.

115 got him fired from Hill's band: See the discussion of Clarke's career in Gitler, 175–176.

115 "To understand that you are black": Baraka, 185.

116 "Bop comes out of them dark days": Langston Hughes, "Bop," from *Best of Simple* (New York: Hill & Wang, 1961), 118–119.

116 "Daddy-o, now you and me": Malcolm X with Alex Haley, *The Autobiography of Malcolm X* (New York: Grove, 1965), 124.

117 "It's another one of those nicknames": Max Roach, interviewed in Arthur Taylor, *Notes and Tones: Musician to Musician Interviews* (New York: Coward, McCann & Geoghegan, 1982), 118–119.

117 "There was a message in our music": Kenny Clarke, in Robert Gottlieb, ed., *Reading Jazz: A Gathering of Autobiography, Reportage, and Criticism from 1919 to Now* (New York: Pantheon Books, 1996), 563.

117 "Miles and Max Roach were speaking like men": Tony Williams, quoted in Greg Tate, "Preface to a One-Hundred-Eighty Volume Patricide Note: Yet Another Few Thousand Words on the Death of Miles Davis and the Problem of Black Male Genius," in Gina Dent, ed., *Black Popular Culture / A Project by Michele Wallace* (Seattle: Bay Press, 1992), 243.

118 bop style spread: in Roy Carr, Brian Case and Fred Dellar, *The Hip: Hipsters, Jazz and the Beat Generation* (London: Faber & Faber, 1986), 12–13.

119 "We're not the kind of people who can sit back": Max Roach, in an amusingly confrontational interview with Frank Owen, "Hip Hop Bebop," *Spin,* October 1988, 60.

119 "Café au Lait Society": Roi Ottley, *New World a Coming: Inside Black America,* 167–185, quoted in Eric Porter, "Dizzy Atmosphere: The Challenge of Bebop," *American Music,* December 22, 1999.

120 "the most dangerous Negro in America": For a good description of racial unrest during the war years, see David M. Kennedy, *Freedom from Fear: The American People in Depression and War, 1929–1945* (New York: Oxford University Press, 1999), 763.

120 threatened a march: See the narrative of the showdown between Randolph and Roosevelt in ibid., 768.

121 Record sales fell: in Gioia, 135. His account is thorough, and he pays attention to financial details.

121 new medium of radio: Ibid., 136.

121 Palomar Ballroom: Ibid., 140.

122 "I criticized Louis": Gillespie with Fraser, 295–296.

122 "You got no melody to remember": Louis Armstrong, quoted in Gioia, 217.

123 Minton's was a scene: Davis with Troupe, 132–133. For more on the black kids dancing at Catherine Market, see Lhamon, 5–20.

123 Monk and Powell sometimes held hands: Ann Douglas, "Feel the City's Pulse? It's Be-Bop, Man!" *New York Times*, August 28, 1998.

124 "there were always some cats showing up there who couldn't blow": Dizzy Gillespie, speaking in Nat Shapiro and Nat Hentoff, eds., *Hear Me Talkin' to Ya: The Story of Jazz as Told by the Men Who Made It* (New York: Dover, 1966), 337.

124 "That's not the way we play": Thelonious Monk, in Douglas, "Feel the City's Pulse?"

125 Weston remembered hanging after hours: Jack Chambers, *Milestones: The Music and Times of Miles Davis* (New York: Quill, 1989), 68.

125 "scientists of sound": Davis with Troupe, 63.

125 "no grinning": Ibid., 83.

125 Davis famously turned his back: For Miles's claim that he simply wanted to hear his musicians, see Davis with Troupe, 356.

125 waged "war with the complicated fact": Stanley Crouch, "Bird Land," in Woideck, 256.

126 "trying to play clean": Charlie Parker, quoted by Levin and Wilson, 70.

126 announcing his desire to study with Edgard Varese: Gioia, 231.

126 Living on 10th Street and Avenue B: Courtesy of Bill Cross, editor of *Metronome*, in Gitler, 48–49.

127 his daughter Pree died: Gioia, 231.

127 most of the New York newspapers: Giddins, "Bird Lives!" in Woideck, 9.

127 Parker wasn't really dead, just "hiding out somewhere": Charles Mingus, quoted in Gioia, 233.

127 "Bird was responsible for the actual playing": Billy Eckstine, quoted in Shapiro and Hentoff, 352.

127 Dizzy would "be sticking his tongue out at women": Davis with Troupe, 9.

128 little in the way of record sales: Giddins, *Visions of Jazz*, 285.

128 maintained that he wore the beret: Gitler, 80.

128 "[T]he black people in the audience were embarrassed by it": George Russell, in Alyn Shipton, *Groovin' High: The Life of Dizzy Gillespie* (New York: Oxford University Press, 1999), 200.

128 Pozo was killed: A good account of Gillespie's partnership with Chano Pozo is in Shipton, 202.

130 "who can deny that globalization": Kennedy, 855.

131 wanted "to create something that they can't steal": Mary Lou Williams, quoted in Shapiro and Hentoff, 341.

131 "the only way the Caucasian musician can swing is from a rope": Art Blakey, quoted in Charley Gerard, *Jazz in Black and White: Race, Culture, and Identity in the Jazz Community* (Westport, Conn.: Praeger, 1998), 9.

132 "tall, thin, white guy": Davis with Troupe, 122.

132 "What bothered them": Minnijean Brown Trickey, member of the Little Rock Nine, interview with author, 1997.

133 "Why'd you put that white bitch on there?": Davis, quoted in Giddins, *Visions of Jazz*, 347.

133 "it was the same old story, black shit was being ripped off": Davis with Troupe, 141.

133 "We were trying to sound like [the white bandleader] Claude Thornhill": Ibid., 119.

135 "something entirely separate and apart": Parker, quoted by Levin and Wilson, 70.

135 "It was the bebop tradition": Coleridge Goode, quoted in Chambers, 67.

6 | The Golden Age of Hip, Part 2

137 "[It's] a story of many restless travelings": Jack Kerouac, *Selected Letters, 1940–1956* (New York: Viking, 1999), 226.

137 Meltzer lined up the affinities: In comparing Beats and beboppers, Richard Meltzer performs his usual free-associative wonders in "Another Superficial Piece about 158 Beatnik Books," in Holly George-Warren, ed., *The Rolling Stone Book of the Beats: The Beat Generation and American Culture* (New York: Hyperion, 1999), 71.

139 "I am not the poet of goodness only": Whitman, "Song of Myself," 66.

139 "Great is Wickedness": Whitman, quoted in Reynolds, *Beneath*, 109–110.

139 "It's all bop": Allen Ginsberg, quoted in Tytell, 101.

140 "At lilac evening I walked": Kerouac, *On the Road*, 179–180.

140 "wild, undisciplined, pure": Jack Kerouac, quoted in Tytell, 143.

140 are at least two worth mentioning: Ginsberg's encounters with Monk are in Michael Schumacher, *Dharma Lion: A Critical Biography of Allen Ginsberg* (New York: St. Martin's, 1992), 295, 348, and "Innerview," an interview with Harvey Kubernik, in George-Warren, 259.

141 fewer than 300 people came to his funeral: Eric Ehrman, "Kerouac Retrospective," in George-Warren, 133.

142 "[I]t went beyond anything we 'planned' ": Allen Ginsberg, quoted in Cook, 242.

142 "absolute personal freedom at all times": The quote, along with an account of Kerouac's Navy career and early years, are in Gerald Nicosia, *Memory Babe: A Critical Biography of Jack Kerouac,* (New York: Grove, 1983), 104, 106.

143 Kerouac returned to New York: For more on Kerouac's return and first book, see the good, myth-chasing essay by Douglas Brinkley, "The American Journey of Jack Kerouac," in George-Warren, 110.

143 a fellow Horace Mann alum: Kerouac's friendship with Buckley and his Horace Mann experiences are dicussed in Brinkley, 109, and Dennis McNally, *Desolate Angel: Jack Kerouac, The Beat Generation, and America* (New York: Da Capo, 2003), 336.

143 $200 scholarship: Schumacher, 23.

143 seeking a bond: Ginsberg's childhood, including the scene with Louis, is treated with sensitivity in Mykal Gilmore, "Allen Ginsberg, 1926–1997," in George-Warren, 227–240.

144 "Burroughs's addicts, Kerouac's mobile young voyeurs": Baraka, from *The Moderns: An Anthology of New Writing in America* (New York: Corinth, 1963), quoted in Charters, *Portable Beat Reader*, 339–340.

144 "the spectralized color of blue cheese": Neal Cassady, quoted in Tytell, 93.

144 "sensitive vehicle for a veritable new consciousness": Allen Ginsberg, quoted in Charters, *Portable Beat Reader*, 145.

144 "Subway Mike had a large, pale face and long teeth": William S. Burroughs, *Junky,* excerpted in ibid., 112.

144 a reformatory kid: Cassady's biographical details are in ibid., 187.

145 "What got Kerouac and Ginsberg about Cassady": Gary Snyder, quoted in ibid., 189.

146 "I have renounced fiction and fear": Jack Kerouac, quoted in Brian Hassett, "Abstract Expressionism: From Bird to Brando," in George-Warren, 25.

146 "The Cold War": Allen Ginsberg, quoted in George Plimpton, ed., *Beat Writers at Work: The Paris Review* (New York: Modern Library, 1999), 58–59.

146 "What kind of war": Edgar Jones, "One War Is Enough," *Atlantic Monthly*, February 1946, quoted in Kennedy, 794.

146 "The burden of my generation": John Clellon Holmes, *Nothing to Declare*, quoted in Charters, *Portable Beat Reader*, 4. I find Holmes defensive and somewhat clunky, but cite him as a window on how the Beats felt about themselves.

146 Thanks to the industrial buildup: For the growth of the American economy, including manufacturing and oil, during World War II, see Kennedy, 857.

147 The country's growth product: Ibid.

147 "a lazy man or a shirk": See Charters, *Beat Down*, xxiii.

147 " 'It's a sort of furtiveness' ": Kerouac speaking to Holmes, from *Nothing to Declare*, quoted in Nicosia, 252.

148 in the church of Ste. Jeanne d'Arc: Brinkley, 113.

148 *"will* to believe," despite "the valueless abyss of modern life": Holmes, in Charters, *Portable Beat Reader*, 6.

148 "literary wing of the environmental movement": Michael McClure, "Painting Beat by Numbers," in George-Warren, 39.

149 " 'Honey, you see, we all thought *experience itself was good'* ": Diane di Prima, *Recollections of My Life as a Woman* (New York: Viking, 2001), 202–203.

149 "the two strands of male protest": Ehrenreich, 52.

149 "the only really genuine experience I feel I've had": Allen Ginsberg, quoted in Graham Caveney, *Screaming with Joy: The Life of Allen Ginsberg* (New York: Broadway Books, 1999), 55.

149 "cultivate the terror, get right into it": Allen Ginsberg, quoted in Barry Miles, *Ginsberg: A Biography* (New York: Simon and Schuster, 1989), 103.

149 "a human voice and body": McClure, quoted in Charters, *Portable Beat Reader*, xxviii.

149 "For Carl Solomon": See the account of Solomon and Six Gallery in ibid., 167–168.

150 Burroughs fatally shot his wife: Tytell, 46.

150 "[We] felt like blacks caught in a square world": John Clellon Holmes, quoted in Tytell, 22.

150 "the myth of Lester Young": Allen Ginsberg, interviewed in Plimpton, 35.

151 "I want to be considered a jazz poet": Jack Kerouac, introduction to *Mexico City Blues*.

151 he hit the Harlem nightclubs: Nicosia, 65–67.

151 "Yes, jazz and bop": Jack Kerouac, interviewed by Ted Berrigan, in Plimpton, 116.

151 "anything but what I was so drearily": Kerouac, *On the Road*, 182.

152 "has exactly the attitude toward the American Negro": Kenneth Rexroth, "What's Wrong with the Clubs," *Metronome*, 1961, repr. in Rexroth, *Assays* (Norfolk, Conn.: J. Laughlin, 1961), and *World Outside the Window: Selected Essays of Kenneth Rexroth* (New York: New Directions, 1987). Though Rexroth was clearly not impartial, his criticism is both sound and reflective of the sniping that set in.

152 "Bird Parker who is only 18": Jack Kerouac, "The Beginning of Bop," *Escapade*, 1959, in Charters, *Portable Kerouac*, 556.

152 "the new White Negro has not *arrived* at black culture": Carl Hancock Rux, "Eminem: The New White Negro," an astute and ungentle essay in Greg Tate, ed., *Everything but the Burden: What White People Are Taking from Black Culture* (New York:

Broadway, 2003), 38. Besides Rux's essay, this book includes an incisive introduction by Tate and a fascinating autobiographical sketch by Jonathan Lethem that
test-drives some of the racial themes he treated more expansively in *The Fortress of
Solitude* (2003).

153 "conformists masquerading as rebels": Robert Brustein, "The Cult of Unthink,"
in Charters, *Beat Down,* 51.

153 Rexroth, who had championed the Beats: For Rexroth's disaffection, see Charters, *Beat Down,* 494; for a more nuanced appraisal, see his essay in same collection, "Disengagement: The Art of the Beat Generation," 494–508.

153 "*[S]elf-expression* and *paganism*": Cowley, 62.

154 "Join the beat generation!": William Manchester, *The Glory and the Dream: A
Narrative History of America, 1932–1972* (New York: Bantam, 1975), 592.

154 "Atlantic is the label in tune with the BEAT": Charters, *Beat Down,* xxi.

154 "You were headed for the Remo": Ronald Sukenick's amusing and idiosyncratic,
if occasionally self-righteous, *Down and In: Life in the Underground* (New York:
Collier, 1987), 18–19.

154 "the images of their disappointment": Anatole Broyard, quoted in ibid., 35.

155 "In actuality," he wrote, "there was only a handful of real hip swinging cats": Jack
Kerouac, "About the Beat Generation," in Charters, *Portable Kerouac,* 560.

156 "Make a mistake": Thelonious Monk, quoted in Douglas, "Feel the City's Pulse?"

156 "jewel center of interest": Jack Kerouac, "Essentials of Spontaneous Prose," in
Charters, *Portable Beat Reader,* 58.

156 "*no revisions*": Ibid.

156 This commandment was somewhat disingenuous: See Brinkley, 112.

157 "[W]hatever it is that Neal represented for them": Carolyn Cassady, in Gina
Berriault, "Neal's Ashes," in George-Warren, 119.

157 "always trying to justify ma's madness": Kerouac on Ginsberg, in Schumacher,
114.

157 "This book is a must for anyone": William S. Burroughs, quoted in Steven Watson, *The Birth of the Beat Generation: Visionaries, Rebels, and Hipsters, 1944–1960*
(New York: Pantheon, 1995).

158 "Those who would have good government": Watts, 607.

158 "the first great American poet to take action": Allen Ginsberg, letter to John Allen
Ryan, September 9, 1955, in Charters, *Beat Down,* 218.

158 "I am the poet of slaves, and of the masters of slaves": Whitman, quoted in
Reynolds, *Beneath,* 109.

159 "solitary Bartlebies staring out the dead wall window": Jack Kerouac, quoted in
Charters, *Portable Beat Reader,* xviii.

159 "I discovered a new Beat Generation a long time ago": Jack Kerouac, quoted in
Brinkley, 119.

159 "It occurs to me that I am America": Ginsberg, "America" (1956), in Charters,
Portable Beat Reader, 76.

159 "I quietly declare war": Thoreau, "Civil Disobedience," in *Walden,* 297.

159 "are presented as mostly motivated": George W. S. Trow, *My Pilgrim's Progress:
Cultural Studies, 1950–1998* (New York: Pantheon, 1999), 202.

160 "And this was really the way": Kerouac, *On the Road,* 9, 10.

7 | The Tricksters

161 "The biggest difference between us and white people": Alberta Roberts, quoted
in John Langston Gwaltney, ed., *Drylongso: A Self-Portrait of Black America* (New
York: Random House, 1980), 105.

162 "lords of the in-between": Lewis Hyde, *Trickster Makes This World: Mischief,
Myth, and Art* (New York: North Point Press, 1998), 6.

162 "The secret source of humor itself is not joy, but sorrow":   Mark Twain, *Following the Equator: A Journey Around the World* (New York: Dover Publications, 1989), 119–124.

163 "Look, up in the sky!":   Richard Pryor, from *Who Me? I'm Not Him,* CD, Polygram, 1994.

165 "As long as you think you're white, I have to think I'm black":   James Baldwin, quoted in Hyde, 237.

165 the terrapin and the deer: Lawrence W. Levine, *Black Culture and Black Consciousness: Afro-American Folk Thought from Slavery to Freedom* (New York: Oxford, 1977), 115. Levine is a reminder of how valuable the liberal-biased scholarship of the post–civil rights era was, even if it is no longer in fashion.

166 "Don't ask me nuthin' about nuthin'":   Bob Dylan, "Outlaw Blues," *Bringing It All Back Home,* LP, Columbia, 1965.

166 Yoruban trickster Esu-Elegbara: Hyde, 111–112, 117n, and Palmer.

166 "individuality, satire, parody, irony":   Henry Louis Gates Jr., *The Signifying Monkey: A Theory of Afro-American Literary Criticism* (New York: Oxford University Press, 1988), 6.

167 "had done teached the black folks":   Zora Neale Hurston, "High John De Conquer," *American Mercury* 57:450–458, October 1943, quoted in Bill R. Hampton, "On Identification and Negro Tricksters," *Southern Folklore Quarterly,* March 1967, 60.

167 "The humorous story is American":   Twain, "How to Tell a Story," in *How to Tell a Story and Other Essays* (New York, Oxford University Press, 1996).

168 "a form of rebellion against fate":   Ernst Kris, *Psychological Explanations in Art,* 1953, quoted in Hampton, 60.

168 "A lot of things are said with words or body language":   Chuck D (Carlton Rydenhour), interview with author in "Armageddon in Effect," *Spin,* September 1988.

168 "The blacks are the great humorists":   Unnamed traveler, quoted in Constance Rourke, *American Humor: A Study of the National Character* (Garden City, N.Y.: Doubleday Anchor, 1953), 71.

168 "If you will hear men laugh, go to Guinea":   W. E. B. DuBois, *Dusk of Dawn: An Essay Toward an Autobiography of a Race Concept,* 148–149, quoted in Levine, 299–300.

168 "the dry mockery of the pretensions of white folk":   W. E. B. DuBois, "The Humor of Negroes," *Mark Twain Quarterly,* Fall–Winter 1943, quoted in Shelley Fisher Fishkin, *Was Huck Black? Mark Twain and African American Voices* (New York: Oxford University Press, 1993), 61.

169 "Down in the jungle near a dried-up creek":   Unnamed source, quoted in Levine, 378.

170 first true American celebrity: For a good discussion of Barnum's biography and hoaxes, see Jackson Lears, *Fables of Abundance: A Cultural History of Advertising in America* (New York: Basic Books, 1994), 265–267.

170 His first great hoax: Wood, 150.

171 "The public," he noted, "appears to be amused":   P. T. Barnum, quoted in Lears, "The Birth of Irony," *New Republic,* November 12, 2001.

171 "For me it was a liberation to lose myself":   Richard Hell, interview by author, 2003.

172 "I think I made it for Richard":   Richard Hell, ibid.,

172 They "looked as deep into my eyes":   Legs McNeil and Gillian McCain, *Please Kill Me: The Uncensored Oral History Of Punk,* exp. ed. (New York: Penguin, 1997), 173.

172 "The Black concept of *signifying*":   Claudia Mitchell-Kernan, "Signifying," in *Language Behavior in a Black Urban Community* (Monographs of the Language-Behavior Lab, University of California at Berkeley, no. 2, Feb. 1971), 87–129, quoted in Fisher Fishkin, 60.

172 "Signifying," as the novelist John Edgar Wideman defined it: John Edgar Wideman, "Playing, Not Joking, With Language," *New York Times*, Aug. 14, 1988.

172 "at a sort of crossroads, a discursive crossroads":   Gates, *Signifying Monkey*, 65.

173 "I fucked your mama":   H. Rap Brown, *Die Nigger Die!* (New York: Dial, 1969), 25–26, quoted in Levine, 346.

173 "And the teacher expected me to sit up in class":   Brown, 25–26, quoted in Levine, 346.

173 "to dozen":   Hyde, 273.

173 "The crowd did not dream when they laid down their money":   Muhammad Ali, quoted in Levine, 350.

174 "I was playmate to all the niggers":   Twain, quoted in Dixon Wecter, *Sam Clemens of Hannibal* (Boston: Houghton Mifflin, 1952), 75.

174 he watched a local overseer kill a slave: Geoffrey C. Ward et al., *Mark Twain: An Illustrated Biography* (New York: Alfred A. Knopf, 2001), 11–12.

175 "All I care to know is that a man is a human being":   Twain, quoted in ibid., 193–194.

175 "as one who receives a revelation":   Twain, quoted in ibid., 30.

175 "Aunt Rachel, how is it that you've lived":   Twain, "A True Story, Repeated Word for Word As I Heard It" (1874), repr. in ibid., 98.

175 "No Huck and Jim, no American novel":   Ellison, "What America Would Be Like without Blacks," in *Collected Essays*, 577–585.

175 "a sound heart and a deformed conscience":   Mark Twain, quoted in Justin Kaplan, *Mr. Clemens and Mark Twain* (New York: Simon & Schuster, 1983), 198.

176 Times Square strip clubs: Bruce's upbringing is traced in Tony Hendra, *Going Too Far* (New York: Doubleday, 1987), 115.

177 "That Bojangles, Christ, could he tap-dance!":   Lenny Bruce, quoted in ibid., 121.

177 "Adolf, my friend":   Bruce, quoted in ibid., 135–137.

178 "The important thing in writing":   Terry Southern, in Eric Pace, "Terry Southern, Screenwriter, Is Dead at 71," *New York Times*, October 31, 1995.

178 "breezy compound of street jive and Madison Avenue knowingness":   Luc Sante, "Everywhere Man," *Village Voice*, May 15, 2001, 116.

179 "I was a nigger for 23 years":   Richard Pryor, quoted in Wil Haygood, "Why Negro Humor Is Black," *American Prospect*, December 18, 2000, 31.

179 "Art is the ability to tell the truth":   Richard Pryor, quoted in Watkins, *On the Real Side*, 559.

179 "the first African-American stand-up comedian":   Ibid., 562.

179 "Pryor belongs to the sassing tradition":   Ishmael Reed, interview with author, 2003.

180 "Well, I've changed music five or six times":   Davis with Troupe, 381.

182 The son of a middle-class sign painter: Ali's background and significance in David Remnick, *King of the World: Muhammad Ali and the Rise of an American Hero* (New York: Random House, 1998), 207, 212.

182 "before he ever got in the ring":   Muhammad Ali, quoted in Ibid., 141.

183 "If the fans think I can do everything I say I can":   Muhammad Ali, quoted in Ibid., 139.

183 He stole albums: Dylan's misadventures get a gossipy treatment in Howard Sounes, *Down the Highway: The Life of Bob Dylan* (New York: Grove, 2002), 56.

183 Jean Ritchie sought credit: Ibid., 132.

183 Dylan's Yakuza borrowings, which were no big deal, made the front page.:   Jonathan Eig and Sebastian Moffett, "Dylan's Lyrics Seem Like An Author's Back Pages—but Writer Sings Praises," *Wall Street Journal*, July 8, 2003. The borrowings are no more than what blues musicians have done from the beginning.

185 "[M]aybe it is not the trickster who is unruly":   Hyde, 279, 300.

8 | Hip Has Three Fingers

186 "People have a reluctant admiration": Chuck Jones, quoted in Kevin S. Sandler, "Gendered Evasion," in Kevin Sandler, ed., *Reading the Rabbit: Explorations in Warner Bros. Animation* (New Brunswick, N.J.: Rutgers University Press, 1998), 162.

187 "It's preliterate thinking": Art Spiegelman, interview with author, 2001.

187 Felix the Cat: There is a good description of early cartoon history, including Otto Mesmer and his famous black cat, in Stefan Kanfer, *Serious Business: The Art and Commerce of Animation in America from Betty Boop to Toy Story* (New York: Scribner, 1997), 39.

188 "All mythical heroes have been exaggerations": Max Eastman, quoted in Matthiessen, 640.

188 "gathered for a weekly bout of sex": Seamus Culhane, quoted in Kanfer, 71.

189 "The only god I ever relied on was Mark Twain": Chuck Jones, interview with author, 2001.

190 "The thing about the [African] voodoo aesthetic": Ishmael Reed to Reginald Martin, "Interview with Ishmael Reed," *Review of Contemporary Fiction*, vol. 4, Summer 1984.

191 "Cohen" and "Coon": Kanfer, 18.

192 his own tie to minstrelsy: Early Warner history is discussed in Hank Sartin, "From Vaudeville to Hollywood, from Silence to Sound: Warner Bros. Cartoons of the Early Sound Era," in Sandler, 73.

192 "the colored people are good subjects for action pictures": E. C. Matthews, *How to Draw Funny Pictures*, 64, quoted in Terry Lindvall and Ben Fraser, "Darker Shades of Animation," in ibid, 124.

193 "Afro-American history is full of examples of 'racist' benevolence": Henry Louis Gates Jr., "Talkin' That Talk," in Gates, ed., *"Race," Writing, and Difference* (Chicago: University of Chicago Press, 1986), 404–405.

193 "You must love what you caricature": Chuck Jones, *Chuck Amuck: The Life and Times of an Animated Cartoonist* (New York: Farrar, Straus & Giroux, 1989), 101.

194 Count Basie and Fats Waller: Norman M. Klein, *7 Minutes: The Life and Death of the American Animated Cartoon* (New York: Verso, 1993), 9.

194 the first color talking cartoon: Kanfer, 81.

195 dependent on royalties: Klein, *7 Minutes*, 53–54.

196 Disney budgets could reach as high as $100,000: Kanfer, 95.

196 "Disney was making Rolls Royces": Jones interview.

196 "I wouldn't work in a shit-hole like this": Leon Schlesinger, quoted in Jones, *Chuck Amuck*, 87.

196 "We never previewed [ideas] for Schlesinger": Jones interview.

196 "a snazzily dressed Gila monster": Jones, *Chuck Amuck*, 89, 92.

196 "Roll the garbage!": Schlesinger, quoted in ibid., 90.

196 "Jeethus Cristh, that's a funny voithe!": Schlesinger, quoted in ibid., 91.

198 "I've never seen more glamour anywhere": Jack Kelson, quoted in Steven Isoardi et al, eds., *Central Avenue Sounds: Jazz in Los Angeles* (Berkeley: University of California Press, 1998).

198 Ross watched a loose-limbed dancer: Klein, *7 Minutes*, 193.

198 Louis Armstrong expressed interest: Lindvall and Fraser, "Darker Shades," in Sandler, 131.

198 forced to delete all references: Walter Lantz's complaints were typical in the industry; see Kanfer, 182.

9 | The World Is a Ghetto

202 "To me, if you live in New York": Lenny Bruce, *How to Talk Dirty and Influence People* (New York: Fireside, 1992), 5.

202 "I wanna be black": Lou Reed, "I Wanna Be Black," *Street Hassle,* LP, Arista, 1978.

203 "might have been a little minstrel": Joshua Neuman and Nancy Schwartzman, interviews with author, 2003.

206 peppered his act with Yiddish: Jeffrey Melnick, *A Right to Sing the Blues: African Americans, Jews, and American Popular Song* (Cambridge, Mass.: Harvard University Press, 1999), 121. Melnick makes compelling arguments for the influence both ethnic groups wielded on each other, and for the impact they had on American pop.

206 a family of Lithuanian Jewish junk peddlars: Louis Armstrong, who spent his life writing his autobiography in print and on tape, wrote about his Jewish roots toward the end of his life after an illness. See Laurence Bergreen, *Armstrong: An Extravagant Life* (New York, Broadway, 1997), 55–57, 267.

206 "Life is not worthwhile without it": Harry Belafonte, interview with author, 2001.

206 "the most modern of modern people": Cornel West, in Michael Lerner and Cornel West, *Jews and Blacks: Let the Healing Begin* (New York: Grosset/Putnam, 1995), 2.

206 Jewish activists and philanthropists: Jonathan Kaufman, *Broken Alliance: The Turbulent Times between Blacks and Jews in America,* updated ed. (New York: Touchstone, 1995), 31.

206 "[m]onkey talk, jungle squeals": Henry Ford, *The International Jew,* chap. 11. A loathsome document.

207 "We thought that we were black": Mike Stoller, interview with author, 2003. Though Stoller's comments out of context can seem naïve, they are not. The problem is that we don't have language for people who are comfortable on more than one side of a line.

207 "Is you black or is you white": Unnamed customer to Phil Chess, in Nadine Cohodas, *Spinning Blues into Gold: The Chess Brothers and the Legendary Chess Records* (New York: St. Martin's Press, 2000), 29.

207 "It was the concept of performance as a spiritual thing": Aaron Fuchs, interview with author, 2003.

207 "One regards the Jews the same way as one regards the Negroes": Voltaire, quoted by David M. Goldenberg, "The Curse of Ham: A Case of Rabbinic Racism?" in Jack Salzman and Cornel West, eds., *Struggles in the Promised Land: Toward a History of Black-Jewish Relations in the United States* (New York: Oxford University Press, 1997), 21.

207 A joke told by African Americans: William Pickens, *American Aesop: Negro and Other Humor* (New York: AMS Press, 1969), 113–115.

208 "That gets very hairy": Jerry Wexler, interview with author, 2003. Wexler's position is understandable. On this topic, the chances for misunderstanding are high.

208 "Are black folks saving nerdy Jews": Bill Adler, interview with author, 2003.

209 "Italians are niggaz": Chuck Nice, quoted in Jennifer Guglielmo and Salvatore Salerno, *Are Italians White?* (New York: Routledge, 2004), 1.

209 The first Jews arrived: Salzman and West, 1.

209 2.5 million Jews: Douglas, *Terrible Honesty,* 305.

209 "miserable darkened Hebrews": From *American Hebrew,* quoted in Hasia R. Diner, *In the Almost Promised Land: American Jews and Blacks, 1915–1935* (Westport, Conn.: Greenwood Press, 1977), 8–9.

210 popular entertainment was ripe: Melnick, 23.

210 Typical of the newcomers: Laurence Bergreen, *As Thousands Cheer: The Life of Irving Berlin* (New York: Viking, 1990), 3.

211 affinity for these coon songs: Ibid., 22–27.

211 "Negro-ist" white man: Melnick, 50.

211 "improvisations of my father's": Harold Arlen, quoted in Max Wilk, *They're Playing Our Song: From Jerome Kern to Stephen Sondheim—the Stories behind the Words and Music of Two Generations,* 153, quoted in Melnick, 173.

211 "Where did *he* get it?": Cantor Arluck, in Wilk, 152–153, quoted in Melnick, 190.

211 established Tin Pan Alley: Melnick, 33.

212 "Jazz is Irving Berlin, Al Jolson": Samson Raphaelson, quoted in ibid., 103.

212 "not a nationality, but a trans-nationality": Randolph Bourne, quoted in Marshall Berman, "Love and Theft," *Dissent,* July 1, 2002.

212 "If the Jews were proscribed": Neal Gabler, *An Empire of Their Own: How the Jews Invented Hollywood* (New York, Crown, 1988), 5–7.

213 "One reason why ragtime, jazz, and blues": Melnick, 23.

213 "minority even more unloved": James Baldwin, "The Harlem Ghetto," in *Collected Essays,* 51.

213 "not only proved their credentials as Americans": Hasia R. Diner, "Between Words and Deeds: Jews and Blacks in America, 1880–1935," in Salzman and West, 91.

213 "the Jewish performers transformed it": Irving Howe, *World of Our Fathers* (New York: Harcourt Brace Jovanovich, 1976), 562–563. Howe does not say how Jewish minstrelsy was more humane for others, or acknowledge that African Americans might not receive it as such.

216 "every colored performer is proud of him": Thomas Cripps, "African Americans and Jews in Hollywood: Antagonistic Allies," in Salzman and West, 263.

216 "I never felt that I was renting the blues": Jerry Leiber, on *American Routes* radio program, Public Radio International, September 11, 2002.

216 "The idea of hip": Wexler interview.

217 "We felt we were authentic": Stoller interview, 2003.

217 "[W]e became more than business associates": Muddy Waters, quoted in Cohodas, 40.

217 "I didn't even sign no contract": Muddy Waters, quoted in Palmer, 162.

217 The complaints against the Chess brothers: Cohodas, 309–310. The definitive records were destroyed.

218 the shadow of exploitation: Early accusations and suits are covered in Melnick, 34.

218 "Those illiterates": Hy Weiss, quoted in Dorothy Wade and Justine Picardie, *Music Man: Ahmet Ertegun, Atlantic Records, and the Triumph of Rock 'N' Roll* (New York: W.W. Norton, 1990), 70.

218 "As a Jew, I didn't think I identified with the underclass": For this quote and an account of the threats, see Jerry Wexler and David Ritz, *Rhythm and the Blues: A Life in American Music* (New York: Alfred A. Knopf, 1993), 227–228. Since I mentioned Wexler's demurral earlier I should point out that in the book he holds little else back.

218 "get rid of that devil real simple": Ice Cube, "No Vaseline," *Death Certificate,* CD, Priority, 1991.

218 "I thought, wow, one of these days, if I play my cards right": Fuchs interview.

219 Black Swan Records: "On the Blackhand Side," in *Wax Poetics,* Spring 2003.

219 Leonard Chess used to empty the change: Cohodas, 52.

219 "Lenny paved the way for all of us": Redd Foxx, in Watkins, 486.

220 "Man, those records caused a traffic jam": Mezz Mezzrow with Bernard Wolfe, *Really the Blues* (Garden City, N.Y.: Doubleday, 1972), 201–202.

221 "I just felt so much more at ease": Adler interview.

221 "They open industries for us": Russell Simmons, "Hip Hop Fridays," available at www.blackelectorate.com.

10 | Criminally Hip

223 "[T]he roots of the counterculture": Albert Goldman, *Grass Roots: Marijuana in America Today* (New York: HarperCollins, 1979), p. 7, quoted in Cecil Brown, *Stagolee Shot Billy* (Cambridge, Mass.: Harvard University Press, 2003), 12–13.

223 "a malignant matriarchal society": William S. Burroughs, quoted in Victor Bockris, *With William Burroughs: A Report from the Bunker* (New York: Seaver Books, 1981), xvii.

224 "It sounded good to me": William S. Burroughs, *Junky* (originally titled *Junkie*) (New York: Penguin, 1977), xii.

225 "constitutes an implicit criticism of traditional mores": Hyman E. Goldin, Frank O'Leary and Morris Lipsius, eds., *Dictionary of American Underworld Lingo* (New York: Twayne Publishers, 1950), introduction.

225 "Looking back now": Jack Black, *You Can't Win*, 2nd ed. (San Francisco: AK Press/Nabat, 2000), 22.

226 "I began to view": Jay Robert Nash, *Bloodletters and Badmen: A Narrative Encyclopedia of American Criminals from the Pilgrims to the Present* (New York: M. Evans, 1991), 6.

227 the Old English word *lagu*: For a discussion of *lagu, utlaga* and the outlaw, see Frank Richard Prassel, *The Great American Outlaw: A Legacy of Fact and Fiction* (Norman: University of Oklahoma Press, 1993), 3–4.

228 the tale took on the twist: Discussion of Robert Hod and Robin Hood in ibid., 10.

228 Another was to use convicts: For a discussion of imported criminals, see Frank Browning and John Gerassi, *The American Way of Crime* (New York: Putnam, 1980), 88, 93.

228 50,000 English prisoners: Convicts were a commodity for trade; see Prassel, 52.

228 France supplied the feminine enticements: Browning and Gerassi, 90.

228 story of Jesse James: Jesse James's biography gets the mythopoetic treatment in Carl Breihan, *The Complete and Authentic Life of Jesse James* (New York: F. Fell, 1953), 183.

228 "halo of medieval chivalry": John Edwards, in Prassel, 127–128.

229 Jesse Woodson James was born: Biographical detals are taken from Breihan, 70.

229 only to die from a fever: Ibid., 71.

229 Accounts of Jesse as an adult: Such descriptions are typical of mythic accounts; see ibid., 85, 87, 190.

229 "an exact account of this hold-up": Ibid., 115–116.

230 "booty is but the second thought": This spectacular misconception by Edwards is quoted in Prassel, 127–128.

230 "Why has the free-running reprobate": Emmett Dalton, quoted in ibid., 262.

232 When he died: For details of Dillinger's fall and his setup by the Lady in Red, see ibid., 281.

232 crime actually dropped in the 1930s: See ibid., 272–273.

232 Harlem heroin kingpin Leroy "Nicky" Barnes: Fred Ferretti, "Mr. Untouchable," *New York Times Magazine*, June 5, 1977.

233 "I need a handkerchief": Ibid.

233 he bought the Apollo Theater: Nelson George, *The Death of Rhythm and Blues* (New York: Pantheon, 1988), 162–163.

235 "Always remember whether you be a sucker or hustler": Iceberg Slim (Robert Beck), *Pimp: The Story of My Life* (Los Angeles: Holloway House, 1987), 74.

235 killing a band of Mexicans "just to see them kick": Ramon F. Adams, *A Fitting Death for Billy the Kid* (Norman: University of Oklahoma Press, 1982), 62.

235 "blue dragoon jacket": Ibid., 44–45.

236 "I would see myself gigantic and powerful": Iceberg Slim, 77.

236 "the insult of rehabilitation": Ann Douglas, quoted in Charters, *Beat Down*, 238.

236 "the greatest storyteller I know": Jack Kerouac, quoted on American National Biography Online, http://www.anb.org/articles/16/16-03457–article.html.

236 "The gangster is the 'no' to that great American 'yes' ": Robert Warshow, quoted in Prassel, 268–269.

237 "In such places as Greenwich Village": Mailer, 340.

237 "What differentiated the characters in *On the Road*": John Clellon Holmes, "The Philosophy of the Beat Generation," in Charters, *Beat Down,* 229.

238 "In case a crime has been committed": Unnamed writer, quoted in Prassel, 326.

11 | Where the Ladies At?

239 "That whole obsession with hip": Kim Gordon, interview with author, 2003.

239 "I can't watch this": This quote, and a good account of the shooting is from MacAdams, 142–143.

240 The daughter of a factory manager: Brenda Knight, *Women of the Beat Generation: The Writers, Artists and Muses at the Heart of a Revolution* (Berkeley, Calif.: Conari Press, 1996), 49–53. Like most books about the Beats, this is too blindly laudatory, but given the absence of women in other accounts, it comes as a necessary corrective.

240 he and Joan lived together: Knight, 49–53.

240 "Her cunt is sweet": Kerouac, *Visions of Cody,* 23.

241 "Hip definitely seems like a male term": Gordon interview.

242 "There were women, they were there": Gregory Corso, quoted in Knight, 141.

242 "a woman without a man didn't exist at all": Di Prima, *Recollections,* 176.

242 a distinctly feminine cast: Thompson interview.

243 "work, produce, consume": Jack Kerouac, *The Dharma Bums* (New York: Viking, 1958), 77.

243 " 'Pretty girls make graves' ": Ibid., with a good discussion in Ehrenreich, 52.

244 "When the world began to change": Hutchins Hapgood, *Victorian in the Modern World,* 152, quoted in Stansell, 225.

244 "Life was ready to take a new form": Mabel Dodge Luhan, *Movers and Shakers,* 151, quoted in Stansell, 40.

244 "trained by the essence of our nature": Frances E. Willard, quoted in Douglas, *Terrible Honesty,* 242.

244 "My people are in no way a part of me": Louise Bryant, quoted in Stansell, 253.

245 "out to hurt their mother": Mary Heaton Vorse, quoted in ibid., 29.

245 did not have children: Douglas, *Terrible Honesty,* 98.

246 "look the whole world in the face with a go-to-hell look": Margaret Sanger, quoted in Stansell, 238.

246 small-press magazines: Ibid., 152.

246 sexual freedom: Ibid., 259–260.

246 "the wife who married for money": Emma Goldman, quoted in Alix Kates Shulman, ed., *Red Emma Speaks: An Emma Goldman Reader* (Amherst, N.Y.: Humanity Books, 1998), 151.

246 "[U]nder the contract of marriage all duties lie upon the man": H. L. Mencken, "In Defense of Women," quoted in Ehrenreich, 7.

247 "whatever their outward show of respect": Ibid.

247 "Feminism is going to make it possible": Floyd Dell, "Feminism for Men," *The Masses,* July 1914, 19, quoted in Stansell, 226.

248 "expend greater effort in their work":   Hugh Hefner, quoted in Ehrenreich, 46.

248 Edie Parker, who earned $27.50:   Joyce Johnson, "Beat Queens: Women in Flux," in George-Warren, 43.

249 "I wanted the life of an outlaw":   For this quote and her early relationship with Kerouac, see Joyce Johnson's remarks in "Panel Discussion with Women Writers," in Charters, *Beat Down,* 629.

249 "It wasn't the moment *then*":   Ibid., 616.

249 "I knew interesting creative women who became junkies":   Anne Waldman, foreward to Knight, x.

249 "surely poetry's representative in the flesh":   For this quote and details of the abusive relationship, see Bonnie Bremser, *Love for a Day,* quoted in Alix Kates Shulman, "The Beat Queens: Boho Chicks Stand by Their Men," *Village Voice, Voice Literary Supplement,* June 1989, 19.

249 Elise Cowen, a Barnard rebel: Knight, 142.

250 "Many, myself included, wanted far more":   Hettie Jones, "Babes in Boyland," in George-Warren, 53.

250 "I sensed that Allen was only,":   Diane Di Prima, *Memoirs of a Beatnik,* quoted in Charters, *Beat Down,* 116.

251 "Di Prima, unless you forget about your babysitter":   Kerouac, quoted by di Prima, *Recollections,* 202.

252 "we didn't do like the Supremes":   Ronnie Spector, quoted in Gerri Hirshey, *We Gotta Get out of This Place: The True, Tough Story of Women in Rock* (New York: Atlantic Monthly Press, 2001), 61.

252 "I cannot make love to Jews anymore":   Nico, and story of Nico in the band, in McNeil and McCain, 10.

252 "The only people who had any money":   Roberta Bayley, interview with author, 2003.

253 "I was always Flash Gordon":   Patti Smith, interview with Penny Green, *Interview,* 1973, available at www.oceanstar.com/patti/intervus.htm.

255 "Hung-up women can't produce anything but mediocre art":   Patti Smith, interview with Nick Tosches, *Penthouse,* April 1976.

255 "For the most part, cool attributes":   Kathleen Hanna, *Girl Power,* repr. in Andrea Juno, *Angry Women in Rock,* vol. 1 (New York: Juno Books, 1996), 98.

256 "The Beach Boys were still singing these happy songs":   Gordon interview.

256 Moving to New York: Alec Foege, *Confusion Is Next: The Sonic Youth Story* (New York: St. Martin's Press, 1994), 45–48, and Gordon interview.

256 "just seemed like a very easy scene":   Jim Sclavunos, quoted in Foege, 31.

256 "They'd take a big hit":   Gordon interview.

256 "What would it be like to be right at the pinnacle of energy":   Gordon, "Boys Are Smelly: Sonic Youth Tour Diary, '87," *Village Voice, Rock & Roll Quarterly,* Fall 1988, October 12–18.

257 "Hey fox, come here":   Sonic Youth, "Pacific Coast Highway," *Sister,* CD, SST, 1987.

257 "when people say, what's it like to be a woman in rock":   Gordon interview.

12 | Behind the Music

260 "Heroin was our badge":   Red Rodney, quoted in Ira Gitler, *Swing to Bop: An Oral History of the Transition in Jazz in the 1940s* (New York: Oxford University Press, 1985), 282.

260 "in the strictest sense of the word":   Terry Southern, in *Paul Krassner's Impolite Interviews* (New York: Seven Stories Press, 1999), 190.

261 "to a certain extent come out of drug-taking":   Norman Mailer, quoted in "Hip, Hell, and the Navigator: An Interview with Norman Mailer by Richard G. Stern," in *Advertisements for Myself,* 381–382.

261 "[i]f marijuana was the wedding ring": Mailer, "White Negro," 340.

261 "the Negro's normal separation from the mainstream": Baraka, 201.

261 from the Dutch *doop*: Jill Jonnes, *Hep-Cats, Narcs, and Pipe Dreams: A History of America's Romance with Illegal Drugs* (New York: Scribner, 1996), 30.

261 "See, most people": *Drugstore Cowboy*, written and directed by Gus Van Sant, DVD (1989; Artisan Entertainment, 1999).

261 "Light up and be somebody": Mezz Mezzrow, quoted in David T. Courtwright, *Forces of Habit: Drugs and the Making of the Modern World* (Cambridge, Mass.: Harvard University Press, 2001), 43.

262 $64 billion on illegal drugs: Office of National Drug Control Policy (www.white-housedrugpolicy.gov), the Motion Picture Association of America (www.mpaa .com) and the Recording Industry Association of America (www.riaa.com). Obviously, the drug figure is an estimate and subject to political manipulation.

262 "no sniffers please": Lou Reed, in liner notes to *Metal Machine Music*, quoted in Victor Bockris, *Transformer: The Lou Reed Story* (New York: Simon & Schuster, 1994), 118.

262 "Then, with Sid trailing along behind me": Dee Dee Ramone with Veronica Kofman, *Lobotomy: Surviving the Ramones* (New York: Thunder's Mouth Press, 2000), 115.

263 "With good white benny tablets": Jack Kerouac to Donald Allen, December 1959, in *Selected Letters, 1957–1969* (New York: Viking Penguin, 1999), 239.

264 A semisynthetic derivative: Sadie Plant, *Writing on Drugs* (New York: Picador, 1999), 6.

264 "Only drugs that were widely used": Courtwright, 69.

264 "I go to this heart specialist": Charlie Parker, quoted in James Gavin, *Deep in a Dream: The Long Night of Chet Baker* (New York: Alfred A. Knopf, 2002), 100.

265 "Diz, why don't you save me?": Parker, quoted in Gillespie with Fraser, 393.

265 Born in Oklahoma: Gavin, 9–12, 47.

265 "It wasn't for cheap thrills that I took heroin": Chet Baker, "30,000 Hell-Holes in My Arm," *Today* (U.K.), February 2, 1963, quoted in ibid., 188.

266 "When you looked at her": Art and Laurie Pepper, *Straight Life: The Story of Art Pepper* (New York: Da Capo, 1994), 83.

266 "I said, 'This is it' ": Ibid., 85–86.

266 "which seek to exist apart": Herbert J. Gans, *Popular Culture and High Culture: An Analysis and Evaluation of Taste* (New York: Basic Books, 1999), 121.

266 "Junk" Burroughs wrote, "is not": Burroughs, *Junky*, xvi.

267 Body Bag, Hellraiser: Ann Marlowe, *How to Stop Time: Heroin from A to Z* (New York: Basic Books, 1999), 34. An evocative drug tale that was controversial because Marlowe suffered little damage for her experiments, and did not pity those who did.

267 "Nonusers wonder why": Ibid., 57.

267 "Junkies run on junk time": Burroughs, *Junky*, 97.

267 "exorcise the darkness": Lou Reed, quoted in Bockris, *Transformer*, 71.

268 "I take drugs just because": Ibid., 85.

269 "negative, strung-out": Details of Reed's life at Syracuse and the early days of the band and the song are in ibid., 71.

269 "I think he might start writing some good songs again": John Cale, quoted in Nick Kent, *The Dark Stuff: Selected Writings on Rock Music*, updated ed. (New York: Da Capo, 2002), 169.

269 his parents sent him: Bockris, *Transformer*, 13, 71.

269 "You can't read a book": Lou Reed, quoted in ibid., 15.

269 "I stopped, and being a little wacky": Maureen Tucker, in Clinton Heylin, *From the Velvets to the Voidoids: A Pre-Punk History for a Post-Punk World* (New York: Penguin, 1993), 23.

270 "gave dignity and poetry and rock 'n' roll to smack": Lester Bangs, "Let Us Now Praise Famous Death Dwarves," in Greil Marcus, ed., *Psychotic Reactions and Carburetor Dung* (New York: Vintage, 1988), 170–171.

270 "because he stands for all the most fucked up things": Ibid., 171.

271 "There was commitment there": John Cale, quoted in Heylin, 10.

271 America's first drug epidemic: Jonnes, 25.

272 passed the Harrison Narcotic Act: See ibid., 47.

272 the artist's stock in trade: Barry Miles, *William Burroughs: El Hombre Invisible* (New York: Hyperion, 1992), 98.

274 "Sal, we gotta go": Kerouac, *On the Road*, 240.

274 "in emphasizing as he does the importance of the 'kick' ": Harold Finestone, "Cats, Kicks, and Color," *Social Problems*, 5(1), 1957, 7.

275 "I don't want your money": William S. Burroughs, *Naked Lunch* (New York: Grove, 1992), 182.

275 "When *you* have a bad day": Parker, quoted in Gillespie with Fraser, 291.

276 "Of that time which we call the present": De Quincey, quoted in Plant, 146.

276 "He'd wasted his entire life": Denis Johnson, *Jesus' Son* (New York: Farrar, Straus & Giroux, 1992), 37–38.

276 "In the nod, I felt less guilty": Marlowe, 45, 58–59.

277 "It was a matter of pushing the envelope": Martin Scorsese, quoted in Peter Biskind, *Easy Riders, Raging Bulls: How the Sex-Drugs-and-Rock 'N' Roll Generation Saved Hollywood* (New York: Simon & Schuster, 1999), 377.

279 "I thought that one used heroin to play": Frank Morgan, quoted in Gary Giddins, "The Scene Is Clean," *Village Voice*, December 16, 1986.

279 "I paid tribute to Bird": Frank Morgan, quoted in David W. Grogan, "Frank Morgan: After Three Decades of Drug Addiction, a Jazz Genius Comes Back from the Depths," *People*, July 18, 1988, 93.

280 "I guess that's when I decided to fail": Frank Morgan, quoted in Giddins, "Scene."

281 "not a turning loose of emotion": T. S. Eliot, "Tradition and the Individual Talent," *Selected Prose of T. S. Eliot* (New York: Harvest, 1975), 43.

13 | "It's Like Punk Rock, But a Car"

282 "Hip capitalism wasn't something on the fringes": Thomas Frank, *Conquest of Cool: Business Culture, Counterculture, and the Rise of Hip Capitalism* (Chicago: University of Chicago Press, 1997), 26. Frank's skeptical analyses are invaluable, though I do not share his sense of betrayal.

282 American ambition: The story of Kroc and the McDonald brothers is told in David Halberstam, *The Fifties* (New York: Villard Books, 1993), 155–171.

283 "so bad that it used to send chills through me": Davis with Troupe, 196.

283 "cannot trust some people who are nonconformists": Ray Kroc, quoted in Halberstam, 165.

283 "The American middle class had come to the end of its Puritan phase": Floyd Dell, *Homecoming*, 360, quoted in Stansell, 335.

284 "the hipster parodied and packaged": Herb Gold, quoted in Sukenick, 113.

285 "When a thing is current, it creates currency": Marshall McLuhan, quoted in Naomi Klein, *No Logo* (New York: Picador, 2002), 71.

285 "one of those cornball ideas": Allen Ginsberg, quoted in Sukenick, 121–122.

286 "Bohemia could not survive": Michael Harrington, "We Few, We Happy Few, We Bohemians," *Esquire*, August 1972, 99, quoted in Frank, *Conquest*, 29.

286 "the fucking needy indie fascist regime": Kurt Cobain, quoted in Charles R. Cross, *Heavier Than Heaven: A Biography of Kurt Cobain* (New York: Hyperion, 2001), 301.

286 "They're hipper than you can ever hope to be": Thomas Frank, "Why Johnny Can't Dissent," in Thomas Frank and Matt Weiland, eds., *Commodify Your Dissent: Salvos from the Baffler* (New York: W.W. Norton, 1997), 44–45.

288 "It was weird": Troy Pierce, quoted in Bunn.

289 "It is our willingness to forgive": Nikki Giovanni, in Tate, *Everything But the Burden,* cover.

290 "things were isolated from their origins": Lears, *Fables of Abundance,* 5.

291 age of advertising revenues: are taken from Douglas, *Terrible Honesty,* 64.

291 "Brevity is the soul of lingerie": Dorothy Parker, ad slogan, in ibid., 66.

291 "Only in America was advertising": Ibid., 65.

291 "Modernism offered the opportunity": Ernest Elmo Calkins, *Annals of an Adman,* 239, quoted in Jackson T. Lears, "From Salvation to Self-Realization: Advertising and the Therapeutic Roots of the Consumer Culture, 1880–1930," in Richard Wightman Fox and Jackson T. Lears, eds., *The Culture of Consumption: Critical Essays in American History, 1880–1980* (New York: Pantheon, 1983), 22.

292 "People don't always drink the beer": Burt Manning, quoted in Leslie Wayne, "How a Popular Beer Fell out of Favor," *New York Times,* March 3, 1985.

292 "If a manuscript was sold to an established publisher": Winifred Bryher, in Fitch, 61.

292 "By the end of the 1940s": Klein, *No Logo,* 7.

293 "What is a brand?": Lance Jensen, interview with author, 2001.

293 faster than any medium: James L. Baughman, "Television Comes to America, 1947–1957," *Illinois History,* March 1993.

294 "Better to live simply": Gary Snyder, "Notes on the Beat Generation," in Charters, *Beat Down,* 518–519.

295 "found in the ideas of people like Jerry Rubin": Frank, *Conquest,* 121.

295 "The only people for me are the mad ones": Kerouac, *On the Road,* 5–6.

296 "Rent a Genuine Beatnik": Schumacher, 320.

296 "get to the so-called squares": Ted Joans, quoted in Sukenick, 118.

297 "None of the kids I grew up with": Kris Parker, interview with author, 1999.

301 "We was young entrepreneurs": Afrika Bambaataa, quoted in Jim Fricke and Charlie Ahearn, *Yes Yes Y'all: The Experience Music Project Oral History of Hip-Hop's First Decade* (New York: Da Capo, 2002), 45–46.

301 "These pioneers made the bold claim": Klein, *No Logo,* 4.

303 "You see Disney going into the cruise business": Frank Biondi, quoted in John Seabrook, "In the Demo: The Power at MTV," *New Yorker,* October 10, 1994.

304 "The indie skateboarders": Klein, *No Logo,* 64–65.

306 "[h]ardly anyone without a pretty strong ambition": Larry Rivers, "Where Has All the Floating Energy Gone?" *New York Times* book review, November 1, 1987, 34.

307 "We're putting money back": Tim Barnes, interview with author, 2001.

308 "exactly the places where the deepest": Allen Ginsberg, letter to Richard Eberhart, May 18, 1956, quoted in Charters, *Beat Down,* 213.

308 "not because it's politically correct": Leon E. Wynter, *American Skin: Pop Culture, Big Business, and the End of White America* (New York: Crown, 2002), 152.

309 "immense, protective power": Alexis de Tocqueville, quoted in Christopher Newfield, *The Emerson Effect: Individualism and Submission in America* (Chicago: University of Chicago Press, 1996), 63.

14 | Do Geeks Dream of HTML Sheep?

310 "Today, coolness isn't outright rebellion": Alan Liu, quoted in Shari Caudron, "Cool Defined," *Workforce,* vol. 77, no. 4, April 1, 1998, 56.

310 "A lot of this stuff was started by a bunch of people on drugs": Patrick Kroupa, interview with author, 2003.

311 "Trust thyself": Ralph Waldo Emerson, "Self-Reliance," *Essays and Lectures* (New York: Library of America, 1983), 260.

311 "True jazz is an art of individual assertion": Ralph Ellison, "Shadow and Act," quoted in Robert G. O'Meally, ed., *The Jazz Cadence of American Culture* (New York: Columbia University Press, 1998), 5.

312 "just as the beatniks anticipated the hippies": Paul Saffo, "Cyberpunk R.I.P.," *Wired,* September–October 1993, p. 90.

313 "You could use the computer as a fulcrum": Kroupa interview.

313 "Working 90 Hours a Week And Loving It": John Markoff, "Saying Goodbye, Good Riddance to Silicon Valley," *New York Times,* January 17, 1999.

313 "Cool is being redefined from how you look to how you think": Margie Mader, quoted in Caudron, "Cool Defined," 56.

314 jukebox inside a '57 Chevy: Shannon Henry, "A High-Tech Hothouse: Mario Morino's New Building in Reston Will Be a Hip Home for Internet Start-Ups," *Washington Post,* November 9, 1998, F12.

314 "Any company in any industry in any location": Sharri Caudron, "Be Cool," *Workforce,* vol. 77, no. 4, April 1, 1998, p. 50.

314 "For most of those young dot-comers": Howard Rheingold, interview with author, 2003.

314 "the information rich . . . the most powerful people": Louis Rossetto, *Wired* prelaunch manifesto, quoted in Gary Wolf, *Wired—a Romance* (New York: Random House, 2003), 34.

315 "The Net used to have a somewhat Bohemian air": Steve G. Steinberg, "Hype List," *Wired,* July–August 1993, 103.

316 "had his own way": Louis Armstrong, quoted in John Atlee Kouwenhoven, *The Beer Can by the Highway: Essays on What's American About America* (Baltimore: Johns Hopkins University Press, 1988), 40.

316 "The union is only perfect": Ralph Waldo Emerson, "New England Reformers," *Essays and Lectures,* 599.

317 "prepare us for acts of improvisation": Brian Eno, quoted in "Gossip Is Philosophy," interview by Kevin Kelly, *Wired,* May 1995.

318 "No class in history has ever risen as fast": Peter Drucker, quoted in "Post-capitalist," interview by Peter Schwartz, *Wired,* July–August 1993, 80.

319 "The traditional factors of production": Ibid.

319 "It somehow goes with the paradigm": DJ Spooky, quoted in Richard Harrington, "Prolific DJ Spooky Mixes Media Projects," *Washington Post,* January 10, 2003.

320 "You're sort of destroying this received object": DJ Spooky, quoted in Hugh Gallagher, "Gimme Two Records and I'll Make You a Universe," *Wired,* September–October 1993, 87.

320 twelve things: Kouwenhoven, *Beer Can,* 42.

321 "Break music is that certain part of the record": Bambaataa Aasim (DJ Afrika Bambaataa), "The Beginning of Break Beat (Hip Hop) Music," Tommy Boy poster.

323 teenagers playing video games: Brian D. Johnson, "Mind Games with William Gibson," *Macleans,* June 5, 1995, 60.

323 "A consensual hallucination": William Gibson, *Neuromancer* (New York: Ace Books, 1994), 51.

323 "a kind of ghostly teenage DNA": Ibid., 57.

324 "This was it": Ibid., 58.

324 breakdown of urban inner space: Dani Cavallaro, *Cyberpunk and Cyberculture: Science Fiction and the Work of William Gibson* (New Brunswick, N.J.: Athlone Press, 2000), xiii.

324 "Whatever appears on the television screen": *Videodrome,* written and directed by David Cronenberg, DVD (1983; Universal, 1998).

325 "The sky above the port was the color of television": Gibson, 3.

325 Hermes typewriter: noted in Saffo.

325 "That was one of the most hallucinatory pieces": William Gibson, quoted in Laurence B. Chollet, "William Gibson's Second Sight," *Los Angeles Times,* September 12, 1993, 34.

326 "in a culture saturated with artificial substances": Cavallaro, 24.

326 "All I did was free up the fashion options": William Gibson, quoted in Stephen Lynch, "Mnemonic Conversion: The Cyberpunk Movement Bemoans the Popularization of Its Image with the Release Of 'Johnny Mnemonic,'" *Orange County Register,* May 28, 1995, F10.

326 "Gibson basically created a whole mythology": Kroupa interview.

326 hacker underground: Kroupa interview and Katie Hafner and John Markoff, *Cyberpunk: Outlaws and Hackers on the Computer Frontier* (New York: Simon & Schuster), 20.

326 "rushing through the phone line like heroin": The Mentor, in "The Conscience of a Hacker," *Phrack,* vol. 1, no. 7, phile 3, quoted in Bruce Sterling, *The Hacker Crackdown: Law and Disorder on the Electronic Frontier* (New York: Bantam, 1992), 85.

327 "What Gibson wrote about didn't exist then": Kroupa interview.

329 "It is the DJ who presides": Bill Brewster and Frank Broughton, *Last Night a DJ Saved My Life: The History of the Disc Jockey* (New York: Grove Press, 2000), 5.

329 no ordinary crank: Steve Ditlea, "Ted Nelson's Big Step," *MIT's Technology Review,* vol. 101, no. 5, September 1, 1998, 44.

329 "the Orson Welles of software": Owen Edwards, "Ted Nelson," *Forbes,* vol. 160, no. 4, August 25, 1977, S134.

330 "Computer Power to the People": Quoted in Wolf, 20.

330 subcultural proclivity: Ibid.

330 Rossetto arrived at Columbia: Ibid., 6.

330 This credo: Louis Rossetto and Stan Lehr, "The New Right Credo—Libertarianism," *New York Times Magazine,* January 10, 1971.

331 launched *Wired*: Wolf is good on details, like the *Ultimate Porno* boondoggle; see Wolf, 8.

331 "Suddenly you could be two Stanford students": Rheingold interview.

332 "The future is already here": Kevin Kelly, quoted in Wolf, 67.

332 "I heard two kids in here, maybe 25": Jim Marshall, interview with author, 2000.

333 progenitor of bling: Hirshey, 23.

335 "Many things that were anchored to the balance of power": Don DeLillo, *Underworld* (New York: Scribner, 1997), 76.

336 "One is Hip or one is Square": Mailer, "White Negro," 339.

336 9.5 million visitors: Romesh Ratnesar and Joel Stein, "Everyone's a Star.Com," *Time,* June 5, 2000.

15 | Everybody's Hip

339 "You know it's gone to hell": Charles Barkley, quoted in Peter Vecsey, "Barkley Looking Like a Real Gem These Days," *New York Post,* October 22, 2000.

347 Immigrants started about 25 percent: Richard L. Florida, *The Rise of the Creative Class: And How It's Transforming Work, Leisure, Community and Everyday Life* (New York: Basic Books, 2002), 253.

347 "The great cultural legacy of the sixties": Ibid., 202.

347 best predictor of economic growth: John Leland, "On a Hunt for Ways to Put Sex in the City," *New York Times,* December 11, 2003.

347 Economists disagree: For Glaeser's analysis, which is less mystical in its causes than Florida's, but with the same effects, see Edward L. Glaeser, Jed Kolko and Albert Saiz, "Consumer Cities," *Journal of Economic Geography* 1:27–50, 2001.

349 Spotted in the early 2000s: Julia Chaplin, "Noticed: A Hat That's Way Cool. Unless, of Course, It's Not," *New York Times,* May 18, 2003.

349 your hat was your honey: Clarence Major, *Juba to Jive: A Dictionary of African-American Slang* (New York: Penguin, 1994), 225.

350 "I have, in fact, worn a fedora hat,": George W. S. Trow, *Within the Context of No Context,* repr. (New York: Atlantic Monthly Press, 1997), 119.

351 Between 1970 and 2000: U.S. Census, "Profile of the Foreign-Born Population in the United States: 2000," December 2001, p. 23–206, available at: http://www.census.gov/prod/2002pubs/p23-206.pdf.

351 In New York, 40 percent: Bruce Lambert, "40 Percent in New York Born Abroad," *New York Times,* July 24, 2000.

351 Latinos in 2001 made up 71 percent: Gregory Rodriguez, "The Nation: Where Minorities Rule," *New York Times,* February 10, 2002.

352 whose numbers doubled: Felicia R. Lee, "Does Class Count in Today's Land of Opportunity?" *New York Times,* Jan. 18, 2003.

352 were living as white: Robert P. Stuckert, "African Ancestry of the White American Population," *Ohio Journal Of Science* 58 (3), May 1958, 155. Stuckert assumes that a constant and estimable percentage of light-skinned people of mixed race will identify themselves as white each year, even though one or both of their parents identified as black. But there is no reason to believe this flow is steady or knowable. The essay is more provocative for the questions it asks than the answers it provides.

354 the beginning of meaning: Hyde, 65. Hermes created meaning by moving Apollo's cattle from one realm to another.

354 "How the fuck can I be white": Eminem, "Role Model," *The Slim Shady LP,* CD, Interscope, 1999.

354 "two souls, two thoughts": W. E. B. DuBois, *The Souls of Black Folk* (New York: Modern Library, 2003), 5.

354 "Of every hue and cast am I": Whitman, "Song of Myself," 62.

355 "stupider than the animals": Carl Jung, quoted in Hyde, 43.

photo credits

index

Page numbers in *italic* type indicate illustrations.